'Coveney has come up with persuasive answers to the questions that leap to people's minds when the name Andrew Lloyd Webber comes up in conversation.'
Daily Mail

'Refreshingly objective . . . pacy . . . insightful'
Independent

Michael Coveney is theatre critic of the *Daily Mail*. He was born in the East End of London in 1948, the same year as Andrew Lloyd Webber, and educated at St Ignatius College, Stamford Hill, and Worcester College, Oxford.

He has worked as a teacher, script reader, trainee stage manager, piano player and journalist. He was editor of *Plays and Players* magazine from 1975 to 1978, and theatre critic and deputy arts editor of the *Financial Times* throughout the 1980s. He went to the *Observer* as theatre critic in 1990, joining the *Mail* in 1997.

By the same author

The Citz
Maggie Smith: A Bright Particular Star
The Aisle is Full of Noises
Knight Errant (with Sir Robert Stephens)
The World According to Mike Leigh

THE ANDREW LLOYD WEBBER STORY

MICHAEL COVENEY

ARROW

Published in the United Kingdom in 2000 by Arrow Books

1 3 5 7 9 10 8 6 4 2

Copyright © Michael Coveney 1999

The right of Michael Coveney to be identified as the Author
of this work has been asserted by him in accordance with
the Copyright, Designs and Patents Act, 1988

First published in the United Kingdom in 1999 by Hutchinson

Arrow Books
The Random House Group Limited
20 Vauxhall Bridge Road, London SW1V 2SA

Random House Australia (Pty) Limited
20 Alfred Street, Milsons Point, Sydney,
New South Wales 2016, Australia

Random House New Zealand Limited
18 Poland Road, Glenfield, Auckland 10, New Zealand

Random House South Africa (Pty) Limited
Endulini, 5A Jubilee Road, Parktown 2193, South Africa

The Random House Group Limited Reg. No. 954009

www.randomhouse.co.uk

A CIP record for this book is available from the British Library

Papers used by Random House are natural, recyclable
products made from wood grown in sustainable forests.
The manufacturing processes conform to the environmental
regulations of the country of origin

Typeset in Plantin by SX Composing DTP, Rayleigh, Essex
Printed and bound in Denmark by
Nørhaven, Viborg

ISBN 0 09 925719 X

CONTENTS

PERMISSIONS

INTRODUCTION AND ACKNOWLEDGEMENTS

Deep in Dickens country in Borough near London Bridge, south of the River Thames, actors and singers are milling around nervously on the first morning's rehearsal of a new Andrew Lloyd Webber musical.

It is the last Monday in April 1998 and *Whistle Down the Wind* is on the road again. While it is not necessarily true that any theatre artist is only as good as his last show, this really is a watershed for Lloyd Webber. The musical was withdrawn in early 1997 after its Washington premiere and some indifferent critical reception. The director Hal Prince has been replaced and the storyline drastically overhauled.

The show has returned to the care of the young Australian director, Gale Edwards, who first put it up on its feet at Lloyd Webber's annual try-out festival in his own back garden at Sydmonton Court, his country estate in Hampshire. On that occasion, in the summer of 1995, with a narration spoken by Martin Sheen, the audience went in expecting to see the outline of a film proposal and came out demanding a stage show.

Since then, Lloyd Webber's Really Useful Group has announced unexpected losses. Staff have been sacked. The composer has parted company with his chief executive, Patrick McKenna. *Sunset Boulevard* has done a lot less well than was hoped, losing its entire

1

investment in America and going out with more of a whimper than a bang in London after a run of just three and a half years.

Yes, just three and a half years! The show had not proved the milk cow the company was looking for twelve years after *The Phantom of the Opera* and seventeen after *Cats* – both still running, both co-produced with Cameron Mackintosh, Lloyd Webber's near contemporary and only rival as biggest cheese in the West End theatre.

In the past few months Lloyd Webber has taken action and taken stock. He is not really aiming for the sky with this one. He seems to know the value of his own score and the worth of the lyrics by Jim Steinman, an outstanding American composer and lyricist in his own right, famously associated with a string of memorable hits for Meat Loaf, Bonnie Tyler and Celine Dion.

The story of three children finding a man in a barn whom they take to be Jesus has been transposed from cinematic black and white innocence in Lancashire, with Hayley Mills and Alan Bates, to the redneck Bible-belt in Louisiana. An even bigger leap, this, than made in Bryan Forbes's charming 1962 movie from the idyllic rural, very Anglo-Saxon, Sussex hinterland of Mary Hayley Bell's original novel.

As the actors form a circle and shift about uneasily on their chairs, the composer explains how, not having been one hundred per cent happy with the Washington production, he has decided to start again.

He says this is a modest musical, but it matters a great deal. When the production team and cast are invited to introduce themselves by name in time-honoured first day of rehearsal style, Lloyd Webber kicks off by declaring himself to be a food critic and part-time composer. (He has written a restaurant and free-wheeling opinion column each Saturday in the *Daily Telegraph* for nearly three years.)

This breaks the ice. Gale Edwards explains that the small town community is being bypassed by the motorways springing up all over that part of the world in the late 1950s. The drawings of the design on the walls of the functional rehearsal room show a stark uncluttered picture of a virtually bare stage with a concrete, incomplete flyover.

That's it. 'This is a tremendous story,' says Gale, 'and it's like a Greek tragedy. It's about change in people's lives, and the catalyst is this criminal, who has murdered within the past forty-eight hours. The children believe he is Jesus. And if this show is about anything, it is about the Jesus within us all. Those of you who know *The Bacchae* by Euripides will know about one man arriving and changing everyone's lives and then moving on.'

I feel a corporate mood of pinching flesh to make sure we are awake. Did she just say that? This sounds more like a play than a show, as (according to Ned Sherrin) one incensed blue-rinsed lady declared on emerging from a torrid evening of Eugene O'Neill.

Jim Steinman, whose long white hair, last cut in 1972, trails down one side of his black leather jacket like a sable fur on an evening gown, brings us back to reality by saying that he used to have a complete crush on Hayley Mills when he saw her in the film in his local downtown cinema. So did we all. Hayley in white ankle socks and cute Wellington boots, pouting and pleading on the brink of freckle-faced adolescence, was the first girl next door for all the boys of our generation, though I suspect Lloyd Webber was more taken with the peppy, knock-'em-dead gutsiness of Judy Garland in the Andy Hardy movies.

Jim, a pleasant, unexpectedly gentle cove who resembles a man lately awoken from a deep coma, a sort of gently grinning Rip Van Winkle of rock, lauds his composer friend's brilliant musical mix of rock, pop, gospel and operatic declamation. That is why he took the job. (He had also nearly worked with Lloyd Webber on *Phantom*, but got involved with a Bonnie Tyler album instead.)

So, with a low-key Lloyd Webber and a laid-back, virtually horizontal Jim Steinman, Gale Edwards will have to be at her most characteristically galvanic over the coming weeks.

There have been several books about Lloyd Webber before, all with some merit and many important details, and I have found them all extremely informative and helpful. The early, unauthorised tomes of Gerald McKnight and Jonathan Mantle contain many useful biographical nuggets, but not all that much in the way of stuff about the shows themselves, except for McKnight's marvellous fourteen pages on the saga of 'Memory' in *Cats*. More recently, Michael Walsh, a music critic on *Time* magazine, decided to put the drama critics in their place and flaunt his staves and time signatures at them. His large volume is monumentally well researched and full of interesting detail which I have gratefully absorbed.

I wanted to do something breezier, faster, something more along the expanded lines of Keith Richmond's excellent but too uncritical survey. The more I have learned of Lloyd Webber's family background, the more fascinating his character and his creative impulse become. For the key to this controversial figure – and Lloyd Webber is controversial on two fronts: as an artist and as a public figure, and the two overlap with alarming regularity – is his constant quest to write musical theatre that speaks to as wide an audience as possible. And I don't think this means that he writes down to anyone, or that he ever resorts to the tried and tested, or the already familiar.

Sometimes his tunes have the virtue of instant familiarity, but that is something else, a trick of his talent. And for all the brickbats, knock-backs, triumphs and fantastic accumulation of wealth, he wants to carry on. As a dominant cultural figure of the age, Lloyd Webber is as widely derided by the chattering classes as he is admired by the broad mass of theatre audiences all over the world.

I wanted to examine this dichotomy and also the secret of his success, as well as his personality, at a time when the musical theatre is in crisis. Theatre, of course, would not be theatre if it were not in a perpetual state of crisis. Our New Labour politicians boast of the achievements of Cool Britannia while it is generally thought totally uncool (you try it in the pub) to say anything positive about Lloyd Webber.

Baron Lloyd-Webber of Sydmonton Court in the County of Hampshire (as he was officially gazetted in February 1997; the hyphen is compulsory with the title, though humorist Keith Waterhouse immediately, and more pithily, dubbed our man Andrew Lord Webber) turned fifty last year. So did Prince Charles.

I see many similarities between the prince and the showman. Both had a lot to prove, and a lot to live up to. Both were temperamentally scarred by family backgrounds and both took an uneasy place in public life, one through inheritance, one through talent and determination.

Both seemed, in a way, old before their time, often culturally removed from it, tortured and stressed by the consequences of that fame. And both were viewed with mixed feelings by the British public while remaining greatly admired and indeed revered abroad. Psychologically, they are virtually peas from the same pod.

When I went up to Oxford in 1967, Lloyd Webber had already been and gone, and nobody talked about him much except David Marks, the outstanding Oxford actor of his generation, who had forged a close and lasting friendship with him the minute they met on a college staircase. As a student in Andrew's college, Magdalen, Marks was now the Oxford University Dramatic Society President and clearly destined for a great theatrical career.

Instead he went into the law. Why not the theatre? Because, he told me, he could never really live with the prospect of being rebuffed. There were outstanding theatre musicians, too, at that time, and many were my friends: composers Nigel Osborne and Nick Bicat and, in my own college, Worcester, organ scholars David Stoll and the late Stephen Oliver, who went on to write the music for the RSC's *Nicholas Nickleby*, a production Lloyd Webber greatly admired and which led to its director, Trevor Nunn, becoming involved first with *Cats,* then with *Starlight Express*, *Aspects of Love* and *Sunset Boulevard.*

All my Oxonian musical friends have pursued careers of musical distinction. But none has made the impact of Lloyd Webber. This is not to do so much with their respective talents, but with the desire for success and fame, a knack and desire for popular approval, and a fanatically single-minded dedication, all of which qualities – some might say flaws – separate Lloyd Webber from the pack.

I am fascinated, too, by the way in which an outstanding and extremely strong-willed individual chooses to excel in an art form that is nothing if not collaborative. Lloyd Webber has never written lyrics for his own music – in the way of Cole Porter, Noel Coward or Sandy Wilson – but knows exactly what lyrics he is looking for.

His professional relationships with a string of lyricists and librettists – primarily Tim Rice, then Alan Ayckbourn, Don Black, Richard Stilgoe, Charles Hart, Christopher Hampton and now Jim Steinman – are particularly important and revealing.

Don Black said that Lloyd Webber changed lyricists

like gardeners. Charles Hart, not to be outdone, said he changed them as often as underpants. And one American collaborator, Richard Maltby Jr, seeing a stream of heavy traffic emanating from the private roads around Sydmonton as he was turning up there, asked Don Black, who was travelling with him in the same car, who on earth all these people were fleeing the maestro's estate. 'Lyricists,' said Black.

But Black also said that if you wanted to paint a big ceiling, it was advisable to hang around with the Pope. Lloyd Webber has been the biggest talent in musical theatre this last half-century. And he changed it for ever in this country. Even more amazingly, he took the public, if not always the critics, with him. It has been an astonishing career and he has emerged not only as a leading composer but as a theatrical showman, producer, artist and self-publicist without rival or equal.

He also lives a life of extraordinary diversity and commitment. He is a leading art collector, a gifted journalist, a horse-breeder, a devoted family man, a notable philanthropist, landowner, serious oenophile and dedicated foodie – with all three wives providing him with an expanded, apparently harmonious family life.

His first wife, Sarah Norris, chose not to comment on her life with Andrew, and wrote me a letter of explanation, which she has allowed me to quote. Her stance is entirely consistent with the dignified position she has adopted over the years. His second wife, Sarah Brightman, embarked on several cheery telephone calls but avoided head-on collision, making it plain that she felt everything that could possibly be said had already been said in newspaper cuttings.

These, of course, I have systematically filleted, both at home, where I have kept a bulging 'ALW' file for many years, and in the superbly maintained cuttings library at Associated Newspapers, publishers of the *Daily Mail*.

Where possible, I have checked the verity of many tabulated tabloid and broadsheet stories against other sources and in conversation with the people involved.

Andrew Lloyd Webber himself has cooperated to the extent of spending many hours and the odd mealtime in conversation with me and my tape-recorder. He has graciously and good-humouredly answered and parried all manner of impertinent questions, performed the entire overture to Rodgers and Hammerstein's *Flower Drum Song* on a restaurant table, taken me on an unforgettable, personal guided tour of his art collection at Sydmonton and ensured access to many of his key colleagues.

None of this he has found necessarily easy or even pleasant to do. He has a short attention span and an understandably ambivalent attitude towards anyone wanting to lay down in words the consequences of an inexpressible urge to create musical theatre based on melody, passion, and popular theatrical harmonics. His energetic jumpiness is one of the most intriguing and alarming things about him.

Madeleine, his wife, has been charming, hospitable and equally cooperative, sorting out photographs and steering me towards areas, especially with regard to the horses, that are entirely new to me. And Andrew's secretarial task force in Eaton Square – Pippa Underwood and Juliet Lamb and, latterly, Emma Hasler – have never been anything but cheerful and helpful when it would have been much easier, and more understandable, for them to be the opposite.

Julian Lloyd Webber, Andrew's brother, has been a generous source of information, not only on the family background but also in the evidence of his own remarkable career, his writing on modern music and his admirable campaign, supported by Andrew, to bring to light the undervalued and forgotten music of their late father, William Lloyd Webber.

At the Really Useful Group headquarters in Tower Street I owe thanks to Sarah Lowry, Marie Curtin and Jeannie Paul, who provided me with facilities, access, interview opportunities and invaluable recorded materials, and also to David Robinson, who advised on permissions and acknowledgements. Thanks are due, too, to the phlegmatic Peter Thompson, mellow prince of PR, and to the following friends and colleagues of Andrew Lloyd Webber who spared time to be interviewed and talked unsparingly of their shared times and tribulations: Rod Argent, Maria Bjornson, Don Black, Peter Brown, David Caddick, Michael Crawford, David Cullen, Gale Edwards, Sir David Frost, David Gilmore, Christopher Hampton, Charles Hart, John Hiseman, Jeremy James-Taylor, Anthony van Laast, John Lill, Gillian Lynne, David Marks, Simon Marsh, David Mason, Trevor Nunn, Elaine Paige, Arlene Phillips, Steven Pimlott, Anthony Pye-Jeary, John Reid, Sir Tim Rice, Michael Sydney-Smith, Wayne Sleep, Bill Taylor, Barbara Thompson, Keith Turner, Kevin Wallace, Marti Webb, and Nigel Wright.

I am especially grateful to my wife, Sue Hyman, for her wisdom, beauty and support; to my editor at Hutchinson, Paul Sidey, a friend with whom I have long wanted to work; and to his assistant, Sophie Wills; to the good offices and friendship of Caradoc King and Penelope Dunn at A. P. Watt Ltd; and to other friends who helped stimulate my researches with ideas and suggestions: Baz Bamigboye at the *Daily Mail*, Nick Bicat, Tom Bower, Shimon Cohen, Bridget Hayward, Sir Nicholas Lloyd, Tiffany Neller, Iphigenia Taxopoulou, Paul Taylor, as well as former crucial colleagues of Lloyd Webber – Brian Brolly, David Crewe-Read, John Napier – who felt unable to talk to me on the record, but were charmingly helpful off it.

Another reluctant witness, and most regrettably absent of all, is Sir Cameron Mackintosh, who has declined to talk to me after a quarter of a century of friendship because of something I said about his not pulsatingly successful recent presentations of *Martin Guerre* and *The Fix*. There is no doubt that the collaboration between Lloyd Webber and Mackintosh on the composer's two biggest hits – *Cats* and *The Phantom of the Opera* – as well as on lesser projects like *Song and Dance* and *Café Puccini* – is one of the most important and influential in modern British theatre.

These two young men – when they were still young – transformed the perception of British musical theatre at home and abroad in the 1980s, created a lifeline for their spiritual home on Broadway and a thriving new industrial landscape on their own territory and were a most remarkable and stimulating double act as the West End theatre old guard reluctantly and then ecstatically took them to their withering bosom.

One of the depressing facts of British theatrical life is that both men look likely to outlive their own legacy. Who will challenge and replace them? And is Lloyd Webber correct in pessimistically sensing that despite all the transformations and excitements of the past twenty-odd years, nothing has really changed at all? We shall see.

PROLOGUE WITH THE BIRTHDAY BOY

On the weekend of his fiftieth birthday in March 1998, Andrew Lloyd Webber and his third wife Madeleine threw a lavish party at Sydmonton Court, their country estate on the edge of Watership Down on the Berkshire and Hampshire borders.

The occasion, and the largest marquee erected in the area since the days of travelling circuses (and not even the combined resources of Barnum, Bailey and Billy Smart could have matched this hundred-foot high monster), was shared by Lloyd Webber's daughter, Imogen, the eldest of the composer's two children by his first wife, Sarah. Imogen would be twenty-one years old ten days later.

Half a life in musical theatre flashed by as guests in black tie and evening gowns mingled in the reception rooms, quaffing champagne, surrounded by the Pre-Raphaelite paintings in the composer's private collection. It was the showbiz party of the decade, an event of unprecedented lustre and luxuriousness.

Lloyd Webber's first wife – known as Sarah One to distinguish her from his second wife, Sarah Brightman (Sarah Two) – was accompanied by her second husband, Jeremy Norris. Imogen's eighteen-year-old brother Nicholas was rallying his pop group, Morgan's Baby, for the cabaret later on; like his father at that age,

Nicholas wavers between academic pursuits and the lure of a life in the music business.

Andrew Lloyd Webber left Oxford after just one term in 1965 because, shortly before taking his place at Magdalen College, he had met an older boy in the music business in London who wanted to write lyrics. Indeed, he and Tim Rice had already sketched out a dozen songs for a putative musical before he had even gone up to Oxford.

Sir Tim Rice was on hand for the bash, benign and merry as ever. Any squabbles or tiffs were on hold. Sir Cameron Mackintosh, producer of *Cats* and *The Phantom of the Opera*, Lloyd Webber's biggest hits after the split with Rice, chuckled mischievously at all and sundry.

There were countless colleagues from the musical theatre, friends from the surrounding villages, the editor of *The Times*, the actress Joan Collins, the concert pianist John Lill, who lodged with the Lloyd Webber family in South Kensington in the early days, Sir David Frost, who first interviewed Lloyd Webber and Rice in the late 1960s on both sides of the Atlantic, and the former Conservative prime minister Sir Edward Heath, who reviewed Lloyd Webber's *Requiem* at its New York premiere in 1985.

After dinner – tian of crab with avocado, foie gras, loin of lamb with truffled mash and crispy leeks, and crème brûlée, washed down with vintage wines from the Sydmonton cellars – the crowd was regaled with an excerpt from the forthcoming *Cats* video projected on a giant screen. Sir John Mills suddenly loomed large as Gus the Theatre Cat ('These modern productions are all very well . . .'), blinking through a true blue crepuscular haze.

Then the cabaret: songs from the new Lloyd Webber musical, *Whistle Down the Wind* – based on the novel of that name by Sir John's wife, Mary Hayley Bell – and a soaring rendition by Dame Kiri Te Kanawa of 'The Heart is Slow to Learn', a Puccinian aria, with lyrics by Don Black, which is one of several songs Lloyd Webber has already stashed away for a projected sequel to *Phantom*.

'Phantom Two' as yet has no storyline, though the novelist Frederick Forsyth – whose spy thriller *The Odessa File*, as a film, had music written for it by Lloyd Webber and his younger brother Julian – is now trying to develop one. One working notion is 'The Phantom in Manhattan', and the rights in such a novella will remain with Forsyth should the composer not respond to the outline.

Forsyth was rubbing shoulders with other literary and theatrical luminaries such as Melvyn Bragg, who scripted the film of *Jesus Christ Superstar* and was for a time a director of Lloyd Webber's Really Useful Group; Trevor Nunn, new director of the Royal National Theatre, and director of no less than four Lloyd Webber musicals; his predecessor at the RNT, Sir Richard Eyre; the producer Robert Fox (who nearly produced *Cats*); Sir Tom Stoppard (who nearly wrote an animated film version of same); and Valerie Eliot, widow of *Cats'* posthumous lyricist, T. S. Eliot.

Media hotshots sprouted among the hot plates: near-legendary talking heads Alan Whicker, Esther Rantzen, Ned Sherrin and Sheridan Morley; easy-listening disc jockeys Mike Read, Susannah Simons and Paul Gambaccini; famed impresarios Robert Stigwood and Harvey Goldsmith; nibbling newshounds Andrew Neil and Nigel Dempster; comedy superstars Rowan Atkinson and Barry Humphries.

The floor was cleared and dancing commenced to the nostalgic, retrogressive rock and roll of Bobby Vee and the Vees (Bobby's three sons).

Lloyd Webber is often quoted as saying that the first records that made a deep impression on him were the march from *The Love of Three Oranges* by Prokofiev (his father, the composer and teacher William Lloyd Webber, bought Andrew and Julian an LP of the *Nutcracker Suite*, but both young boys, to his absolute horror, immediately preferred and loved the Prokofiev piece on the flip side) and 'Rock Around the Clock' by Bill Haley and the Comets. These two items in fact encapsulate precisely what he has done as a theatrical composer: he has worked consciously and unavoidably in the slipstream of early and mid twentieth century classical music while, as an ambitious populist, embracing the innovations, both barbarous and technical, of rock.

There was nothing forced about this. The family home in South Kensington was an echo chamber of every type of music. The place was a bit like some kind of nightmarish rehearsal studio, with Andrew scraping on a violin and banging out his own tunes on the piano, Julian practising diligently at the cello, their father William turning up his own gramophone records of Rachmaninov and the Romantics and both boys rocking round the clock – in their smart grey jumpers and short trousers – at every opportunity.

Julian's favourite early pop recordings were those of Bobby Vee, songs like 'Take Good Care of My Baby' and 'Rubber Ball'. So here is Julian dancing ecstatically with his second wife to the real live version. After an hour or so, and in the small hours of his actual birthday, Lloyd Webber and Tim Rice suddenly join Bobby Vee on stage and deliver an impromptu, word-perfect rendition of several hit numbers by the Everly Brothers, the American pop duo they both admire above all others.

In the birthday booklet circulated as a guide to menus and events, Lloyd Webber recalls the last major shindig, his wedding party for Madeleine seven years previously which was first of all delayed by snow and then partly

14

undermined by the Gulf War. Also, 'some bounder' from Lambourn – a clear reference to his newfound circle of friends in horse breeding and training circles – had swiped all the Veganin. 'Hopefully this time things should go more smoothly . . . no amazing horrors have emerged in the long-range weather forecast department and threats of Gulf War II seem to have receded, at least for the time being [Sadam Hussein was refusing to allow United Nations people to inspect his defence arrangements]. My supply of Veganin is in the safe.'

He pays tribute to Madeleine's talents as the new, third hostess of Sydmonton. At lunch the next day, Peter Brown, one of Lloyd Webber's longest-serving associates, suggests that the Brigadier's daughter and former international horse-rider should be dubbed an honorary Field Marshal for her achievements in organising the weekend.

The couple's first son, Alastair Adam Lloyd Webber, aged six, is invited to cut the birthday cake decorated with edible posters of all the hits. His father helps him seize the knife: 'Right, which show shall we destroy first?' Alastair chooses *Jesus Christ Superstar*.

It is hard in all this hullabaloo to remember the creative role played by Sydmonton and Lloyd Webber's annual informal festival there – he tries out most new shows in a converted chapel in the grounds at an annual summer weekend gathering of colleagues and friends.

But on the Sunday morning, at a Thanksgiving Service in the nearby church of St Mary's Kingsclere, the Rev Canon Don Lewis – a Sydmonton Festival stalwart for twenty years – ringingly evokes the Biblical command of Elijah – 'Send me a minstrel!' – and lauds the spiritual dimension in Lloyd Webber's music. He invokes a school hall performance many years ago by underprivileged children in his parish in Wales of *Joseph and the Amazing Technicolor Dreamcoat*. 'The kids and the parents still live in the memory of that performance, and sing all the songs. It never leaves them.' The music of the service includes the opening chorale of *Whistle Down the Wind*, in which Jim Steinman's lyrics express religious certainty with a piety entirely ironic in terms of what follows in the show.

But Lloyd Webber's tune is, like all good hymns, instantly rousing, and the small, slightly hungover congregation, remnants of the previous night's carousing, give it everything: 'The nights have been growing darker, So much darker now than sin; We'll open the vaults of heaven, And the answers are there within!'

In the small organ loft the local choir sings a growling, moody 'Sanctus' by William Lloyd Webber, Andrew's father, who died in 1982, and this is skilfully elided with the rhythmically upbeat 'Hosanna' from Lloyd Webber's own *Requiem*, written in memory of his father shortly afterwards.

On this same Sunday, BBC Television devotes its religious slot *Songs of Praise* to Lloyd Webber's music and an interview conducted in the gardens at Sydmonton. He comments on the bohemianism of his family: when his mother, Jean, died in 1992, he says that he was in Los Angeles and no-one told him. He pays tribute to his father, William, usually known as Bill, a composer 'out of his time', whose gifts for melody and orchestration he certainly inherited.

And the *Variations* that he wrote in the first place for his cellist brother Julian are performed by the original jazz and rock musicians in the magnificent Victorian church of St James the Less in Westminster, the first beneficiary of Lloyd Webber's philanthropic Open Churches scheme which he founded in 1994.

'Do you pray?' asks his interviewer, Pam Rhodes. 'Yes.' 'Who do you pray to?' 'I don't know . . . I do believe there is something we don't understand . . . and it's impossible to contemplate infinity.'

St James the Less, with an amazing Italian Gothic

interior and a glorious mural over the chancel arch by G. F. Watts, is situated on the Vauxhall Bridge Road, a five-minute walk along the same street from the theatre where *Starlight Express* has been playing these past fourteen years. And a stone's throw from the playing fields of Westminster School where Lloyd Webber developed his lifelong interest in religious architecture, painting and the English choral tradition – 'one of the most precious things we have'.

Lloyd Webber's first musicals with Tim Rice were based on Biblical subjects and his latest, with Jim Steinman, pitches the simple, innocent faith of children against the more cynical version of their parents. 'Any Dream Will Do' sings Joseph in one of Lloyd Webber's most lilting early compositions, and that simple comforting expression of optimism and belief is something to which Lloyd Webber has returned full circle in the journey from *Superstar* to *Whistle*.

That arc in his career is fully illustrated in the birthday concert at the Albert Hall a couple of weeks later. The stars turn out in force on the stage: Antonio Banderas, Glenn Close, Donny Osmond, Dame Kiri Te Kanawa, Bonnie Tyler, Boyzone, Elaine Paige, Michael Ball, Sarah Brightman, Julian Lloyd Webber. As these sorts of galas go, it is an exceptional evening, brilliantly staged by Steven Pimlott on a pair of scenic, interconnecting musical staves designed in black and white by Mark Thompson.

The band is arranged in full view under the energetically-wielded, non-stop baton of Michael Reed. The spectacle ranges from the heart-rendingly simple – Donny Osmond, as relaxed as Andy Williams, singing 'Any Dream Will Do' with a chorus of seated children clutching coloured balloons which float towards the roof; to the imposingly theatrical – Antonio Banderas and Elaine Paige strutting sexily among a massed phalanx of mourning extras in a filmic recreation of *Evita*.

Amazingly, Banderas reveals later in the evening that this is his stage debut, and that he first wanted to go into showbusiness on account of seeing *Jesus Christ Superstar* in Madrid in 1974.

Another British stage debut is that of Glenn Close, who recreates her Broadway triumph as Norma Desmond in *Sunset Boulevard* in a glittering gold and black gown and toque, like some exotic, armour-plated armadillo. Another splash of colour among the black and white is provided by Andrew's brother Julian in a red football jersey proclaiming his lifelong devotion to Third Division strugglers Leyton Orient.

He leaps on to the stage like a whirling dervish and rips through the *Variations* Andrew wrote as a result of a fraternal bet laid against Orient being demoted at the end of one particularly sorry season in the East End. Orient survived, and Andrew was obliged to write one of his most vivid and inspired pieces.

The concert is greeted by accusations of hubris and pretentiousness in *The Times*, and by some heavy-handed sneering in the *Independent*. Lloyd Webber is someone who writes musicals for people who don't much like musicals, we are told, by someone who presumably likes them even less than the rest of us.

Others, from gushing columnists to the former Prime Minister, John Major, opine that Andrew Lloyd Webber has given untold pleasure to untold millions. The fearless *Independent* man says that on the occasion of his retirement he will give even more pleasure to even more millions.

None of this knockabout ever involves any analysis but a sort of gut reaction to the phenomenon of Lloyd Webber's career, his bullish knack for self-promotion and the way in which his work proceeds inside an elaborate professional bubble of his own making. This does create a problem in the critical evaluation of the work itself. So much seems to get in the way of dispassionate assessment when the life of a Lloyd Webber musical is surrounded by hyperbole and bound up in the fate of his company. Genius for marketing and a quick eye for the main chance are part of this story. But only part.

The life of the musical theatre in Britain is a much wider subject. For the moment, as the prince of musical theatre historians, Mark Steyn, sagely notes, Lloyd Webber is the only hope for commercial musicals. Such artistic enterprises are not the preserve of normal people. Abnormal people write them, and Lloyd Webber fits the bill. He has passion and he has self-belief. He also has an abundance of talent that shades, I believe, into genius.

When he finally takes the stage at the Albert Hall he thanks Tim Rice, without whom, he says, he might never have gone this far, or indeed this way. It is a touching moment because it sounds slightly out of character. Gauche and even clumsy in physical motion – he admits to vertigo at the thought of getting out of bed, and his manner of walking (short, clipped steps, feet daintily pressed to the ground) is that of someone suddenly re-acquiring a basic skill after years of not bothering – he seems genuinely moved. 'Musicals, whether small, medium or big, are alive and well as long as someone wants to write one and someone wants to produce one . . . When I started to do this, nobody believed in it at all. People said it was an old form and you had to be the Beatles or Elvis Presley.'

The evening is dedicated as a charity to the National Youth Music Theatre of which Lloyd Webber is chief sponsor. In thus turning his words, and the stream of hit songs, into a statement about the continuity of an art form, he cleverly transcends the vanity of his own celebration. His musicals are performed all over the world and his fame and wealth easily exceed anything achieved by the century's two other great British musical theatre figures, Ivor Novello and Noel Coward.

Novello, largely and unjustly forgotten today, worked within the operetta tradition and kept the home fires burning. Coward, a composer, dramatist and lyricist of rare metropolitan wit and wisdom, kept them crackling; he was his own greatest invention and our own patriotic answer to Cole Porter. After them came the pleasant parochialism of Julian (*Salad Days*) Slade, the stylish nostalgia of Sandy (*The Boy Friend)* Wilson and gifted Cockney earthiness of Lionel (*Oliver!*) Bart.

But love him or hate him, Lloyd Webber soars over all these past two decades, dominating, and to a large extent defining, the contemporary musical theatre in a series of highly popular compositions imbued with an original rock-lyrical brand of vivid musical eclecticism, teeming melodiousness and supreme theatrical flourish.

The first Lloyd Webber show I saw was *Jesus Christ Superstar* at the Palace Theatre shortly after it opened there in 1972. *Hair* had arrived from New York to announce the Age of Aquarius and The Who had written *Tommy*. But the London musical theatre was really still stuck in, and stuck on, the past.

Its attempts to sound up to date were usually of flesh-crawling awfulness. The West End musical that opened just before *Superstar* was something called *Pull Both Ends* in which a cracker manufacturing concern, its output threatened by a workers' strike, ended quite happily after a few harmless kerfuffles with everyone singing and pulling together. The critical response ensured a hasty demise: 'Not so much a cracker as a damp squib' was a typical review headline. Despite allusions to industrial strife during the Ted Heath government, its musical language was more suited to an audience old enough to remember the Ted Heath band.

Andrew Lloyd Webber's career, on the other hand, has been a fascinating attempt to marry new musical idioms with new sound technology, new ways to dream with old standards of artistry. None of his shows is set in the contemporary world, but for their audiences they strike contemporary chords.

A conservative by nature, Lloyd Webber is an artist who wants to make money while making new waves, and his unique contribution has been duly recognised by his political peers: the music of the knight is now the music of the lord!

In the still air of the Albert Hall, as the cheers and the encores die away, Lloyd Webber sits quietly at the piano and plays while a young girl sings. He presses the keys as if his life depends on them. And he seems to withdraw inside a private reverie as the years roll back to a noisy London apartment where a very small boy with bright eyes and a short temper insists on playing his own tunes instead of doing his piano practice. We are just eavesdropping.

ONE

HOME ALONE IN SOUTH KENSINGTON

Andrew Lloyd Webber was born in the maternity wing of the Westminster Hospital on 22 March 1948. He was christened without any hyphens seven weeks later in All Saints, Margaret Street, Marylebone, the church where his father, William Southcombe Lloyd Webber, had been organist and choirmaster; and where, as a serving soldier in the Royal Army Pay Corps, he married Andrew's mother, Jean Johnstone, in 1942.

It was all that neat and tidy. However, family life in Harrington Court, the huge red-brick block of spacious mansion flats next to South Kensington tube station, was anything but. Vivid is one word to describe it. Another is bohemian. Another, noisy.

Harrington Court is a dilapidated relic of former Victorian red-brick glory. The Arabs moved in during the early 1970s – the area became known as 'Saudi' Kensington and long-term residents like the Lloyd Webbers were forced out.

But you can still get an idea of what the place must have been like before becoming the run-down pile of today: the legend of 'service apartments' over the main entrance is a dodgy advertisement unleavened by the sight of dowdy, cheap net curtains hanging in not very clean windows above the ground-level parade of shops. The whole block, shops and all, is owned by the Princess el Bandri who, for reasons best known to herself, has allowed the apartments to become entirely unoccupied and untended. Inside the apartments there were high ceilings, a long hall and large, comfortably appointed rooms leading off on either side. Money was scarce in the Lloyd Webber family and the furnishings, though plentiful, were scruffy. Lloyd Webber recalls that there was more linoleum than carpet on the floors, and a Murphy fold-up bed was kept in the sitting room. But this was a prime site in one of the smartest parts of town, and there was plenty of room to live noisily together and retreat privately behind closed doors. The apartment was rented by Lloyd Webber's grandmother, so the family were sitting tenants. When the landlords sought to develop the property in the early 1970s, the ever-tenacious Jean negotiated three smaller nearby flats in exchange for the one large flat and one adjacent small apartment the family by that time occupied. When they finally all moved out in 1973, they went literally just around the corner to Sussex Mansions on the Old Brompton Road.

This whole area, bounded by Knightsbridge and Kensington Gardens to the north, Chelsea and the Thames to the south, gives (or at least, gave) a background of comfort and privilege to anyone resident within. There is a plethora of good restaurants, flighty upper-class girls at secretarial colleges, and an enclave of world famous museums on the doorstep – the Victoria & Albert, the Natural History and the Science.

The Albert Hall and the Royal College of Music are a few hundred yards away. And, travelling eastward, it is no distance at all to the even grander squares and streets of Belgravia, where the young Lloyd Webber as a schoolboy at Westminster would develop his passion for Victorian churches and paintings.

One day, when he could afford it, he would buy homes in Eaton Square and Chester Square: however far he roamed, to the Sydmonton Estate in Hampshire, the Trump Tower in New York, to Cap Ferrat in the South of France, Kiltinan Castle in County Tipperary, he would always remain defined by this special part of London.

Harrington Court is in Harrington Road and continues, across the Gloucester Road, into Harrington Gardens, where Gilbert of Gilbert and Sullivan lived at Number Thirty-nine in the 1880s. There is a story of how Gilbert, incensed that his music-writing partner had pooh-poohed a new storyline, exploded so furiously that an old Japanese executioner's sword crashed to the floor and gave him the idea for *The Mikado*.

More plausibly, the scholars insist, Gilbert was merely inspired by a Japanese exhibition of the day in Knightsbridge – and the fact that the department store Liberty's was selling many fabrics and dresses in the Japanese style. But the volatile working relationship of Gilbert and Sullivan was not all that dissimilar to that of their modern successors Tim Rice and Andrew Lloyd Webber.

Number Ten, Harrington Court was on the top floor at the right-hand side of the building. The place was full of pianos, cats, musicians and gramophone records. And it was primarily the fiefdom of neither William nor Jean, but Jean's mother, Molly. Molly lived there first of all with her two daughters, Viola and Jean, and later with Jean and her husband and their two boys. As the family expanded, so she acquired the lease on a small adjacent apartment where she lived alongside the younger musical brood. Her own marriage to an officer in the Argyll and Sutherland Highlanders had fallen apart after the birth of her three children – Alastair, Viola (Andrew's vaunted Auntie Vi, who became a crucial influence in his life) and Jean, who was the youngest.

Molly Johnstone had obtained a divorce – an unusual enough occurrence in those days, the late 1920s – and

moved her family from Eastbourne in Sussex, where
Jean had been born, to Harrow in Middlesex. Alastair
attended the famous public school nearby and was
about to take up a place at Cambridge University when
tragedy struck. He was drowned, aged eighteen, off the
Dorset coast in a boating accident. Molly, stricken with
grief, sold up the family home, gathered up her
daughters and took a lease on the apartment in
Harrington Court.

Once the girls had been seen through school, she
found work as a doctor's receptionist and promptly fell
in love with her employer. Fate promptly dealt another
unkind blow to Molly. For the doctor, George Crosby,
one of the first general practitioners to have access to
insulin, fell in love with Molly's elder daughter, Viola.
And married her.

This peculiar development was not openly talked
about in front of the rest of the family. Years later,
Andrew and his brother Julian confirmed that they were
never told outright about this 'incestuous' development
– a modern, inverted version of Phaedra falling
hopelessly in love with Hippolytus, son of her husband
Theseus in the plays of Seneca, Euripides and Racine –
but enough nudges and winks were exchanged for them
to be pretty sure about what had happened.

Molly presumably found consolation in her faith. She
was a deeply religious woman and a regular member of
the congregation at the City Temple Church, where
Leslie Weatherhead, a very distinguished Methodist
preacher, was the minister. Her Christian devotion went
hand in hand with the sort of firebrand left wing politics
espoused by another great Methodist minister of the
day, Donald Soper.

It is hard now to imagine the impact of a man like
Weatherhead on his parishioners and beyond, but when
Donald Soper died at the end of 1998, many of his
obituarists recalled the great Methodist triumvirate of

Weatherhead, Soper and William Langster. Of Langster it was said that he loved God, of Weatherhead that he loved sinners and of the even more flamboyant Soper that he loved an argument.

Jean absorbed Soper-style soap-box socialism and Christianity – Soper always insisted that Christianity was incompatible with capitalism – with her mother's milk. She was a dour, serious, deeply unworldly woman. Viola could not have been more different. She was loud, large, demonstrative and theatrical. She worked as an actress during and shortly after the war. She never achieved any great success although Andrew remembers her being on more than nodding terms of acquaintance with John Gielgud and Vida Hope, the charismatic director of Sandy Wilson's great musical hit, *The Boy Friend*.

Vi was the antithesis of her younger sister, who was shy, serious, anonymous-looking and rather intense. Vi wore big hats and floral dresses. Jean never spent a penny on clothes for herself and indeed acquired most of her wardrobe in later life from the Oxfam shops.

Endearingly, she never made any sartorial concessions towards Andrew's glittering first night parades or smart gatherings at Sydmonton. And the sisters, even when Vi moved out of Harrington Court, did not get on at all well. The fact that Andrew, as he grew up, became closer to Vi than to Jean would have been a cause of yet more domestic irritation in a household increasingly riven with artistic and temperamental flare-ups.

While Jean was seeking salvation on her own and other people's behalf, Vi was booming around London with her theatre chums and even concocting, years ahead of its time, something referred to by Andrew and Julian as the Gay Cookbook. This unpublished opus was full of rather saucy descriptions of how to make Coq au Vin ('Take one cock firmly by the hand . . .') and such homiletic aphorisms as 'Too Many Cocks Spoil the Breath'.

When she married George, Viola retired promptly from the stage and moved in with him above the doctor's surgery in Weymouth Street, which bisects the more famous medical thoroughfare, Harley Street.

Jean, a student at the Royal College of Music where she met William in 1939, remained in Harrington Court. And that is where William joined her after their marriage in 1942. After the war, he continued to work at the college as a teacher and examiner. There had been no music previously on Jean's side of the family, but she loved her studies and became not only an expert in the appreciation of talent in others – fanatically so, you might say – but also a fine teacher in her own right. She specialised in teaching piano to very young children and eventually took a job at the little Wetherby pre-prep school in Rosary Gardens just around the corner from Harrington Court.

William, or Bill as he was generally known, was a budding composer of Romantic music and was recognised as one of the outstanding organists of his day. He was just seventeen when appointed the youngest ever fellow at the Royal College of Organists.

There had been music on his side of the family, but not all that much. His father, also called Bill, was a local tradesman and plumber along the King's Road in Chelsea. He had married Mary Winifred Gittins in 1913 and was an amateur chorister with the Bach Choir and the Oriana Madrigal Society. He also worked with the BBC Chorus and the George Mitchell choir – later the Black and White Minstrels – on radio.

Young William had a strong Anglo-Catholic church background and won a scholarship to the Mercers' School, one of London's oldest educational establishments, founded to help bright boys from poor families (it closed in 1959). He was a prodigy, appearing on the radio in his early teens and winning an open scholarship to the Royal College of Music.

He was soon giving organ recitals all over the country. He also began to compose his own music, unashamedly in the vein of his beloved late Romantics such as Rachmaninov and César Franck. Like Jean, he too was shy, but – unlike her – given to dramatic mood swings and melancholic fits of depression.

This shows in the music Bill wrote, as indeed I believe it shows in the music of his first son. There is anguish and distress in quite a lot of Lloyd Webber's music from *Superstar* onwards. Bill was certainly a severely repressed and secretive cove and I think that the emotional dam-bursting we find in much of his son's sweeping musical theatre moments is all part of a deep and complex hereditary temperament.

The concert pianist John Lill, who later came to know the family very well, describes Bill as one of the six or seven really great musical minds he has encountered in his career (this short list includes the conductors Sir John Barbirolli and Sir Adrian Boult), and that, like his two sons, he had an almost hysterical sense of humour.

But he felt at odds with modernism in musical taste, and struggled to have his work performed. He even wrote under a pair of pseudonyms – Peter Wade and Clive Chappell – but it is not clear which aspects of his personality occupied which identity. Julian thinks the Wade work Bill felt to be inferior, and states that the Chappell stuff is mostly short piano pieces with a romantic base veering into jazz chords.

Andrew is convinced that Bill would have liked to have gone off and written film scores, but that the war, and other circumstances, intervened. 'He certainly could have been like Muir Matheson, but in the end I don't think he had it in his personality to make that leap. He had a hugely academic caste of mind, which I don't. He could take down an entire orchestral score if somebody played it. And his knowledge of the art of fugue was second to none.'

Bill wrote one children's musical, *Pinnochio*, staged by students at the Royal College in 1946. But mostly he wrote choral music, lush orchestral pieces and some really rather beautiful nocturnes and serenades. Some of this lost and forgotten work has lately been released on a new CD, *Invocation*, performed by the City of London Sinfonia under the direction of Richard Hickox. All of it is interesting and some of it – especially a nine-minute, atmospheric, almost cinematic orchestral item called *Aurora* – full of melody, yearning and turbulence.

In *Serenade for Strings*, which he wrote at the age of twenty-five, you can sense real talent and promise. An interpolated slow movement, written in an Indian summer burst in 1980, when he suddenly started to write again after years of inactivity, has the sort of gorgeous, full-on melody, complete with theatrical throb quotient, that his son might have been proud to include in *Sunset Boulevard*. There is a distinctive melancholic undertow, too, in a lovely triple of miniatures called *Invocation*, which gave the new album its title.

'My father's music is entirely about latent sexuality,' says Andrew. 'His *Aurora* is just about the most heightened piece of music I've ever listened to. I remember hearing it on an old 78rpm record we got made from a BBC tape when I was a child. Even thinking about it makes me cry.'

In the end Bill gave up and, after his two sons were born, didn't write anything at all for many years. He gave up the idea of a composing career. The family was generally poor, in a genteel sort of way but, on Molly's side at least, it had quite a classy background. As Bill was living in her flat with her daughter, he was expected to start earning enough money to send his children to fee-paying schools.

Shortly after Andrew was born, Bill resigned from his concurrent post as organist at All Saints in order to devote more time to his role of Professor and Examiner in Theory and Composition at the Royal College of Music.

And the new baby was a bit of a handful. Jean sometimes blamed this on Bill's pet monkey which had attacked her when she was pregnant, scratching and biting her hands, thus earning instant dismissal to a zoo. Forty odd years later, Jean said that when Andrew arrived, 'He never stopped screaming until – well, just about now.'

'When he was little,' said Bill when Andrew was the subject on *This Is Your Life* in 1980, 'he was forever jumping and bumping around the place, making a dreadful din and disturbing all the neighbours at three o'clock in the morning.' The only successful soporific, apparently, was the Latin American dance music of Edmundo Ros and his band. Bill placed records of Edmundo and Co on his creaky, wind-up gramophone turntable while Jean rocked the little terror to sleep.

Everyone loved cats. There were two called Sergei and Dmitri in honour of the great Russian composers Prokofiev and Shostakovich. And Bill, owlish and bespectacled, was seldom seen around the flat without Perseus (or Percy), the beautiful Siamese specimen, perched on his shoulder like Long John Silver's parrot. As both of his sons proceeded to embark upon distinguished musical careers – Andrew as a composer, Julian as an internationally acclaimed concert cellist – Bill withdrew to his study and wrapped himself against the cruel world in a shroud of nostalgia and regret. Not that he didn't relish their success, to a degree. He did, but it made living with his own comparative failure all the more difficult.

By the time Julian arrived in 1951, Andrew was fiddling around on the piano keys, but showing early signs of not wanting to take his practice all that seriously. This drove Jean nuts: 'He always played his instruments in a *completely* unorthodox manner! All the pieces he was supposed to play, he wouldn't touch. He wanted to play his own tunes, and no others.'

Another opportunity for dramatic high jinks arose when Andrew upstaged Julian's newborn baby status by undergoing an operation for appendicitis. He howled, bawled and carried on in a manner Jean always claimed he perfected for tactical use in later life. One of his mollifying presents in hospital was a picture book of castles, and it is possible that the lifelong interest in architectural ruins took hold there and then.

As well as banging imperfectly about on the keyboards, Andrew turned to the violin and the French horn. In due course, Julian rebelled even more totally than his brother against their mother's demanding piano tuition and, much impressed by a performance of *The Sorcerer's Apprentice* at an Ernest Read children's concert at the Royal Festival Hall, decided he wanted to learn to play the cello.

By the middle of the 1950s the cacophony in Harrington Court must have been stupendous. Julian noted the crescendo in his entertaining memoir, *Travels With My Cello*: 'My father's electric organ, mother's piano, grandmother's deafening (she was deaf) television, elder brother's astounding piano and French horn and my own scrapings on the cello and blowings on the trumpet by themselves would have made the cannon and mortar effects of the *1812 Overture* seem a bit like the aural equivalent of a wet Sunday morning on Hackney Marshes . . .'

There was a lot of screaming and shouting as well. Bill and Andrew were the prime culprits on this front, says Julian. Bill, especially, for all his apparent taciturnity, was prone to extreme bouts of violent temper.

'He nearly killed me once. He had two pedigree pet mice. One of them got out and of course the cat got it. It was my cat. And my father started smashing up this cat, which I pulled away from him. At which point he tried to strangle me to death.' Molly and Jean intervened and saved the situation, but nobody considered the outburst to be anything out of the ordinary.

In the flat below, the fine old character actor Carlton Hobbs, best known as Sherlock Holmes on radio, must have cast many a despairing look ceilingwards. But he was known to complain only twice in twenty years: once when Julian, like some incompetent hod-carrier, dropped a large bag of heavy bricks on the floor; and secondly when Andrew's tireless stamping on the loud pedal finally proved too much even for this stoical thespian.

It is conceivable that those dropped bricks were part of the toy theatre building operation supervised in Harrington Court by Auntie Vi. It was made of wooden bricks and blocks, the walls were fully wallpapered, there was red plush curtain and an elaborate revolving stage, made from a gramophone turntable and inspired by the revolving farewells on the *Sunday Night at the London Palladium* programme on television. There was even a primitive sound system. Andrew – bashing out his tunes on the piano – would be impresario, producer, composer, writer and stage manager, with Julian pressed into service wherever he was needed, moving toy soldiers and properties around the set, sometimes with every sign of reluctance.

Andrew had made his first public appearance on the cover of a magazine at the age of three, when Jean placed a full-length photo of him playing his violin with *Nursery World*. But now he was moving into show-business proper. Those first infantile compositions, written from the age of six or seven, were published in the *Music Teacher* magazine in 1959 in a selection titled *Toy Theatre Suite* with a fulsome critical appreciation saying that the pieces 'which are clearly the product of a gifted child of one of our most distinguished musicians, will be enjoyed because of their natural and spontaneous qualities.'

They do survive, these little tunes, but Lloyd Webber declares they are all dreadful, apart from one, which was recycled as a ragtime soft-shoe number for Tim Rice's easy, charming King Potiphar lyrics in *Joseph and the Amazing Technicolor Dreamcoat* ('Potiphar had very few cares, He was one of Egypt's millionaires, Having made a fortune buying shares in Pyramids; Potiphar had made a huge pile, Owned a large percentage of the Nile, Meant that he could really live in style, and he did').

Meanwhile, Julian had acquired a scaled-down cello and took the Grade One examination at the age of five. The extent of his precocity may be measured by the confession that he played all the pieces from memory and was too small to read the sight reading paper placed on the music stand in front of him, so he simply made it up. He was on his way.

In 1956 Andrew left Wetherby, where his mother was a teacher, and was sent to Westminster Under School. This was an exclusive prep school, affiliated to Westminster School itself, occupying two tall houses on the south side of Eccleston Square behind Victoria Station (the new Under School opened in Vincent Square in 1981).

Jean was ambitious for him to be an academic historian, as Andrew himself had already professed his lifelong ambition to be Chief Inspector of Ancient Monuments to the Ministry of Works. This passion ran parallel to his musical prowess, much as it still does today. He loved the countryside in a way that any town child does who remembers the first thrill – as Lloyd Webber certainly does – of rushing through a dark train tunnel to the limitless infinity of a green and gold horizon. He started collecting ordnance survey maps with train-spotting obsessiveness.

The romance of ruined buildings was tied up in this,

and Lloyd Webber recalls having a heated argument, aged about seven, with his father on the restoration of Tintern Abbey. Dad said it should be restored, little Andrew vehemently demurred, arguing it should be preserved as a ruined building (an attitude he disavows today).

This architectural enthusiasm began to dominate family holidays, and excursions were often planned to include, at Andrew's insistence, a detour to a ruined castle or abbey. He even started writing books about these places, and never once thought that his future lay seriously with music. The earliest dream he can recall is of being taken to Fountains Abbey in Yorkshire.

His masters found him to be a naturally precocious pupil with a facility for words as well as music. But he was getting fed up with being pushed forward as a historian by his mother – he was always a year younger than the other boys in his class – and recalls a life-changing experience when asked to play the violin in a school concert. 'I said I'm not going to do that, I'm going to play six songs and I'm going to dedicate each one of them to masters in the school, which I did from the stage. Because of the reaction of the other kids, I knew that there was something very different that I would be interested in doing . . . I was about nine or ten and I'd written all the songs myself.'

Despite this success, and against the expectation of the masters themselves, he failed to secure the internal scholarship awarded to the outstanding boy of each year going on to the main school. But forward he went, anyway, aged thirteen, after taking the ordinary entrance examination, in the autumn of 1961. At the same time, Bill was appointed director of the London College of Music, then going through a bad patch, according to Julian, although – surely not because – James Galway was teaching the flute.

Andrew remained a day boy for his first two years, but

then became a boarder as a result of winning a foundation scholarship in an examination known as the Challenge. Andrew really felt he left home at about this time. Although, as a boarder, he would return at week-ends and during the holidays, life now revolved around his new school, his determinedly renewed interest in making something of his musical talents, and the increasing number of theatre visits arranged for him by Aunt Vi.

In truth, he was also mighty glad to get out of Harrington Court. One of the consequences of his mother's ambition for him was that he had been catapulted forward at an unusually early age. But he astonished his housemaster, Frank Kilvington, head of Rigaud's, by delivering a detailed project on English castles complete with drawings and diagrams.

And he had written, in a furious inky scrawl, to the Ministry of Works thus:

I have been making a tour of the buildings on the Welsh border, and in the course of this two or three horrible examples of decaying buildings were visited. The first was Usk Castle. This is covered with ivy and plants to the extent that one can hardly make out the periods of construction. An old lady who appears to own the site told me that it was almost impossible to consolidate the remains owing to lack of finance.

An even worse example can be seen at Clun. The castle here is owned by the parish council and it is in a terrible state. The keep, which is somewhat unique in that it uses one side of the motte as a wall, stands almost to its full height, but a huge split has appeared from top to bottom. It is completely overgrown and no attempt is being made to excavate or, more important, to consolidate remains . . .

The last is at Whittington in Shropshire which, I understand, has been offered to you for preservation, but due to lack of finance you are hesitating to accept. This is the most terrible state of affairs and surely something can be done about it.

Yours sincerely,

Andrew Lloyd-Webber (Aged 13)

Note how the errant hyphen pops up uninvited, presumably because usage at school by others had decreed an occasional appearance in the face of which, and on semi-official occasions, the owner simply caved in.

Knowing of his musical ability, and anxious to revive the house's fortunes within the school, Kilvington instigated a series of concerts and performances and teamed Lloyd Webber with an older boy, Robin St Clare Barrow, who wrote the lyrics.

Their first show, and Andrew's official stage debut, can be dated Christmas 1961. Posterity does not record audience response to *Cinderella Up the Beanstalk and Most Everywhere Else!* but Andrew's music was all over the show and he performed a well-received Russ Conway impersonation at the piano.

He sat papers in Maths, French, English, Latin and History in order to win the Challenge prize and become a member of College House. This was the elite corps in an elite school. There were forty boys in College House. They were known as Queen's Scholars and were entitled to be the first people to cry 'Long live the Queen' (or King) at any Coronation ceremony. They wore academic gowns at all times, and morning dress for Sunday services in the Abbey. The prize also went towards the cost of boarding and must have been very welcome to his parents, though they hardly put themselves out to help him celebrate.

This triumph was marked instead by Aunt Vi, who whisked Andrew off for dinner in Camden Passage, Islington, and treated him to an honest Italian nosh-up in the Portofino. The restaurant, complete with Neapolitan waiters and red checked tablecloths, is much the same today. Aunt Vi treated her favourite nephew to his first serious bottle of wine, an experience Lloyd Webber still cherishes as a milestone. She ordered a 1961 bourgeois claret, and the fellow has simply never forgotten it.

Back in Harrington Court, there had been some curious upheavals owing to Jean's eagerness to encourage new talent. Bill's reluctance to push his own work forward had driven her first to distraction, and subsequently to embark on a campaign of belittlement. Then she switched her attentions elsewhere.

Even before Julian was born she had fastened on to a tenor from Gibraltar, a wartime refugee, called Louis, about whom no-one remembers anything, least of all his surname. Jean simply decided this chap was a great singer, but there are no extant recordings either to confirm or confound her infatuation. Julian simply says that Louis became a fixation, that his father wasn't very happy about it, and that in time the intense friendship fizzled and petered out.

One begins to wonder about Jean's private life and the price of Bill's obstinacy and reticence. There was, apparently, a string of proteges. But one above all is of special significance. And his arrival on the scene, and indeed in the family home, helped distance Andrew even further from his mother. He came to feel supplanted in her affections by an outsider whose musical gifts she prized higher than his own.

John Lill (b. 1944) was – is – an exceptionally intelligent working class boy from the East End of London imbued with a rare musical ability. He was plucked and nurtured by Jean in the manner of a

Shavian prototype, and his extraordinary and rapid rise to international stardom – culminating in a London debut at the Festival Hall in 1963 and his victory in the Tchaikovsky competition in Moscow in 1970 – was in large measure due to the intervention of the Lloyd Webber family in general and to Jean in particular.

Largely self-taught and, by his own admission, immensely headstrong, Lill had breezed into the Royal College from Leyton County High School thanks to the self-sacrificing efforts of his parents, both factory workers. Interestingly, at the time he met the Lloyd Webber family, aged about fourteen or fifteen, his cramped, impoverished household in Buckland Road suddenly had to accommodate an unexpected baby sister.

Maybe, like Andrew fortuitously becoming a boarder at Westminster, Lill wanted out. But he could not possibly have planned what happened: he was definitely chosen. He met the boys at orchestral rehearsals in the junior department of the Royal College in the last gasp of the 1950s. On Saturday mornings, Lill, a star pupil in the junior college, was helping out in the percussion section where both brothers had opted to take up a second instrument.

On Haydn's Military Symphony, Andrew played cymbals and Julian the bass drum; and both practised their parts at home, which must have provided a little additional torture for poor old Carlton Hobbs beneath. (One is reminded of Max Wall's misguided boast about practising the trumpet: the neighbours threw stones and broke all the windows so they could hear him better.)

John Lill, who played the tympani, found himself chatting to Julian, whom he remembers as an immaculately dressed little boy, very correctly spoken, with a high-pitched squeaky voice. One day, Julian announced that Lill was invited to lunch with his parents. 'Meeting these people was quite a shock to me,'

Lill says. He must have felt like one of the nonplussed weekend visitors of the Bliss family in Noel Coward's *Hay Fever*. His first impression was of total eccentricity, the second of an unfamiliar but seductive domestic situation of what struck him as unwonted luxury: immense rooms, top-class pianos, the odd carpet. He really felt he had landed in Paradise.

Jean knew about Lill's outstanding record at college and he flabbergasted his hosts by sight-reading a tricky piece of Bach at the piano after lunch and immediately playing it back from memory. He became an instant fixture in the flat, and Jean would insist on him staying the night in a spare bedroom, so that he was on hand for college and slipping inexorably under her spell.

Back in Leyton, Lill's parents gladly accepted that he was flying away into a new stratosphere. Young John stayed with them over the weekends – he was playing piano in the Thatched House pub for pocket money – but living a new life courtesy of the Lloyd Webbers in town. 'Thanks to Jean and the family, I met people, and got my London debut. I played Rachmaninov's Third Piano Concerto at the Royal College with Boult conducting, and they organised people from the press to come along to rehearsals.'

But even Lill himself acknowledges that, by the early 1960s, Jean was becoming over-possessive. He even felt sorry for the boys. 'My own mother wasn't always totally delighted at the prospect of them coming over to Leyton every Saturday, which they did.' Jean wanted to see John's family, and while she sat there gurgling over John's baby sister and unwittingly undermining the confidence of the exhausted Mr and Mrs Lill, Julian sloped off and crossed the road to watch Leyton Orient playing soccer at Brisbane Road. He would become a lifelong fan of the club.

But there was an even more bizarre aspect to this new friendship. Jean, like her mother, was deeply religious and also psychic. She believed that you could make contact with the dead, and indeed much later on entered into some serious psychic investigation with John Lill, who had himself discovered a capacity for psychic experience during his musical preparations. As a child, he was acutely aware of forces working through him when he played and he often exclaimed to his mother that he didn't know how his fingers were working in such a demonic fashion.

Lill did not take his psychic dabblings any further with Jean until about 1970. He won an open scholarship to the senior part of the college in 1961 and made his debut at the Festival Hall in 1963. Throughout this period the Lloyd Webbers kept a bed available to him in the flat, and Jean would always leave out a cold meal for him when he came in at night. He spent a lot of time with the boys and even went on family holidays.

Like Andrew, he had a passion for the music of Prokofiev – he remembers Andrew's interest in crazy orchestrations, and Prokofiev's accentuation of the tuba was a firm favourite – and he also shared the family's enthusiasm for Rodgers and Hammerstein. Bill had told Andrew he could call himself a real composer the day he wrote anything as good as 'Some Enchanted Evening'. But he recalls especially laughing a good deal with Andrew. Both were big fans of *The Goon Show* on radio. 'Andrew was much the more difficult and highly strung of the two boys, less sociable, but clearly intelligent and gifted. I used to have a beaten-up old Jaguar car and we used to go away for afternoons in the Cotswolds. We'd find a tea shop and sit there ordering more and more hot water and trying to extract as many cups as possible from the one pot. By the time we got to our fifteenth cup we'd be laughing ourselves silly.'

The Lloyd Webber parents, apart from the annual holidays, tended to leave the boys to their own devices. Julian remarks that it was in many ways a very strange upbringing: 'I've often thought that if Andrew and I had turned out to be drug addicts we could have quite easily turned round and said it was all due to our family background. We were allowed to do what we wanted to do all the time. I had this fascination with the underground system. And I was allowed, at the age of nine, to travel all over it on my own. I had this odd ambition to visit every single underground station, and I did, which must have been quite dangerous.'

Jean thought that John Lill and Andrew would be interested in a concert for unusual instruments somewhere near King's Cross. Indeed they were, but the fartlike reports of the tuba in a Vaughan Williams concerto for that instrument soon had them on the brink of a serious giggling fit. They then exploded in laughter at the sight of a man Andrew remembers as 'the biggest I've ever seen' who wobbled on to the stage to play a very small flute, a sopronino, in a piece by Telemann. Lill and Lloyd Webber were asked to leave during the interval and continued braying uncontrollably along the Euston Road for another hour or so.

Jean and Bill did not take their sons to the theatre all that often, but Aunt Vi would suggest outings to the hit musicals of the day such as *My Fair Lady*, which Andrew saw from the gods but without Stanley Holloway, who was off that night, 'so I remember not seeing him'. He saw *West Side Story* and, in the cinema, *South Pacific*. The pleasure he took in Rodgers and Hammerstein was extremely unfashionable among boys of his age, a fact to which he alluded in an affectionate tribute to the great partnership he penned for *Time* magazine in June 1998: 'It was 8.30 a.m., May 19, 1961 . . . There was an uproar as I entered the common room, where we boys were supplied with the daily newspapers. "Have you read your heroes' reviews, Lloydy?" "Look, *The Times* says the show is treacly" "Webster, look at *this* one." *That* one said something to the effect that "if you are a diabetic who craves sweet things, take along some extra insulin, and you will not fail to thrill to *The Sound of Music*."'

If nothing else, 'Lloydy' continued, he had learned his first lesson in creative theatre advertising, for the quotation 'You will not fail to thrill to *The Sound of Music*' was blazened across the front of the Palace Theatre for many years afterwards as the show became the longest-running American musical in London theatre history.

Around this time, the budding composer sent a score to Harold Fielding, a leading West End producer of musicals, and he had responded encouragingly and suggested he write to the agent Noel Gay. 'So I did, and indeed they did look after me for about a year but there was nothing much doing, especially as I was still at school and only thirteen or fourteen! There was no real tradition of active musical theatre anyway, at that time, apart from Harold, who would have been the only one. And I wasn't ready.'

Another escape route now offered itself in the South of France. George Crosby had retired and he and Aunt Vi bought a house on the Italian coast at Ventimiglia, near the French border. George fancied his knowledge of classical music, so became a butt of a joke played by Andrew and Julian. They had heard a discordant piece for the cello by one George Crumb on the radio, so they decided to make a tape of 'a new masterpiece for cello and piano by George Crumb', as (if) heard on the BBC, and titled 'Spasms for Cello and Piano' by Lloyd Crumb. This consisted of random bangings and grindings climaxing in a massive 'In a Monastery Garden'-type tune. Posterity does not record Uncle George's response, but the jape certainly shows us where the lads stood on the pretentious burblings of the avant-garde.

'Lloydy' aka 'Webster' spent as many holidays as he could in Ventimiglia and would often take the most liked of those jeering school chums along as well. The British film director Ronald Neame was a neighbour, and Andrew remembers meeting him shortly after he had finished making *I Could Go on Singing* with Judy Garland.

The film, when he saw it, made a big impression. So did the performance of Maria Callas in *Tosca* at Covent Garden in 1964. His memory is unequivocal. 'I absolutely fell in love with it. Although I didn't know it at the time, it was the performance that brought Puccini back into some sort of respectability. My father thought that Puccini was the greatest composer who ever lived. Neither of us was able to go to a performance of his music without leaving the auditorium in floods of tears.'

At school he had produced another end-of-term show with Robin Barrow called *Utter Chaos, or No Jeans for Venus*. Then, in 1964, he took sole charge of a musical revue, *Play the Fool*, containing thirteen pop songs but none of his own; he was now flexing his tender producer's muscles. Everyone was now mad about the Beatles, and it had certainly not escaped Andrew's notice that two former Westminster schoolboys, Peter Asher and Gordon Waller, known as Peter and Gordon, had climbed to the top of the charts with 'World Without Love', a lilting, wistful song written by Paul McCartney. This was the peg of his show, and the items included such favourites of the day as 'Terry' by Twinkle and the Trekkers.

In the previous year, he had sent a demo tape of a song he had written to the record company Decca, and they had passed it on to a record producer called Charles Blackwell. The song was published and led to a contract with the music publishers Southern Music. Blackwell was a client of a budding agent, Desmond Elliott, who dutifully trotted along to Westminster School to see these end-of-term efforts of the infant prodigy. He was impressed.

Coincidentally, Elliott had also got to know a self-assured, very tall boy, the son of a family friend, who had been to school at Lancing College in Sussex. Timothy Miles Bindon Rice had recently left a job as a trainee solicitor in Baker Street and joined the EMI record company as an assistant trainee. He had run a pop group at school called the Aardvarks and was determined to be the next Cliff Richard. Desmond Elliott told him about Andrew Lloyd Webber.

Andrew was barely sixteen when he took his A-levels, but he hardly distinguished himself, passing History and English with the low grades of D and E. He had been put up by the school for a closed scholarship at Christ Church, Oxford, but was rejected. He entered himself for an entrance exam to Magdalen and surprised everyone by winning an Open Exhibition in Modern History.

He had written an idiosyncratic and highly personal paper on Victorian architecture and had been summoned to the college for interview by K. B. McFarlane, one of the most eminent medieval historians in postwar Britain. According to the playwright Alan Bennett, who was a pupil and friend of McFarlane's in the late 1950s, he was a gentle and compassionate man nonetheless feared for his acerbic and deflating comments. He was usually to be found in his college rooms, deeply ensconced in an armchair with a cat on his knee. Bennett, memorialising McFarlane in the *London Review of Books* in September 1997, added that 'as one came in, the last smell was always the fish that was put out in the vestibule for the cats.'

On his way to the interview, Lloyd Webber came across one of these cats, a Siamese, hanging about outside McFarlane's door and picked it up. The professor suddenly appeared and asked Lloyd Webber to go in. He clung on to the cat throughout the interview. McFarlane liked what he had written in the general paper and asked him a trick question, one he no doubt always threw at boys from Westminster, viz. what is the date of the nave of Westminster Abbey? Webster was not to be confounded: 'Hang on, I thought, we weren't born yesterday . . . we all know it's the first example ever in English architectural history of someone continuing 150 years later in exactly the same style . . . so with his cat in my arms, and in spite of the wretched A-level results, I thought I had a chance. I went off that evening to George Street to see Gene Pitney singing at the Oxford Apollo, or New as it was then called.'

He was indeed offered the History Exhibition a few weeks later and gratefully accepted. He was all set to begin his new life at Oxford in the Michaelmas term of 1965. But he had made a new friend, who was not going to Oxford. On 21 April 1965, Tim Rice had written, out of the blue, to Lloyd Webber from his flat in Eleven Gunter Grove, near Fulham Broadway, SW 10:

> Dear Andrew, I have been told that you 'were looking for a "with-it" writer of lyrics for your songs' and as I have been writing pop songs for a short while now and particularly enjoy writing the lyrics I wondered if you considered it worth while meeting me? I may fall short of your requirements, but anyway it would be interesting to meet up – I hope!

When they did meet up, Andrew told Tim that he had written eight musicals. He played some of the tunes. Tim was impressed. He said they should give it a whirl.

TWO

OXFORD BLUES, RICE RHYMES AND BIBLE BELTERS

Tim Rice, nearly four years older than Andrew, was the son of an aviation businessman and a classic product of middle-class Middle England. He was tall, blond, confident, easygoing and blazingly genial. He loved cricket, pop music, pretty girls and gave a good impression of taking nothing at all very seriously. He was the absolute antithesis of everything in Andrew's rather more tortured temperament and conditioning.

The Rice family lived in comfortable respectability in Hatfield, Hertfordshire, and Tim – one of three brothers – was packed off to Lancing College in Sussex, where his contemporaries included Christopher Hampton (who became and remained a close friend) and the younger David Hare, two future playwrights of some significance and equally impressive social polish and self-confident demeanour.

He left Lancing in 1963, spent a year at the Sorbonne in Paris and became an articled clerk in a solicitor's office while trying to break into pop music. His mother was a freelance writer and had met Desmond Elliott, then a one-man band of an agent, at a writers' function and told him of her son's fanatical interest in pop music and a book he was keen to write about the pop charts.

When Tim went along to see him, Elliott said there would be no market for such a book – he was proved spectacularly wrong when Rice and his brother Jo, together with disc jockey Paul Gambaccini, published the *Guinness Book of Hit Singles* in 1977, a long-running, regularly reprinted bestseller – but expressed interest in the pop song the ambitious youngster had written and had actually seen produced.

At this point, Elliott put Rice in touch with Lloyd Webber, and the best known collaboration in British musical theatre since Gilbert and Sullivan was born. The duo met up shortly after Rice wrote the April letter. Tim went along to Harrington Court and Andrew played him various tunes and half a dozen songs he had written for a musical he had already mapped out with his school friend Robin Barrow. Rice went off and overhauled the lyrics completely, and by the time Andrew went up to Oxford, the first Rice/Lloyd Webber musical was written.

The Likes of Us was a musical about Dr Thomas John Barnardo, an Irish doctor and philanthropist who founded a mission for destitute children in the East End of London in 1867, and subsequently a number of similar institutions in greater London – the Dr Barnardo's Homes. The subject was obviously inspired by Lionel Bart's urchin-rich, long-running Cockney crowd-pleaser *Oliver!* (which had opened in 1960 and was the longest-running West End musical until *Jesus Christ Superstar* came along). But it might also have been suggested by Leslie Thomas, one of Elliott's first clients, himself a Barnardo boy and soon to make a successful transition from journalist to popular novelist.

Although nothing in the mostly unremarkable, sub-Bart-ish score could have tickled Rice's rock and pop-picking ambitions, there were enough spirited and rhythmically animated moments to hold his interest. Leaving Rice behind, Lloyd Webber took an Italian summer holiday with three Westminster friends, visiting Florence, Rome and Assisi, indulging their talkative passions for art, architecture and music. Last port of call was Ventimiglia, where Aunt Vi was on hand to spoil them with exotic home cooking and a steady flow of good wine.

Andrew went to Oxford in October 1965, and moved into well-appointed top-floor rooms in the New Buildings in Magdalen, next to the deer park. One of the first other freshers he bumped into was David Marks, a francophone law student from Manchester Grammar School who was also, like Andrew, an exhibitioner with added privileges, and resident in the New Buildings.

Marks – dapper, neat, vocally resplendent, technically adroit beyond his years – would prove to be the outstanding student actor of his generation, a brilliantly funny Ford in *The Merry Wives of Windsor*, an astounding exponent of Molière and other high comedy, and a ruthless undergraduate politician who elbowed his way to the presidency of the Oxford University Dramatic Society via playing Rosencrantz in the Oxford Theatre Group's acclaimed world premiere of Tom Stoppard's *Rosencrantz and Guilderstern Are Dead* at the Edinburgh Festival in 1966.

He ducked out of an obvious acting vocation and is now a leading barrister specialising in insolvency; he is unlikely, therefore, to have any meaningful professional dealings with his former Oxford chum. But he was immediately taken up by Lloyd Webber, or 'Lloydy' as he called him, who told Rice that he had found the next Laurence Olivier, although he had never seen Marks act. 'He just knew!' says Marks, who was staggered by the Lloyd Webber rock and roll record collection and swept along by his enthusiasm. He also spotted his nervousness and vulnerability, which expressed itself in his pulling at a woollen jumper he always wore and plucking at his shirt cuffs.

Most of all, Marks remembers Lloyd Webber's quickness and cleverness, though he did little work and spent most of that one term of eight weeks doodling at the piano. Marks was instantly assigned the role of Barnardo, and Tim Rice visited the pair in Oxford a couple of times to see how things were coming along. By the end of the year, in the Christmas vacation, a demonstration tape had been made and Lloyd Webber had been granted a sabbatical leave of two terms to sort out the show before returning to take up his place in the following academic year. His tutors felt, anyway, that he was too young and, certain that he was promising academic material, said he would benefit from starting again a year later. And a year older. Of course he never returned.

Lloyd Webber expected to find wonderful theatre in Oxford and says that he simply didn't, though this was a pretty good era, with future professionals like Michael Palin, Terry Jones, David Wood (who appeared on the demo tape of *The Likes of Us*, and later in the composer's only outright flop, *Jeeves*), Maria Aitken and Braham Murray all making their marks. And Marks soon making his.

In 1964, the Experimental Theatre Company, the ETC, had created a great stir with an anti-capital punishment revue, *Hang Down Your Head and Die*, which later came into the West End. And in February 1966, the OUDS would present Christopher Hampton's reputation-making first play *When Did You Last See My Mother?* which, like the Barnardo show, had been written before the author came up to the university.

Desmond Elliott advised against the Oxford presentation of *The Likes of Us* that Marks and Lloyd Webber had planned, and as soon as the link in London with Rice was renewed, there was no great argument about this. Elliott, who had persuaded Leslie Thomas to have a look at the libretto prepared in Oxford by Marks and Lloyd Webber, was angling for a London production that never happened, despite his efforts at publicity. In January 1966, the *Daily Express* plugged the venture and asked the question: 'After Rodgers and Hammerstein, Lloyd Webber and Rice? A long-distance forecast which could be right.'

In fact their partnership would prove more measurable against Rodgers and Hart, but this first mention in the national press was a nice early indication of the sort of 'dream team' publicity to follow. The musical was never performed, the songs never published, and Desmond Elliott would soon disappear from the duo's lives only to re-emerge in 1971 with an unsuccessful High Court writ claiming commission and damages amounting to five per cent of all Rice and Lloyd Webber's *Superstar* album earnings on the grounds that he had put them together and paved the way for their success.

Elliott could hardly feel too peeved judging by the mushy fruit of *The Likes of Us* collaboration as it survives on a crackling tape. Barnardo is discovered as a young man in the Edinburgh Castle, an East End gin palace, a dive of ill repute, beset by waltzing sluts and a foxtrot stirring of his social conscience.

He comes across two homeless children who declare, showing him their den across the chimney tops, 'It doesn't matter if it snows/The likes of us are meant to die outdoors.' Some strident chords indicating local resentment at Barnardo's do-gooding interference presage Pilate's stonking sneer in *Superstar* and, like Jesus, Barnardo is defined as a social pest and meddler, a blighter fit for being run out of town.

Equally, Barnardo is seen as a Christ-like man alone – until he finds a good woman, Siri, whom he finally regales with a reasonably expansive melody, and the more expensive wedding gift of the Edinburgh Castle as a home of hope and virtue. There ensues a right old Cockney knees-up with a company cuppa char and an invitation to stir away all misery. The music is at best jaunty, stock material. But one song shines: 'Love Is Here', a jangly, fast melody with a characteristic Lloyd Webber optimistic key change, has charm and character; the composer banked it in the melody file and dusted it down a few years later as 'Travel Hopefully' in *Jeeves*.

Rice looks back philosophically on a first collaboration that was basically a bad idea but which at least proved to him that he could work well with Andrew. And Andrew, in turn, was 'smitten' with Tim, and now says that he left Oxford only because of him. John Lill drove up to collect him in Bill Lloyd Webber's car, and after Christmas with the family, Andrew decamped to Ventimiglia again to take advantage of Aunt Vi's ever brimming hospitality. He also felt slightly unwanted at Harrington Court.

Molly had acquired a small three-bedroomed flat adjacent to Number Ten on the top floor, with access across a small outside balcony from the main living room. She occupied the master bedroom in 2A and was soon flanked on either side by John Lill in a smaller bedroom and Tim Rice in the third and smallest retreat.

Both John and Tim, who were charged nominal rents, often had girls round for the evening, and the corridor would resound not only with musical mayhem, but also to the chattering and giggling of scantily clad visitors zooming up and down while a totally unfazed Molly simply turned up the knob on her television set.

John's career was gathering pace, greatly supported by Bill and Jean, and Tim was working closely with Andrew. Tim had left the law firm and taken a lowly job with EMI, soon moving into Norrie Paramor's office. Paramor's major clients included Cliff Richard, with whom Tim would develop a lifelong friendship and professional relationship. For now, he was under instructions to sally forth and find new talent. Some of it obviously came round to Harrington Court for supper and afters.

Bill and Jean Lloyd Webber did not really mind that Andrew had no intention of going back to Oxford, but they did not mind a little less when he agreed to sign up for a year's part-time course in orchestration at the Guildhall School of Music and enrolled for a further academic year at the Royal College of Music. During this period he and Tim worked steadily away at pop songs. They got along fine, though Tim kept away from family business and the not infrequent family arguments.

When Tim read in the *Evening Standard* about their Girl of the Year, a publicity competition won by a singer called Ross Hannaman, he rushed out to see her performing at a club. He liked her, seeing more than a touch of Marianne Faithfull in her style and indeed her look, and he persuaded EMI to give her a contract. He and Andrew then wrote a couple of records.

The first Rice/Lloyd Webber single, performed by Ross Hannaman and recorded in June 1967, was 'Down Thru' Summer' and it had a tune Lloyd Webber banked for a big show later on. The B-side was unpromisingly titled 'I'll Give All My Love to Southend'. The second single, recorded in October 1967, used themes from Beethoven's 'Für Elise' and Dvorak's *New World Symphony*. Another pop song, 'Kansas Morning', was a cleverly disguised steal from the First Movement of Mendelssohn's Violin Concerto and would emerge in *Superstar* as Mary Magdalene's poignant 'I Don't Know How To Love Him'.

None of this was really leading anywhere. Nor was Ross Hannaman's career. Eventually she married a rock musician, had a family and ran a dress shop in Notting Hill. But the two lads' working method was fixed: Andrew would supply the music and Tim would find lyrics to fit. What comes first, music or lyrics, goes the old question, and Irving Berlin's answer was 'the phone call'. But, with the rare exception of setting words by

T. S. Eliot, or from the Church's liturgy, Lloyd Webber always kick-started his songs and his projects with his tunes.

The Barnardo musical was shelved and none of the records was successful. But Rice and Lloyd Webber were busy and they were getting known. Word of their activity reached Alan Doggett, a music master who had taught Julian Lloyd Webber in Westminster Under School and had moved to Colet Court in Hammersmith, the preparatory school for St Paul's across the road.

Doggett had become friends with Bill and Jean and in late 1967 he asked Andrew if he would be interested in writing a brief pop cantata for the annual school concert. A Biblical subject would be ideal, he said, mindful of the little tradition of that sort of unbuttoned Christian sing-along represented by such pieces as Herbert Chappell's *The Daniel Jazz* (which he had produced the year before), Michael Flanders and Joseph Horovitz's *Captain Noah and His Floating Zoo* and indeed Benjamin Britten's exemplary *Noye's Fludde*. Tim Rice flicked idly through *The Wonder Book of Bible Stories* and proposed the tale of Jacob's son, Joseph, whose dreams and splendid coat of many colours landed him in trouble with his brothers, who then sold him into slavery in Egypt.

There, Joseph becomes a prophetic guru to the Pharaoh, predicting years of plenty, then of famine, and guides the country through the recession to economic renewal. His father and his brothers, having become refugees from Canaan, turn up and beg for food, the magical coat goes missing, is found again, and the tribe is joyously reunited as Joseph ascends in a blaze of colour and a chariot of gold.

On 1 March 1968, the story was related by a singing narrator and an eager school chorus and orchestra, conducted by Doggett, and spun along merrily for just twenty minutes. Andrew played the piano and Tim

53

delivered a much practised Elvis Presley routine as the Pharaoh in '1957 Rock time': 'I was wandering along the banks of the river, When seven fat cows came out of the Nile, a-ha, haa (Bop-shu-wah-doo-wah, Bop-bop-shu-wah-doo-wah); And right behind these fine, healthy animals, Came seven other cows that were skinny and vile, a-ha, haa (Bop-shu-wah-doo-wah,etc).' Pharaoh's dream is interpreted by Joseph in the irresistible couplet, 'All these things you saw in your pyjamas, Are a long-range forecast for your farmers.'

The mixture of brash, trumpet-tongued musical statement, unforced, relaxed melody and well-turned, racy lyrics ('And when Joseph tried it on, he knew his sheepskin days were gone . . . He looked handsome, he looked smart, he was a walking work of art') was a winner. Musically, the little score was streets ahead of *The Likes of Us*, with a lilting fluency in Joseph's dream, an expressive, minor key soliloquy in waltz time ('Close Every Door To Me') and the pleasantly mobile 'Any Dream Will Do', which remains one of the duo's most enduringly, and endearingly, popular songs and which uses a stiffening choral counter-melody to add sinew and dramatic effect.

The dazzle of the coat was conveyed in a one-note litany which sparkled simply as the words slowed and defined themselves like a separation of all the colours in the rainbow. That coat was red and yellow and green and brown and scarlet and black and ochre and peach and ruby and olive and violet and fawn and lilac and gold and chocolate and mauve and cream and crimson and silver and rose and azure and lemon and russet and grey and purple and white and pink and orange and blue.

The reception was good and Bill Lloyd Webber suggested that they could make the show a little longer and present it a few weeks later in the Central Hall, Westminster, where he was the resident organist. Thus a concert was announced in aid of the new drug addiction centre based there, and John Lill was roped in to play some piano pieces. Bill played the organ and Julian – on the brink of taking up his scholarship at the Royal College – volunteered to play the Saint-Saëns cello concerto.

Thus bolstered, on Sunday 12 May 1968, a slightly expanded, twenty-minute-plus *Joseph* was given in front of a packed audience of nearly 3,000 people, and the 'modoratorio' as Rice dubbed it was reinforced in the rhythm section with the addition of a pop group called the Mixed Bag – whose lead singer was David Daltrey, a cousin of Roger Daltrey of The Who – and Tim Rice once again shaking his hips.

The audience included many parents of the singing schoolboys, including Derek Jewell, the pop and jazz critic of the *Sunday Times*. To everyone's amazement, a review duly appeared on the following Sunday, 19 May 1968, under the heading 'A Springboard Called Joseph': 'The quicksilver vitality of *Joseph and the Amazing Technicolor Dreamcoat*, the new pop oratorio heard at Central Hall, Westminster, last Sunday, is attractive indeed. On this evidence, the pop idiom – beat rhythms and Bacharachian melodies – is most enjoyably capable of being used in extended form.' Jewell noted the 'very beautiful melody' of 'Close Every Door To Me' and concluded that *Joseph* 'bristles with wonderfully singable tunes. It entertains. It communicates instantly, as all good pop should communicate. And it is a considerable piece of barrier-breaking by its creators.'

The concert was also reviewed by Merion Bowen, the composer Michael Tippett's lifelong partner and amanuensis, in the *Times Educational Supplement*. He was less enthusiastic than Jewell, but he insisted that *Joseph* 'offered abundant evidence of the composer's talent. Contact with the wider world may deepen his vision, but he certainly has the skill and talent to become a successful composer/arranger.'

Bowen also complimented Julian on his 'superb account of the concerto', though Julian himself, who had never played in front of so many people before, was stricken with nerves and convinced that he had performed badly. He beat a hasty retreat from the hall's back door, where he was confronted by an excited teenage schoolgirl – the younger sister of one of Andrew's friends, David Ballantyne, who was a singer and guitarist in the show – who told him he was brilliant and asked for his autograph. Six years later, after the friendship had been cemented at Andrew's twenty-first birthday party, she became Julian's first wife.

Norrie Paramor was impressed by the *Sunday Times* review and agreed to make a recording of the piece at Decca (where he had moved from EMI). Simultaneously, the music publishers Novello said they would publish the piano score. When they did so, Andrew wrote a short preface announcing that the score had been prepared for schools and youth clubs, acknowledging his father's help in arranging it from the rough draft. Even more significantly, Novello bought out the rights to *Joseph* for 100 guineas: in 1991, Lloyd Webber's Really Useful Group would pay Novello/Film Trax £1m to buy them back.

At the same time, Andrew sent another copy of the *Sunday Times* review to a property man called Sefton Myers at the suggestion of David Ballantyne. Myers was a patient of Ballantyne's father, a doctor in Walton-on-Thames. He was also dabbling in showbusiness and trying to launch Ballantyne as some sort of pop star. His showbiz adviser was another property man, David Land, who managed the Dagenham Girl Pipers and several even less distinguished outfits. He and Myers were backing lots of ventures – their company was called New Ventures – but none was really taking off.

Lloyd Webber went to see Myers at his offices in Charles Street, Mayfair, and talked to him about a museum of pop memorabilia. He really wanted to see if he could squeeze any money out of him. He was desperately hard up, despite the mini-windfall from Novello, and had moved from Harrington Court a couple of hundred yards round the corner into a basement flat in Gledhow Gardens.

Myers made encouraging noises and passed the record of *Joseph* Andrew left with him to Land, who loved it the minute he played it. He and Myers offered Rice and Lloyd Webber a basic weekly salary, an office to work in and their services as management. Andrew leapt at this offer, though Tim was a little less sure. 'I was going out with a Jewish girl called Sarah whose old man had heard of Sefton Myers, but no-one knew anything about David Land, and my parents were worried about me leaving the comparative security of Norrie Paramor's office.'

But they took the plunge and signed up with New Ventures. The deal seemed good, in the sense that it formalised the writing partnership and encouraged that essential ingredient of self-belief. They were placed under a three-year contract as songwriters, being paid £2,000 each (£38 a week) in the first year, £2,500 in the second and £3,000 in the third, as advance against all royalties, with options that could extend the agreement to ten years. Myers and Land would also take a 25 per cent commission of all earnings.

Land worked out of an office the size of a broom cupboard in Wardour Street, and kept in touch on a day to day basis with Andrew and Tim across town in Charles Street. The lads had the occasional lunch with Myers, but they mostly dealt with Land. And they clocked into the Mayfair office on most days to send off letters, make phone calls and write songs together. For their next show, Land suggested they consider another Biblical subject, adding that, whatever they did, he – as a good practising Jew – would be grateful if they steered clear of Jesus Christ.

Meanwhile, there was a third performance of *Joseph* in St Paul's Cathedral on 9 November, as part of a Festival of Youth organised by Martin Sullivan, the Dean, and an early pioneer in the happy-clappy school of Church of England clerics. Not content with sending his prayers skywards, the publicity-prone priest had even sent himself in the opposite direction, like some trendy counterweight to devotion, by parachuting from his own dome.

There was a feeling now that *Joseph* had had its day. Lloyd Webber said that the St Paul's performance – which was slightly expanded to include 'Potiphar' and one or two other items for the first time – went as well as it possibly could, 'but we felt that *Joseph* had gone about as far as it could and we decided to have a go at writing something else'. However, they would return, like their hero, to the beginning.

One year after *Joseph*, in the summer of 1969, Julian had a debut brush with the grown-up world of professional theatre, just ahead of Andrew, when he appeared fleetingly as a musician in William Gaskill's Royal Court production of *The Double Dealer* by Congreve (the cast included Nigel Hawthorne, the late Richard Beckinsale and Judy Parfitt). The Court, in nearby Sloane Square, had recruited a few students from the Royal College to play an entr'acte. On the second night, Julian missed his entrance but somehow escaped the wrath of the demanding Mr Gaskill.

Tim and Andrew knuckled down to work on a second cantata for schools called *Come Back Richard, Your Country Needs You*. This was performed, again under the direction of Alan Doggett, at the City of London School, where Doggett was now teaching, in November 1969. It was much longer than *Joseph*, running at about forty minutes, and was in part a satire on the Love and

Peace sloganeering of the day. One number, 'Those Saladin Days', which had been recycled from an unsuccessful candidate as the British entry in the 1969 Eurovision Song Contest, was in turn refitted with cheeky new lyrics as 'King Herod's Song' in *Superstar*: 'Prove to me that you're divine, change my water into wine . . . prove to me that you're no fool, walk across my swimming pool.'

For the couple were now immersed in something in an altogether different league, despite David Land's plea to give Jesus a wide berth. The Richard the Lionheart story was told in tandem with that of his minstrel, Blondel, and the subject lay dormant until Tim resurrected the show, entirely rewritten as *Blondel*, and with music by Stephen Oliver, at the Old Vic in 1983. It was not a success.

The last months of 1969 were taken over by their excitement in recording and releasing a song inspired by Tim Rice's fascination with Judas Iscariot, and in particular with Bob Dylan's great song 'With God on Our Side'. Andrew had been hit with a stirring tune while rushing down the Fulham Road to buy an old Ricky Nelson album. He came out of the shop with this unassigned theme running through his head and the tune had subsequently bugged Tim for several weeks.

Another idea as a *Joseph* follow-up had been the First Book of Samuel, and so at first that tune had an opening lyric of 'Sam-u-el, Sam-u-el, this is the first book of Sam-u-el,' but Tim preferred his own alternative version, 'Jesus Christ, Jesus Christ, who are you, what have you sacrificed?' When finally issued, the title of the single was 'Superstar' from the (as yet unwritten) rock opera *Jesus Christ Superstar*. The title came about, according to Andrew, in a conversation with the late Mike Leander of MCA Records, who later produced all Gary Glitter's hits.

Tim's story is that he spotted a picture of Tom Jones

in the *Melody Maker*, and the caption read 'Tom Jones, the World's Number One Superstar', and he thought, why not stick that in? 'And of course *Jesus Christ Superstar* is a brilliant title. We were a bit shocked about what we'd done, just as Andrew had been a bit worried about *Joseph* being too slangy. But of course it was its being precisely that – slangy and funny – that made it work.'

Rice pondered the Dylan song, especially the line, 'I can't think for you, you'll have to decide; did Judas Iscariot have God on his side?' This set the tone and he wrote out the entire lyric one Sunday morning before lunch at his parents' house in Hatfield. Since the age of ten, Tim had harboured an ambition to write a play about either Pontius Pilate, or Judas, and to bring on Jesus as an incidental character.

No interest in such a piece, with or without music, was evinced by a single theatrical management. The Grades, even Robert Stigwood, who was to figure prominently later, turned down the idea at this stage. David Land offered the song around, but all the big record labels turned it down as being far too controversial.

Finally, Brian Brolly, a canny, rugby-playing and immensely charming Irishman who was London boss of MCA-UK, a subsidiary of Music Corporation of America, owners of Universal Studios and four big recording labels, agreed to make the record. And Martin Sullivan, who had encouraged the duo to take Jesus down from the stained glass windows when approached with the idea, supplied a blurb for the dust jacket:

There are people who may be shocked by this record. I ask them to listen to it and think again. It is a desperate cry. 'Who are you Jesus Christ?' is the urgent enquiry, and a very proper one at that. The record probes some answers and makes some comparisons. The onus is on the listener to come up with his replies. If he is a Christian let him answer for Christ. The singer says, 'Don't get me wrong, I only want to know.' He is entitled to some response.

The singer asking the questions was Judas, just as the narrator had highlighted Joseph's dilemma, Che Guevara would question Evita's career and Joe Gillis would view the tragedy of Norma Desmond face down in his swimming pool. The framing device gave a setting, and a distance, to the song, and the subsequent drama; indeed, you might argue the Lloyd Webber catalogue of musicals offer the most successful application of Brecht's alienation technique on the British stage.

One of Tim's best friends at EMI had been the singer Murray Head, and he agreed to head up the single with the Grease Band, a group of session musicians who had backed Joe Cocker, and the all-female Trinidad Singers from Notting Hill. There was also a 56-piece orchestra, including strings from the London Philharmonic, for which Andrew supplied the first of his spectacular studio orchestrations.

The opening effect was entirely dramatic. Eight bars of grandiose chords announced a classical ambition and segued into the rumbling rock and bustling soul of Judas's frenzied inquisition. Then back to the opening chords, this time sung a cappella by the girl backing group, with bass guitar joining in, then the repeated eight bars with full percussion and rapidly bowing violin section. Then all the elements were wrapped up in a full rhythm section and a darting brass counter-melody. It was a fantastic setup, Lloyd Webber's first essay into full orchestra and rock band megamix, with all the various elements climactically unleashed while the structure was retained, with Head raving on in his distinctive, rasping voice.

The single was recorded in Barnes in October 1969, and released to virtually no British reaction in the following month, although it crept into the lower reaches of the US Hot 100 in the very last week of the Sixties. Rice recalls that the BBC more or less banned it, though David Frost featured the song on his TV show, prompting headlines such as 'Public schoolboys in Jesus row'.

But news was arriving from mainland Europe that the single was becoming a cult hit in gay underground bars, and Brolly convinced his fellow MCA executives that there was more life in this. MCA therefore commissioned the full album at a cost of £14,500, and in the middle of December Andrew and Tim booked themselves into the Stoke Edith Hotel in the Herefordshire village of Stoke Edith. They had a room each and a piano in one of them. Five days later, the score was complete. Andrew had not raided any of his previous material, apart from 'Kansas Morning'. They were ready to go.

THREE

JESUS ROCKS AND THE GOOD TIMES ROLL

Between the release of the *Superstar* single and the release of the full double album a year later in October 1970, Rice and Lloyd Webber enjoyed their last few months of obscurity. Bizarrely, Tim stayed on for a while in Harrington Court (though he soon moved out to Bayswater) after Andrew had decamped just two minutes around the corner to Gledhow Gardens.

Aside from business contacts, Andrew met two people who became central in his life over the next decade or so: sixteen-year-old schoolgirl Sarah Tudor Hugill, his future wife, whom he came across at a party in Oxford; and David Crewe-Read, his future best friend, who lived in the flat above his at Number Ten, Gledhow Gardens.

Sarah was a quiet, shy, friendly creature whose father was a research chemist and director with the sugar manufacturers Tate & Lyle. Ironically, Sarah was found to be diabetic a few years later. And coincidentally, she was a sixth-form pupil, studying for her A-levels, at Queen's Gate School, an exclusive all-girl establishment situated deep in the heart of Lloyd Webber territory, virtually adjacent to both Harrington Court and Gledhow Gardens.

Pert, short, pretty and long-haired, Sarah played second clarinet in the school orchestra and was affectionately nicknamed 'the vole' – a creature whose speedy metabolism necessitates eating every twenty minutes. Sarah was never renowned as an over-hearty eater: 'I haven't got any whiskers and all the usual parts are there. I don't think it is because I look like a vole. It's just that I've got a rather squeaky voice.'

Crewe-Read could not be more different. Tall, more beaky than squeaky, noisily upper-class and full of the joys of spring even in deepest midwinter, he became Andrew's buddy and unofficial court jester for the next twenty years: 'We had a great time knocking spots off each other,' is how Crewe-Read remembers it. Lloyd Webber's endless piano-playing during the composition of *Superstar* drove his new neighbours to distraction and Crewe-Read and his then wife Lisa took to banging on the floor with a poker.

Eventually, Andrew invited them downstairs, and an instant friendship was struck based on a shared interest in Victorian art and architecture and a deeply unfashionable enthusiasm for the Pre-Raphaelite Brotherhood. Crewe-Read was an antique furniture dealer specialising in pine cupboards and tables; in 1972 he would open his own shop, the Pine Mine, on Wandsworth Bridge Road, where he still operates today, selling and acquiring antique furniture and making pine pieces to order in the on-site workshop. Until a serious falling-out over commissions on purchases and some disputed payments, Crewe-Read would act as Lloyd Webber's art adviser and sales-room representative.

For the moment, though, the new friends concentrated on the more affordable pleasures of eating and drinking. It was a source of wonder to David Land that even before he had any money to speak of, Andrew founded an informal dining club which he called the Eating Out Club and through which he commanded the best tables in the best restaurants, whither he would frog-march his friends to sample the most adventurous of menus.

With work more or less finished on the double album, Tim and Andrew paid their first visit to New York in June 1970 to see the American amateur premiere of *Joseph* at the College of the Immaculate Conception in Douglastown, New York. They were, says Andrew, 'incredibly well looked after' by their hosts and billeted in the Harvard Club on West 44th Street, a beautifully appointed, hushed, discreet and wood-panelled enclave in the heart of Manhattan, a stone's throw from the theatre district.

The producer was a certain Father Huntington who, amazingly enough, turned out to be distantly related to Sarah Hugill's parents, though nobody knew this at the time. The production led to a lot of interest in the piece among schools and colleges, but the show never arrived on Broadway until 1982.

In London, Rice and Lloyd Webber were finding their way around the new post-Beatles music scene. Although *Superstar* had been conceived as a stage show, they were temporarily resigned to seeing it into the world as an album. Andrew was determined to be a success in a new sort of musical theatre; he loved *South Pacific* and *The Sound of Music*, but the West End had been shaken up by *Hair*, the tribal rock protest musical announcing the Age of Aquarius, and The Who had composed an avowedly rock musical, *Tommy*, that contained theatrical possibilities.

Tim was always more phlegmatic about theatrical endeavour and remains so to this day. He has never been a theatrical animal as Andrew was and was much more interested in writing hit pop songs. Success in musical theatre, he believed, was what happened to other people, not to him. And anyway, he much preferred the buzz and rush of a rock concert to that of a Broadway musical. But he loved good words in pop songs, especially those of Lieber and Stoller, Eddie Cochrane and Buddy Holly.

But he also loved the dry, conversational wittiness of middlebrow favourites like Flanders and Swann, Paddy Roberts, Alan J. Lerner and Tom Lehrer. 'I was very keen to write that sort of thing, so writing for the theatre gave me more of a chance to go in that direction. But I've never really been captivated by the theatre. I nearly was. Then I met too many people I couldn't stand, and I always disliked the artificiality of it. But then, the pop world is just as bad, really!'

Rice had already developed an impressive network of colleagues in the pop industry, and Lloyd Webber was becoming known as a name to watch. One of his future collaborators, the wizard keyboard player and composer Rod Argent, had been at school briefly with Rice and vividly remembers bumping into Andrew at a party in Ennismore Gardens. He told Lloyd Webber how much he liked the orchestrations on the *Superstar* single, saying that they sounded positively Handelian. The fledgling composer surprised him by replying, 'Oh, dear boy, if it's anything it's Strauss.'

Argent had been the driving force behind the Zombies, one of the more successful Beatles-influenced pop groups of the mid-1960s and the first since the Liverpudlian quartet to have a homegrown song – 'She's Not There' – climb all the way to Number One in the American charts. By the end of 1968, the Zombies were splitting up and Argent formed a new group called Argent, featuring the Zombies' lead singer Colin Blunstone.

He launched the new band in a showcase at the Institute of Contemporary Arts in the Mall and both Tim and Andrew had come along, partly because they were interested in Blunstone singing Jesus on the *Superstar* record. In the event, Blunstone's record company wouldn't release him and the young songwriters had the great good fortune to sign up Ian Gillan, the lead singer of the legendary heavy metal group Deep Purple.

Although Argent and his fellow Zombies hailed from working class backgrounds in Hertfordshire, they were a brainy bunch and had acquired hatfuls of O-levels and A-levels at school. The pop world was suddenly full of bright, quintessentially English young men, many of them from public school. So there was nothing strange about Rice and Lloyd Webber mixing in. Mick Jagger had studied at the London School of Economics and was at least as keen on cricket as Tim Rice. Most of Manfred Mann were clever public schoolboys. The core of Genesis had been to Charterhouse.

The recording of the double album featured a representative sample of the best pop musicians of the day. Murray Head extended his extraordinary performance on the single as Judas. Ian Gillan was an amazingly effective, and affecting Jesus, his voice a pickled, rasping gurgle. And Mike d'Abo of Manfred Mann sang Herod's camp number. Paul Raven – yet to find fame and notoriety as Gary Glitter – was a priest, the gloriously gifted Madeline Bell sang in support and the role of Mary Magdalene was taken by nineteen-year-old Hawaiian beauty Yvonne Elliman whom Andrew had found singing 'Blowing in the Wind' for £5 a night plus drinks in a club along the King's Road. Barry Dennen, who had appeared in *Hair*, sang Pilate with an incisive and histrionic grace that became his trademark. Lloyd Webber recalls that the album was recorded as the IRA cranked up their mainland bombing offensive, and that Alan O'Duffy, the recording engineer, was a cheerily dedicated Republican, though not a sympathiser to the IRA campaign of violence.

The album was totally original, totally exhilarating. The music had tremendous energy which, blending with Rice's cynical, quizzical lyrics, never stood still for a minute. Quite apart from the songs themselves, the score was full of fragmentary moments that belied an unusual talent: the melodic phrase, made almost in passing, on

Judas's 'It seems to me a strange thing, mystifying . . .' and Jesus' angry riposte in Mary Magdalene's defence.

Lloyd Webber's taste for unusual time signatures made a stunning debut in Mary's 'Everything's Alright', a number that bowls along, five syncopated beats in a bar, like an undulating hillside or gentle wave. There was the majestic entrance to Jerusalem – 'Hosanna Heysanna Sanna Sanna Ho, Sanna Hey Sanna Ho Sanna, Hey JC, JC won't you fight for me? Sanna Ho Sanna Hey Superstar' – the concerted soul shout of 'Christ you know I love you' and the howling anguish of the vulnerable hero in the Garden of Gethsemane. And as Jesus died on the cross, the orchestra gathered in one of the most sweeping and melancholy of all melodies.

And of course there was 'I Don't Know How to Love Him' with its Mendelssohn quotation. All criticism rightly compares and contrasts with other precedents and examples and William Mann, *The Times*' chief music critic, writing in *The Gramophone*, described that final swelling theme as 'Grandson of Barber's *Adagio*' but he also praised the lyrics and libretto, its skilful incorporation of imagery from the Gospels, and the consistency in style of diction.

Mann also made comparisons with the fierce, Eastern European modernist composers Ligeti and Penderecki. A later critic and biographer, Michael Walsh, took up this point and declared that Lloyd Webber had clearly been 'listening to Ligeti's eerie *Atmospheres* (used by Stanley Kubrick to depict the cold void of outer space in his film *2001: A Space Odyssey*) and to Penderecki's brutal choral work *The Passion According to St Luke*, both sensations of the late-1960s avant-garde.'

Criticism can become a form of trainspotting and Walsh, memorably defining the style of the *Superstar* musical idiom as 'a semiconscious agglutination of rock, show music and classical influences', detected bits of Greig's Piano Concerto in the theme symbolizing

Judas's betrayal, Carl Orff's *Carmina Burana* in the Gethsemane scene and the 'ominous trudge' of Prokofiev's 'Battle on the Ice' from *Alexander Nevsky*. This sort of game is usually more entertaining than illuminating, the point surely being that no-one writing music seriously in the middle of the twentieth century does so in a vacuum sealed off from what has happened since – in Lloyd Webber's case, especially since – Prokofiev and Stravinsky.

Years later, when Dmitri Shostakovich, arguably the greatest composer of the twentieth century, and certainly one of its greatest artistic spirits, came to London shortly before he died in 1975 to attend the British premiere of his Fifteenth Symphony, he asked to go and see a performance of *Jesus Christ Superstar*. He was so impressed by what he heard and saw that he went back the following night to see it again. Julian Lloyd Webber says that Shostakovich confessed that, but for Stalin, he might have tried to have written in such a way himself.

But it was the subject matter as much as the music that caused the stir that followed the album's release. In 1966, John Lennon had declared that the Beatles were more popular than Jesus, and there was even a short time when it seemed possible he might make the most of both reputations by taking the lead in the stage version of *Superstar*. A more secular approach to religion – die-hards would call it blasphemy – was part of the mood of the time. And even that mood was not all that new.

The medieval Mystery plays had shown the human side of the Passion. The more ambivalent, sexual connotations of *Superstar* – expressed in Judas's symbiotic fascination with the people's pin-up and Mary Magdalene's confused devotion as expressed in her best song – were also part of the cultural currency. Nikos Kazantzakis' sensational 1955 novel, *The Last Temptation of Christ* (filmed many years later by Martin Scorsese with Willam Dafoe and Harvey Keitel as Jesus and Judas), was at least as interestingly outspoken. And Pasolini's breathtaking 1964 black and white film *The Gospel According to St Matthew* gave a modern credence to the story of a closed community battling against, and baffled by, mystical imperatives. *Superstar* might well have been breaking down barriers but it was also tuning into the *zeitgeist*. Even so, the album, released in October 1970, was not initially successful in Britain. 'It was a stiff,' says Andrew, and when he and Tim received a call summoning them to New York a few weeks later to promote the album, he had no idea what to expect. When they stopped off the plane on their second visit to New York, they were suddenly famous. The recording was the talk of the city and was careering up the charts. MCA Records booked them into the Drake Hotel on Park Avenue. 'The food was filthy,' says Andrew. 'God, all the food was terrible in New York in those days. But the Drake had a good wine list which I felt we should explore at MCA's expense. Trouble was, the bottles had been stored badly, and so that was all awful, too.'

The important thing, though, was that all the talk was of converting this record into the stage show its perpetrators had originally desired. Managements, including the all-powerful Lord Delfont in London, who ran the Stoll Moss group of theatres on Shaftesbury Avenue, were now calling them at all hours.

They made a whistle-stop tour of major cities, including Los Angeles and Montreal, where they participated in question and answer sessions on their rock opera. But Robert Stigwood, Lloyd Webber recalls, was the only one sensible enough to send round a car and take them to dinner. They were delivered to Stigwood's New York apartment and ended up as part of his empire. Robert Stigwood was an Australian rock and theatre impresario (still is) who had run into financial trouble but was now back on the scene managing the Bee Gees and Cream.

His theatrical stock was rising with his stake in shows such as *Hair* and Kenneth Tynan's nude revue *Oh Calcutta!* He had recently launched a publicly quoted company in Britain. And he knew that Sefton Myers, aged only forty-three, was terminally ill with cancer and that Myers' family wanted a buy-out. When Rice and Lloyd Webber arrived, another guest, who was secretly negotiating with Stigwood to join his company, was watching with interest from the sidelines. This was Peter Brown, close associate of the Beatles and their late manager Brian Epstein. Brown was trying to extricate himself from Apple, the Beatles' company that was now run by Alan Klein, and hoping to switch horses and run Stigwood's American operation.

Brown was English suave personified in New York, though his origins had been ordinary. A boyhood friend of Brian Epstein in Liverpool, he had become Epstein's personal assistant. Epstein had died of an accidental drug overdose in 1967, and Brown had been uneasily and unhappily assimilated into the new Apple company. Working with Tim and Andrew would be a welcome doddle after his experience. 'The Beatles weren't laid back at all. Paul was a monster, very opinionated and bossy. John was fascinating, mercurial, not always easy to be with. George was difficult from the point of view that he was always feeling left out, not getting his due. And Ringo was always the nice guy. So it was a very good training ground. No matter how impossible Andrew can be at times, and he can be, the saving grace is always that there is a mind there. If you stick with it, you talk him down and get back to his mind. It's not as if you are dealing with a fool. He is highly, and deeply, intelligent.'

Rice was impressed by Brown's presence at the meeting because of his Beatles connections (Brown was particularly close to John Lennon), Lloyd Webber not at all. Still, the deal went through. Stigwood – recognising, says Brown, that the smart thing to do was not to pursue the theatrical rights on *Superstar* but to seek the management rights, and therefore control – bought out the contract with Myers and David Land, with the proviso that Land remained the boys' personal manager.

Thus, in an exchange for shares in an unweaned company and a cash advance against future royalties, Stigwood bought a 51 per cent interest in New Ventures, leaving Land with 49 per cent. Stigwood also took over the rights to 25 per cent of Rice and Lloyd Webber's earnings over the next eight years. By making deals with himself as the management, he also in effect owned all rights to stage and film production of their works in the English-speaking world.

At the time this must have seemed like a gamble, but it paid off handsomely. The *Superstar* album met with an ecstatic reception in America. *Time* magazine identified a quasi-religious revival in pop music (citing Simon and Garfunkel's 'Bridge Over Troubled Water' and the Beatles' 'Let It Be'), hailing *Superstar* as a modern-day passion play that might enrage the devout but ought to intrigue and perhaps inspire the agnostic young. Within a year Myers had died, much missed by Lloyd Webber, who respected his civilised mind and always regretted not having his advice on how to handle the *Superstar* phenomenon.

MCA in London retained the rights on the record as well as all publishing and performing rights but, as the record took off, Stigwood browbeat them into doubling their royalties (from the usual 2.5 per cent to 5 per cent), which now included his own 25 per cent, in return for a portion of future Rice/Lloyd Webber compositions. Then, for a further cash payment of £80,000 plus another large slab of his shares, he bought out Land completely and set up his own company, Superstar Ventures, to publish all future works of the authors. He owned them lock, stock and barrel. Land was retained as a manager.

The double album played for ninety minutes divided into three-minute slabs and, for an effective concert or theatrical performance, no libretto was needed. There was no impulse behind the composition of a 'through-sung' musical beyond making it make sense as a record. Christopher Hampton, Tim's old friend at Lancing, had kept in touch – he had been mightily impressed by the performance of *Joseph* in Westminster Hall – and had been asked to go and talk to them about the possibility of adding a libretto, but when he sat down and listened to the record, he could not see where such a contribution could go and sensibly enough talked himself out of the job.

Concert performances were by now springing up all over America, and in February 1971 – as the album hit the top spot in the US charts – Rice and Lloyd Webber, with David Land, returned to New York to discuss strategies. Stigwood was tracking down these unlicensed performances and wiping them out with legal action. The rewards, as he owned the grand rights, would justify the costs.

Peter Brown, who had been appointed Stigwood's organisation chief in the States, met them on arrival late one Sunday night and was hoping they would all be too tired to go out to dinner. Tim and David Land were indeed looking for their beds. But Andrew wanted dinner. Brown took him off to a Greek restaurant on Lexington Avenue and got along so well with him this time that the dinner lasted five hours. They have been firm friends ever since.

It was Brown's job to police the pirate productions, often with difficulty as local judges were often disinclined to act against their neighbourhood schools, even though money was changing hands on the door. One of the solutions Stigwood came up with was a tactic to dominate this market by putting out his own concert version, like a rock and roll tour.

Yvonne Elliman sang Mary Magdalene, the young folk rock singer Jeff Fenholt (later to appear in the Broadway premiere) appeared as Jesus, Carl Anderson (later in the film) was a black Judas, and the whole caboodle was beefed up by a twenty-strong choir and a thirty-two-piece band. This proved an unmitigated triumph. The first authorised live concert performance was given to an audience of 12,000 people in Pittsburgh in July 1971. In Brown's words, after a four-week tour visiting nineteen cities, 'it was raining money', and by September a second tour was on its way. There followed a college tour. And then Stigwood licensed performances all over the world.

Andrew had long since asked Sarah Hugill to marry him, but her parents insisted, not unreasonably, that she should first take her A-levels. He was besotted with her and always said that he was lucky enough to meet her before there could be any suggestion that she was in love with his success more than with him. On 24 July 1971, they were married in the church of the Holy Cross in Ashton Keynes, Wiltshire, and the music included works by the bridegroom.

Sarah moved into Gledhow Gardens. Andrew had already helped dispose of the sudden rush of money by acquiring a Victorian farmhouse with a barn and six acres at East Knoyle, near the market town of Shaftesbury in Dorset. Summerlease was not a grand property, but it was homely and inviting, and Andrew indulged his new hobby of pinball machines by installing several of them in the barn. They had a swimming pool added. The money was starting to roll in, and Broadway beckoned.

Rice always preferred that concert tour version to any later stage production, but being on the road with his partner he found a bit like travelling with a maiden aunt. 'Of course, Andrew was married, and I wouldn't say that I was carrying on like Led Zeppelin. But if I went to a show on the road in America, or subsequently in Germany, there were always lots of lovely actresses hanging around and it wasn't too difficult to have a nice evening and not check into your hotel!'

Finally, on 12 October 1971, Rice and Lloyd Webber made their Broadway debuts when *Jesus Christ Superstar* was produced at the Mark Hellinger Theater on 51st Street. They had been installed in adjacent suites in the Waldorf Astoria working on rewrites and a pleasant new song, 'Could We Start Again, Please'. Jeff Fenholt and Yvonne Ellison continued in their roles as Jesus and Mary Magdalene, joined by Ben Vereen as Judas and Barry Dennen as Pilate. The initial director, Frank Corsaro, was replaced by Tom O'Horgan, who had directed *Hair* and had been brought in with the brief of 'theatricalising' an oratorio. Everyone learned the hard way, and too late, that this was an unnecessary approach.

What Lloyd Webber now describes as the most depressing night of his life became a religious circus, with huge angels swinging about on psychedelic wings across shimmering, surreal sets by Robin Wagner and a full battery of laser beams, smoke and wind machines. There were dancing dwarfs and lepers and a crucifixion scene set on a dazzling golden triangle. The composer, opposed to O'Horgan's appointment all along, concedes only that the beginning was very clever. 'The floor of the stage was vertical and, as it went down, people swarmed over the top of it, like ants.'

There was an immense amount of ballyhoo. Stigwood flew over a contingent of British arts reporters and put them up in the Plaza thus ensuring fair and objective comment. The cost of the staging was three quarters of a million dollars, but the advance booking amounted to over a million, and the show ran for nearly two years. So it was certainly not a flop, despite receiving a spirited hammering from the New York critics. John Simon said it was closer to rock bottom than rock opera while the British critic Clive Barnes, who was the *New York Times* man, said that while this was the best score for an English musical in years, he detected an undefined air of smugness in its daring.

But it was undoubtedly a landmark, one of the greatest in musical theatre history. The evangelist Billy Graham inveighed against it, the Mark Hellinger Theater was picketed by the National Secular Society with leaflets dubbing the show 'Jesus Christ Supersham' and one irate nun carried a banner declaring 'I am a Bride of Christ, not Mrs Superstar!'

After this came the deluge. A few years ago at a musical theatre conference convened by the playwright David Edgar at Birmingham University I inadvertently referred to the show as 'Jesus Christ Superstore'. Mark Steyn later observed that even Cameron Mackintosh would draw the line at such a concept, even though he 'made a multi-million dollar marketing phenomenon out of that starving urchin girl from *Les Mis* and scored the third biggest-selling perfume in America with Esprit de Phantom (you too can have the sophisticated fragrance of a hideous misfit who lives in the Paris sewers).'

Steyn may well be right that *Superstar* laid the foundation for the global marketing of musicals that characterised the 1980s. But Lloyd Webber's first reaction to the Broadway production was to return to basics, strip away the veneer and insist on an austere London production more suited to the rawness and simplicity of the work itself. To this end, the Australian director Jim Sharman was recruited to do the opposite of Tom O'Horgan's extravaganza.

Sharman had already directed the acclaimed Australian premiere in Sydney and his similarly simple, uncluttered production which opened at the Palace Theatre on 9 August 1972 was an instant hit. The top price seat cost £2.50 and the advance bookings amounted to a quarter of a million pounds. It cost £120,000 to put on, went into profit after twenty-two weeks and became the longest-running musical in West End history, overtaking Lionel Bart's *Oliver!* with its 2,620th performance on 3 October 1978 and closing in 1980 after playing for 3,358 performances and taking £7m at the box office.

The London cast included another sand-blasted voice in Stephen Tate's Judas, a sympathetic and good-looking Jesus in Paul Nicholas, the huge and lustrous Dana Gillespie as Mary Magdalene and Paul Jabara as Herod. Sharman's production was stark, gripping, dignified and very moving.

The chorus of unknowns included Floella Benjamin (who later became a household name on children's television), Diane Langton, Elaine Paige and Richard O'Brien. O'Brien, a brilliant singer and artist, had been cast as chorus and understudy to Paul Jabara on the understanding he would take over as Herod after three months.

When the time came, O'Brien was quickly succeeded by Victor Spinetti in the role – seen as more of a straw-boater type than a diabolic trans-sexual – and Sharman, disappointed in the management's decision, consoled O'Brien with the promise that they would work together again. They did, a few months later, on a Sam Shepard play in the Theatre Upstairs. And this led directly to their collaboration in the same venue on O'Brien's *The Rocky Horror Show*, which he had started to compose as a reaction to his differences of opinion with Robert Stigwood over Herod.

Julian Lloyd Webber will never forget the British opening night of *Superstar* for something his brother said. After a reception with the cast, Andrew joined the closest members of his family for dinner in the strikingly ordinary Norfolk Hotel opposite Harrington Court.

Julian remembers his father's sister saying, in a very proud, English way, 'You must feel you've really done it now, Andrew.'

Andrew replied, in total seriousness, 'I shall never think that I've done it unless I can go into the record stores and see the shelves packed with the Greatest Hits of Andrew Lloyd Webber. Like Richard Rodgers.' Julian knew his brother well, but even he was struck with the way he said this without a trace of emotion: 'Writing one hit show for him, if that's what it was going to be, wasn't going to mean very much. He wanted, even then, to be the best there had ever been.'

The show has outlived its own notoriety and survives in a score of vibrancy and great power, as witnessed in many revivals. A 1973 Tokyo version which visited London in 1991 portrayed Judas as a desperate outlaw, Caiaphas and the priests as magnificently attired, and magnificently sung, kabuki soldiers and the amazing Jesus of Yuichiro Yamaguchi as a stern warrior of still and ferocious theatrical presence. Herod's swimming pool song was brilliantly misconveyed by a shrieking transvestite tossing his fan and slipping off his sandals as a high-class kimono-reversing courtesan.

The record sleeve of the original album was an exploding yellow sun, which opened out like a star with childish drawings of Jesus inside. But a subsequent sleeve – dun-coloured brown with a gold relief design of praying angels shaped as a curling laurel wreath – became an iconic theatre poster of the age. You could even catch a glimpse of it on the inside of the frozen train out of New York in the marvellous 1997 film *The Ice Storm*, in which the betrayals and miseries of modern marriage were decimated in emotional impact by the acting of a bunch of kids. Going against the tide was the theme, too, of the 1996 London revival's poster, Christ in a white dhoti charging across Waterloo Bridge in the rush-hour stampede of office workers.

The packaging of theatre brought with it the allied minor industries of publicity, marketing and image placement. One of Stigwood's key associates, the producer Bob Swash, brought on board a new publicity outfit called Cue Consultants, comprising Anthony Pye-Jeary and Peter Wright, who were based at the Greenwich Theatre and had gathered early West End experience by their involvement in transfers from Greenwich to Shaftesbury Avenue of plays by Peter Nichols, Michael Frayn and John Mortimer. With *Superstar* they joined the big time.

Wright became a close friend of Lloyd Webber for several years, but Pye-Jeary would stay the course after he left Cue Consultants in the early 1970s and would work with him closely on all aspects of poster design, graphics and publicity on every show thereafter. Lloyd Webber takes an avid interest in all aspects of such matters and when his input is positive, Pye-Jeary says, it's as exciting as hearing him play a new tune. 'Andrew has more original ideas – about everything – than most people. It's as simple as that.'

The two of them became habitués of Le petit club français, where Bob Swash had introduced Pye-Jeary as a member. This marvellous place in a little street off St James's had been set up by the French Resistance during the war and was always on the verge of bankruptcy. Patronised by all sorts, including writers and journalists, you could eat a plate of fine charcuterie, sample the best cheeseboard in London and sup good wines for just a few pounds. 'Andrew and I have been talking about opening a similar sort of place for about ten years without doing anything about it,' says Pye-Jeary. 'The idea really is to have the sort of place one would want to go to oneself.'

Within a week of *Superstar* opening, *Joseph* received its professional premiere at the Edinburgh Festival in a Young Vic production by Frank Dunlop. It formed part of a show called *Bible One – Two Looks at the Book of Genesis* at the Haymarket Ice Rink, moving down to London at the Young Vic and on to the Round House, produced by Stigwood and Michael White, for a short season in December. The first part of *Bible One* was an adaptation of the Wakefield Mystery Plays, from the Creation to Jacob.

When Stigwood moved the Round House presentation into the West End in February 1973, that prologue was replaced with a new mini-musical by Rice and Lloyd Webber, with a script by television comedy writers Alan Simpson and Ray Galton, called *Jacob's Journey*. It was a catastrophe and soon withdrawn, leaving *Joseph*, now running at nearly an hour's length with the addition of a couple of new songs and many reprises, to win new friends on its own. Gary Bond scored a big personal success as Joseph and he would become one of the unofficial Lloyd Webber ensemble regulars, and another close friend.

Alan Doggett, still running his children's choirs, was again in charge of musical direction. There was another early important link forged on this revival. The Young Vic cast included Jeremy James-Taylor as one of Joseph's brothers, and he would one day be in charge of the National Youth Music Theatre of which Lloyd Webber became an active and generous patron in 1993.

James-Taylor recalls one incident during Granada Television's filming of the production over one hectic day in their Manchester studios. 'It was frantic: all these kids, a donkey, a genuine golden Rolls-Royce and Andrew leading the band with Alan Doggett in the pit. The director wanted the last bit done in one uninterrupted take after lunch. Everyone went for it, the snowflakes were falling, the Rolls was standing by, the kids straining at the leash. We were almost there and, as the band hit the last chords, the majestic theme of *Jesus*

Christ Superstar – dah-dee-dah, dah-dee-dah . . . – came blaring out of the pit.

'The director came rushing out of his box yelling and screaming, the whole take was ruined and the band collapsed in fits of laughter. Andrew simply stood up with his hands above his head and said, 'Sorry, my idea,' and the whole thing had to be done again. The brilliant thing was of course that it *was* a great idea and has in fact become a standard joke quotation at the end of most productions of *Joseph*, certainly any I've been involved with, ever since.'

Superstar also found its way quickly on to celluloid, work on the feature film beginning in Israel in 1972. Lloyd Webber spent, he says, a hysterical three days with David Land in Israel. Land became increasingly obsessed with the effect of this gig on his own Jewishness. As the two of them walked around the rapidly developing city of Tel Aviv, he even started regretting that Andrew wasn't his own son and Jewish into the bargain. And Land loved bargains – he used to send out cheques and encourage people to save them as autographed souvenirs instead of cashing them in.

And he loved terrible jokes. In the chauffeur-driven limousine one day they saw a man standing by a dead camel at the side of the road. Land wound down the window and yelled, 'What's the matter, buster, Wall Street gone through the floor?' In Jerusalem, Lloyd Webber was fascinated to learn of the history of the Wailing Wall and was happily regaled with a long lecture on the subject by the tourist guide. When this was over, Land turned furiously to Andrew and said, 'See, now you know never to ask anybody Jewish about the Wailing Wall. He's made us an hour late for lunch!'

The director, Norman Jewison, did not get on at all with Land. This may have been something to do with the fact that when Land first arrived on the set, Jewison was heavily involved in a very complicated shot in a hot, dry wind, and Land simply strode up and said, 'I've got a message from Robert Stigwood. Will you kindly stop fucking around and get on with this movie.'

The film script was by Melvyn Bragg, the cinematography by the estimable Douglas Slocombe, and the score conducted by André Previn. The critical reception in 1973 was fairly derisory, but the film stands up today as both theatrically intelligent and cinematically interesting. We are watching a fit-up show by a travelling troupe of hippies in the desert. Once you accept – as a ritual, as an impromptu day trip? – that the busload of rocky thesps comes out of nowhere, erects a whole lot of scaffolding around some ancient ruins, does the business, then goes home without any sign of an audience, you can actually enjoy the movie.

There is even something for the MTV generation with the occasional use of freeze-frames, throwback 1970s choreography in a flurry of flared jeans, bare midriffs and Afro hairdos and the Las Vegas-style descent of the dead Judas in a white slashed costume on an illuminated stage surrounded by shimmying groups of angelic chorines. The myth lives on while the man, in a chillingly contrasted next scene, trudges towards Golgotha for the anguished finale. The cast return to their bus, shaken and becalmed, to the accompaniment of the gorgeous 'John 19:41' theme and the sight of a simple bare cross silhouetted in a blood orange sunset.

Yvonne Elliman, who had been with *Superstar* from the outset, appeared as Mary, Ted Neely was Jesus, Barry Dennen, Pilate and an impressive Carl Anderson was reinstated as Judas. Zero Mostel's son Joshua is a fat and funny Herod with yellow shades and a medallion who has commandeered a chorus of high-stepping transvestites in the shimmering blue heat haze of his sybaritic coastal inlet and who turns up in his leopardskins like a giggling sadist for the flogging entertainment.

A high wind rattles through most of the scenes and the

military threat of Pilate's soldiers, attired in mauve vests, silver helmets, fatigues and desert boots, is enforced with the beautiful, sinister effect of tanks materialising in the heat haze over the horizon and the swift passage across the sky of a lone fighter plane as the chorus hymns 'Good old Judas', the traitor bought with a bag of blood money.

By the end of 1972, Lloyd Webber felt confident enough to assume a voice, as well as a place, in the world. Having joined the country set in Dorset, he wrote to *The Times* in November complaining about vast buildings resembling aircraft hangars being put up without proper planning permission. This was to be the first of a steady stream of missives to what used to be known as 'the top people's newspaper' on the subjects of rural affairs, architecture and high taxation of high earners such as, suddenly, himself.

Tim Rice had been the relaxed, easily approachable one for a couple of years with Andrew looking surly and unsure of himself with his floral shirts and curly long hair. But increasingly Andrew revealed a flair for public utterance and over the years would slowly become an adept manipulator of the media and eventually, like Rice, a polished exponent of the opportunities that opened up in the print and other media.

Rice reacted to the sudden rush of fame and fortune with a feeling that he better make the most of it, because it might not last. '*Superstar* was so big, but looking back we probably didn't make as much money as we should have done, though we still made an awful lot. Every time I received another cheque I never thought I was getting enough. But equally, I never thought I should have been getting more. It was strange.'

He and Andrew had formed their own little company called QWERTYUIOP – the top row of letters on the typewriter, but Andrew was already thinking bigger. He had every intention of getting away from Robert Stigwood as soon as he could. Tim was more relaxed about this, and more dedicated to the friendship and counselling of David Land. Andrew remembers crossing a road in Knightsbridge with Tim around this time and Tim saying to him, 'The big problem with you, Andrew, is that whatever you try and do, you are always going to be thought, because of the way your mind works, to be selfish. I get away with it because I'm the other side of the coin.' That is, the kind of guy who doesn't seem to care about anything.

I am not at all sure that Tim didn't care about anything. It just didn't show as much. And he certainly had no taste for the corporate wrangling and empire-building that Andrew was soon going in for in a big way. They were a remarkable couple, these boys, immensely gifted and clever, and they now had the world at their feet.

The extraordinary success of Andrew and his younger brother in the concert halls had an odd effect on their father back in Harrington Court. Suddenly, Bill was being congratulated all the time. But this, Julian reckons, only made him feel worse about his own non-achievements. And Bill used often to say that it all made him feel as though he had done nothing at all. Andrew had left home, really, when Bill had started drinking a little more, so he was unaware of the problem. Julian used to hear his father go into his study late at night, play some of his music on old 78 records and sob his heart out.

Across the way in the second flat, John Lill was less aware of Bill's drinking, while agreeing that he certainly liked a few in the evening. Jean would cross the balcony, or buzz the intercom, and report that Bill would like John to come across for a drink at 7 p.m. 'He had a little corner where he assembled an extraordinary array of cocktails.' But Lill never remembers seeing Bill drunk in the afternoons when he was still teaching at the Royal College. 'On the other hand,' says Lill, 'you can see the combination of things building up against Bill leading to a need to escape through alcohol.'

Not the least of these was a strong-minded wife who had given up on her husband's right to her encouragement. There were other unusual aspects to life in Harrington Court. Jean's psychic powers had found a resonant alliance with her young pianist protege. Lill's sense of dead composers directing him as he played had led to a meeting with Sir Robert Mayer, the ancient conductor and proselyte of children's music, on the eve of entering the Tchaikovsky competition in Moscow in 1970.

Mayer had no idea that Lill was fascinated by spiritual matters, but he played him a tape on which he had recently recorded the voice of a long-dead pianist and Beethoven specialist, Artur Schnabel. By use of a voice phenomenon, Mayer could apparently transfer a spiritual force on to a blank tape. Lill heard Schnabel speak, using nicknames for Mayer that only Mayer would know. And he heard other voices.

Simple radio equipment was all that was required, connected to a tape recorder. This lit the fuse of Lill's interest to the extent he felt compelled to try it himself. The first and only time he ever succeeded in getting a voice on the tape was the first time he tried it. The voice said, 'Music portrays your life, please get in touch, I've got so much to tell you.' The voice belonged to Jean's dead brother, Alastair, who had drowned at sea aged eighteen.

After that, John and Jean had felt it mandatory to try things out. Generally, they sat down together late at night as if it was the most natural thing in the world and waited for the dead to get in touch. Lill's realisation that this power is available to all was, he says, the most exciting experience of his life. He took down about three notebooks full of their psychic investigations – about one per cent of their ten-year-long, intermittent sessions

– and now stores it all on computer, protected by a password. 'I will,' he says, 'never let it out of my sight. I feel I should publish the contents, but not yet . . .'

They never made contact with Bill Lloyd Webber after his death in 1982, but they did hear from an intermediary that Bill had made contact with his beloved Rachmaninov. Lill has never considered pursuing these psychic methods of communication with anyone else but Jean. 'I do have persistently strong visions and feelings,' he says, 'and I do know when people are around.' It is extraordinary to think of them, the Madam Arcati of South Ken and her internationally famous house guest, rapping on the windows of the next world while poor old Bill vegetated morosely down the corridor in his study, and while Julian started to tear round the concert halls and Andrew, with Tim, was taking the world by storm with a religious rock opera. You could even contemplate turning it all into a musical.

One of the reasons Lill had for going to Moscow and, fortunately, winning the competition was to try and help his parents move house. They had steel bands on either side of their small terraced property, and they had not slept properly for five years. With the prize money Lill bought them a house nearby which is now owned by his sister. His widowed father is in sheltered accommodation on the other side of Leytonstone, where his son and daughter visit him once a week.

Time was up, too, in Harrington Court. Molly had died and the whole block of apartments, and the shops on the ground floor, were bought up by Arab landlords. Julian was incensed because the new owners had no legal right to force out the residents; they just ran down the services, failed to repair the lifts or maintain the building in a general way. So people started to leave.

Julian advised staying as long as possible so that they were given a better deal. In the end, the Lloyd Webbers were offered three flats in Sussex Mansions, a few minutes' walk away on the Old Brompton Road, for their two. John Lill took one, Julian took another – where he lives to this day – and Bill and Jean took the third, two floors below. The rents were reasonable, and controlled.

What could Tim and Andrew do next? Tim says that while Andrew has always been an 'I've got to do another show' type, he always thought, 'Well, I'll only do another one if I really want to.' Their temperamental approach to work was that of the congenital obsessive and the discerning amateur.

There were a few ideas sloshing around. Tim joined the new Capital Radio station as a disc jockey. He was driving to a dinner party somewhere in London at the end of 1973 and was late. And, because he was late, he caught the end of a programme about Eva Péron on his car radio. The name rang a vague bell and intrigued him.

Andrew had already toyed with the idea of something by P. G. Wodehouse, to whom both he and Tim were devoted. Tim was not all that keen on a P. G. Wodehouse musical. As for Eva Péron, Andrew said to Bob Swash, 'I really don't want to do another piece about an unknown who rises to fame aged thirty-three and then dies . . .'

FOUR

JEEVES HEAVES-HO ON THE FEAST OF EVITA

One idea for their next show did not even make it on to the drawing board. In early 1973 Tim and Andrew went to see a preview of *Billy*, a John Barry musical of Keith Waterhouse and Willis Hall's play with lyrics by Don Black, at the Theatre Royal, Drury Lane, and arranged to have dinner afterwards in the Inigo Jones restaurant (these days, L'Estaminet) in Covent Garden.

Tim discovered he had left his coat at the theatre and went back to retrieve it. There, he became embroiled in a long chat about the show with the authors, told them what needed doing and, much to Andrew's annoyance, did not return for a couple of hours.

Over the delayed desserts and coffee, Andrew's fury simmered until he found himself agreeing with Tim that this was a terrific idea for a musical show: a man goes to a theatre, leaves, realises he has forgotten his coat, returns, becomes embroiled in a long chat about the show with the authors, tells them what needs doing . . . and ends up playing the leading role.

Tim did play a leading role in *Evita*, but only in the sense that he instigated and conceived the show while Andrew was much more taken with the notion of a Jeeves musical. P. G. Wodehouse himself described his novels as musical comedies without music and, although he made encouraging noises when approached by Lloyd

Webber, it is clear from some letters that have recently come to light that he was less than smitten with the project. That did not, of course, invalidate the attempt.

Through Bob Swash, the playwright Alan Ayckbourn, also a Wodehouse fan, was approached to write a libretto. This he did, concocting a fiendishly complicated but suitably silly plot derived distantly and in part from *The Code of the Woosters*. The main plot points of the pursuit of a much-prized silver cow-creamer and the theft of a policeman's helmet were omitted. Instead, the adaptation was framed in a village hall concert where Bertie Wooster is unadvisedly improvising after a string on his banjo has snapped. (When, at the Hay-on-Wye literary festival of 1998, the iconoclastic journalist Christopher Hitchens unexpectedly pronounced *The Code of the Woosters* to be his favourite funny book, the novelist Muriel Spark replied that there was not a single character in Wodehouse you would not wish to take out with insecticide.) Tim Rice, who had sensed that he was entering a retrogressive, shrinking world of English musical theatre rather than building on the rock concert excitement of *Superstar*, retired from the fray and left a bemused Ayckbourn feeling conned into doing the lyrics: 'Already the thing was becoming a bigger commitment than I had already envisaged,' he told me soon afterwards.

'I don't think I could ever collaborate with another writer, but I did find collaborating with a musician very stimulating.' When he and Lloyd Webber visited the frail and ancient Wodehouse at his home on Long Island in January 1973, to show him their outline sketches and play him the score, the writer professed himself flattered and satisfied by their efforts thus far.

I attended the final Saturday matinee at the Her Majesty's in May 1975 just three and a half weeks after it opened. It was my second date with my future wife, so I dare say my defences were down, doubly so as our first date had been at an extremely trying Royal Shakespeare Company production of *Love's Labour Lost*. I saw a muddle of scattergun plotting and mixed musical idiom scaled up beyond its potential to fill a large stage. I also saw charm, wit, quite a funny show and heard some amazingly facile and well-turned lyrics by Ayckbourn. Three or four songs were really fine – they would be retained in the drastically improved and scaled down re-write Ayckbourn and Lloyd Webber cooked up twenty-one years later. The critics had attacked *Jeeves* with venom, hearing horror stories from the out-of-town run in Bristol and knowing only too well when they were on to a sure-fire loser. Nothing unusual in that for musicals on the road. *Guys and Dolls* was such a flop on tour that it had been withdrawn altogether, emerging six months later as a big hit.

And the Gershwins' *Strike up the Band* lasted a fortnight on its pre-Broadway try-out, opening two and a half years later, with an overhauled book – and the new title song, as well as 'I've Got a Crush on You' – as a New York smash. And what had been the advance word in *Variety*, the showbusiness bible, on *Oklahoma!*? 'No Girls, No Gags, No Chance.'

You never know with musicals, as you never know with plays. Anything can happen and hearing a score for the first time is a notoriously difficult undertaking. Still, *Jeeves* seemed jinxed. The director, Eric Thompson, renowned for his Ayckbourn productions, had never helmed a West End musical, and the first read-through, with music, lasted five and a half hours. When it opened in Bristol, it ran a mere four and a quarter. And the cuts made it incomprehensible so that, as the musical director, the late Anthony Bowles, said, 'people began to do things that didn't make any sense'.

Even the star had never been in a musical. David Hemmings, that beautifully ageing cherub of a film actor, who seemed such ideal but unexpected casting as Bertie Wooster – his blue-eyed sang-froid, suggested Ronald Bryden in a wonderful review in *Plays and Players*, implied perfectly a progression, with no intermediate stops, from choirboy chubbiness to clubman tubbiness – drove Lloyd Webber to distraction: 'He would never go to bed, and during the previews you'd find him doing magic tricks for some travelling salesmen at three in the morning in the hotel bar, even though he'd have rehearsal early next day.'

Tim Rice believes that, even in its re-worked, 1996 reincarnation as *By Jeeves*, it is very nice stuff but not something to stir the pulses for ever. 'And I think I was in the pulse-stirring business.' He told Andrew at the time that he thought the low point was reached in a song called 'Summer Day' – which Lloyd Webber was particularly pleased with: 'I was so cross that, without telling him, I promptly re-used it in *Evita* as 'Another Suitcase in Another Hall', and to this day he's never noticed!' So it went on. Eric Thompson was sacked on the Friday before the show opened, Ayckbourn taking over as director.

Ronald Bryden's savvy, good-natured and partly corrective review appeared too late. He declared the book to be the most literate and genuinely witty a British musical comedy has offered since Sandy Wilson's *Valmouth* but he reckoned the score went downhill after Bertie and the Drones Club chorus flung themselves with joyous abandon into 'Banjo Boy', 'a heaven-made marriage of Broadway zip and the Wodehouse world where the height of bachelor chic was a collection of American one-steps for one's tinny, horned Victrola.'

All the same, Ayckbourn said that they badly needed Hal Prince, or someone like him. Oddly enough, Lloyd Webber then received a letter from Hal Prince, the essence of which was, 'You can't listen to a show if you can't look at it. Bank that score.' This was the second time Lloyd Webber had heard from the legendary Broadway director.

The first was in 1970 when a telegram arrived at Harrington Court saying, 'I am the producer of *Cabaret, West Side Story* and *Fiddler on the Roof*. Please call re rights to *Jesus Christ Superstar*.' It arrived soon after Rice and Lloyd Webber had flown to New York for the first time and been smartly wooed by Robert Stigwood.

This time, Lloyd Webber rushed to meet him and did so at the Savoy, where Prince's diagnosis of *Jeeves* lodged with the composer for ever. He said that a small show had lost its identity. That the music couldn't shine in a sea of sets and costumes. And that there had obviously been so many problems that any baby had disappeared down the plughole, with the bathwater, long before previews. Lloyd Webber banked the score.

The director, Eric Thompson, was asked on television if the critics had killed the show. 'No, the show killed the show,' he replied. Steeled by Hal Prince's advice, Lloyd Webber resolved that he would prepare any new show to a far better state of pre-production readiness in future. Thus was born the idea of the Sydmonton Festival, and in June 1975, soon after he went running back to Tim and his *Evita* project, he mounted a try-out for all the try-outs on Midsummer's Eve with an informal concert in St Mary's Kingsclere featuring his brother and Yitkin Seow the pianist.

Summerlease, the Dorset retreat, had proved too far from London to maintain, and became a loss-making factor (of about £40,000) in a general property shake-up around this time. Andrew had already traded in the Gledhow Gardens basement for a six-storey house in Knightsbridge, 37 Brompton Square. Now, in early 1975, Brompton Square was sold for a profit of £100,000. Sydmonton had been acquired for £170,000 with the house and twenty acres of land as collateral. Everything was mortgaged because, in those days, you could still benefit from tax relief on mortgages.

He also bought a two-storey basement and ground floor flat, this time in the Belgravia heartland he would occupy for the next twenty years or so. 51 Eaton Place became the London pad, with offices installed in another, adjacent house at 11 West Eaton Place.

This period, between *Jeeves* and *Evita*, saw the formation of the Really Useful Company, designed to promote and protect Lloyd Webber's work, and the arrival on board of Brian Brolly, the champion of *Superstar* at MCA. The name Really Useful derived from that of James, the really useful engine in the children's idyllic puffer stories – trains bossed around in the countryside by the Big Controller – by the Reverend E. W. Awdry. The hundred one-pound shares were divided between the two company directors, Andrew and Sarah.

The wealth that had accrued from *Superstar* propelled both authors into the top tax bracket, though for a time each drove the modest cars they preferred, Tim a Triumph, Andrew a Mini. Andrew was especially exercised over the amounts of money being sliced out of his earnings firstly by Stigwood and secondly by the taxman. From the rarefied library of the Savile Club in Brook Street, where he was a new member, he wrote to *The Times* in May 1974 on the injustice of the 83 per cent taxing of high earned income and the 98 per cent taxation of high unearned income: 'The only ways for a British person to make money are to be an entrepreneur, speculate, inherit the money, win the football pools, or emigrate; but you cannot earn it.' This would remain a common theme until Mrs Thatcher changed the tax laws in her 1979 government in favour of high earners like Rice and Lloyd Webber.

Sydmonton also fulfilled the boyhood ambition of owning a fine country house. The place would exert a central influence on Lloyd Webber's future life and there is nowhere in the world where he feels more comfortable, more at home. The property stands in some of England's most beautiful scenery, but it is not an intimidating or even architecturally coherent place.

Various outhouses and stabling yards have been added and improved over the years, but the main approach through the front gates is a dramatic avenue lined with majestic lime trees narrowing to a thickly hedged lane that suddenly opens to a fairly unimposing prospect of the house from the side. The glorious landscape, which includes a large lake dotted with swans and full of fish, has many fine paddocks, paths and copses, marked off with clumps of beeches and cedars.

The earliest visible signs of the house date from the sixteenth century, though Sydmonton Court was mentioned in the Domesday Book as a grange of Romsey Abbey. There was a major reorganisation in the early 1950s after a period of first disuse and then deterioration while serving as functional accommodation for several hundred American servicemen during the last war. The north face looks at first eighteenth century, but is in fact a Victorian 'Georgianisation' with windows inserted in sixteenth century brickwork.

More or less simultaneously, Tim had bought a country house in Oxfordshire, Romeyns Court in the village of Great Milton, where he laid out his own cricket pitch. In August 1974 he had met and married Jane McIntosh, a secretary working at Capital Radio. Shortly before their marriage, Jane had left a note for her colleagues on her typewriter: 'Gone abroad with Tim Rice.'

One of their jaunts was to Buenos Aires, where Tim was getting seriously stuck into Eva Péron. He was content to maintain a low profile on that trip because the planned stage and film presentations of *Superstar* in the city had met with fairly strong, indeed preemptive, critical reaction: 'The theatre where the stage show was scheduled to open was burned to the ground and the cinema due to show the film was bombed. I am not sure exactly who was responsible but, after that reaction to our work, mere words from theatre critics hold no terror for me.'

Rice's old schoolfriend Christopher Hampton, now an established young playwright, was also living in Oxfordshire at this time, and was intrigued by the Eva Péron project. A keen student of modern history, Hampton happened to have a book called *Great South American Leaders* on his shelves in which Chapter Five was about Eva Péron and Chapter Six about Che Guevara. He loaned Rice the book and takes the slightest of minor credit for the fact that the great surprise of *Evita* was the bracketing of these two charismatic figures in the way they were in the show.

Rice and Lloyd Webber were determined to make their partnership thrive, despite marked differences in their approach to work. Andrew simply couldn't understand, for instance, why Tim should want to disappear to Japan the minute that *Superstar* had opened. There was still work to be done and future projects to discuss. Off his own bat Andrew had done a couple of film scores in this period, though he was not seriously tempted in this direction because of the minimal control a composer could exert over his output.

But he had supplied an interesting, atmospheric soundtrack for Stephen Frears's *Gumshoe* (1971) starring Albert Finney and Billie Whitelaw and, after meeting Aunt Vi's neighbour, Ronald Neame, in Ventimiglia, an even moodier score for Neame's version of Frederick Forsyth's *The Odessa File* (1975). Tim had supplied lyrics for one song in the first and for the opening song, 'Christmas Dream', in the second, sung by Perry Como in the spirit of festivity: 'Watch me now, here I go, all I need's a little snow.' This lyric was mistakenly taken as a paean to cocaine, something that had never entered Rice and Lloyd Webber's minds, let alone their nostrils.

One item in the second commission, which was composed with an input from brother Julian, was a fugue for cello, rock group and full orchestra. The brothers liked this section best of all, and Julian – who felt Andrew had written some of his best music to date on this film – kept badgering him to write something more extended for him to play in the concert hall.

This would not happen for a couple of years, and only then after a bizarre bet struck on the fate of Julian's beloved Leyton Orient at the end of the 1976/7 season. Orient, as usual, were in peril of relegation from the Second to the Third Division, and the bet obliged Andrew to write a piece for Julian to play if Orient survived.

The fate of the O's was in the balance until the last day of the season, when they managed a 1-1 draw with Hull City and stayed up by the skin of their teeth. 'Andrew was never convinced they could manage that draw,' says Julian, 'but I just *knew* the lads would pull through.'

As a result of the result, Andrew wrote his *Variations on a Theme of Paganini*. And Julian enjoyed what he still describes as 'undoubtedly the proudest moment of my life': presenting a special gold disc made by MCA Records to the club chairman on the pitch at Brisbane Road before a game against Leicester City.

Andrew himself remained always immune to the appeal of soccer, but in 1974 Tim had a bunch of tickets for an evening match between Chelsea and Sunderland at Stamford Bridge and invited the brothers along. Andrew was much taken by the floodlit theatrical atmosphere and was quite shaken by the ferocity and uniformity of the chanting, some of which was racist and directed at black players.

The rhetorical world of *Evita*, the savagery of the crowd scenes is partly rooted in that experience, as well as in the stamping audience participation in Gary Glitter concerts of the time. For the speech patterns of Juan

Péron, Lloyd Webber had a strong schoolboy recollection of hearing a recorded broadcast of Oswald Mosley addressing a crowd.

The public dimension of the Eva Péron story, and indeed her grisly rise to power, was not initially as appealing to Andrew as it was to Tim although, ironically, in real life, Andrew had already shown a marked taste for dominating table-fulls of accountants and business colleagues to an extent that simply left Tim cold. But the Evita story was not really Andrew's kind of tale and he found her a deeply unsympathetic character. 'And yet, perhaps because she died when she did, it is hard not to admire something about her. She must have been furious when she found that she was ill. That is why her story intrigued me. I am sure that Puccini would have adored her.'

As *Jeeves* closed in May 1975, he and Sarah took up an invitation from Gary Bond to visit him on holiday in the Greek Islands. Andrew was, as usual, preoccupied with work and had not really thought about his wardrobe. Bond – who died tragically young, of Aids – always used to say that the funniest thing he had ever seen was Andrew having to wade ashore in his long velvet jacket and rolled up trousers when a ferry had unceremoniously delivered the couple to the appropriate beach. It also happened to be a nudist beach, and as Bond introduced him to his fellow revellers, who were hanging loose in every sense of the word, Andrew simply did not know where to look.

He was probably still thinking of Eva Péron and how he would rush back and find a way, after all, of writing about the two sides of Eva's life, the glamorous and the tragic, that might work musically and dramatically. More straightforwardly, Tim felt that, as a dramatic heroine, despite her power lust and selfishness, she had one quality going for her, and she had it in spades, indubitably: style.

And Tim was always clear about the defence of the project. 'If your subject happens to be one of the most glamorous women who ever lived, you will inevitably be accused of glamorising her. The only political messages we hope will emerge are that extremists are dangerous and attractive ones even more so.'

Eva's life story, from her origins in a poor country village in 1919 to her escape to the big city as a model and actress, her snaring of Juan Péron and her drive to political power and iconic cult status, ending in death from cancer in 1952, was sketched out in the detailed synopsis Tim handed over to Andrew on a working trip to Biarritz.

The first thing the composer then wrote in a year, 1976, dedicated to the writing and recording of the *Evita* white album, was the tune that became 'Don't Cry For Me, Argentina'. That lush, soaring, strangely ambivalent song of a leader's relationship with her adoring public became the duo's first and totally unexpected UK chart-topping single in February 1977.

Without lyrics, Lloyd Webber was moved by the plight of a doomed woman isolated from the crowds who made her, and fascinated by Tim's concept of Che as a musical alter ego offering not only background information to the audience but also a running, cynical commentary on Eva's career. He also thought of Judy Garland's last, tragic London concert at the Talk of the Town in the late 1960s. He had been there to see her mess up the 'Trolley' song and stutter through 'Over the Rainbow'. He noted how her anthem had turned around to destroy her – 'And that was the genesis of how I felt we should make the big song work.'

Tim Rice knew at once that the big tune should be the big hit, but his lyrics aimed to do three things at once and would therefore conspire, they believed, against any obvious pop chart success. The tone was deliberately banal, as in a Hollywood Oscar acceptance speech, and the first point was that Eva was being deliberately insincere, seducing the audience with more style than content.

Secondly, there was an element of a love song, and thirdly the song had to work as a bridge between Péron's presidential election success and her own plea for popular sympathy. And there was poetry: illusions internally rhyming with the solutions they promised to be, the girl you once knew dressed up to the nines at sixes and sevens with you – the lover, the country.

There was thus a firm theatrical conditioning to the creation of the album, which took five months to make. Into the recording studio at Barnes they went with Paul Jones (of Manfred Mann) as Péron; Colm – then C. T. – Wilkinson, who had taken over as Judas in *Superstar*, as Che; Tony Christie in the Tony Christie role of the Latin nightclub singer; and Barbara Dickson – whose career had taken off after West End success in Willy Russell's Beatles fantasy, *John, Paul, George, Ringo . . . and Bert*, plucked from the Liverpool Everyman by Bob Swash – as the discarded mistress singing 'Another Suitcase, Another Hall'.

In the role of Evita they cast Julie Covington, a raw, brilliant, untrained singer who had made several records of songs by Clive James and Pete Atkinson (in her Cambridge revue days she had played a fairy alongside yours truly in an Oxbridge production of *A Midsummer Night's Dream*) and who had lately enjoyed success in the TV series about an all-girl rock group, *Rock Follies*. One of the subsequent sticking points was that Covington – who began to believe with some of her friends that Rice and Lloyd Webber were too obviously commercial to be serious – refused to publicise the album, and the chart-busting single. She then turned down the lead role on stage.

The title line of her hit song was added in some time after the main recording session. There were several grisly alternatives, according to Rice, of which the most likely was 'It's Only Your Lover Returning'. In the first statement of the tune, as a counter-melody in Che's critical 'Oh What A Circus' – itself a high-flying rocky-rhythmed chart success for David Essex, the first stage Che – during the opening funeral scene, the dead Eva had uttered the line 'Don't Cry For Me, Argentina'. Andrew suggested they stick it into the main song and see if it worked. 'On the one hand,' says Tim, 'it didn't make sense. But on the other, it did: she's dishonestly implying that she needs their sympathy.

'The irony is that she was conning people without them realising what she was saying, or understanding it. Which is precisely what happened with a mega hit with people who had no idea it was part of a show. In a way, it proved that we'd got it right. We had conned the world into thinking it was a beautiful pop song. And it *is* a beautiful pop song! But it's really not conceived as such.'

It was not as if a musical about Eva Péron was any kind of commercial guarantee of success. Nobody in Britain really knew who she was, and Mary Main's definitive biography was only published here once the Rice/Lloyd Webber album was a hit. Before then, the rough tape was played at Lloyd Webber's first Sydmonton Festival proper in 1976.

The tapes were played, lunch taken and after a decent tea-time interval, a black-tie dinner was followed by a larky debate. This became the social pattern in following years, with extensions into the Friday night and beyond into the Sunday afternoon (after church, and lunch) when a cricket match was played on a local pitch and, in later years, croquet on the Sydmonton lawns. After the Sydmonton *Evita* premiere, the whole opera – Lloyd Webber was quite unabashed about using this definition from the off – was re-mixed and about fifteen minutes of material either cut or re-written.

The project was now ready to go forward to the stage, but in the meantime Lloyd Webber got on with the business of honouring his brother's winning bet. The *Variations* Julian reckoned the best piece of music for the cello since Britten. It was a brave undertaking. Paganini's theme had already been taken to the variation cleaners by Brahms and Rachmaninov, Schumann and Liszt, and more recently, in the jazz idiom, by Benny Goodman and John Dankworth. But Julian relished not only his brother's winning phrases but also his instinctive understanding of the capabilities of the cello – all he suggested adding was some double-stopping in the final variation.

There is something unbuttoned in the composition of both *Evita* and *Variations* that remains, in my view, unmatched in Lloyd Webber's writing before and since. In the first, he was liberated by the option of Latin rhythms-into-rock, and wrote vocal lines that floated over sambas, rumbas and tangos in a fantastic melodic profusion. There was also a new determination to write theatre music in the sense of numbers for politicians, soldiers and 'descamidos' (Eva's peasants, the shirtless) that moved the nature of the musical theatre enterprise forward from oratorio to, well, yes, opera.

Rice's lyrics were an inspirational match in numbers like 'Rainbow High' where the triple time swooped across Eva's embodiment of star quality in the beauticians' salon: 'They need to adore me, so Christian Dior me . . . I need to be dazzling, I need to be rainbow high . . . It's vital you sell me, so Machiavel me . . . I'm their saviour, that's what they call me, so Lauren Bacall me,' and the money keeps rolling in to the sound of a hot shuffle, seven beats in a bar sequence that acts like a career travelator in Eva's money-raising pitch for her (corrupt) foundation.

Lloyd Webber was now lit up by the challenge of the subject and the showbiz take on it. A mood of requiem colours the score, oscillating between the Latin mass and the Latin dance, the saint and the sinner embodied in the one character. She was the new world Madonna with the golden touch, a line that reverberated years later when the film came round. There was only one out-and-out pastiche number, 'On This Night of a Thousand Stars' for the small town nightclub singer, Magaldi, but even that manages to sound like an authentic item.

The conjunction of convenience between Péron and Eva is ingeniously expressed in the entwining duet 'Surprisingly Good For You' and there is a parallel number for Eva and Che, encircling each other in the showdown Waltz that enfolds a Beatles quote right at the end in a number of simple melodic quality that Lloyd Webber felt, not unreasonably, paid suitable theatrical homage to his great hero Richard Rodgers.

The newly established English National Opera – opera sung in English on an official subsidised basis had finally arrived in 1973! – offered to produce *Evita* at the Coliseum under Lord Harewood's chairmanship. But Andrew knew what he really wanted. He wanted Hal Prince – who had lately produced Stephen Sondheim's *Company* in London – and he wanted a money-spinning hit. He flew to Prince's holiday hideaway on Majorca with the score, determined to build on the encouraging contact Prince made after the *Jeeves* fiasco. 'We went down the road to his local bar where he quizzed me for hours on end on musical theatre. I did okay, we got along fine. We knew we could and should work together.'

While negotiations proceeded for the stage production, he got down to more work on the *Variations*. He knew he had to assemble the right people. At first, the evolution depended on a chance encounter entirely consistent with the improvisatory nature of the piece. In the London offices of MCA Records, the secretaries used to play the latest releases and one caught Andrew's attention as he was passing down a corridor. He stuck his head round a corner and said that whatever he was hearing was exactly the sound he was after.

The record was by Colosseum Two, a jazz rock combo run by the percussionist John Hiseman, with Gary Moore, who had made his name with Thin Lizzy, on lead guitar, John Mole on bass guitar and Hiseman's wife Barbara Thompson – who was just founding her own electric jazz group, Paraphernalia – on saxophone and flute. The group was the son of Colosseum, the world's first jazz rock group that Hiseman had launched with enormous success at the end of the 1960s.

Hiseman had never really heard of Lloyd Webber. Theatre wasn't his 'area' and his musical life was defined by endless touring, headlining concerts at the Albert Hall and European festivals. At Andrew's invitation he went across to Eaton Square and listened to him romancing the piano for forty-five minutes. He was impressed by the fact that Andrew knew what he wanted. The others in the group huffed and puffed, but Hiseman persuaded them all to go down to Sydmonton for a week's rehearsal culminating in the second Sydmonton Festival in the summer of 1977.

Before they set off Hiseman received a call from David Land saying that Andrew had marked out some passages for improvised flute and saxophone, and did he know anyone who might be able to help out. So at a preliminary rehearsal in London, Hiseman introduced Barbara: 'I could see the look on Andrew's face which said, "Oh no, he's rowed his bloody wife in . . ." but within twenty minutes he'd forgotten all about me and the boys and was courting Barbara, because of course she's a brilliant player and he recognised that immediately.'

Julian was fully established as a cello soloist and now married to Celia Ballantyne, the girl who had rushed up to him after the *Joseph* performance. He joined the group at Sydmonton, along with Don Airey, Rod Argent and David Caddick as keyboard players. Argent's second group had broken up and he was starting to broaden his musical base. He had lately been involved with a laser exhibition at the Royal Academy and one of his compositions for it had been released as a single by MCA.

Caddick was a young musician from Doncaster who would become another close and important colleague. He had studied at the London College of Music with Bill Lloyd Webber and had got to know both Bill and Jean well. He had recently graduated and was fully intending to make a career in classical music but was filling in as a substitute keyboard player on *Jesus Christ Superstar* while David Cullen was away working on some orchestrations. He had gone home to Yorkshire and when he returned from the pub with his father one Sunday lunchtime, his mother said that Andrew Lloyd Webber had called. He had never met him. An extra keyboard player was urgently needed in Sydmonton and Jean had recommended him and given Andrew his telephone number.

The cello part was written, also the woodwind with indications for extemporisation from chord symbols, and most of the piano. Hiseman took care of the percussion and Caddick and Argent worked on synthesizers to create the unique sound of the two dozen variations. This collaborative and highly creative manner of working, with Lloyd Webber knowing exactly what he wanted, became central to his output over the next few years. With Hiseman, Thompson, Argent and Caddick, these Sydmonton rehearsals, culminating in the weekend festival, saw the genesis of *Cats, Requiem* and *Starlight Express*.

And the process was nannied along by Bridget – 'Biddy' – Hayward, Lloyd Webber's former PA, now a director, at the Really Useful who had acquired a weekend cottage in the nearby village of Ecchinswell and who kept everyone happy. Biddy hailed from a Roman Catholic, Army background and was everyone's favourite godmother. She was also one of the very few people Lloyd Webber ever confided in. She remembers going to meet Caddick when he arrived for the first time and made such an impression on everyone with his good manners and good looks – and beautiful legs. It was a hot, idyllic summer. Andrew and Sarah's first child, Imogen, was in her pushchair. Meals were served in Sydmonton round the kitchen table, or in Biddy's cottage.

Lloyd Webber himself lived as usual on the edge, never relaxing, even when things were going well, always anxious about the sound system, the dampness in the church which was still in a pretty ramshackle state, fighting all the time for the highest of standards. This approach impressed Hiseman, Thompson and Argent who were not exactly new to the business themselves. Argent was a bit worried as to how he was doing until at the end of 'a bloody hard week's work' Biddy came up and said that Andrew thought that what he was doing was marvellous and had been saying so to everyone else. 'I was impressed by that. He didn't come up and say fatuous things to my face, but made sure everyone else knew that he thought I was doing OK, or better. That made a big impression on me. He's always very generous and positive with his enthusiasm and I respect that. It's sometimes not easy for him to say what he thinks to people, it's easier sometimes perhaps if he makes a big drama out of things going wrong. But that's how he is and deep down he's always positive and enthusiastic.'

The premiere of *Variations* was on the Saturday morning as the second part of a cello concert. In the first half, Julian was due to play some sonatas with the pianist who had played with him in the previous year's try-out, Yitkin Seow. Unfortunately, Seow had been delayed in Belfast where he had given a concert the night before, and was unable to get himself on to an early shuttle flight. As a result, *Variations* was played twice, which nobody much minded, least of all the record executives from MCA, who were feeling more confident the more they heard.

When Seow eventually turned up in a terrible fluster around lunchtime, Andrew was so furious he refused to speak to him. This sent Julian into a parallel rage at his brother and he declared that he would have nothing more to do with the project he had initiated before tearing into the house, going upstairs and packing his suitcase to leave. Somehow his wife Celia managed to calm everyone down and peace was restored.

The music was a showpiece for the performers, and not just Julian. It switched between energetic riffs and floating, almost hallucinogenic floating tunes, some of them quite a long way from the original theme. There is a rich fecundity in the writing that bears comparison with anything Lloyd Webber, or indeed anyone else, wrote in the 1970s and 1980s. The statement of the theme is kicked off by the surprising cello and driving drums of Hiseman. And Thompson on saxophone has some of the most beautiful writing, the ninth variation being a new tune altogether with a jazzy soft drum solo.

The Latin rhythms of *Evita* had obviously spilled over into *Variations*, with a funky bossa nova recurring between other hornpipe motifs and an extraordinary, galloping Wild West climax bringing the piece full circle to the first variation. There are some witty, stylish evocations, close together, of Jimmy Hendrix's wailing lead guitar, the Shadows' twangy rhythms, and of Prokofiev's *Romeo and Juliet*. But the overall, distinctive sound is of the rock and jazz synthesis. The piece is, above all, the most enormous fun.

Variations became a bestselling Number One album in early 1978 and Lloyd Webber's favourite composition. Even at this distance, and after its later transposition to the stage, he says there is not a thing about it he would alter, not a note. When it was being recorded, Lloyd Webber's friend Jamie Muir – whose father, Frank Muir, the humorist, had spoken at the first two Sydmonton Festival debates – brought along Melvyn Bragg, with whom he worked, to the Morgan Studios. Bragg promptly asked if he could adopt the opening as his signature tune for his new television arts programme *The South Bank Show*. One graphic moment in the title sums it up: a flash of lightning as God creates Man at finger stretch, as in a cartoon version of Michelangelo's Sistine Chapel, the clear implication being art as a popular explosion of styles.

Evita finally hit the stage on 21 June 1978, a hot night with summer crowds milling round the Prince Edward, newly reopened as a theatre after many years as a cinema. The theatre, previously known as the London Casino, had been restored to its former glory by the Delfont Organisation who owned it, the palazzo-style brown-brick facade wedged into the very heart of Soho on the corners of Greek and Old Compton Street. The venue had housed another Latin American dame in its first ever production in 1930, *Rio Rita*. Since then, the place had been a cabaret-restaurant and an increasingly popular stage for ballet, pantomime and revue. More recently, it had been, with the Coliseum, the home of Cinerama. A short-trousered Lloyd Webber had indeed seen 'This is Cinerama' there when he was about eight years old.

The atmosphere was electrifying, the roads outside jammed with black limousines and crowds of first-nighters in midsummer evening wear, jackets thrown over shoulders, floral print dresses rippling in the breeze. The mood was that of a carnival or fiesta, the sense of anticipation high, not least because this was Hal Prince's British musical debut. Lloyd Webber, who had loved Prince's productions of Stephen Sondheim's *Company* and *A Little Night Music*, had flown to Majorca, played him the score, and subjected himself to that rigorous grilling on what he felt about musical theatre.

Prince had kept Rice and Lloyd Webber waiting because of another engagement. And when he started work they began to have doubts. His first idea was to have three Evitas, as he believed the role was too demanding. Then there was a tremendous wrangle over the casting. Julie Covington had walked away from both publicising the album and the opportunity of singing her hit number on stage. Hal Prince wanted to cast an American actress called Bonny Schoen, who was flown over to audition in a shoot-out for the role with a little-known dynamo called Elaine Paige.

Paige had appeared in the chorus of *Hair* and *Superstar, Grease* with an unknown Richard Gere and *Billy* with Michael Crawford, and had also featured in a doomed musical called *Maybe That's Your Problem* about premature ejaculation; which, needless to say, came off early. But she had also worked with Joan Littlewood at Stratford East and was just breaking into good dramatic roles on television. She felt she was finished with musicals.

In fact, she was just starting. She won the role which she suddenly wanted very badly and became indelibly associated with a show that ran for eight years in London, nearly five on Broadway, where it won seven Tony Awards. Much of this was due to Prince's brilliant sleight-of-hand production. The content, as a theatre piece, could strike you as thin. But the accumulation of stage pictures and statements, oiled by Larry Fuller's slick, strutting group choreography, was simply stunning.

The lighting was supplied by David Hersey, who would go on to light most of the big West End musicals of Cameron Mackintosh and Lloyd Webber, including *Cats* and *Les Misérables*. He is best known now for what he calls the 'light curtain', an intense sheet of light he first used in ballet. And he proved a master of defining the space on a stage with blocks of light. 'Another Hersey trade-mark, if you like,' he told an interviewer years later, 'was first seen in *Evita*. The script called for lots of blackouts, and I suggested . . . the use of white-outs instead – where we freeze a moment at the end of a scene in a blaze of light. We did that and it became one of the dynamics of the evening.'

The encapsulation of the story in cinematic flashback was a master stroke, and scene after scene was staged with a steely, pointed precision. Elaine Paige came high-flying melodically over the infectious samba chorale as she descended on Buenos Aires, Big Apple. Péron (Joss Ackland) and the generals defined the art of the possible in politics in a reductive game of musical chairs, and the rapid changes in a political culture of coups and putsches in a revolving door.

The gesture of public address was also conveyed in the body language of Eva, and Paige played her with a diamond-hard brilliance and edge that made her seem like a poisonous, but exotic, bird. David Essex was rather more flaccid as Che, but that was in the nature of the role and his many fans appreciated the way he made the sardonic commentary part of his own relaxed and smiling stage persona.

Critical reactions were mixed, Bernard Levin declaring in the *Sunday Times* that he had spent one of the most disagreeable evenings of his life, inside or outside a theatre. He also rated 'Don't Cry For Me, Argentina' a melody somewhat inferior to those he would hear as a boy improvised on a saxophone outside the Albert Hall by a busker with only three fingers on his left hand.

Peter Hall confessed to his *Diaries* that he had encountered 'the cult of the kitsch again, inert, calculation, camp, and morally questionable. I fell out of step with popular taste.' It was the old *Arturo Ui* question: could you make a musical with a wicked hero, as the glorious spoof in the Mel Brooks movie *The Producers* had anticipated with the 'Springtime for Hitler' number. What next, cried Levin, unmindful of that movie, a musical about Hitler? Similarly, in New York, John Simon would excoriate the show as an 'artfully produced monument to human indecency' and urge the readers of *New York* magazine not to help fill the coffers of 'these two amoral, barely talented whippersnappers and their knowing or duped accomplices'.

Nothing in the show, however, condoned Eva Péron's career, any more than Shakespeare condoned arch villains like Macbeth and Richard III by giving them the glamour of poetry and privileges of centre stage. Lloyd Webber was surely right in saying that he could not imagine any intelligent person going to *Evita* and coming away with anything but the idea that she was a fairly grisly piece of work. And the last twenty-five minutes, including the scene in the bedroom, he counted the most daring passage of harmonic and musical writing he had yet done.

The show made its way in the world. Hal Prince repeated his London triumph on Broadway with Patti LuPone – another unknown whose name would be made by the show – as Eva and Mandy Patinkin as Che. The film rights were sold and nothing happened for nearly twenty years, though Lloyd Webber, Rice and David Land made a million in selling them on.

In Argentina, where the show was banned, a 'correct' version of their own was staged by the right-wing arts establishment; it was apparently so anodyne and dreadful that coachloads of theatregoers went down to Brazil to see the real *Evita*. And in Austria, a film director was sentenced to two years' imprisonment after arranging for the actress playing Evita to be beaten up so that his own girlfriend could take her place.

There was something else about the piece. It seemed to catch something in the politically strife-torn air of Britain in the mid-1970s. This was a volatile, dangerous time in British politics, with a weak Labour government standing helplessly by while the stock market wobbled. The show took its energy from a spirit of football hooliganism, violence, private armies and a growing need for someone to take control.

Prophetically, the arrival of one strong woman on the London stage preceded the arrival of another in Downing Street, in the following year's General Election.

And in 1981, the new, abrasive Prime Minister was unwittingly entwined in the legend of Eva Péron by going to war with Argentina over the issue of British sovereignty in the Falkland Islands. Mrs Thatcher became a legend in her own crunch time. She was not renowned as a theatregoer, but she did like *Evita*. Indeed, she returned several times to watch the Casa Rosada scene from the back of the stalls.

As the writer Trevor Grove, himself raised in Buenos Aires, expressed it, 'Although Argentinians were so desperately bitter about their eviction from the Falklands, their defeat had a thoroughly beneficial outcome, leading to the ejection of the brutal military junta and their country's return to democracy after decades of shame.'

Britain's good name abroad was renewed in the Thatcher years, and the Prime Minister developed what became commonly known as a special relationship with America, and specifically the White House of President Ronald Reagan. The 1980s would herald a boom time, too, for the British musical in a transatlantic show-business alliance running parallel to the political one, and Lloyd Webber led the way. He was loosening his ties with Robert Stigwood and gearing up to take more charge of his own affairs. And the partnership with Tim Rice would be more or less dissolved.

For the moment, though, their partnership had produced an enduring classic of modern musical theatre, one that would be produced in perpetuity. And their careers were set. Andrew had recovered from *Jeeves* and Tim had been proved right about their choice of subject matter, 'Had *Evita* flopped,' he says, 'Andrew might have given up, I don't know. And I would have just gone on and been a disc jockey.'

The world was changing. And not all for the better. In the spring of 1978, Aunt Vi died in the retirement home in Brighton that Andrew had bought for her and George. And in February of the same year, Alan Doggett, who had worked on the white album of *Evita*, threw himself under a train. He was still teaching and running his boys' choirs but he was threatened with allegations about his private life and preferred not to risk public disgrace. The tragedy is that it later emerged there was nothing on the files that was ever going to make any kind of case against him in court. Lloyd Webber remains convinced that Doggett would never have been guilty of taking advantage of any young person in his charge: 'His main talent was in helping children to make music. He was convinced that every young person had music in him or her, and that it was never too late to stop learning.'

Any dream will do.

FIVE

SONG AND DANCE OVER JELLICLE CATS

Just as *Evita* opened in June 1978, the BBC was completing work on a television series about British songwriters. The last programme was devoted to Rice and Lloyd Webber, and the rehearsal pianist was David Caddick, who was also assistant musical director on *Evita*. He tutored the singers on the finer points of the songs from the latest hit. Marti Webb sang 'Buenos Aires' and also 'I Don't Know How to Love Him' from *Superstar*. Webb – who had starred opposite Tommy Steele in *Half a Sixpence!*, sung Nancy in the first London revival of *Oliver!* and appeared in *Godspell* alongside David Essex, Julie Covington and Jeremy Irons – later succeeded Elaine Paige in the title role of *Evita*, having sung two performances a week during the early part of the run.

Quite innocently, she became a pawn in the struggle of disassociation from Rice that Lloyd Webber instigated. The ten-year management contract with Robert Stigwood was up, and Lloyd Webber's affairs could now be handled entirely by his own Really Useful company, which he ran with Brian Brolly. Sarah and he held thirty-five shares each in the company and Brian Brolly thirty. Biddy Hayward remained closely involved. The performance rights on *Joseph*, *Superstar* and *Evita* remained with Stigwood, though Lloyd Webber was of course paid royalties as the composer.

From this time, a split with Rice was inevitable not so much because of differences or disagreements but because Lloyd Webber was taking control of his own artistic destiny. Rice stayed with Stigwood's partner David Land, who continued to manage his affairs. He had also become closely involved with Elaine Paige, and their affair, though discreetly conducted over the years, soon became public.

He and Andrew were talking about a song cycle for Paige, and indeed went so far as to open talks with Thames Television. But the next thing Rice knew was that the song cycle was now being written by Andrew with another lyricist, Don Black, and was going to be performed by Marti Webb.

Looking back, Rice is relatively sanguine about the whole affair. 'After *Evita*, Andrew and I never had a real split but we kind of drifted apart. If I'd had another great idea like *Evita* maybe we would have gone on. But I didn't. My heart wasn't really in the song cycle because I didn't know what I wanted to say in it. I was looking for something more exciting and once Andrew got going on *Variations* and *Cats* I thought I'd better find something to do on my own . . .'

Don Black had written lyrics for *Bar Mitzvah Boy*, an unusual, fairly average hybrid of an Anglo-Jewish musical by Jule Styne (the composer of *Gypsy* and *Funny Girl*) based by the writer Jack Rosenthal on his own television play. The show had opened a few months after *Evita* and Hal Prince sent Black a cable saying he liked his contribution.

Lloyd Webber got to hear about this, also liked what he heard of Black's work, and took him to lunch in Walton Street. They returned to Black's Knightsbridge flat and the composer revealed that he'd always wanted to do a one-woman show. (Black assumed he meant write one, not perform one.) Black said that he could envisage one about an English girl going to America, working there and trying to find the right man. 'In fact,' says Lloyd Webber, 'there was a quite specific English girl we both knew and we modelled the show on her. I can't remember her name and I don't know what happened to her.'

Lloyd Webber sat down at the piano and played a couple of tunes he already had floating about, Black recorded them on his cassette tape and suggested the girl went from New York to Hollywood; they quickly wrote 'Capped Teeth and Caesar Salad', a swingy-rhythmed, sun-tanned sort of a catalogue song which includes a stonewalling telephone conversation with an office secretary in the middle of an acrid view of Tinsel Town: 'Capped teeth and Caesar salad, bloodclot Beverly Hills, when business starts to dip, wheel out the glucose drip . . . It's like a wonderland, except the laughter's canned . . . I'll call you back and – have a nice day.'

The nameless girl starts off writing home to her mother in Muswell Hill from New York, where she is living with a man who bores her rigid. Then she meets Sheldon Bloom the film producer and goes to Hollywood. After latkes and laughter, tears and borscht, she's back in New York. She meets a younger man, whom she loves but who leaves, and she drifts into a bitter, half-committed affair with a married man ('It's not the end of the world if he's married, making do is nothing new . . . It's not the end of the world to chase rainbows, I'll be fine when I find mine'). Marti Webb sang the cycle at the 1979 Sydmonton Festival, and a recording was made in February 1980 just as Webb succeeded Paige full-time as Evita.

Black had nothing to prove. He had a career already. And he was ten years older than Lloyd Webber. Hailing from Hackney in the East End of London, where his parents were of Russian Jewish immigrant stock, he had been a journalist on the *Musical Express*, a record plugger in Denmark Street, a stand-up comic and a writer for Matt Monro – 'Walk Away', the story of an older man and younger woman was a classy 1962 Number One hit – as well as of many film scores. In 1967 Dean Martin had presented him with an Oscar for his lyrics to John Barry's 'Born Free'.

He had been around songwriters all his life but had never met anyone like Lloyd Webber. 'He is a very bizarre kind of character, you can see he's besotted with the musical, which is strange, because when you're with him it's very uplifting. You come out and you think, this guy is sensational, he's out there on his own. Who else is there like this? Then of course he can talk with the same passion about lots of other things. Whereas Marvin Hamlisch, for instance, talks about music and the baseball game, and that's it.'

Musically, *Tell Me On A Sunday* contains several of Lloyd Webber's best tunes and is inventively harmonic throughout. Again, Rod Argent, John Hiseman and co made a crucial Sydmonton input around phrases that recur as full tunes and a core of songs that express powerful emotional turmoil and defiance. Marti Webb had the right sort of voice for this. Basically an untrained coloratura, she could belt higher up the range than most singers without having to break from her 'chest' voice into her 'head' voice.

'Take That Look Off Your Face' was a good example of this technique, given a punchy musical accompaniment that sounded like the beaty, snazzily reverberative Motown arrangements of Phil Spector. And the title song had lyrics full of internal rhymes ('I'd like to choose how I hear the news') and a touching evocation of remembered outings – 'Take me to a park that's covered with trees, tell me on a Sunday, please,' the second line rhymed in subsequent, wistful choruses, with 'Take me to a zoo that's got chimpanzees,' and 'Find a circus ring with a flying trapeze.'

By the time the cycle was recorded, Lloyd Webber had

made a new pact with a producer with whom he would transform not only the musical theatre on both sides of the Atlantic but with whom he would also raise his own fortunes to a previously unimagined level. If *Superstar* followed the dawning of the age of Aquarius, *Cats* heralded the age of the musical Midases: Lloyd Webber and Cameron Mackintosh. Myths proliferated and showbiz millionaires made good copy in a political era where the Thatcherite imperatives of self-help and self-improvement held sway.

In November 1979, Cameron Mackintosh was responsible for organising the Society of West End Theatre Awards ceremony in the Grosvenor House Hotel. *Evita* had swept the board, but the performed excerpts were bedevilled by microphoning faults and technical problems. In his acceptance speech, Lloyd Webber said, '*Evita* only became a great show because it had one of the world's greatest directors, Hal Prince, directing it. That's exactly what this cabaret needed tonight.'

Reports of an ensuing drunken brawl have been exaggerated – by the mischievous David Land, for one – but Mackintosh owns up to the fact that, replete with celebratory claret after an exacting afternoon and evening's work, he went tottering across the room to Lloyd Webber's table where he subsided quietly at the maestro's feet. After being helped from the premises, he passed out on the floor of his taxi.

A few days later, Lloyd Webber contacted Mackintosh and invited him to lunch at the Savile Club in the New Year. They hardly knew each other at this point. Mackintosh had gradually made his mark in the West End without exhibiting all that much in the way of good taste. His early years of second-rate tours and gloriously misguided ventures such as a stage adaptation of the long-running radio serial *The Dales* were marked, however, by his absolute dedication to, and enthusiasm for, all kinds of musical theatre, from Lionel Bart and Julian Slade to David Wood's children's shows and 'The Best of Broadway'. In 1976 he consolidated his growing status in the West End by co-producing *Side by Side by Sondheim*, one of the first, and one of the best, compilation shows, which did a lot to establish Sondheim's reputation in Britain, building on the previous year's big London success of *A Little Night Music*.

Two years later, he set a precedent that was to have profound historical consequences: supported by money from the Arts Council, he mounted a better than average revival of *My Fair Lady* at the Leicester Haymarket starring Liz Robertson. The time-honoured gap between the profit-oriented commercial theatre and the design and directing skills more sharply prevalent in the subsidised sector was closing. The erosion of this traditional apartheid would be a feature of the Thatcher years, a key factor in the success of *Cats* and a phenomenon that ironically ensured the survival of the big subsidised companies while achieving the political goal of undermining them, or at least making them see pragmatic sense in a harsh funding environment.

One of the talents Mackintosh had noted in the subsidised sector was Trevor Nunn, artistic director of the Royal Shakespeare Company since 1968. Nunn had been on a hot streak since his *Nicholas Nickleby*, co-directed with John Caird, had taken London and New York by storm in 1979/80. He had also staged a winning version of *The Comedy of Errors* with a musical finale and a riotous revival of Moss Hart and George S. Kaufman's Broadway-to-Hollywood fable *Once in a Lifetime*. He knew how to 'put on a show'. His *Nickleby* production team included the designer John Napier and the lighting designer David Hersey; the musical staging of *Errors* and *Lifetime* was by Gillian Lynne, a veteran of West End musicals who had worked at Stratford-upon-Avon with Nunn for several seasons. All three would be crucial to *Cats*. Lynne was already in place for *Cats*, whatever happened, and she, in Lloyd Webber's recollection, was the crucial conduit to nabbing Nunn.

Although Nunn was a classic example of the working class lad come good through grammar school and university (like Peter Hall, who had founded the RSC in 1960 and whom he would follow eventually into the top job at the Royal National Theatre, he came from Suffolk and made his early reputation at Cambridge), he never recognised any frontier or borderline between various categories of theatrical expression. In his final year at Cambridge, the *wunderkind* produced both the Foot-lights Revue and *Macbeth* for the Marlowe Shakespeare Society. He was as familiar with Shakespeare's sonnets as he was with Peter Cook's already famous funny sketches.

But he was undoubtedly looking for new challenges and a change of pace. In 1978, after what he says were ten punishing and exhausting years, his artistic directorship had been shared, at his own request, with Terry Hands, with the proviso that both could occa-sionally work away from the company. His first outside job was *Cats*. He had been approached by Lloyd Webber, who was much impressed by *Nicholas Nickleby*, with a request to listen to a tape of *Tell Me On A Sunday* with a view to its theatrical possibilities. Nunn advised writing a second cycle for a man and inter-leaving his set of songs with the woman's until they converged in a duet.

That idea was noted and filed away. 'The next I heard from Andrew was a message saying that he wanted to talk to me about a major musical and I immediately thought, great, some mighty work to follow *Evita* – which I thought was absolutely stunning – a great novel adaptation, maybe *The War of the Worlds*. When he said that he'd got settings of ten poems in T. S. Eliot's *Old Possum's Book of Practical Cats* I really did experience a crash of disappointment. I couldn't believe my bad luck that he was talking about something that didn't involve Tim Rice and which could only have a limited audience appeal.'

By then, ten settings of the poems had been given as a cycle – along the lines of *Tell Me On A Sunday* – at the 1980 Sydmonton Festival, performed by Gary Bond, Gemma Craven and Paul Nicholas. T. S. Eliot's widow Valerie, who supported the enterprise throughout, sat in the church among the other guests, liked the songs and afterwards showed Andrew a cache of relevant unfinished fragments, unpublished poems and letters, including one in which Eliot pondered the possibility of ending Old Possum's collection with a poem about dance. The idea of a musical was born.

Before approaching Nunn, Lloyd Webber had bearded Hal Prince on the subject. He knew he needed some magical concept, or brilliant trick, to transform a song cycle into a show. Prince was sceptical, wondering if the enterprise was a metaphor for British politics, with cats representing Disraeli, Gladstone and Queen Victoria. 'Hal,' Lloyd Webber replied patiently, 'it's about cats.'

The making of *Cats*, on the face of it an entertainment of total simplicity, was at first a process of trial and error suddenly unlocked by an important discovery. Nunn's anxiety over a lack of narrative was challenged by Cameron Mackintosh. Under pressure, Nunn envisaged a delightful small show set in Fitzrovia, with potted palms and dinner jackets and two pianos, with the cats poems supplying a social critique. Absolutely not, said Cameron and Andrew. They were thinking fullscale musical, full orchestra, lots of dance, Gillian Lynne choreographing.

Nunn still demurred, saying that there had to be an idea for a storyline. 'And it is entirely conceivable that while I was playing for time, other people were being

ALW, aged four, on his first day at Wetherby pre-preparatory school
in South Kensington

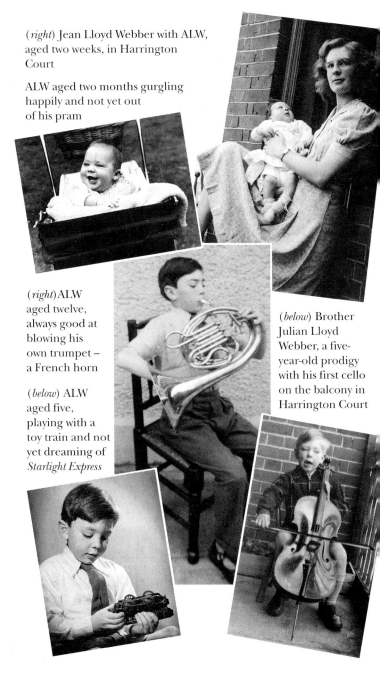

(*right*) Jean Lloyd Webber with ALW, aged two weeks, in Harrington Court

ALW aged two months gurgling happily and not yet out of his pram

(*right*) ALW aged twelve, always good at blowing his own trumpet – a French horn

(*below*) ALW aged five, playing with a toy train and not yet dreaming of *Starlight Express*

(*below*) Brother Julian Lloyd Webber, a five-year-old prodigy with his first cello on the balcony in Harrington Court

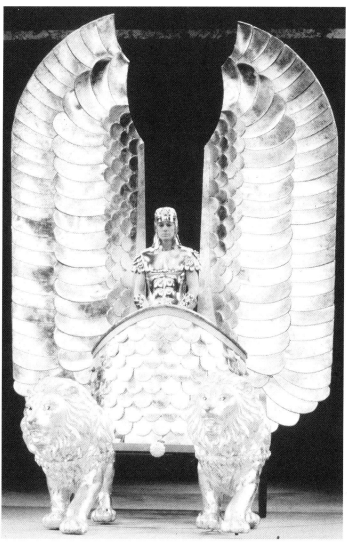

Jason Donovan in his chariot of gold at the climax of the
1991 London Palladium revival of *Joseph and the Amazing Technicolor
Dreamcoat*. Joseph, the first collaboration of ALW and Tim Rice,
was originally presented at the Colet Court School in
Hammersmith in 1968

Jean and William Lloyd Webber, ALW's parents, in the 1970s

ALW's first marriage, to Sarah Hugill, in Wiltshire in 1971.
The couple are joined by Tim Rice (*far left*), Robert Stigwood
(*centre*), and David Land (*far right*)

Jesus Christ Superstar.
The second Rice/
Lloyd Webber
collaboration, one of
the biggest smash
hits in the history of
musical theatre, was
first issued as a
record in 1970,
premiered on
Broadway in 1971
and, in the following
year, in London

ALW enjoying a
party with Imogen
and Nicholas, his
children from his
first marriage

The first flush of success for music director David Caddick, producer Cameron Mackintosh and ALW: they worked together on *Cats*, *Song and Dance* and *Phantom*

(*Below*) David Hemmings and Gabrielle Drake in the original production at Her Majesty's of *Jeeves* in 1975. ALW's collaboration with Alan Ayckbourn was his only real flop, but the show was successfully revamped and relaunched as *By Jeeves* in 1996

Sarah Brightman with a relaxed-looking ALW at the opening night of *Starlight Express* in 1984, five days after their marriage

Elaine Paige sings 'Don't Cry For Me, Argentina,' the big song from *Evita* at the Prince Edward in 1978. A recording had been issued two years earlier

Cats, which opened to sensational
reviews at the New London in
1981 and has been running there,
and all over the world, ever since

asked, and that I was the tenth person they had asked anyway. That's how musicals get set up.' Nunn then read a poem Eliot had not included in *Old Possum's*, about a man in a pub called the Princess Louise who meets someone who talks to him about types of cats. This was among the cache of poems Valerie Eliot had handed to Andrew after the Sydmonton song cycle, and was Eliot's first clue that there might be a context for his poems; at the end of the poem, the poet follows the little man and arrives in a sort of cat world. Here was the genesis for 'Jellicle Cats'.

There followed the proposition that there should be no humans at all, that everything physical should be cat-scaled and that, in Nunn's rough scheme, the audience should be attending a ritual of the Jellicle tribe – the Jellicles being the street cats of this area – and that Old Deuteronomy should be their leader. By this time it was tacitly agreed that Nunn was on board and he stipulated the participation of Napier and Hersey. When word got about of what was happening, incredulity was rife. 'Once we got started,' says Nunn, 'people, when they enquired after the show, had great trouble disguising their amusement at the seeming badness of the idea.'

The key to it all was a lost fragment, 'Grizabella the Glamour Cat', which Valerie had passed on to Lloyd Webber. This comprised just eight heart-breaking lines – Eliot deemed them too upsetting for children to read and had pulled them from the published text at the last minute – about becoming so marked by mortality as to be unrecognisable.

Nunn forged a link between the tragic state of Grizabella and the notion of renewal beyond Eliot's mysterious Heaviside Layer, which he proposed treating as a heavenly region, a limbo district where certain cats had access to their other eight lives. The ritual could pivot on the election of a cat deemed worthiest by the Jellicles of this privilege on this particular night.

The show became woven into Nunn's RSC routine. During the final few weeks of rehearsals and previews he would start the day in his horse-shoe shaped Aldwych office, walk a few hundred yards round the corner to the New London Theatre and return to the Aldwych in the evening. The New London, brainchild of the great architectural designer Sean Kenny, had opened in 1973 and become something of a white elephant. It housed lacklustre shows and boring conferences but offered the possibility of the sort of environmental staging Nunn and Napier envisaged.

The television programme *This Is Your Life* was recorded in the New London, and when Lloyd Webber was the victim in 1980, he sat through the proceedings dreaming of what this theatre might do. After the recording, he left the reception and ran down to the Aldwych to grab Nunn and bring him back to have a look. They found a man who showed them Sean Kenny's revolving floor, which had never been exploited. Nunn was completely astonished and told Andrew this was a momentous discovery. The place had also become a conference centre, and there was considerable resistance to any dodgy theatrical project that would threaten that source of revenue. Bernard Delfont, who owned the building, brokered a deal involving a second mortgage on Lloyd Webber's Sydmonton Court. If *Cats* were to fail, Lloyd Webber faced financial disaster, if not indeed ruin.

Thus, in a rush of enthusiasm and possibly misplaced confidence, the great revolving outdoors rubbish tip was conceived, with a spectacular apotheosis made possible by the discovery in one of Eliot's letters of his proposal that eventually the cats were to go 'Up up up past the Russell Hotel, up up up to the Heaviside Layer.' The cats on a cold tin roof inhabited a world of scaled-up newspapers, Coke bottles, tyres, scrap iron and all the detritus of a consumer society while a hydraulic escape route to the world beyond, excitingly lit by Hersey, took the theatrical experience into the realms of a Steven Spielberg movie.

Having Napier and Hersey around him made Nunn feel at home in the commercial environment; not only that, he had persuaded Judi Dench, his favourite actress, and an RSC associate, to play Grizabella. At that stage most of the casting was doubled up, with each performer playing two cats.

Judi Dench liked the sound of Grizabella and her lynchpin role and, for the other feline, asked if there was an old moggy who lay in the sun on a wall and slept a lot: the Gumbie cat was hers! Two weeks into rehearsals in Chiswick, dancing in front of Wayne Sleep, Dench as the Gumbie cat emitted a sudden shriek and stopped in her tracks. She had torn her Achilles tendon and went straight to hospital for an operation.

That focused everyone's mind on another problem: the big song that was needed as an emotional climax for Grizabella. The next morning, Lloyd Webber came in with the as yet untitled 'Memory' tune, which had nearly worked its way into *Evita* as an aria for Juan Péron. As he played it, Nunn claims to have turned to the others in the room and told them to remember the day, the *hour*, they first heard the next smash hit by the composer. No-one shouted out, 'When I last heard the opening bars of Ravel's *Bolero*,' but that's another issue. The tune dated from when Lloyd Webber had thought of doing a one-act opera about the race between Puccini and Leoncavallo to write the first *La Bohème*. Puccini's wife hears the 'Memory' tune as Leoncavallo's response to 'Your tiny hand is frozen' and remarks bitterly that if only her Giacomo had come up with a tune like that, he would have had a big hit!

Lloyd Webber remembers playing the tune to his father at the time and asking him if it sounded like Puccini. Bill blinked and replied, 'No, it sounds like ten million dollars!' All the same, the composer had played the tune rather reluctantly that morning to Trevor Nunn. The rest, as they say, is history.

Words were commissioned from Roger McGough, the Liverpool poet, who wrote a funny poem, says Nunn, that was not a singable lyric. The situation would nearly repeat itself a few years later when, at the suggestion of Nunn and John Caird, the poet James Fenton was invited to provide lyrics for *Les Misérables* by Alain Boublil and Claude-Michel Schönberg. He did so on a deal that gave him a small percentage of all future world grosses on the show. His lyrics, though fine, were not considered quite right for the project and were replaced by those of Herbert Kretzmer – you wouldn't necessarily want to quote Herbie, but you could always hum him – leaving Fenton the richest unsung lyricist in the annals of musical theatre.

Next, Tim Rice declined the invitation to chip in, then Don Black wrote a couple of versions that 'didn't work', so in desperation, over the weekend, Nunn sat down and read through all of Eliot's poetry and decided there was probably something in 'Rhapsody on a Windy Night' in *Prufrock*:

> Twelve o'clock.
> Along the reaches of the street
> Held in a lunar synthesis,
> Whispering lunar incantations
> Dissolve the floors of memory
> And all its clear relations,
> Its divisions and precisions.
> Every street lamp that I pass
> Beats like a fatalistic drum,
> And through the spaces of the dark
> Midnight shakes the memory
> As a madman shakes a dead geranium.

Personalising the imagery as experienced by Grizabella and binding in snippets from other *Prufrock* poems, Nunn's words for the flowing triple-time melody began:

> Midnight.
> Not a sound from the pavement.
> Has the moon lost her memory?
> She is smiling alone.
> In the lamplight the withered leaves collect at
>   my feet
> And the wind begins to moan . . .
> Every street lamp seems to beat a fatalistic
>   warning.
> Someone mutters and a street lamp gutters
>   and soon it will be morning.

His idea was to hand over a rough outline to a real lyricist, but Lloyd Webber said that was it, and that is what Judi Dench in plaster rehearsed in a darkened theatre – the rehearsals had moved into the Her Majesty's in the Haymarket – lit by a naked bulb after the rest of the cast had left for the day. 'We worked on it for an hour and a half and it was unforgettable. It is heartbreaking to think that nobody saw her.'

But as Nunn, a seasoned *Hamlet* director, well knows, when sorrows come, they come not single spies, but in battalions. Dench rejoined the cast on crutches and in plaster but fell off the stage while rehearsing and injured herself all over again. She reluctantly withdrew from the show. Cameron Mackintosh rang Elaine Paige and asked if she would come and help out. The previous night, she had heard a snippet of the backing track for the 'Memory' melody on her car radio.

She was determined to find out if she could record the song and, making a mental note, got out of her car and rushed to her front door – the disc jockey had said he would play the whole of the track after the midnight news. As she rushed, a bedraggled black cat wrapped itself around her legs and followed her indoors. The cat was a stray and stayed with Paige until the day he died. With Paige on board after a cloak and dagger dinner with Nunn in Covent Garden, Tim Rice suddenly re-emerged as a potential lyricist for 'Memory', much to Lloyd Webber's delight. A new lyric duly arrived and Nunn was ordered to rehearse it, though he felt it did not do the job required and was too recognisably written in the voice of a human.

Paige sang the Rice lyric at the first preview, but Nunn was distraught because he felt the content of the show was bleeding out of it. 'Memory' was prefigured at various points in order for the big number to work when it came – and yet he didn't want to appear to be defending something he himself had written and which obviously had commercial possibilities because of the tune.

He talked to Rice on the telephone but Rice was reluctant to change anything because Andrew had said he was perfectly happy with it. In the end, Nunn says, Mackintosh took the decision to go back to Nunn's lyric. By which time, Paige, who had been singing both Rice's and Nunn's and sometimes muddling them together, was more disposed towards the Rice version she had instigated by joining the show and helping everyone out. In the end the Nunn version did prevail and Paige had a big hit.

Rice was pretty angry. 'My lyric rapidly turned from being a lyric everyone was happy with to one that nobody was happy with. Elaine was stuck in the middle of all this. I was delighted for her that the song did become such a big hit, but less delighted that I had lost out on a couple of million nicker!'

Wayne Sleep, a principal dancer with the Royal Ballet and a tireless populariser of dance with his own specially formed group, Dash, was on hand to witness both

Grizabellas, and to create a few minor ripples of his own. He admired the way choreography was so integrated into a theatre show – 'before *Cats*, most directors in England just used choreographers for dance breaks.' But he was unsure of the ensemble nature of the piece that guaranteed him two solo spots, one of which was slow to appear. Eventually, he says, he retired to his dressing room until he got his way.

He also visited Judi Dench in hospital, bearing commiserations. Like Nunn, he loved what she was doing, the musical talent she evinced without having a great musical voice. 'She was going to sing "Memory" in a husky, broken-down voice, a cat whose life was on the ebb – Elaine interpreted Grizabella's solitude and lameness through movement and sang the song with a haunting, dynamic bravado.' Grizabella hung around the periphery of the Jellicle ball like a terrible warning to the others. Her tattered grey costume was in stark contrast to the rest, which were sprayed body-stockings made of Lycra and lurex, with knitted bibs and leg-warmers, simple rope tails and wigs of yak hair that could stick out and not droop under lights.

A few days before the opening, Wayne Sleep found a half-drowned cat in the corner of the Covent Garden piazza, near his flat in Long Acre. It was black with a white bib and two white flashes on his face – an almost exact replica of Sleep's Mr Mistoffelees costume. The dancer gave the cat a stroke and it followed him home. Sleep already had another cat who did not take kindly to the new arrival, so the stray was billeted with his manager's secretary's family in the country. But, like Paige's feline follower, this was taken as an omen of success, even though so much had gone wrong.

One actor, Jeff Shankley, damaged a cartilage, another was fired and at one point Gillian Lynne – who was devising a cat world of movement using elements of classic, jazz and modern dance in a manner unprecedented on the British stage – stopped for two days suffering from exhaustion. The musical director was replaced, and on top of everything else, a row developed over billing. Wayne Sleep, whose ego was as mighty as his talent – the godmother of British dance, Dame Ninette de Valois, dubbed him 'the greatest virtuoso dancer the Royal Ballet has ever produced' – wasn't planning on being a chorus member of a cat team.

The production team had succumbed to the poster idea of yellow cat's eyes on a black background, with moonlit dancers flitting through the eyes like fiery pupils. The notion had been cooked up at DeWynters – Robert DeWynter's advertising and graphics agency founded by his great grandfather, where Anthony Pye-Jeary had now fetched up alongside a brilliant graphic designer, Russ Eglin – and had nobody's name above the title. In fact, at first, it had nobody's name anywhere.

Mackintosh told Sleep he didn't want to clog up the poster with names, otherwise it would look as though a mouth had appeared. 'Fine,' said Sleep, 'give it some whiskers as well.' So his name did appear, as well as those of Paul Nicholas (as Rum Tum Tugger), Brian Blessed (as Old Deuteronomy) and Elaine Paige. Other fancy unbilled felines included Sarah Brightman, Bonnie Langford, the late Geraldine Gardner, Finola Hughes, Sharon Lee-Hill, Susan Jane Tanner, Stephen Tate and Ken Wells.

It was a hand-picked company, designated to explore and convey the curious characteristics of cats, described by Gillian Lynne as 'aloof, hypersensual, cold, warm, completely elastic and very mysterious'. Set pieces were constructed to stand within the overall night on the tiles: the exotic theatre of Growltiger's dreams of the Siamese, including the Ballad of Billy McCaw, with its fine parody of a duet from *Madam Butterfly*; the savage cat fight for Macavity; the fantastic playground atmosphere of the driving number for Skimbleshanks the railway cat, complete with his engine improvised from old wheels and dustbin lids.

The opening night was delayed because of Judi Dench's injury, but it seems incredible now to relate that the most successful musical of all time nearly never opened at all because of a shortfall in the capitalisation. Having re-mortgaged his Sydmonton property, Lloyd Webber invited a group of film executives to listen to him playing the score on the piano. They were not impressed. Finally, three-quarters of the £450,000 capital needed was raised from small investors.

Anyone with £750 to spare could take out one unit of investment. If you took more, you would have made one of the most amazing killings of all time. One cast member changed his mind, and returned his £750 because he smelt disaster. Rod Argent on keyboards felt optimistic, but could only afford the one unit. It has earned him somewhere near £50,000.

Lloyd Webber had cut his ties with Stigwood and struck out alone. He was on a hiding to nothing. And he knew enough to know that everything in the musical theatre is a throw of the dice. But from the first preview he was confident of the show being a hit. 'The first act went okay. At the second preview, the second act didn't. And I remember the third preview very well. I was with Sarah and we decided we wouldn't see the show, but would pop along after dinner in Boulestin. At the end, I just looked at the audience, and I said to Sarah: "We're not down at Sydmonton tonight. Lets's go to Annabel's." When we got there, the doorman said, "What are we going to do about a hotline for tickets?" The word had just got around and it was clear we were going to fly. There was no hanging around. It didn't matter what anyone was going to say. For some reason, this kind of strange show had just taken off.'

It is hard now to realise how unexpected *Cats* was. I

stood on a railway station in Stratford-upon-Avon a couple of years ago while two visiting American school-girls discussed their schedule. 'What are you doing this weekend?' asked one. 'Buckingham Palace, Hyde Park, the Tower of London . . . and *Cats*,' said the other. 'Have you read the T. S. Eliot poems it's based on?' asked the first girl. 'No. I know nothing about it. Except it's got cats in it. And it's got a cool poster.' Indeed it has. Those yellow eyes have stared out of the blackness for seventeen years.

I've seen *Cats* several times, but I shall never forget the first night at the New London on 11 May 1981. The rubbish tip heaved and moved during the overture and lithe girls and chaps in bits of fur and body-stockings crept among the audience, bottoms proud, claws at the ready. Then the explosive opening number, the antici-patory 'Jellicle Ball' with its speeding rhythms, anthems, key changes and irresistible high spirits. Sean Kenny's revolutionary space had at last realised its potential. With *Cats*, the place was suddenly like a mixture of the National Theatre's Epidaurus-inspired Olivier auditor-ium and the rackety in-the-round Round House.

What was that sad, twangy, synthesized but not synthetic sound behind it all? Rod Argent, who by now had a share in a shop called Rod Argent's Keyboards in Denmark Street had imported the first Prophet Synthesizers – the first polyphonic synthesizers – from Los Angeles, and Lloyd Webber seized immediately on their potential. In *Variations* there is a totally original and compelling coalition of real and synthesized sound. In *Cats*, the nighttime jangled howl of the mobile moggies and capering kitties is characterised by that glistening cascade of the spangled synths.

On the night, the score struck home as thoughtfully accommodating towards Eliot's rhymes, continuously inventive and also sounded like a conscious effort to change gear towards fantasy and romance. *Joseph* was the school play, *Superstar* the rock concert, *Evita* the Latin opera, *Jeeves* the English musical comedy and now *Cats* the vaudeville. The eclecticism of Lloyd Webber's music, an aspect of his own volatile character, was only matched by the unpredictability of his theatrical endeavours.

The reception was wild bordering on crazy as the critics dashed from their seats. As they did so, Brian Blessed came to the front of the stage and raised his hand, asking the audience to leave quickly and quietly as there was a bomb scare. A standing ovation was cut off at the knees. The scare turned out to be a hoax, at a time when such japes were as common and unsettling as the real thing without bloodshed. The call had been made just before 'Memory' was sung, but the stage doorkeeper couldn't find anyone authorised to stop the show. So 'Memory' and the finale went ahead uninterrupted. Lloyd Webber's fortune, and career, may have hinged on that incident.

Oddly enough, when *Cats* was premiered in Australia, the Sydney first night in the presence of the prime minister Bob Hawke was similarly disrupted by a bomb scare. You'd think the people who do this sort of thing would choose more appropriately murderous musicals, such as Sondheim's *Assassins* or *Sweeney Todd*. (In fact, Sondheim did attract one of the most famous non-hoaxes with *Pacific Overtures* at the Winter Garden, the New York theatre later occupied by *Cats*. Some chap rang up to say that there was a bomb in the house. The theatre was cleared before they established this was a dissatisfied customer who had hated the show the night before and had rung up to say that the show *would* bomb, not that he would bomb the show. The show bombed anyway.)

The London critics were enthusiastic, though Irving Wardle in *The Times* felt a vast input of talent failed to take fire with an organic work, and that the orchestrations were more remarkable than the basic material. Michael Billington in the *Guardian* paid his highest compliment by insisting that a great poet had not been let down. The energy and whoosh of a theatrical event is not always what critics respond to first of all, but musical theatre at its best can and should destroy all defences, and *Cats* did that.

The fall-out was far more mega than the show itself, which remains modest, muscular, and appealing to all cat-lovers over the age of ten. When it moved to the drastically altered and heavily gutted Winter Garden in New York, in October 1982, the show opened to a new Broadway ticket top-price of $45 and an all-time record advance of ten million dollars. I visited the office of the Shubert Organisation in New York at the time, and watched the co-producer Bernie Jacobs flash up the figures on his office computer. His watery old eyes were sparkling like topaz and for a man who was about as athletic as a tree-bound sloth you could even say he had a spring in his step.

This was the start of a transatlantic tie-in between the Shuberts and Lloyd Webber and Mackintosh that would keep Broadway afloat for the next decade. The production team were all on their way to becoming millionaires, and the show was soon as heavily marketed and exported as *The Merry Widow* had been in its heyday.

Frank Rich, newly appointed on the *New York Times*, who was to give all of Lloyd Webber's shows a fairly rough ride, acknowledged the primal theatricality and fantasy world of *Cats* as satisfying a real audience hunger, though the even sterner Robert Brustein in the intellectual magazine *New Republic* averred that *Cats* could have been an effective small cabaret piece 'with the help of talent, imagination and a little taste'.

Playing the old 'sounds like' but 'sounds worse than' card, Clive Barnes opined that the lyrical passages are to

132

Puccini what Richard Addinsell's *Warsaw Concerto* was to Rachmaninov, thus conferring a degree of seriousness on Puccini and Rachmaninov of which neither had been deemed worthy by the Clive Barneses of *their* day. Still, the show, like *Evita*, won seven Tonys, in the categories of musical, score, book, director, featured actress (Betty Buckley as Grizabella), costumes and lighting.

It has become fashionable to say that you don't have to understand what is going on in *Cats* to have a good time. This is as popular and misleading a myth as the one about Lloyd Webber being only a mega-musical man, or the other one about his shows being obvious commercial propositions before they even open.

The songs repay attention even if they don't feed into the narrative drive that has always seemed to me imposed rather than endemic, despite Nunn's best efforts. This attention is easier to advance if your language is English, and for all the translation help given to foreign tourists, I really don't see how you 'get' *Cats* if you come from Osaka. Sure, you have quite a good time at the show. But Bustopher Jones swaggering around St James in his white spats, the battle of Pekes and Pollicles and the knockabout clowning of Mungojerrie and Rumpelteazer are all quintessentially English conceits, rooted in a specific topography and reeking of the music hall.

A later song of Lloyd Webber maintained that love, love chan-ges everything. But in truth it was *Cats*, and the reduction in tax rates, that chan-ged everything. The fortunes of Cameron Mackintosh and Lloyd Webber for a start. Thanks to Mrs Thatcher's tax changes, this was the first major hit show on which Lloyd Webber could retain a substantial amount of his earnings. He and Mackintosh shared 25 per cent of gross profits and rocketed into the millionaire bracket; and, more importantly, the undisputed front seat of West End management power.

In their wake – although it is fair to say that posters, like press releases, are the cries of John the Baptist before the saviour or the sacrifice arrives – DeWynters grew like Topsy, until by *Cats*' 'seventeenth phenomenal year', a staff of four had grown to one of a hundred, with offices in Leicester Square and New York, a publishing department, a design studio, advertising and information task forces, and a new media wing creating CD-Roms and websites for shows all around the world. Today, they even have their own glass blower who makes neon signs.

The marriage of Trevor Nunn to the classical actress Janet Suzman broke up and he married Sharon Lee-Hill, who pranced nimbly as Demeter every night. Designer John Napier also left his wife for Donna King in the *Cats* chorus in New York. It was, indeed, showtime. School was out, the living was easy. Soon Andrew would exchange one Sarah for another, though not during *Cats*. Bizarre though it sounds, Wayne Sleep was having an affair with Sarah Brightman at this time. 'It didn't bother me,' he says, 'I'm gay anyway, but we had a hanky panky time; she's a sexy girl and was always way out.'

When *Cats* opened on Broadway, Lloyd Webber achieved a new record of having three shows running simultaneously in London and three in New York. *Cats* joined *Evita* and a re-vamped, two-act version of *Joseph* (the 1976 New York premiere at the Brooklyn Academy was a flop) that came steaming in from the East Village and ran for nearly two years. The last authorial hat-trick in Broadway musical history had been in the 1950s, when Rodgers and Hammerstein could boast *Carousel, South Pacific* and *The King and I* running side by side, a triple crown Lloyd Webber could only dream about, and no doubt would, as he moved later into the romantic realism of *Phantom* and *Sunset*.

Still, the achievement to date was recognised in full by *Time* magazine, who made Lloyd Webber only the fifth

British artist to merit its cover story: he followed Charlie Chaplin, Gertrude Lawrence, Julie Andrews and Paul McCartney. And *Time* music critic Michael Walsh's extensive and exhaustive essay became the basis of an important book. In the full flush of their early success, in the summer of 1981, Lloyd Webber and Mackintosh had travelled to New York together on the *QE2*. 'That was when I first saw,' said Mackintosh, 'what a marvellous marriage we made together, in theatrical terms. Andrew is the most talented man I shall ever work with in my life, I know that.'

That trip was a riot. Andrew had also taken Sarah One and young Imogen along for the ride, and they all cringed at the frightful food served up in the Queen's Grill by a Scottish fellow with a meat cleaver. Lloyd Webber and Mackintosh took especial delight in a terrible onboard theatre company called Theatre at Sea, who rendered Neil Simon's fizzing quartet of comedy gems, *Plaza Suite*, entirely mirthless. 'We giggled uncontrollably at that, for all the wrong reasons, of course. On the food front, after five days it became like being in hospital. So I phoned ahead from the ship to New York and booked a table at Le Veau d'Or, whither Cameron and I repaired the minute we docked in the harbour.' It was a very hot summer in New York, and as they first walked past the Winter Garden, where *Cats* was to be presented, Mackintosh told Lloyd Webber that he really didn't want to produce theatre in this town. 'Take a tip from Robert Stigwood,' advised Lloyd Webber, 'who says that if you're going to be serious about working in the theatre, you simply have to work, and succeed, in New York.'

In London, *Evita* and *Cats* were joined in April 1982 by *Song and Dance*, the final, not totally satisfactory theatrical pairing of *Tell Me On A Sunday* and *Variations*. Wayne Sleep played out his nine-month contract in *Cats* and was on the look-out for new dance material for his group Dash. At a party, he suggested *Variations* to Lloyd Webber, whose first idea for a pairing was between the song cycle and *Cats*. But crossing the Atlantic on that *QE2* trip, Mackintosh seized on the idea of the song cycle paired with *Variations*, and suggested the title *Song and Dance*.

The show came with the subtitle 'a concert for the theatre', a tacit admission of defeat, really. Placed in the cavernous acres of the Palace Theatre on Cambridge Circus, the song was never matched with the dance, though some token effort at a 'relationships' cross-over was implied by director John Caird. A ludicrously ambitious idea of somehow telling the life story of Paganini in dance was ditched at Cameron Mackintosh's suggestion that the trump card in *Variations* was the personality of Wayne Sleep.

There was plenty of that to go round, but not enough to make any kind of story out of *Variations*. Instead, with choreographer Anthony van Laast – who had danced with Sleep and had progressed from a classical training via jazz and contemporary dance to working on pop videos with Kate Bush – he devised a phantas-magoric showcase for his leaps, turns, tap-dancing riffs and high-speed spinning top impersonations.

The music raced through his veins. He had persuaded Lloyd Webber to dress up a hornpipe variation with a complex and witty tap routine that built into Broadway brassiness. Against the suppleness of the best new tune – which, ironically, did not sound so good once it had the words of 'Unexpected Song' added to it – the dancers moved in kaleidoscopic motion as in a soporific garden of delights where Sleep was left awake.

That song capped the dance and brought back Marti Webb in some forced liaison with the dancers for an unconvincing finale. Her character in *Tell Me On A Sunday* had nothing to do with *Variations* unless she had found her ultimate man under the duvet in Sleep.

Marti Webb had a privately invented name for the girl, that of her Irish grandmother, Annie Maguire.

A terrific new song was written by Black and Lloyd Webber for the show – 'The Last Man in My Life' which unaccountably disappeared when Sarah Brightman recorded the role on television, and also when Bernadette Peters played it in New York in 1985. This was an engorged song of physical fulfilment, and it achieved liftoff on the first night. Another new song not on the original album was the boppy 'Married Man' which Webb delivered with a smiling, kooky, cynical acceptance of her mistress role: 'She and I can cover each mood, one will be on heat while the other's subdued . . .'

The attempt to Americanise, supposedly authenticate, *Tell Me On A Sunday* for a New York audience, was a dismal failure, Richard Maltby Jr's tinkerings with Don Black's lyrics insensitive to the fact that Black's heroine's absorption of American detail was filtered through her predominantly Muswell Hill persona. Bernadette Peters would not have been seen dead, or even half alive, in Muswell Hill.

Variations, too, suffered in the crossing to New York. Frank Rich had come over to London and declared that Wayne Sleep had out-danced the choreography, which he didn't like anyway. Within two weeks of the notice appearing, Anthony van Laast was no longer going to New York, nor was John Caird, nor was lighting man David Hersey. Lloyd Webber could have made a few phone calls, but he didn't, and all concerned felt terribly aggrieved. Two or three years later, he apologised profusely to van Laast.

Nor did Wayne Sleep go to New York. His role in *Variations* became that of an official boyfriend, Joe, of the girl in *Tell Me* – now given the name of Emma and a job as a milliner. And the dance was overhauled by Peter Martins of the New York City Ballet. The show was not a wild success, but it did run for over a year, just as *Song and Dance* ran for over three in London. The musical components had strong audience appeal, and it was at the least extraordinary that such a concert could fill a West End theatre for so long.

Owning some of those theatres, and controlling what went into them, was a natural progression. As *Song and Dance* opened, Lloyd Webber and his Really Useful Company were confident of acquiring the Old Vic as a home for new British musicals. Somehow, news of his sealed bid of £500,000 was leaked to a Canadian impresario, David Mirvish, who was passing through London.

He and his father, 'Honest' Ed Mirvish, theatre owners and renowned restaurateurs and cheap shopping magnates in Toronto, gazumped the bid with an offer of £550,000 – and the theatre was theirs. They proceeded to refurbish the Old Vic at a cost of £2m and then presented many admirable but loss-making seasons of productions by Jonathan Miller and Sir Peter Hall before putting the Old Vic back on the market – for an estimated price of £7m – in 1997.

Having also failed to get his hands on the Aldwych and, later on, the declining Round House in North London, Lloyd Webber finally announced in August 1983 that he had purchased the freehold on the Palace Theatre for £1.3m. The Palace had not been on the open market probably because, as Sir Emile Littler, who had managed the theatre for thirty-seven years, said in a short, emotional handover speech, 'It is no good owning a theatre without things to put on the stage.' He was paid £200,000.

Lloyd Webber and Cameron Mackintosh were the new kids on the West End block, with the product and the power to put things on the stage. The composer was now the only creative artist in London to own a theatre and there was an appropriateness to the acquisition of a Grade II listed building, a magnificent monument of high Victorian architecture, as noted in a congratulatory telegram to Lloyd Webber on buying 'the ultimate Victorian art work'. *Song and Dance* was still running there.

The place had opened in 1891 under the management of Richard D'Oyly Carte as the Royal English Opera House, with a presentation of Arthur Sullivan's *Ivanhoe*, a lavish and ludicrous extravaganza written when the composer was enduring one of his not infrequent tiffs with Gilbert, and notable chiefly for the huge popularity of a numbingly trite song, 'Ho! Jolly Jenkin.'

The theatre was sold on in 1892 to Augustus Harris and became known as the Palace Theatre of Varieties. In addition, *Jesus Christ Superstar* had run there for years, and Lloyd Webber was besotted with the idea of restoring the venue to its highest former glory. This he did, supplying a belated response to John Betjeman's 1959 complaint that the veined marbles, a distinctive feature of the interior design, had been defaced with a coat of plum-coloured paint: when the paint was scraped off, the marble and Mexican onyx panels were revealed undamaged. And by 1987 the magnificent terracotta frontage, three huge bays filled with dozens of tiny arched windows, was fully restored. By which time, *Les Misérables* was immovably installed.

Biddy Hayward had left the Really Useful at the end of 1982, but she was wooed back to take charge of the Palace – which for a time had a pleasant restaurant situated in the splendidly ornate and mirrored circle bar – and also to back up Brian Brolly's supervision of the RUG's first foray into production of work other than Lloyd Webber's. This came about through Lloyd Webber's longstanding friendship with the director David Gilmore, whom he had met while Gilmore was running the Watermill Theatre at Newbury, near Sydmonton.

In early 1983 Gilmore was coming to the end of a term running the Nuffield Theatre in Southampton and received in the post *Daisy Pulls It Off*, a spoof girls' school play in the style of Angela Brazil novels, written by an unknown playwright, Denise Deegan. He unhesitatingly put it on with a completely unknown cast (including the subsequently much better known Alexandra Mathie, Kate Buffery and Samantha Bond) to packed houses and rave reviews.

London managements visited, and so did Lloyd Webber. The distinguished producer Michael Codron went to Gilmore's office in the interval and said he loved the show but would only present it in London with two stars in the leading two roles. At the end of the show on the same night, Lloyd Webber told Gilmore he would take it, lock, stock and barrel with the Nuffield cast.

The plot was just the sort of asinine, jolly hockey sticks jape designed to appeal to Lloyd Webber's Wodehouse-ian side. Set in 1927 at the Grangewood School for Young Ladies, the annual school play presented the story of a scholarship girl, Daisy Meredith, surviving resentful snobbery and beastliness to emerge victorious as the heroine of the hockey pitch and a clifftop rescue. And there were gymslips galore.

Lloyd Webber volunteered to write a school song for the West End opening, and did so anonymously. The rousing anthem was attributed in the programme to Beryl Waddle Browne, the school's headmistress and a brilliant anagram dreamed up by Richard Stilgoe with whom Lloyd Webber was at work on his next blockbuster. When the show made its way to New York, *Time* magazine fulsomely reviewed this song, oblivious to the anagrammatised identity of its composer, and the quotation lauding the unknown Beryl was proudly displayed outside the theatre.

The association with Gilmore would lead to further collaborations on the Howard Goodall/Melvyn Bragg coalminers' musical, *The Hired Man*, and the riotous Ken Ludwig backstage farce *Lend Me A Tenor*, while Really Useful would also present a brilliant rhyming period pastiche play *La bête*, starring the indomitable Alan Cumming, and the late Edward Duke's one-man Bertie Wooster show, *By Jeeves* (that title would come in handy later on).

When *The Hired Man* opened at the Astoria in November 1984, Milton Shulman of the *Evening Standard* predicted a failure for Lloyd Webber. He then put his money where his mouth was, saying the show would certainly fold before the following February and that if it didn't, he would buy Lloyd Webber lunch at the Dorchester. For his part in the bet, Lloyd Webber would fly Shulman to New York for the premiere of his *Requiem*. Neither won, with *The Hired Man* struggling on a little past the date set, but not sufficiently to warrant triumphalism on the producer's part. The solution was a friendly lunch in Lloyd Webber's London house at which Shulman – a neighbour who lived in Eaton Square – provided the Dom Perignon champagne.

Lend Me A Tenor at the Globe in 1986 also produced a pleasant critical brush. Jack Tinker of the *Daily Mail* was less than enthusiastic about the play but said that he wished he could afford to go and live in the sumptuously designed setting. Lloyd Webber wrote to the *Mail* saying that an emergency board meeting of the Really Useful had unanimously decided to deliver the set free of charge to Jack Tinker when the show closed, so that he could live happily in it ever afterwards. 'The only snag is,' concluded Lloyd Webber, 'that the favourable reaction of the vast majority of Jack Tinker's colleagues means that the delivery date will almost certainly be many years from now.' (The show ran for just ten months, but Jack continued to live in Brighton.)

Gilmore tells a wonderful story of producing *Song and Dance* in Australia, abetted by Anthony van Laast.

One night in Adelaide they visited a strip club, having been told this was the place to find a late-night drink. Suddenly, Brenda the Naked Contortionist appeared, placing her body in poses that defied all previously known anatomical knowledge. 'She had not a stitch on, and was completely covered in oil. Our eyes were out on stalks. One had no idea that a lower region of the anatomy and the human head could be placed in such intimate conjunction. And she did all this to a recorded soundtrack of the Music of Andrew Lloyd Webber!'

There were seismic changes in Lloyd Webber's personal life. Three weeks after attending the New York opening of *Cats* in October 1982, Bill Lloyd Webber was taken ill and, after an operation in hospital, his kidneys gave out, and then his heart. He was sixty-eight. He had seen his sons triumph as, respectively, composer and solo musician, and at least his own reputation as a teacher and musical figure had been recognised with the CBE in 1980. But he was undoubtedly a sad man, and his sadness made a lasting impression on both his boys.

Years later, when publicising the new CD of his father's music, Julian even revealed that Bill had been so unhappy that he had tried to encourage him to leave his mother. 'Three years before my father died, he fell in love with Justine Bax, one of his music students. She was twenty-five. He was sixty-five. She used to come to our home so I guess my mother knew about it.' Bill was spurred by this dalliance to start composing again, and a highly emotional composition called *Romance*, written for Justine, was included on the new CD. Why did he not break free at this late stage? He told Julian that he simply couldn't, that it was impossible to leave Jean after so long. 'But I think this mirrored his attitude to his own music,' says Julian. 'He simply didn't have the guts to do it.' He had given up the ghost long ago, despite this late flurry of excitement.

At the end of 1982, Andrew Lloyd Webber had gone

to see one of his *Cats* girls, Sarah Brightman in a children's opera, *Nightingale*, based by Charles Strouse on a Hans Christian Andersen story, at the Lyric in Hammersmith. He was drawn there by two rave reviews which commented on her extraordinary soprano voice, and remembers seeing the late Jack Tinker there on the same night. 'Jack hated the piece but loved Sarah, and I begged him not to be too nasty. I was indeed very much taken by Sarah's voice, and by the little hamster she kept permanently in her dressing room. We had hardly noticed this side of her talent in *Cats*, as she had only played the chorus role of Jemima.' He poured out his admiration at a small gathering in the Zanzibar Club, then a popular theatrical haunt in Covent Garden, after the show. *Nightingale* was a visually remarkable production, with Brightman investing her chirpy grey nightingale with spectacular coloratura trills and soaring melodic lines.

And Lloyd Webber was bewitched. Their friendship grew to the point where he was brazenly escorted by Brightman to the first night party of *Daisy Pulls It Off* on 18 April. Sarah Lloyd Webber accompanied her widowed mother-in-law home for a simple dinner in Sussex Mansions. Andrew issued a short statement: 'I want to record that my affection for Sarah is still very great, but unhappily we will be seeking a divorce in the near future. Sarah Brightman and I have known each other professionally for several years. Only recently has our relationship developed.'

SIX

SAGAS OF SARAHS, STARLIGHT WITH REQUIEM

In a symmetrical buzz of nomenclature, Sarah Brightman was herself married to an Andrew, Andrew Graham-Stewart, a record executive and producer with Virgin. The two Sarahs became Sarah One and Sarah Two during a period that was tricky all round and especially painful for Sarah One, who had seen Andrew through his early years and shared his joy in their two children, Imogen and Nicholas.

Sarah One was quiet, private, thoroughly sensible and dependable. Sarah Two was, well, exactly the opposite. On the day she auditioned for *Cats* she escaped death by a whisker. She stood by the piano in a blue wig and a skimpy dress, made the right sort of impression, the sort that might leave an audience shouting for miaow, and left.

She set off to Hertfordshire in her white Triumph sports car and, halfway along the M1, accelerated to overtake a French lorry. The lorry did not see her and carved her up badly. She spun out of control, turned over completely and crashed into a wall. When the car stopped spinning, she groggily noted that the roof had caved in. She managed to punch out the back window and climb through it. As she did so, the car burst into flames.

A few years later, she said to David Crewe-Read: 'Do

you realise that, after Charles and Diana, Andrew and I are the most famous couple in the world?' Unlike Diana, she cheated car-death at high speed. But in a tragic aftermath, her own father would be found dead in a car of his own self-inflicted volition. There was nothing safe or predictable about the Brightman family.

Born in August 1961, Sarah was the first of six children. The family lived in Little Gaddesden, prime golfing territory, north of Hemel Hempstead and St Albans in Hertfordshire. The house was seven hundred years old and had been the home of Edward III's surgeon, John O'Gaddesden. Grenville Brightman, Jewish and comfortably off, had a building company which specialised in mock Tudor houses. His wife Paula, a Roman Catholic, had been a topless dancer in West End nightclubs, notably Murray's.

Following in her mother's twinkly footsteps, Sarah had been a stage school prodigy and a member of the television dance group Hot Gossip, founded by the choreographer Arlene Phillips in 1976 in Maunkberry's club in Jermyn Street. Hot Gossip had moved, cult following intact, to Country Cousin in the King's Road.

When the television and video director David Mallett was looking for a successor to Pan's People, who graced *Top of the Pops* for several years, he saw a photograph of Hot Gossip and signed them up. At this point, Sarah Brightman joined the group and reinforced the wicked, raunchy image of girls behaving badly. They made a sensational TV debut on the late Kenny Everett's show and soon afterwards Sarah made a record, 'I Was Married to a Starship Trooper', that went to Number One.

So if anything, *Cats* was a bit of a come-down for her. The marriage to Andrew Graham-Stewart – she had married him in 1979, aged eighteen – was obviously unconventional. During the run of the show Sarah not only enjoyed the company of the fizzingly antinarcoleptic Wayne Sleep but also sustained a friendship with a 46-year-old property developer, Max Franklyn, who had teenage sons by a former marriage and who commuted between London and Minorca. She openly professed her love for Franklyn. She was a free spirit, and emitted the musky smell of forbidden fruit.

It was this that flattened Lloyd Webber, who had never really thought about girls and stuff all that much. He was steady as a rock with Sarah One, and he was suddenly smitten, helpless to resist. His profile, though not exactly low, was relatively modest until this period in his life. He clearly had no over-developed interest in clothes, no sense of vanity when it came to haircuts. Cars were functional assets, not a luxury. He ran a 1939 prototype Mark V Bentley that he had bought off a Swansea scrapheap in the early days, and he kept an old jeep and an ordinary BMW. Nothing fancy.

But now the spotlight was on him because he had abandoned the mother of his children for a scarlet woman, clearly a visible embodiment of sex on two rather lovely legs. In July 1983 Sarah One sought a divorce as the petitioner, citing Andrew's admitted adultery, and Sarah Two filed for divorce from her estranged husband. The first went through in July, the second in September.

Sarah One moved with Imogen and Nicholas into the Really Useful office premises in West Eaton Place while Andrew found new offices in Greek Street, Soho. Sarah Two was installed in a flat in Eaton Square. Andrew later bought a house in Oxfordshire for Sarah One and the children after lawyers had sorted out the settlement of money, property and a trust fund.

Around this time Sarah One went to New York to visit her sister, Olivia, who worked there and, as in her days with Andrew before he was wealthy enough to keep a New York apartment, she stayed with the inscrutable, ever devoted Peter Brown. 'Andrew found out and was furious with me for harbouring his ex-wife who, he said, had just taken him to the cleaners! And I said, fuck you, she's my friend as well. He was angry for a while, but he soon got over it.'

Two years later, in July 1985, Sarah married Jeremy Norris, six years her junior. An affable, cuddly bear-like character, he was a free magazine management executive in Oxford whom she met on a health farm in Berkshire. Their marriage, followed by a reception at the Berkeley Hotel, coincided with a Sydmonton Festival weekend; Tim Rice went to the wedding.

It is one of the most remarkable facets of the Lloyd Webber story that he has managed to maintain a more than civilised relationship with Sarah One; indeed, you might say they are best friends. Sarah Norris now says: 'In the fourteen years to 1983 when I was with Andrew, lots happened of course; much happiness as well as some deep sorrows. For me, lots has also happened in the fourteen years since. In particular, my marriage to Jeremy and the happiness and stability he has brought into the children's lives have been an enormous source of pleasure and contentment, enabling me to forge a richly satisfying and private way of life. Jeremy has also been immensely successful in his important role as stepfather while, at the same time, ensuring that the children, and indeed all of us, have a healthy and continuing relationship with Andrew.'

One of the other important things about Lloyd Webber's career is the element of organic growth. I dare say all our lives are like this, progressing from point to point with the assistance and participation of an expanding company of recurring people, but there is, in his case, a marked interconnecting tissue of friendship that is maybe typical of how everything works in theatre and entertainment. And maybe surprising in one so seemingly aloof, or impossible. Rod Argent's wife, Cathy, for instance, was a dancer who grew up with

Arlene Phillips, both working with the great jazz dance teacher Molly Molloy. When Hot Gossip emerged, Cathy danced with them for a while and organised an outing to Maunkberry's for Lloyd Webber, Hal Prince and a few others.

So Lloyd Webber met Phillips before he met Brightman. In fact, after that first meeting, he talked to Phillips about *Cats*, still in embryo. Later, she told him about a rollerskating sequence in a film she worked on – *Can't Stop the Music* – when she was pregnant, and how she had to learn how to rollerskate, and then stop careering around the streets of Los Angeles on skates because of her condition. By the time Lloyd Webber came back to her on his new idea for a musical about trains, Phillips had also been involved in pop videos all over the world with Elton John, Boy George and Queen.

The Really Useful Company held the rights in the children's train stories about Thomas the Tank Engine and his puffing chums, and Lloyd Webber wanted to make a series of animated cartoons, with Thomas singing the leading role. 'I couldn't get it off the ground and let the rights go. I was ten years ahead of my time. It *still* should be an animated feature film. Look at what happened with *The Little Mermaid* and *The Lion King*.'

So, the original working title for the new suite of rock and roll and country music pastiche songs was 'Trains', but by the time of the 1982 Sydmonton Festival try-out, this had become 'Starlight Express, or the Magic Toot'. In this form, the show was really a Cinderella story, with Rusty losing a piston and going all over the country trying to find it and fit it back on. 'It was very funny,' says the composer. He denies pinching the eventual title *Starlight Express* from a minor, charming piece for children by Edward Elgar; he was unaware of the Elgar piece at the time and has still not heard it to this day. Elgar's music was written for a Christmas performance at the Kingsway Theatre in 1915. *The Starlight Express* was based on a fantasy play, *A Prisoner in Fairyland* by Algernon Blackwood, and advocated the redemptive powers of children's 'stardust'. There was about an hour of incidental music, including nine or ten songs, most of them written for the characters of the Organ Grinder and the spirit of Laughter.

Interestingly, Elgar's light, exuberant music, full of atmosphere and nostalgic evocations, was a throwback to his own delight in children's entertainment. And he signed the score, which he wrote at the age of 58, 'Edward Elgar, aged 15.' Lloyd Webber, too, was keen on regressing to childhood. As with *Joseph* he envisaged, initially, something for schools and said so in the Broadway programme note. The Really Useful Company were the sole producers, so it is a surprise to learn that the resultant show apparently came about in spite of the producer's, i.e. Lloyd Webber's, wishes.

The idea of a competition, a race, was Trevor Nunn's, he has said: 'I hope Trevor and my other collaborators will forgive me for saying that despite the commercial success the show has had in London, something of the joy and sense of pure fun that was the original intention seemed to get lost and *Starlight Express* was not quite what we intended.' Trevor Nunn, not surprisingly, feels differently about this disclaimer: 'Andrew kept saying this was a sweet little show about Thomas the Tank Engine. The evidence of the score is the opposite to that. As I have analysed and interpreted the material back to Andrew, it is clear that the narrative is presented through the intelligence of a child who has not only an obsession with trains but also a record collection, and that the child imagines different kinds of locomotives to be represented by different kinds of contemporary music or pop.'

This schism of intention is almost unprecedented in a hit show of this kind. Clearly, *Starlight* as realised in the theatre is '*Cats* Mark Two', with obvious parallels. Just as as you can pair *Superstar* with *Evita* – both have leading characters who died at the peak of their fame, aged thirty-three, and both were counterpointed, in music and temperament, by critical commentaries (by Judas and Che) – you can think of *Starlight Express* as a variation, three years later, on *Cats*.

Both are entertainments, with avuncular, wise old Papa in *Starlight* succeeding Deuteronomy as the referee; Rusty, like Grizabella, born to lose but coming through to win against all the odds; and the supporting anthropomorphic cast exchanging cat fur and pussy paws for robotic railway rocker gear and rollerskates.

At least Lloyd Webber and Nunn agreed on one thing: *Starlight* was never meant to be anything more than fun. Any child between the ages of seven and eleven who sees the show reckons it is the best thing ever. And one of my sharpest memories of the old *Critics' Forum* on BBC Radio Three is the exuberant response of both John Carey and Hilary Spurling, two of our most intellectually formidable critics, pulling down their pants, almost, and declaring what a great time they had at the show.

There were two clear intentions. One was Lloyd Webber's deeply felt tribute to the age of steam, the romance of train journeys, and that abiding affinity between American popular music and the railroad. 'There is a romance,' he said, 'about trains and there is natural rhythm about them which suggests music. I remember going from Chicago to California by train and that was a great journey, though somewhat slow. I think I was finally convinced when I saw how excited my son Nicholas became when he first saw those enormous engines.'

The other was the idea of theatrical motion. At the early workshop Lloyd Webber convened with Nunn, designer John Napier and Arlene Phillips, performers who could skate took part, and Tracey Ullman sang Pearl, the observation car. The nightmare about dancing on skates was that it might all turn into an ice-show.

Arlene Phillips was determined to make the dance theatrical, and the racing like a sporting event. Skates allowed freedom of arm and body movement.

But something else happened in the preparation. Lloyd Webber's music began to catch something in the air in the early 1980s, a confluence of rollerblading, street dancing, body-popping, rap and video pop culture that exerted a much wider appeal than most everyday musicals. There is some grain of the truth in the jaundiced assertion that *Starlight Express* was aimed at people who don't like musicals. Refreshingly, it was also aimed at people who don't like theatre.

Like *Cats*, it was an event, a gleeful rush of a show, a vaudeville, a marvel and an entertainment. It still is. Richard Stilgoe, an adept wordsmith and highly skilled revue performer who had made his name as a kind of TV lounge pianist and middlebrow wit, was invited on board as lyricist – he had contributed to the opening number of *Cats* – and did a job wittily worthy of Tim Rice, though without, perhaps, the killer punch of genuine slangy idiom.

The environmental requirements dictated an adaptable venue like the Round House or a concert arena at Earl's Court. Instead, the choice, or the chance, fell on the Apollo, Victoria, an art deco cinema near Victoria Station which had oscillated between terms as a picture house, concert venue and last ditch ballet date. Nunn and John Napier moved in with a vengeance. They tore out a thousand seats (leaving about 1,500), installed rollerskating ramps for a bowl effect, and a gantry-style railway bridge which raised and parted, video screens to both 'record' an instant experience and solve a problem with sight-lines, retractable crash barriers and two race tracks in the circles.

It was a phenomenal redesign, costing over half of the record-breaking £2m production budget and far more drastic than anything done at the New London for *Cats*.

Napier aimed to place the performers on a continuing spiral raking right around the auditorium. Nunn saw this effort as part of the new convergence of British popular entertainment and British classical theatre, stemming from the moment when Hal Prince and Andrew had invited Timothy O'Brien – an associate designer of the RSC – and his costume specialist colleague Tazeena Firth to design *Evita*.

Such ingenuity and imagination had only been made possible by the subsidised theatre, said Nunn, which encouraged continuity of effort between artists in a creative and partly protected atmosphere. Just as, thanks to Lloyd Webber and Tim Rice, an expansion of the subject matter in musical theatre had been complemented by a challenge to its form deriving from a readiness to write for all the electrically energised resources of the recording studio and then see if it could work on stage.

The first night impact was extraordinary, like seeing a Spielberg movie in the flesh, or visiting Space Mountain in Disneyland. The event's theatre-ness lay in its brash denial of anything traditionally associated with theatre. It pushed out the barriers separating fairground, vaudeville, rock and roll concert and private pinball machine fantasy – and this must surely lie at the root of its perennial success with audiences. The show became an ultimate theatre experience by not being like theatre at all.

A race was announced from the heavens. This later became the voice of a young boy specifically instructed by his mother to go to bed. In the middle of the stalls what then happened was like sitting in the middle of a roller rink, with Scalectrix fantasies exploding all around and that huge metallic bridge floating into the night air.

The theatre shuddered and brought forth the international contestants like ethereal baseball players in Darth Vader masks topped with miners' lights, gallivanting and grooving to the steady, dirty beat of 'Rolling Stock' ('I'm just the fastest thing you'll ever see, that streak of lightning you just missed was me; Don't stop now, you gotta keep it going all night . . .'): Espresso from Italy, Bobo from France, Nintendo from Japan and the Prince of Wales from Britain (inevitably delayed and rather soppy looking, with big ears). This was as visceral and physically exciting an opening number as the Jellicle prologue in *Cats*. In both cases, you could argue that the show strenuously tried to follow the initial blast but never quite lived up to it.

The slick diesel Greaseball, an Elvis-like descendant of the Pharaoh in *Joseph*, was pitted against the sweet, unassuming Rusty, a steam engine stand-in for his ageing Poppa, with no chance in the modern world. And standing alone was the graceful, bisexual Electra, robotic figure of computerised danger and adaptability: 'I am electric, feel my attraction . . . I am electric, the future is me . . . ACDC, it's OK by me, I can switch and change my frequency.'

Here was a new tin man in a re-worked *Wizard of Oz* fable, heart and guts showing through the pantomime of disguise. The women – in a light-hearted, misogynistic sort of way – were detachable railway carriages hoping to get hitched: Ashley, the smoking car, Buffy the buffet car, Dinah the uncoupled dining car with a crush on Greaseball, and Pearl. The eroticism was not exactly subliminal, nor was it sexy beyond the athletic intimations of those gyrating, sliding limbs and buttocks. But it was fast and graphically embedded in songs about hitching and switching, pumping iron and whistling that had a naive, metallic honesty.

The musical was a pastiche songbook, but it also surged out like a stage version of the film *Rollerball*, ironically asserting the values of steam engine over diesel, and using every available trick of technology to do so. There was a positively physical dimension of pleasure in the sound – conceived by Martin Levan and supervised by David Caddick – which tumbled in great synthesized washes around the auditorium, brass and saxophones blazing away in the live band under the main thrust stage area.

Later on, as Lloyd Webber added more music, he turned to Don Black for the words in one of his most seductive pop tunes, 'Next Time You Fall In Love'. To say that such a song is, musically, infinitely superior to anything you hear in the pop charts these days is, in my view, only stating the obvious. The authentic sound of genuine synthetic charm was also apparent in Poppa, the voice of a brand of spiritual washing powder called Starlight Express that floats down to earth like the twinkling shop fronts on Fifth Avenue at Christmastime; David Hersey's lighting made you feel as if you were inspecting a major city from the air by night.

This boost you need in yourself if you are to achieve anything, as Trevor Nunn put it, came across as a Thatcherite instruction to just jolly well pull yourself together and get on with winning. To that extent, *Starlight Express* belonged philosophically very much to its time. And it caught the mood of street rap and rollerblading in the urban young. It was also, as a theatrical event, miles ahead technically of any other show in London. Interestingly, constant adjustments continue to be made to the physical and musical language of the piece, a necessary tactic in a work partly rooted in pastiche and satirical intentions: the targets keep moving.

In this context, the London opening became the source of one of the most cherishable first-night hitches in theatre history. Papa's microphone packed up just as he hit the lyric, 'Dark days ahead when the power goes dead' which only goes to show, as Raymond Briggs memorably observed, that 'The Light at the End of the Tunnel' (the title of the song in question) is invariably that of an oncoming train.

A spokesperson explained afterwards that a BBC Radio Outside Broadcasting van had turned on their signals to tape audience reactions at the end of the show, but that their system started interfering with the onstage mikes. Lloyd Webber, en route to the aftershow party, said part jokingly, part furiously, that he fully intended to withhold his BBC licence fee for three years. He couldn't be totally displeased, though. Not only had the show gone well up to that point. He had also just married Sarah Two.

Five days previously, in fact, just in time to introduce Sarah Brightman to Her Majesty the Queen at the royal gala charity preview on 22 March 1984 – his thirty-sixth birthday. The ceremony took place at the registry office in Kingsclere, near Sydmonton, with Mr and Mrs David Crewe-Read and Sarah's parents as sole witnesses and guests.

Most of their friends were surprised. Even today, Andrew's third wife, Madeleine, thinks he should have got the obsession out of his system by having a short, sharp affair. She also feels he was egged on in his obsession by David Crewe-Read, who often brought out the boyish, public school breadroll-chucking side of Lloyd Webber's character. Tim Rice was quietly amused that his old partner had fallen for another woman, especially as he had always been so disapproving of his affair with Elaine Paige. He could see at once that this was a doomed relationship between two highly volatile people.

But Lloyd Webber is rarely someone who works things out in advance, or with any great degree of calculation. He is always instinctive, impetuous, honest with himself. And, rather like Sir Peter Hall, he is not a part-time flirt or adulterer: he falls in love and he gets married. And Arlene Phillips knew the effect Sarah Brightman had on him, because she knew her as well as anyone did: 'Sarah has deep and secret qualities. She tapped something in

Andrew, and I think she really loved him. There was a reciprocal effect of his music on her and her voice on him. And she really is so wildly different and daring. I'd been working on one of her videos and I remember her getting ready for a party with Andrew, wearing a very tiny Christmas tree of a rubber dress – there really wasn't a lot to it. I looked at them both, and it was so bizarre. And that was all part of the fun and excitement for Andrew.'

The party was for the opening of *Little Shop of Horrors* in the West End, and Andrew said to Arlene that he couldn't possibly take her looking like that. Arlene advised Sarah that what she was wearing was more of a costume than a dress, so she went home to change. Arlene had told Andrew that Sarah would change the course of his life, and he remembers the lunch where she said so, vividly. 'She's a strangely psychic person, Arlene,' he says. 'There's a great deal more to her than meets the eye.'

Most of the reviews found fault with *Starlight* along the lines of a millionaire being let loose in a toyshop. Michael Ratcliffe in the *Observer* thought that 'the mountain labours marvellously for more than two hours and brings forth a mouse'. The races were repetitive and the storyline, such as it was, not always clear; but these weaknesses were ironed out over the years. John Napier defended the extravagance and expenditure: 'It's not just buying toys. When people accuse us of squandering money they tend to forget we are giving skilled people full employment, with British equipment and know-how, proving that we can do it better than the Americans.'

And Nunn was equally proud of his work: 'Whatever else you care to say about it, *Starlight* pushes back frontiers. It could only be happening *now,* not possibly even ten years ago. Andrew's music reflects what has been happening very, very recently – the social changes, the disco revolution, the birth and growth of the robotic age and so on. It is *hugely* in advance of the technology you find in most theatres.'

The show was not as successful on Broadway, where it finally arrived in 1987. Economics dictated the use of a more traditional theatre, the Gershwin, but the cost was over $8m, making it the most expensive Broadway show ever. Frank Rich jeered at Lloyd Webber going 'funky' and alleged that his soul music lacked true soul. It barely ran two years, but *Phantom* was already up and running in London and Broadway-bound to scotch any fears of commercial vulnerability. Lloyd Webber was always sceptical of the show's chances on Broadway and had avoided the opening. 'It would have been much better in an old film studio we found near Brooklyn Bridge, and indeed would have been infinitely better suited to almost anywhere in America other than Broadway.'

A cartoon by Gerald Scarfe appeared in the *Sunday Times*, with Lloyd Webber's head drawn on to a locomotive and the caption echoing the lines of W. H. Auden in the film documentary *Night Mail* about the night train steaming from London to Scotland accompanied by the chugging, lyrical music of Benjamin Britten: 'This is the Webber train crossing the border, bringing the cheque and the postal order.' Jokes about 'Andrew Lloyd Banks' were common currency by now.

He was keen to write something new for Sarah to sing and he also had the idea of writing a requiem Mass in memory of his father. Sacred music was an important part of his early life, and not just because his father was an organist. Any schoolboy at Westminster was drenched in the atmospherics of the liturgy and church services. The composer Nick Bicat makes the interesting point about Lloyd Webber that he has always been 'very carried away with the environment of art' – the atmospheres of churches and theatres, of paintings and architecture – and this is maybe what fuels more than anything his creative instinct as a theatre writer.

Lloyd Webber told John Higgins of *The Times* what a

deep impression the memorial service for Ralph Vaughan Williams in Westminster Abbey had made on him. And how, as a thirteen-year-old, he had crossed the Abbey yard through a thick fog for the first London performance of Britten's *War Requiem*, one of the greatest (and last) English popular pieces in the oratorio tradition.

Having set T. S. Eliot to music, it might be a plausible task to set the Mass to a theatrical structure: 'The whole idea,' says Lloyd Webber, who wrote vocal parts for a boy, a soprano, a tenor and chorus 'was that the boy was the innocent, the girl a sort of girl child, and the tenor the voice of the adult. And as the adult voice emerges there is this celebration that can happen, but it's cut off in its prime as the girl comes in again with the "Dies Irae" and we bring the whole thing back to nothing, almost in anger.'

The idea had lodged for some time. He had been approached as early as 1978 by Humphrey Burton, then director of arts programmes at the BBC (and subsequently a critical biographer of Leonard Bernstein), about writing a requiem for the victims of the troubles in Northern Ireland. Bill Lloyd Webber's death in October 1982 was the spur. And two months later, a young journalist on the *Daily Express*, Philip Geddes, whom Lloyd Webber knew and liked, and who had just interviewed him, was killed by the IRA Christmas shopping bomb at Harrods. The composer had also read, and been affected by, a story in the *New York Times* about a young Cambodian boy who had been forced by terrorists to choose between killing his mutilated sister and being killed himself. He killed his sister.

By December 1984, after the ritual try-out at the Sydmonton Festival, he was ready to go into the recording studio, having worked closely on the orchestrations with David Cullen and secured the services of the distinguished conductor Lorin Maazel and the great

Spanish tenor Placido Domingo. Sarah Brightman sang soprano and Paul Miles-Kingston the boy treble, with Martin Neary directing the Winchester Cathedral Choir.

What emerged was a rough barbaric score, shot through with moments of great tenderness and some furious fugue-like overlapping in the 'Dies Irae'. The 'Hosanna' introduced by Domingo is racily rhythmed, then chopped down before Brightman and Miles-Kingston sing the beautiful 'Pie Jesu' that, astonishingly, found its way into the British Top Ten. The album did astoundingly well, too, but Lloyd Webber always remained surprised – and very chuffed – by the popular success: 'The last thing on my mind was that it would have wide appeal,' he said – though a promotional video directed by Stephen Frears with Brightman and Miles-Kingston singing 'Pie Jesu' in a derelict urban landscape did not do any harm. 'When I wrote *Starlight Express* I really worked hard to produce something that would contain a selection of pop singles, and they all failed. This thing comes out in Latin and in ten days it's at Number Three . . .'

'Pie Jesu' was a beautiful item with the two voices descending in thirds against a setting as simple as that in Faure's *Requiem*, the only other requiem that replaces the words 'Agnus Dei' with 'Pie Jesu'. There all similarity ends, though there is a touch of Faure-ness in the calm translucence of the writing. Lloyd Webber, like Faure, had not scored for violins at all, leaving the voices, especially the boy's, more clearly offset against the chamber orchestra. You do feel passion everywhere in the score, and none of it is corny or routine.

'Pie Jesu' was the only single ever issued by the HMV Classics department, thanks chiefly to the advocacy of Anna Barry, an assistant in the department, who liked it very much. Lloyd Webber himself offered to pay for the printing of 200,000 copies. Later, Barry left HMV to run the classical division at the Really Useful and had the idea of the affordable high quality Classics on CD that Marks & Spencer took up. This was another idea ten years ahead of its time, and Barry moved on to join Phillips, where Julian Lloyd Webber is one of her charges.

The *Requiem* followed the accepted order of the church service, just as the countless requiems of Palestrina, Berlioz, Mozart, Dvorak and Brahms and others had done. Lloyd Webber said that it was, to date, the most personal of his scores and Lorin Maazel preempted the accusation of it sounding like other requiems: 'No-one can possibly write great music on his own. A composer needs others to stimulate him, to firm up his fancy. Even in Beethoven you can hear the composers he admired – Weber, Gluck, as well as Haydn. I think that this is a piece that's really inspired, an important statement.' And you can certainly hear Stravinsky and Ravel lurking within the surprise elements in the piece, and the violence.

The world premiere was given in St Thomas's Episcopal Church on Fifth Avenue in New York on 24 February 1985. The composer insisted on the same personnel as on the recording. 'I was determined to try and get that unique choir sound that only we have in our English choral tradition. We take it for granted because it sits on our doorstep. Everywhere in the world they try to reproduce it. No-one can.' Which is why the whole Winchester Cathedral choir was flown to New York to be reunited with Domingo, Brightman and Maazel.

I'm not quite sure how this happened – I was working on the same newspaper at the time – but Edward Heath, the former British Prime Minister and amateur conductor, wrote a review in the *Financial Times*. He admired the piece inordinately. The first, and greatest, *Financial Times* music critic, Andrew Porter, was less overwhelmed, but certainly positive, if a mite barbed, in the *New Yorker*, finding it a 'felt' work and an honest one: 'The effects are obvious, but they are effective . . .

This is unchallenging music, unless the challenge is to a listener to set aside any ideas of development, difficulty and such subtlety as informs the varied repetitions of the "Agnus Dei" in Verdi's *Requiem*.'

The London premiere followed in April in Westminster Abbey and all proceeds went to the Sussex emergency services and Royal Sussex County Hospital for their work after the IRA bombing of the Grand Hotel in Brighton in the previous October, during the Conservative Party conference. Mrs Thatcher had been a target. Five people had died, many were seriously injured. The performance was attended by Mrs Thatcher and many of her Cabinet ministers.

The *Requiem* would have a further life as a ballet by the late Kenneth MacMillan and indeed in other concert and dance formats. Anthony van Laast staged a version on a double-bill with *Variations* at the Omaha Opera House, of all places, where Fred Astaire began his career and the British opera director Keith Warner was in charge for a while. Somehow, van Laast turned the *Requiem* into a story about a car crash in which the two principals, who had been in the car, sang the tenor and soprano parts while two dancers acted out their roles.

This unpromising sounding project is an example of the way in which Lloyd Webber's growing reputation transformed the lives of many colleagues such as van Laast, whose entire subsequent career (and not inconsiderable wealth) is based on his association with Lloyd Webber on *Song and Dance*. He already had a career but he then entered, as he says, a different league.

As 1985 drew to a close, there were big rumblings on both business and artistic fronts. Lloyd Webber was persuaded by Brian Brolly that the future of the company lay in expanding its interest and going public. A more short-term objective was to raise the money needed to complete the expensive programme of renovations on the Palace Theatre. The Really Useful's board was expanded from comprising just three executive directors (Lloyd Webber, Brian Brolly and Biddy Hayward) to include several non-executive directors who would take the company towards a flotation on the stock market in the New Year.

These were Tim Rice, back in the fold and still sporadically engaged in creative discussions with Andrew; Madeleine Gore, a theatrical investor, and friend of Biddy's, who worked at N. M. Rothschild Asset Management, specialising in large private portfolios; Sir Richard Baker Wilbraham, another Lloyd Webber investor and a director of J. Henry Schroder Wagg, the merchant bank charged with handling the flotation; and, as chairman, Lord Gowrie, an affable and highly civilised politician with special interests in poetry and painting who had memorably resigned from the government as Minister for the Arts saying that he could not afford to live in London on a ministerial salary of £33,000 a year.

Thus, on 20 December 1985, the company changed its name from the Really Useful Company Ltd to the Really Useful Group plc and was registered as a public company. The figures to June 1985 show that the company's profits had gone from £1.7m to £2.6m, with Lloyd Webber owning a seventy per cent stake and Brolly thirty per cent. They estimated the costs of renovating the Palace would amount to £3.5m.

At that year's Sydmonton Festival there had been a promising try-out of the first half of the songs for a new musical, *The Phantom of the Opera*. In the obsessive tale of a deformed opera ghost's love for a virginal soprano with a heavenly voice, Lloyd Webber had hit upon a story of power and passion that would take him further towards his operatic goal of emulating Rodgers and Hammerstein. And although the *Requiem* had been a great success for Sarah Two, he still yearned to establish her at the forefront of the musical theatre and operetta of his day.

SEVEN

GOING PUBLIC WITH A PHANTOM PASSION

Two British musicals based on nineteenth and early twentieth century popular French novels, subjects of proven cinematic pedigree – *Les Misérables* and *The Phantom of the Opera* – went global in the mid 1980s and, alongside *Cats*, formed a power base of achievement in London, New York, Europe and, eventually, the Far East and Asia. All three were produced by Cameron Mackintosh, two were written by Lloyd Webber, two were directed by Trevor Nunn. And *Les Misérables* was written by two Frenchmen who had been inspired by *Superstar*.

This was the supposed era of the blockbuster, though the term is best applied to the phenomenon of each show's success rather than to its style. The most palpably extravagant of all Lloyd Webber shows, if you don't count the staircase in *Sunset Boulevard*, has always been *Starlight Express*. *Cats* is less an overwhelming physical experience than a hard and fast rooftop fiesta with funny and tender bits of music hall *schtick*.

Les Misérables, directed by the *Nicholas Nickleby* team of Trevor Nunn and John Caird, and designed by *Cats* and *Starlight Express* wizard John Napier, gave every appearance of growing organically out of Nunn's Royal Shakespeare Company style, though Mackintosh had acquired the rights in the show three years before the 1985 Barbican presentation. What Mackintosh called 'the underdogs' musical' took off at the same time as Live Aid; poverty gave rich pickings.

Just as in New York, where the two most influential and successful musicals of the late 1960s and 1970s – *Hair* and *A Chorus Line* – came out of Joseph Papp's dedicated forcing house, the New York Public Theater, so the talent in the state-subsidised RSC was endemic to the rise and rise of Mackintosh and Lloyd Webber. Trevor Nunn's triumphs created the post-Trev notion of directing as a money-spinning activity. No directors ever got rich until he came along. Even Peter Hall, who founded the RSC in 1960 and was once married to Leslie Caron, missed out, his one pre-Trev Broadway musical, *Via Galactica*, being one of the biggest flops ever seen on Broadway.

This may not prove much beyond tax-payers having an interest in commercial theatre, but the consequences were far-reaching. Following Nunn's example, the best young directors lined up to cash in with Mackintosh and turn their backs on the theatre that had nurtured their talent. Nunn was unique in that he had actually run the RSC and would then show them all up by disembarking the musicals gravy train and returning to run the Royal National Theatre in 1997.

In between, Nicholas Hytner made a million on *Miss Saigon* and went to Hollywood, Steven Pimlott hit the jackpot with the 1991 Palladium revival of *Joseph*, Sam Mendes made a killing with *Oliver!* for Mackintosh, also at the Palladium, and Declan Donnellan learned the hard way that supping with the devil entailed taking a long spoon: he came a lone cropper when his production of *Martin Guerre* for Mackintosh ended in tears and a stony silence on his part whenever the subject was raised.

These were the best directors of their generation and,

along with Deborah Warner – for whom directing a Lloyd Webber musical might be as unlikely as Lloyd Webber collaborating with Peter Brook – they sidestepped the demands and headaches of running the greatest theatres in London, let alone the regional houses.

The result was that by the end of the 1990s, the future of live theatre in Britain was reaching a crisis point whereby a combination of factors – standstill funding from the government, almost total capitulation to the great gods of sponsorship and commercial expediency, and a thinning out of talent and product in the regional theatres – was turning into a recipe for disaster.

All theatres, encouraged by critics who had forgotten that the greatest public theatres, the Greek and the Elizabethan, played to the widest popular audiences, were downsizing and re-adopting the studio theatre elitism of the London fringe in the 1980s. Lloyd Webber and Mackintosh knew the value of the fringe. The former had bailed out the Almeida Theatre in Islington when local funding suddenly dried up, and the latter sponsored the rebuilding of the powerhouse Tricycle in Kilburn after a fire demolished the auditorium.

But they were the only two practitioners really reaching out to the ticket-buying public. There was a new religion of musicals which supplied spiritual nourishment to the masses craving something bigger and better than a diet of television soap opera. And however much artists protected by subsidy turned up their noses, they were not achieving anything comparable on their own. Like Nunn and his acolyte directors, the mountain had to go to the twin-headed Mohammed.

Mackintosh, having moved in on the RSC, now moved in on the National, with money for musicals (notably *Carousel* and *Oklahoma!*), and support for the Sondheim culture which permeated the South Bank in both British musical theatre personnel besotted with

Sondheim and National productions of his musicals (Sondheim had the intellectual respectability that has always eluded Lloyd Webber) – *Sunday in the Park with George*, *Sweeney Todd* and *A Little Night Music*. But he did not overpower, or emasculate, the National's overall operation, even if he helped keep it afloat.

The RSC undoubtedly – no doubt unfairly – suffered in the public eye because of Nunn's commitment to musicals, but Richard Eyre, who ran the National for ten years before Nunn arrived there, had nothing to do with the musicals he approved under his wing, apart from producing one himself – *Guys and Dolls* – that put the whole Sondheim caboodle firmly in the shade. Eyre was busier directing the plays of David Hare – notably his great trilogy (*Racing Demon*, *Murmuring Judges*, and *The Absence of War*) about the Church, the law and the Labour Party – which proved to be the spine and backbone, even the raison d'être, of his ten-year tenure from 1986.

Nunn's greatest defence of having done *Les Misérables* at all would be that he kept the RSC afloat because of the steady and considerable income accruing to the company in subsequent years. By the time he took over at the National, the RSC was hanging on to its past reputation like a whore touting for business and kind looks wherever they might be found, and the National was set on a course of commercial programme planning that seemed far removed from the idealism of a permanent ensemble company exploring the world repertoire of great drama while instigating momentous and challenging largescale epic plays of its own.

The whole world was dumbing down, as if everyone had forgotten why art mattered, what justified the expenditure of public funds upon it, and where exactly the axe should fall. Money for the arts from the Lottery funds was proving a two-edged sword, building programmes diverting attention from the work itself, as symbolised in the career of Stephen Daldry, the charismatic young director of the Royal Court.

Daldry's personal contribution during his period in office was a stunningly successful revival for the RNT of J. B. Priestley's *An Inspector Calls* (which was globally cloned and made *him* seriously wealthy) and the supervision of a Lottery funded rebuilding programme that ripped the heart out of the Sloane Square headquarters and inadvertently rejuvenated the West End list by laying siege to the Duke of York's and the Ambassadors.

At the same time, David Hare left the National, along with Richard Eyre, and threw in his lot with the fashionable Almeida. The overall state of affairs became too much for him. Hare gleefully weighed in with a savage review of a book called *Creative Britain* by Chris Smith, the Minister of Culture. This review appeared in the *Observer* on the eve of the announcement of Hare's knighthood in Tony Blair's June 1998 Birthday Honours:

> An aimless tangle of bureaucratic structures scandalously ensures that the Royal Shakespeare Company is allowed to do dismal work with lavish, unmerited subsidy, while brilliant young theatres like the Bush, the Almeida, the Traverse and the Royal Court offer fifty times the RSC's vitality on a fraction of its resources. The National Theatre is encouraged to waste £31.25m decorating its shell to resemble a ringroad shopping mall – stick in a branch of Knickerbox and the effect will be complete – while not spending a penny to improve its notoriously flawed auditoria.
>
> Meanwhile, Richard Eyre is invited to squander his firepower on the comparatively trivial question of whether London should serve opera in one hall or two, while the much more important drama schools, orchestras and regional companies are just expected to go hang.

Writing in the same edition of the *Observer*, Susannah Clapp even went so far as to say that the Royal Court and the Almeida now occupied the positions once held by the National and the RSC. However extreme and absurd that statement, the bubble had finally burst around the illusion of unassailable cultural monoliths.

Some faltering of confidence in the fate of big musicals would invariably follow, but the 1980s in Mrs Thatcher's Britain were full of business expansion and optimism. In this context, even before *Phantom* opened, the flotation of Really Useful, powered by the sensational profit-making performance of *Cats*, was a landmark event.

The company had been formed as the association with Robert Stigwood came to an end and so named because Lloyd Webber had acquired the rights in the Reverend Wilbert Awdry's 'Thomas the Tank Engine' children's stories, one of which featured James the Really Useful Engine. One scheme, in collaboration with Johnny Hamp, head of light entertainment at Granada Television, was that pre-*Starlight* animated film, until it became clear that the costs were prohibitive. Lloyd Webber also had a company, Escaway – the name an elision of 'escape' and 'getaway' – which controlled his personal finances, the Steam Power Music Company which owned publishing rights in his music, and Oiseau Productions, formed to produce Sarah Two's records.

Throughout the 1980s, papers filed at Companies House showed that Lloyd Webber was earning well over £1m a year; and that was just his personal spending money, a fragment of his overall wealth. In 1986, the sale of five million shares at 330p each in the Really Useful Group realised a staggering £12.8m for the composer and his sidekick Brian Brolly; Lloyd Webber reduced his holding in the company from 70 per cent to 38.2 per cent, making a tidy £8.96m in the process, while Brolly's 30 per cent holding was cut back to 16.4 per cent, yielding him a neat £3.84m.

Really Useful had flown solo as producers of *Starlight Express*, but Lloyd Webber was in cahoots again with Mackintosh on *Phantom*. His own company raised 60 per cent of the £2m budget and Mackintosh, having safely seen *Les Misérables* on its way as a high profile transglobal milk cow, raised the rest. Ideally, of course, the Palace, now owned by Lloyd Webber, would have been the perfect venue for *Phantom*. But in one of those strange twists of fate, the theatre had already been promised to Mackintosh for the transfer of *Les Misérables* from the Barbican.

This nearly did not happen. As usual with all big musicals, the critics had been divided on the virtues of the Victor Hugo extravaganza. Mackintosh had even called a meeting of his investors to ask them if he should transfer the show. They advised that he should. The RUG board felt that the Palace was the right home for *Phantom*, but Biddy Hayward argued emotionally for honouring the commitment to Mackintosh. Her victory ensured a rental income of £1m a year for over ten years on *Les Misérables* and ensured the triple whammy of *Cats*, *Phantom* (which now moved across town to the no less suitable, but much smaller, Her Majesty's) and *Les Mis*, the three most successful musicals in history and the cultural indicator of the Thatcher boom years.

We can see this with hindsight. At the time there was no such grim sense of rewriting the history books. The Lloyd Webber/Mackintosh alliance was in fact characterised by a lot of fun and laughter. Practical jokes were constantly pulled on each other. On one occasion, Mackintosh was taking his entire office staff on a jaunt to Scotland, with an overnight stay in a hotel in Perth.

After the two carloads of revellers set off, the RUG office personnel, merrily swilling champagne in West Eaton Place, telephoned the hotel to cancel the reservation. The spirit of their first riotous lunch in the Savile Club was maintained by the two young Turks across their professional lives. Trevor Nunn recalls that in auditions he often had occasion to ask them both to leave the room when their giggling got out of control.

The idea behind *Phantom* had been shared by Lloyd Webber and Mackintosh from an early stage, and originated in the quest to find a suitable showcase for the talents of Sarah Two. After her success in *Nightingale* in Hammersmith, she had been invited to play Christine Daaé in Ken Hill's *The Phantom of the Opera*, which started life in Newcastle before arriving at another invaluable London satellite theatre, the Theatre Royal at Stratford East, Joan Littlewood's old stomping ground.

There was some speculation as to the identity of the old ghost. Years earlier, the West End producer Donald Albery had loaned Littlewood a handsome chandelier, which hangs to this day over the stalls. After a decent interval, Albery had asked for it back. 'Come and get it,' said Joan. Littlewood herself had long since departed, but the late Ken Hill was one of her final proteges: actor, writer, director, something of a link with the past and a signal to the future.

Brightman either could not, or would not, take up the offer, but Lloyd Webber and Mackintosh, fascinated by the project, paid a courtesy call once the show had garnered some pretty decent reviews. 'A night of murder, mystery and song,' was how the theatre billed the show, based on Gaston Leroux's 1911 novel and decked out with music of the day – the story is set in 1881 – by Gounod, Verdi and Offenbach. Here were magic tricks and art nouveau decorations, a fake chandelier which fell to the stage, garrottings and a generous helping of that post-Littlewood Stratford East brand of knees-up jollity which is either a) refreshing, liberating, delightful; or b) nauseating, tiresome, embarrassing, depending on your frame of mind or state of equilibrium.

In his new role of producing other people's work, Lloyd Webber, abetted by Mackintosh, decided to try and make a West End success of Ken Hill's production, adding more music of the period – Delibes and Massenet – and some Gothic details from Lon Chaney's still terrific 1925 movie version. He telephoned Hill the next day and talked about enlarging it, and putting Sarah Two in the main role. When they next met, Hill remembered Andrew 'sitting down and playing a song he had written for my *Phantom* which is now in his *Phantom* . . . then it became harder to get him on the telephone, and after a bit of messing around, Cameron told me he was going to do his own version.'

Later in 1984, Lloyd Webber and Mackintosh flew to Japan for the Tokyo opening of *Cats* – presumably aimed at the few Japanese who weren't yet rich enough to become tourists and see the show in London – and bumped into Jim Sharman, who had directed the best productions of *Superstar*.

Sharman advised Lloyd Webber to write a new score himself, on the basis of the novel having a great romantic plot. At some stage, at Sharman's suggestion, the project was mentioned to the composer/lyricist Jim Steinman, whose work was keenly admired by both Mackintosh and Lloyd Webber – his songs for Meat Loaf and Bonnie Tyler, full of sunsets and storms and broken hearts, were often theatrical mini-epics in themselves. Sharman himself was unavailable to direct, Steinman was up to his eyes in a new Bonnie Tyler record, and the idea was temporarily shelved.

But the idea had taken hold. And when, a few months later, Lloyd Webber came across a second-hand copy of the original, out-of-print novella on a bookstall in New York, he took this to be an omen. He prepared a plot outline, working on the second act while in Australia, ignoring all antecedent adaptations, and *Starlight* lyricist Richard Stilgoe elaborated on this to prepare the version first shown at Sydmonton, a version the show's eventual director Hal Prince never saw because he didn't want to. Apart from the Lon Chaney film – which became an influence on the design – there was a less spectacular re-make starring Claude Rains in 1943, a bad Hammer horror movie starring Herbert Lom in 1962 and Brian de Palma's highly enjoyable mid-1970s rocky horror show-type version, *Phantom of the Paradise*. Also in 1975 there had been a stage version by Edward Petherbridge and the Actors Company he then ran with Ian McKellen.

It was a strangely fortuitous choice of material. Lloyd Webber found the story frankly incredible and knew that an audience had to either buy into it and stay there or bale out and forget the whole thing. The scalp-tingling quotient and weird possessiveness of the fable is worthy of comparison with Bram Stoker's *Dracula* or Mary Shelley's *Frankenstein*.

The hokum of the story was entirely redeemed for Lloyd Webber in a footnote that turned and then fuelled the whole enterprise: the dead body of the Phantom was found with Christine's ring on his finger – 'Gaston Leroux pillaged his story from all over the place, from the tale of Paganini at one point, from every conceivable penny dreadful. But actually deep inside it somewhere is a marvellous confection that works brilliantly.'

The other irresistible factor, and one that inspired his most heartfelt and romantic music to date, was the Opera House monster's role as the spirit of music addressing his public through the conduit of a beautiful voice. Having arranged for Christine to score a triumph in Gounod's *Faust*, he orders her to participate in either his wedding Mass, or the requiem to accompany his destruction of the Paris Opera. The imposition of his own will on the repertoire, the wooing of the virginal star with a view to full possession of her body and artistry, even the parallels with Paganini whose theme he had set to variations: this show would be Lloyd Webber's own wedding Mass with Sarah Two.

Between the excerpts from the first draft of the first act at Sydmonton – with a peculiar song for the Man in the Iron Mask – in the summer of 1985 and the second Sydmonton try-out in the following July, even more dramatic parallels asserted themselves. Collaborative theatre, especially in the musical sphere, is a harsh business. There are two key fatalities in the novel: the scene shifter who knows too much and the concierge put in charge of the Phantom's box at the expense of Mme Giry. The evolving musical's victims were Stilgoe himself, whose lyrics were fiendishly clever but not romantically resonant enough – he was replaced on the show by a complete newcomer, Charles Hart; and the pop singer Steve Harley.

Harley, former lead singer with Cockney Rebel, had been virtually promised the role of the Phantom, having recorded the title song with Sarah Brightman under the supervision of Mike Batt and then recorded a lushly extravagant video directed by Ken Russell. The video was unveiled on Terry Wogan's television chat show in early 1986 and the song climbed to Number Seven in the charts. Cliff Richard and Sarah Brightman also released a single from the show, 'All I Ask of You', but Cliff was saving his casting shock for a decade later, when he played the sultry Heathcliff.

The surprise announcement, and a complete masterstroke, was that Michael Crawford would play the Phantom opposite Brightman, and the publicity machine went into overdrive. Crawford, an acknowledged star of the front rank, had a national following due to his portrayal of the stupid but loveable Frank Spencer in the television comedy series *Some Mothers Do 'Ave 'Em*, a role derived from an astonishing, acrobatic stage performance in *No Sex Please, We're British*. His musical pedigree was impressive, too, from his days as a boy soprano singled out by Benjamin Britten to his West End triumphs in *Billy* and *Barnum*.

Fortuitously, he shared the same singing coach, Ian Adam, as Sarah Brightman. Crawford had been going to his house for lessons since 1974. One day, as he was finishing, Andrew and Sarah were sitting downstairs in the kitchen waiting for the next slot in Adam's schedule. As Crawford remembers it, 'When I'd gone, Andrew came charging up to Ian and demanded to know who was that singing. When Ian said it was me, Andrew apparently said, "I think we've found our Phantom."

'I was still appearing in *Barnum*. Andrew invited me over to his office in the Palace Theatre and played me the overture to *Phantom*. The hairs stood up on the back of my neck, and did so every night I played the role for the next three and a half years. As I listened, my head dipped and I went up on my toes. The performance started right there. And I never tired of doing it. The show always took me there.'

Crawford had been inspired as a child by seeing Danny Kaye live at the London Palladium. 'Danny Kaye, I knew, had done what he did that night a thousand times. But for me it was new, fresh, startling and amazing. I've never forgotten that when I go on a stage each night. There's someone out there for whom it's a first time. And each audience is a different entity, a new challenge.

'I could never play the Phantom as a monster. I loved playing him, and I love the character. The cut of the jacket was very important to me because I had to rely so much on my arms and legs. The secret was that the Phantom was a great romantic role, and that is how I hope I played it.'

Crawford, whose career was to be transformed by this performance, especially in America, where he was known only from his appearance in the film of *Hello, Dolly!* directed by Gene Kelly, was one of last few genuine leading men, in the sense that he was big enough, and good enough, to lead a huge company by example from the front. Like Gillian Lynne, he had exercised according to the Pilates technique for years and had, in Lynne's words, 'a very with-it body. We did a company warm-up every day during rehearsals and Michael did not miss a single session. We worked very closely on all the movement in the show.'

Lloyd Webber at first turned from Stilgoe to Alan Jay Lerner, of all people, the lyricist of *Brigadoon, My Fair Lady* and *Gigi*, which titles certainly qualified him as champion romantic, or at least sentimental, writer as ringingly as his many marriages had. Lerner once said that he loved women so much that he kept all the bills to prove it. His advice to Lloyd Webber was not to ask too many questions of the plot, because it worked. He didn't think the composer was in too much trouble, and he considered the score his best to date.

But then his terminal cancer kicked in and he had to withdraw altogether. (It was around this time that the entirely apocryphal exchange took place – Lloyd Webber swears that it didn't; Lerner was such a good friend to him – 'Alan, why do people always take an instant dislike to me?' 'Because, dear boy, it saves time later on.') In desperation, Andrew sheepishly asked Tim Rice if he could help out, but Rice was plotting the West End opening of *Chess* with Bjorn Ulvaeus and Benny Andersson of Abba.

A new writing competition finally came to the rescue. The Vivian Ellis Award is designed to find and encourage new musical theatre writers. In 1985, the winners were George Stiles and Anthony Drewe with the first draft of their Rudyard Kipling musical, *Just So*. The judges included Mackintosh, Lloyd Webber and Don Black, and they were equally impressed by the writer of a musical version of *Moll Flanders*, which was awarded third prize. 'I remember saying to Andrew,' recalls Black, 'there's a kind of freshness and originality there, a lyrical approach. It was witty, it rhymed and it was well crafted. And then when you met the boy – he was very young – you realised how clever he was. He played the piano, he arranged music, he spoke a lot of languages. And he looked like Pierce Brosnan.'

Charles Hart was just twenty-five, a Cambridge graduate with a fine theatrical background. His parents had met when acting in the company at Stratford-upon-Avon and his grandparents were the renowned director Glen Byam Shaw and the actress Angela Baddeley. As a teenager destined for a career in classical music, he saw his grandmother in Sondheim's *A Little Night Music* when she took over the role of Desirée Armfeldt from Hermione Gingold in London. He was completely bowled over, and lost to musical theatre.

After Cambridge, he spent a year at the Guildhall School of Music, then found odd jobs as a keyboard player and auditions pianist. He spent fifteen months in the pit at Wyndham's Theatre playing for every one of the 511 performances of Sue Townsend's *The Secret Diary of Adrian Mole Aged $13^{3}/_{4}$* with songs by Ken Howard and Alan Blaikley throughout and just beyond 1985.

A year after meeting Black and Lloyd Webber, Hart received a telegram from Cameron Mackintosh. When he got in touch, Mackintosh asked him if he would be interested in doing something 'on spec'. Hart was on the dole and penniless and in no position to say 'No' to anyone, least of all Mackintosh. He provided some sample lyrics to the songs Mackintosh sent round – he knew whose they were, but not what they were – and was immediately engaged. His first 'real job' was, in a sense, one from which he would find it very hard to recover. The deal was fair and the billing 'most generous'.

He never collaborated with Stilgoe, working from a score where many passages of music and lyrics had not been completed. Time was short, and he was given a full rein, turning round several new versions of all the major songs, though in most cases Lloyd Webber was sufficiently wedded to the Stilgoe lyrics to revert to them. In the end, Hart reckoned that eighty per cent of the lyrics were his, twenty per cent still Stilgoe's. 'By the time I was on board, Richard wanted out of the whole project, understandably enough. But he was very nice to me over the telephone when we did have to talk, and he made a potentially awkward situation a lot easier. I thought the show would be a success. But I had simply no concept of how it would multiply.'

Another musicals debutante was Maria Bjornson, the designer, who had been a formative influence on the early days of Scottish Opera, where she had designed a complete Janáček cycle for David Pountney. She was less well known in the theatre, but it so happened that Cameron Mackintosh was passing through the Barbican on *Les Misérables* business with Trevor Nunn when he saw the start of a production she had designed of *The Tempest* (with Derek Jacobi as Prospero) on the main stage. A ship made mostly of materials disappeared at the end of the first scene with an almighty whooshing sound, the sail into the flies and the prow below the stage.

Many of Bjornson's ideas were in place at the first Sydmonton try-out: the chandelier that tracked forward over the audience instead of just dropping, the curtains rising and parting as the Phantom's boat tracked forward through an arch into his lair. The speed and flexibility of the designs were always paramount, though as she watched directors join the project then depart, she wondered if any of her inventions would survive.

She had sent some drawings out to Hal Prince's holiday home in Majorca, and he had liked them. But then there was a falling out between Mackintosh and Prince, then for a time the director was going to be Nicholas Hytner, then it was Trevor Nunn, with whom she had several meetings, then it was – at Lloyd Webber's absolute insistence – Hal Prince again. 'By this time,' she says, 'all I had left was my fear and my portfolio!'

'I don't think *Phantom* warrants a mind as good as Trevor's, in a way,' said Lloyd Webber years later. 'And there would have been a lot more furniture. We needed a real showman, and that's what we got with Hal. Trevor, if I remember rightly, had drawings from John Napier with the chandelier on the stage. It would have been an entirely different sort of musical.'

Bjornson only had several meetings with Prince before the show hit the stage, but they were all inspirational, she says. 'Directors who really know how to work with designers are rare. When they can, they become a diving board for your own work. I remember so well what Hal said to me at the very beginning: "I see drapes thudding to the floor in blackouts. I see voices talking in the blackness. And I see dark Turkish corners." And I knew exactly what he meant. We talked about the films, especially the Lon Chaney version, and I went to the Paris Opera and took hundreds of photographs.'

The Turkish corners hint implied antimacassars, silks and swagging and that was what Bjornson provided, as well as the gilt caryatids and proscenium of the Paris Opera, and a huge, stage-filling staircase for the 'Maskerade' opening for the second act. Lloyd Webber still talks of Bjornson's design being 'feminine' and she certainly responded to the submerged sexual repression in the story in a remarkable way.

The centrepiece of the first act, the heart of the matter, really, is the sequence in which Erik the Phantom abducts Christine into his lair. In the Lon Chaney film, this is the erotic heart of the story, too, and depends for its disturbing physical impact on the descent, an act of sexual abduction, down a huge spiral staircase.

The Phantom materialises in Christine's mirror and

the sequence ends with her smashing a mirror in his den, which he has prepared as if it were a bridal bed-chamber. The music goes from the title song to the Phantom's outpouring of his credo, 'The Music of the Night' and Bjornson devised a zigzagging motion of descent, with the lake rising in a mist dotted with candles and the boat coming through like a sinister gondola on a Venetian canal. It was a filmic, ritualistic, soft-handed approach to a difficult but thrilling scene, and the staging of it matched the music all the way: this remains to this day one of the most amazing sequences I have ever seen in any theatre.

The Phantom needs Christine as a singing servant, and his title song becomes a journey of seduction in which she starts vocalising strangely at his behest. Sarah Brightman's highest register expressed the weird orgasmic side effects of his bestial act of possession, summarised in his insistence that she lets her darker side give in to the power of the music that he writes: 'Night-time sharpens, heightens each sensation, darkness stirs and wakes imagination, silently the senses abandon their defences . . .'

Bjornson had psychologically penetrated the Phantom's lair, bearing in mind Erik the Phantom's reputation as the world's greatest ventriloquist and prince of conjurors: he could appear anywhere and throw his voice round corners. She was also interested in the nature of his pain. 'When you're obsessed with someone, you keep dreaming of how it's going to be when they finally arrive. It never happens, we all know that, but Erik has planned the whole thing, and from there we came up with the idea that he had a mirror for her to use and then he would smash it because he wouldn't like to see his own reflection and behind it would be the bride's dummy.'

One of the best examples of how Lloyd Webber often writes his music as theatre is contained in the way he dealt with the unmasking, which on film is a simple matter of close-up and in the book is a matter of private revelation. He took as a clue the scene in Leroux where Christine describes being alone in the lair with Erik: 'Presently I heard the sound of the organ; and then I began to understand Erik's contemptuous phrase when he spoke about operatic music. What I now heard was utterly different from what had charmed me up to then. His *Don Juan Triumphant* (for I had not a doubt but that he had rushed to his masterpiece to forget the horror of the moment) seemed to me at first one awful, long, magnificent sob. But, little by little, it expressed every emotion, every suffering of which mankind is capable. It intoxicated me . . .'

Whereas in the book, the Phantom insists on Christine being allowed to sing Marguerite in Gounod's *Faust*, Lloyd Webber made the Phantom's own opera the work to be performed in the second act, and his unmasking in the role of Don Juan both an ironic come-uppance and a sensational humiliation in front of many characters, in his own composition, on what was supposed to be a night of triumph.

Musically, this was the overlapping of the operatic repertoire and Lloyd Webber's own heightened rock operatic style, with the new excitement of 'The Point of No Return' and a tender reprise of 'All I Ask of You', probably the show's best song and one first given to Christine and her true love, the childhood sweetheart Raoul ('No more talk of darkness, forget these wide-eyed fears, I'm here, nothing can harm you, my words will warm and calm you').

The concentration of the plot on that love triangle, too, was one of Lloyd Webber's most notable innovations, and the score is full of provisional and conditional musical statements of adoration, counterpointed with the more ferocious and satanic demands of the Phantom. Audiences absorb these things subliminally, and their half-realised knowledge of what is going on, expressed in the audible words and implied in the inexpressible music, is what gives a show like *Phantom* its huge popular and theatrically hypnotic appeal.

Artistically, Lloyd Webber hit an absolute bullseye in a show that was not only deeply personal but also perfectly structured, with the mirror image of the Phantom's music pursuing him in the murder hunt, the music box of memory tinkling away at either end of the show, and Christine as the ideal muse and Angel of Music confusing her dedication to the memory of a dead father – and Lloyd Webber certainly had his own father sitting on his shoulder – with the magnetic pull of a demonic composer.

The story was indeed strong enough to take care of itself and, although Trevor Nunn was obviously disappointed not to be involved, Hal Prince's participation guaranteed the mobility and theatricality Lloyd Webber wanted to maximise his emotional effects. As Charles Hart remarks, any actor looking for motivation had to go and look elsewhere as far as Prince was concerned. If someone asked why they had to move downstage at any given moment, Prince would snap back, 'Because that is where the light is.' And the subject would be closed.

While not exactly one of the most notorious directorial martinets, Prince is a phenomenally well organised and disciplined director whose greatest gift is for matching images and scenic composition to the subject matter in hand. He is less able, as Lloyd Webber discovered on their later collaboration on *Whistle Down the Wind*, to fix any problems of plotting and narrative.

He is the master of the broad sweep and mood of a show, less concerned, as Nunn is, with the small detail. He also has the confidence in his ability that only comes with years of experience and recognition, and feels threatened by no-one. He was happy, for instance, to leave the two scenes in the opera managers' office entirely in the hands of Gillian Lynne, whose opportunities for choreography were limited.

Prince had 'pre-conceived' the whole production, and everyone knew what he wanted. On the first day of rehearsals in a community hall in Vauxhall, south London, he sported a trademark safari suit, spectacles pushed up on his suntanned temples and declared that *Phantom* was about the sexuality of freaks, quoting Gaugin and Auden on the impotent murderer myth.

He wanted to tell the story with a sense of staccato and thought of Stravinsky's *Les Noces*. A thunderstorm should be brewing all night and he was adamant about using the old Victorian stage machinery in the Her Majesty's. This, he admitted, would provide Cameron Mackintosh with a problem when he toured the show. 'Don't worry,' piped up the irrepressible producer, 'I've just bought a Black & Decker!'

He was looking not for reality, but the truth in a place, the theatre, paralysed by fear of an incomplete human resident. As he spoke, Maria Bjornson fiddled with her set model, in which she had joyously responded to Prince's emphasis on speed and lightness of texture. The show would have only one opaque curtain and the main scenic prop, the travelator that would expedite the descent to the lair.

She had shown him the set model a few weeks earlier. For any designer, this is the moment of truth and greatest vulnerability. And for Bjornson, especially so, as she was the untried, unknown member of the production team, jostling against quite an array of mostly male egos. The day before Lloyd Webber and Mackintosh were due to arrive at her basement flat for the first viewing, Prince called to say that he was going back to America, that she had not worked hard enough, that she didn't really know what she was doing or how to show a model.

The distraught designer believed at the time that this

was just Prince being capricious, but he might also have been disappointed in her marked lack of fussing assistants, the chaos in her flat and the general impression of muckiness given by scaffolding outside and sketches and materials all over the floor inside. In the event, Prince did not go back to America but turned up at the appointed time with the other two.

Bjornson's address, amazingly enough, was 11 Gledhow Gardens. 'Andrew had noted it in earlier correspondence and of course when he arrived he was absolutely thrilled, because not only had he lived next door; he was in the exactly adjacent basement flat and I had been there all that time and never knew who he was. I used to bang on the wall when the piano went on and on, but I never really saw him at all.' The model showing went with a swing and Lloyd Webber never queried Bjornson's work except to defend some item of expenditure Mackintosh might want to sacrifice. (Another Gledhow Gardens resident at the time Lloyd Webber lived there was Penny Gummer, the wife of John Gummer, former Cabinet Minister in the governments of both Mrs Thatcher and John Major; Andrew didn't know her, either, though she and her husband came in later life to be two of his closest and most constant friends.)

'There was always this competitive animosity between Andrew and Cameron. Andrew said after the showing that if his music was as good as my set, we were going to be all right. I think he was a little frightened, or at least suspicious, of me. But he was also very generous.

'I noticed working on *Phantom* and later on *Aspects*, and it made a big impression on me, that there were three men he was absolutely obsessed by: Tim Rice, Trevor and Cameron. He would talk about them non-stop. They were like intellectual lovers to him, and those relationships are the sort women don't have. He was always interested in what they thought, and they were his three mentors. And he either loved or hated each of them at any given time.'

Bjornson also sensed something crucial to the anguish that is so prevalent in *Phantom*. 'Designing is a lonely activity and I also knew about being single and about unrequited love. And I think Andrew knows about that. I think that is absolutely how he felt about Sarah. She never gave him the whole of herself and I'm sure that is what also bred this need to write this musical. If they had been truly happy, we would never have had *Phantom*.'

One key decision to be taken was what sort of mask the Phantom would wear. The idea of the half-mask was Bjornson's, who had worn a hat-maker's Paisley with a half-mask, and egrets coming out the top, to a fancy dress party at Sydmonton. Mackintosh was at first sceptical: 'I don't mind a *glimpse* of Michael Crawford but the audience is going to feel cheated, in a funny way, if they see too much of him.' Only Bjornson held out against the idea of a full-face mask and when she showed a drawing of her proposal to Michael Crawford he became interested.

Crawford told Bjornson he would think about it for a week, and he went off with photographs of the set model. A few days later, he rang to tell her which side of the face the mask should be worn. He had gone through the whole show, with the model of the set, and guessed where his moves would probably be – before Prince had even begun blocking them – and worked out that the audience would see the mask side most in the first act, when he was playing the organ.

And in the second act he would have the masked side ripped off in the lair so that the audience could see his deformed face. The make-up was arduous and complicated, with a bald pate placed over his head, then a full facial make-up, including a lot of latex and two contact lenses, one white and one dark blue, then a wig, then the half-mask. All the elements had to match up because the wig had to tie in with the hairline. The process took about ninety minutes, though sometimes Crawford would stretch this time in interviews to add a little mystique. Crawford conveyed anguish, pain and frustrated potential through that mask, and in the chill, sleek demeanour he projected in body and voice.

It was a superb performance by a genuine star, and the first night, 9 October 1986, signalled a return of sex, glamour, wonderful costumes and designs to the West End musical stage after quite a long absence. Her Majesty's proved ideal, large enough for the operatic element, intimate enough to make frightening the continual presence of the phantom haunting a building on which he had been engaged as an engineer.

The quiet beginning, with the auction of Opera House properties, including the music box with a toy monkey, the broken chandelier, and an allusion to the mystery of the Phantom, is ruptured when the chromatic organ chords crash out, joined by rock percussion and then, second time around, full orchestra. This gives way to the riotous magnificence of a rehearsal for 'Hannibal', a pastiche of Meyerbeer grand opera. Two new managers survey the scene and the chorus girl Christine Daaé emerges from the background, transformed in a starring role with 'Think of Me' at the gala, a simple tuneful song in which she celebrates her father's memory. Her sweetheart Raoul watches from a box.

The balancing of operatic pastiche with his own idiosyncratic rock romanticism is a distinctive feature of Lloyd Webber's score, with unusual intervals and adventurous harmonics that help the melodies unfold. A song like 'All I Ask of You' has leaps of a ninth going down, and then up a major seventh, which are certainly unusual but also memorable; the song became an instant classic. And the first act 'Il Muto' is both funny, surprising and melodic as a baroque item, with the

Phantom undermining the soprano Carlotta's voice with that of a croaking toad, and the backstage panic covered with a diverting dance of country nymphs. The Phantom's instructions are conveyed in handwritten notes, the first scene in the managers' office complemented in the second act by a complex septet.

The music is on a constant switchback between the surface sunniness of romantic opera and the heart of darkness in the Phantom's labyrinth. A good example is the trio that develops out of 'Wishing You Were Somehow Here Again' by the dead father's mausoleum in the second act. There is an overpowering sense of grief and loss in this passage, sandwiched between the bustle of the Don Juan opera rehearsal and the fateful performance. 'Angel, or father, friend or Phantom' . . . the muddle in Christine's mind is expressed in a mixture of ecstasy and confusion, with Raoul intervening as Erik closes the net of his sexual deceit.

Michael Crawford has a lifelong custom of fully inhabiting any theatre he appears in. He clocks in after lunchtime, deals with his post, takes a nap and settles into a rigorously observed routine of preparation. His occupation of Her Majesty's, as the Phantom, was therefore doubly appropriate. Because of his exacting standards, he carried the show, onstage and off, in the true style of a leading man. Bjornson recalls being summoned to his dressing room after the first night. 'Oh God,' she thought, 'what have I done now?' And all he said was, 'You and me, girl, we've done this.' And of course she was thrilled to bits.

Michael Crawford's life changed as a result of his triumph. He played the Phantom for a year in London, then opened the show in New York, moving on with it for eighteen months to Los Angeles. Over the next ten years he would become a top flight cabaret and concert performer, often with the music of Lloyd Webber, but broadening his act to include items from other shows in his career. In a curious way, like the Phantom himself, he would haunt large auditoria and pulverise audiences with his solo interventions and iron artistic whim. Could he ever possibly recover his rightful place at the head of a troupe, or was he destined to roam alone and abroad for ever?

With their love story played out nightly on stage, the cast album shooting up the charts to Number One, and his wealth multiplying by the minute, Andrew and Sarah came under more press scrutiny than ever. I think that it's from around this time that the backlash sets in, the tone of envious jeering and childish rudeness that characterises quite a lot of press comment on Lloyd Webber from the late 1980s. By early 1987 Tim Rice was looking closer at another idea that had first come his way, *Aspects of Love*, and in which Andrew was certainly interested. He said of their possibly renewed liaison: 'I need the money and he needs the credibility.'

They had collaborated on *Cricket,* a short piece of eleven songs commissioned by Prince Edward for the Queen's sixtieth birthday party at Windsor Castle in June 1986. Tunes would re-emerge in *Aspects*, but without Rice's lyrics. Still, they were back on terms, and when *Cricket* was repeated that year at the Sydmonton Festival, alongside songs from *Phantom*, Tim Rice was an avuncular presence at the festivities, even taking part in the ritual debate following Saturday night's black-tie dinner and identifying a crowd of dejected supplicants in a Burne-Jones painting on the dining room wall as dissatisfied customers leaving a Cameron Mackintosh production.

In 1984 Rice had opened his new musical, *Chess*, with music by the boys of Abba, in the Prince Edward, scene of *Evita*. This was an ambitious, rather tangled story of love in a cold war climate and probably deserved a better critical fate than it received. This was no worse, and in some quarters a good deal better, than the reception afforded *Evita* and *Les Misérables*, and almost everyone liked the songs, especially when sung by Elaine Paige and Barbara Dickson, Murray Head and Tommy Korberg. The latter made a sensational London debut as the Russian challenger for the world chess championship. Trevor Nunn, a late replacement for the fatally ailing Michael Bennett, supplied a magnificent spectacle of chorales, operatic domestic scenes and *Evita*-like bobbing company tableaux.

Chess was a reasonable success in London, where it ran for three years, but it came a terrible cropper in New York, with unseemly wrangles over the production and the recruitment of an American playwright, Richard Nelson, to overhaul the libretto. Rice was deeply upset by this failure, but he knew he had written some fine songs and that maybe the show's time would come again. Meanwhile, he had many irons in the fire, one of which was his participation on the RUG board.

With *Phantom* up and running, Brolly and the board set about exploiting the success of the *Requiem*, launching a classical record collection with Marks & Spencer and keeping an eye on the productions of *Cats* now running in Los Angeles, San Francisco, Vienna, Budapest, Oslo, Hambug and Helsinki, as well as in London and New York. *Starlight Express* had completed a thousand performances in London and was still going strong, and heading for Broadway. The share price had risen by 40p since the date of issue, and the group was on target for a first year profit of £4.3m.

Lloyd Webber's earnings in the year to June 1987 were shown as £5.5m: £4.84m in royalties from fourteen productions of *Cats*, plus *Phantom* and *Starlight*, and half a million from dividends through his percentage ownership of RUG. More importantly, perhaps, the Really Useful Group was honoured in April 1987 with the Queen's Award for export achievement. Musicals were the new diplomacy.

As befits a high-ranking ambassador, Lloyd Webber had just acquired a villa in the village of St Jean on Cap Ferrat in the South of France. The restoration of the Palace Theatre exterior was completed at a cost in excess of £1m, with a small grant from English Heritage. He bought a second-hand twelve-seater Hawker Siddeley 125 jet for about £2m, and a cache of jewels for Sarah from the Duchess of Windsor's collection. And in September, with New York plans for a New Year opening of *Phantom* hotting up, he spent £4m on a twelve-roomed, double-storey penthouse in the garishly gold Trump Tower on Fifth Avenue, with views of Central Park and neighbours including Steven Spielberg, Johnny Carson and Sophia Loren.

Publicity comes with these sorts of activity. There were even rumours of rockiness in the marriage, with hotly denied stories of Sarah running around with old boyfriends surfacing with some regularity. But there was good stuff, too. After the horrors of the Hungerford massacre, ten miles from Sydmonton, Lloyd Webber arranged a charity performance of the *Requiem* for the families of the victims in the St Nicholas parish church at Newbury. £70,000 was raised in all.

At another, more light-hearted charity dinner and auction, Sarah's knickers were knocked down for £410. Perhaps underwear was on the agenda because of a slight problem with toilet facilities at Her Majesty's. Michael Crawford and Sarah were obliged to share the same star lavatory, or trudge the length of a corridor to use the one belonging to the chorus. There was a slight kerfuffle over who should have the private privy and in the end Mackintosh sanctioned the building of a new one for Sarah. 'Any rumours of a row are a flash in the pan,' he said, 'it's simply a case now of Two Loos, No Trek.'

Sarah left *Phantom* in London after six months fully expecting to open on Broadway in January 1988. She did, but not without a struggle. American Equity vetoed her casting on the grounds that she was not a big enough star to justify exemption from the rules governing foreign artists taking work from local talent. This absurd posturing of the actors' union was insulting and nonsensical – it would recur, with racial overtones, when a furious Mackintosh was denied taking Jonathan Pryce to New York as the slanty-eyed Engineer in *Miss Saigon*.

While RUG directors flew frantically between London and New York trying to salvage the situation, Lloyd Webber suddenly snapped and ordered the company's finance director, Michael Sydney-Smith, to call a press conference at which the composer would announce that *Phantom* would not be opening in New York. He first of all wanted to know why only Sydney-Smith was in the office. 'Because all the others are in the air trying to solve the problem,' replied Sydney-Smith, who then advised restraint, as the effect of such an announcement on the shares of a company newly floated on the Stock Exchange could be catastrophic. He reminded Lloyd Webber that he was no longer free to take such draconian steps alone. At this stage, Lloyd Webber had resigned from the board and was a non-executive director of the RUG. But there was a public company to consider, and the remaining executive directors, of whom Michael Sydney-Smith was one, carried grave responsibilities to their shareholders.

Lloyd Webber turned white with fury over the telephone. Sydney-Smith swears he heard him do so. And then he heard an utterance he has never forgotten: 'Michael Sydney-Smith, could you pick up your pen and your briefcase and walk out of Greek Street and never see or talk to me again.' After a long pause (no slamming of receivers on cradles), Sydney-Smith carried on talking. And so did Lloyd Webber. The rage abated like a summer storm and disappeared into the conversation.

The matter was never mentioned again. And the differences with American Equity were resolved.

While Michael Crawford was justly hailed by the New York critics, some venomously personal attacks were launched on Brightman, suggesting she acted like Minnie Mouse on Quaaludes and that she couldn't act scared on the New York subway at three in the morning. The advance booking was phenomenal and to this day *Phantom* is a packed-out hit on both sides of the Atlantic. John Simon declared that the only areas in which the show was deficient were book, music and lyrics, while Frank Rich accused Brightman of 'simulating fear and affection by screwing her face into bug-eyed, chipmunk-cheeked poses'. Lloyd Webber roundly declared that Rich was a man who knew nothing about love. Rich said the show was 'long on pop professionalism and melody, impoverished of artistic personality and passion'.

Back in London, the contact with Prince Edward through the commission of *Cricket* had a most unexpected consequence. The young man who was fourth in line to the throne of England joined the Really Useful Group as an office assistant. Each day, he would leave one Palace and go to another in Cambridge Circus, where he learned the ropes and the art of tea-making from Bridget Hayward. His working name was Edward Windsor.

What other contribution he might have made rests in the realms of speculation, for in a couple of years' time Biddy had left the RUG, together with five colleagues including Edward ('Pickle with that cheese sandwich?') Windsor, to start her own producing company, Theatre Division. It was a tough wrench, and not one with a happy outcome. Relations between Lloyd Webber and the woman who had been closest to him in professional terms for the longest period of his life had become irreparably strained.

Partly this was to do with the areas of diversification the RUG were investigating. Biddy thought that theatre production – as in the RUG's association with *Daisy Pulls It Off, Lend Me a Tenor*, and so on – was a more suitable strand of activity, and one to which she was enthusiastically dedicated. But the other RUG directors overruled her and went about trying to fix film, television and video deals, buying an electronic publishing company and forming a record company. Brian Brolly had expressed the aim of creating 'a fully fledged communications and creative company' with arena tours of *Starlight* around America financed by Japanese money to the advantage of British shareholders, and investment in TV commercials and corporate videos.

As it happened none of these activities, even those that actually got off the ground, proved really profitable. At least the outside theatre activity looked more plausible and convincing. But only *Daisy Pulls It Off* was a great success, earning back its investment nearly three times over and running for three years. *Lend Me a Tenor* just about broke even. Other ventures, such as Griff Rhys Jones in Brecht's *Arturo Ui*, Howard Goodall's and Melvyn Bragg's *The Hired Man* and the Puccini cabaret, *Café Puccini*, developed with Robin Ray and Cameron Mackintosh, and co-produced with Mackintosh, were dismal failures. The kudos of being seen to be a lively West End producing outfit was offset by the disappointment to investors – and probably audiences – that the shows themselves weren't actually by Lloyd Webber. They were loss leaders.

Diversification was in truth something that sounded good on the Stock Exchange, with overtones of developing into a media group, like Virgin or Granada, with tentacular powers and revenue-producing activity. But the management structures were never concomitant with such ambitions, if indeed those ambitions were ever serious. The RUG remained small and to a certain extent cosy. It was never really the sort of operation that should have gone public.

Diversification, in the RUG's case, really meant dilettantism. And projects like the Marks & Spencer record deal were under-promoted from within the company and soon bit the dust. Psychologically, too, none of this was really anything that interested Lloyd Webber. His sole purpose in having his own company, he always insisted in later years, was to produce his own work to the highest possible standards.

One acquisition soon to have dangerous repercussions was that of the Aurum Press, the publishers of *The Outsider*, an unauthorised critical biography of Robert Maxwell by the smart investigative journalist Tom Bower. Maxwell had already issued a writ – and Tom Bower had counter-sued over a letter Maxwell had written to Lloyd Webber about him, Bower – when there were further upheavals on the RUG board.

A year after the flotation, relations between Lloyd Webber and Brian Brolly had become tricky. The show-business lawyer Keith Turner, who had joined the company in early 1987, noted these rifts. He never understood whether the flotation – which Lloyd Webber was beginning to regret – had come about as a result of Andrew persuading Brian to go public, or the other way around. Brolly, he reckoned, was inexperienced in the particular problems of 'interfacing with city analysts' and that while Andrew was demanding more personal attention, the notoriously thorough Brolly was more concerned – rightly, in all probability – about running a public company.

The new reality of these responsibilities to share-holders caused the ructions. And Brolly became doomed in Lloyd Webber's eyes, a source of unassuagable irritation. Thus in October 1988, Brolly left with a golden handshake of £800,000 in lieu of his pension expectations. At the same time, Tim Rice resigned from the board – fed up with the internal wrangling – and was instantly threatened with a writ for criminal fraud on the basis of manipulating share prices; this blew over when it was understood that the shares he held as a non-executive director were sold on merely because he wanted out. ('I didn't make a killing but I certainly didn't make a loss,' he says.)

Lloyd Webber promptly returned to the board as an executive director. Brolly's place was taken by Keith Turner, who had been legal and business affairs director at the Stigwood Organisation just as Stigwood bought out David Land and Sefton Myers. He had struck up a friendship with Andrew, and with Tim, which had lasted down the years. He became a quiet tower of strength in the company. Brolly, who had first launched Rice and Lloyd Webber by his act of faith in the *Superstar* album at MCA Records, put his shares up to the highest bidder (the market price had almost doubled since the launch to 633p) through the Swiss Bank Corporation.

That bidder was none other than the litigious Robert Maxwell, deploying yet more of his illegally appropriated pension funds to spend more than £10m on acquiring a 14.5 per cent share in the RUG. By February 1989, the new managing director of the RUG, John Whitney, a former director-general of the Independent Broadcasting Authority, was mouthing sweet nothings such as 'We're very comfortable with Mr Maxwell's position' to the *Financial Times*. But Maxwell had an agenda. He wanted Tom Bower's book withdrawn. Lloyd Webber, to his eternal credit, stood firm, backed solidly by Keith Turner. And the issue would be resolved around the buy-back of the company that became increasingly a top project of Lloyd Webber's.

He felt relatively at home in this new heady world of boardroom financial power play. It was, after all, his choice, however much he disclaimed certain developments over the years. A fanatical games player – indoors, rather than outdoors – he had invented a hard-to-follow (I am assured by board-game players I know), Monopoly-style parlour game called *Calamity!*, 'the international high-risk insurance game' in which the participating syndicates – Hook, Crew-Lyne & Floater; Puffin, Money & Bagges; and Sir Rodney Grapeshotte (and others), etc – vied for ascendancy and, in a way, reflected his own obsession with ownership, takeovers and creative partnerships.

His own destiny as an artist was now inextricably linked with the fortunes of a company of his own devising. It was, and would remain, a Frankenstein and Monster plot, with the experimental artist developing a schizoid relationship with the powerful body he had set in motion. By temperament and inclination, Lloyd Webber wanted nothing to do with it. But he felt he had to come back on the board 'because the company was bleeding to death'. Whether he ran the company, owned the company, sold the company or spurned the company, there was no way round it. As the Stephen Sondheim lyric goes – 'in comes company'. And his company was his income.

This dramatic Faustian pact – one which drove Tim Rice even further away from any chance of future reconciliation ('I'd talk to Andrew about anything if I could get past his six secretaries', Tim would say later on) – created all sorts of fascinating problems and tensions.

At the end of the day, Lloyd Webber exists as a man with a talent in a room with a piano. Then, if he's ever happy, is when he's happy. But circumstances, success, the need to survive, the need to prove something perhaps to his parents, the need to be a winner, had driven him into a whole new ball game, let alone board game. Had it?

He is undoubtedly a victim of his own personality, something readily identified by his brother, Julian: 'We are driven, both of us. There are people who wouldn't have gone on writing all these shows; there are people who wouldn't be as intense about their work as I am. But there's not much we can do about it! But no, I don't think we want to prove anything to anyone. We want to prove something to ourselves. I find it strange that, on top of all that, Andrew has created this corporate life around himself . . . but then, he's a very complex character . . .'

Julian himself blames the end of his marriage to Celia on his work. He was, he admits, really married to his much-prized cello, a beast whose travel requirements alongside his master on aeroplanes were demanding and often precarious. He split from Celia after ten years of marriage in 1986 – she continues to work for Hyperion Records – and three years later married a girl he had seen across a crowded supermarket in the Old Brompton Road.

Zhora Ghazi, twelve years younger than Julian, turned out to be an Afghan princess in exile, and a Muslim. She and Julian settled into Sussex Mansions – with a country cottage bolthole, and a big garden, near Chipping Camden in Gloucestershire. Julian rates himself a beer connoisseur and is a stalwart in his local pub. He is also, I think, the first person to point out that lager is an anagram of his favourite composer, Elgar.

For a time, Julian kept pet turtles called Hoddle and Waddle, named in honour of two wonderfully creative footballers associated with Tottenham Hotspur and England. (He once kept, in Harrington Court days, pet tortoises called Boosey and Hawkes in honour of the music publishers.) His focus of interest moved on to his and Zhora's son David, an eminently suitable six-year-old cousin for Andrew's new young family, for whom Julian – a suppressed composer, he readily admits – wrote a sweetly sentimental little piece, 'Song for Baba', as the infant slept.

In stark contrast, the high-rolling financial life of his older brother continued apace. Big changes were also afoot in Andrew's personal life. And there was a new show, *Aspects of Love*, a chamber work of tangled emotions and fleeting sentiment that seemed like a contradictory *cri de coeur* amidst all this visible hard-nosed activity. In May 1989, RUG made £4m in a property deal, selling a Victorian school in Tower Street near Cambridge Circus, intended as a possible head-quarters, for £7m, and renting it back for that purpose as a brand new, functionally designed small office block. The location was perfect, on the edge of Covent Garden, just around the corner from the Ambassadors Theatre and the restored theatrical restaurant, the Ivy.

And in July 1989 he finally got his hands on Watership Down, the rabbit-rich, eminently arable, beautiful green landscape surrounding Sydmonton in the heartland of the British countryside, memorialised by Richard Adams in his stories. There is a lot to be said, in Lloyd Webber's case, for the aphorism that the man loved the country so much he wanted to own it all. Sydmonton had been acquired by the Kingsmill family from King Henry VIII after the dissolution of the monasteries in 1542. The price had been £760. In 1986, when Lloyd Webber bought the adjoining 1200-acre Sydmonton estate from Charles Clifford-Kingsmill, the price was £2.3m. This included the village of Sydmonton and the farms of Canon's Heath and Cowhouse.

Two years earlier, he had lost out on the deal, rather like losing out on the Old Vic or the Aldwych. Phillip Coussens, a computer tycoon, had bought up Watership Down as an extravagant retreat after his wife and two sons had been tragically killed in a helicopter accident. But he was now moving to the South of France with his second wife. Lloyd Webber now owned as far as he could see and way beyond. And as if to fully confirm his appeal to the editors of house, home and garden magazines – not to mention *Hello!* whom he never particularly encouraged – he bought a property in Eaton Square that would knock your eyes out and do your head in.

It was the prime location that had played host to countless television episodes of *Upstairs, Downstairs*. And it cost £10.5m. Number Eleven, Eaton Square. This was an act of appropriation by Lloyd Webber symbolising his journey from Harrington Court in South Ken to the top of the tree in Belgravia. He never really liked the place, and has only just managed to sell it – moving round the corner to the much tidier Chester Square – but felt he was indulging a whim of his wife; maybe even launching a last ditch bid to keep her for himself. The purchase coincided with the sale of the penthouse flat across the road to the bestselling American novelist Sidney Sheldon.

Eaton Square was built between 1825 and 1853 by Thomas Cubitt, the man responsible for the East front of Buckingham Palace and Osborne House, Queen Victoria's beloved retreat on the Isle of Wight. The house was listed after extensive renovations in 1954. There were ten bedrooms, three reception rooms, a billiard room, a ninety-foot atrium with swimming pool, jacuzzi and sauna complex and two mews cottages reached through a double-height conservatory. The cottages would house Lloyd Webber's personal office (and piano), with secretaries, for most of the 1990s.

The recent history of the house would have made a good subject for a musical. It had been owned by the former wife, Soraya, of the arms dealer Adnan Khashoggi. She once decorated the wall of one of the reception rooms with the blasted remains of an Israeli air force jet, not a happy omen for the author of a musical film, *Jesus Christ Superstar*, that received a quarter of its four million dollar budget from the Israeli government.

Soraya rented the house to a Nigerian chieftan, Okerentogba Thompson who, once settled in with his two wives and twenty children, had difficulty paying the bills. The house was sold on eventually for £2.5m, to a company who used it as an entertainment facility and tax haven and instigated all the changes that Lloyd Webber now inherited, including green marble flooring and the grand conservatory.

In November 1989, it was announced that twenty-eight top company directors in Britain earned more than £1m from their own shares. They included David Sainsbury and – a man who was to figure as dramatically as Robert Maxwell in the coming months of RUG trading – the Australian landowner and property magnate Robert Holmes à Court. Sixty other directors, including Lloyd Webber, made more than half a million. He was, like it or not, now part of some material board game of his own devising. And changes, both private and personal, would be convulsive.

In addition, he kept his eye on the ball by bringing forward a musical he had thought about for some years. It combined tangled love relationships, a sense of the landscape in the South of France and a nostalgia for better days. It was an escape, perhaps, from the realities of the imprisoning corporate life he had made for himself.

EIGHT

ASPECTS OF LOVE AND MONEY

When *Phantom* opened, Lloyd Webber's friend and mentor Peter Brown told him that he would never be anything but a success in his life, even if he did nothing else, or merely had a string of flops. 'But he didn't believe me. He's simply not interested. He's only interested in what happens next, the next baby.'

And despite all the brouhaha in the Really Useful, and the imminent collapse of his second marriage, the next baby was soon up and running. Jake Eberts, the film producer who ran Goldcrest Films in the mid-1980s, had talked to Tim Rice after *Evita* opened about a 1955 novella by David Garnett, a minor member of the Bloomsbury Group surrounding Virginia Woolf and Lytton Strachey. His hedonistic story of love among the artists had the appeal of *La Bohème* in a more sophisticated and sexually liberated climate.

As early as 1980, Rice and Lloyd Webber had gone away to the South of France, and stayed in Eugenie-les-Bains near Pau, *Aspects of Love* territory, and had a very good time eating, drinking, playing on pinball machines and talking a lot about nothing in particular, least of all musicals or plots. They came very close to going ahead around 1982, but Rice ducked out of the project altogether, realising the material wasn't his bag after all. The first draft emerged at the 1988 Sydmonton Festival as a delicate, touching, Mozartian piece with lyrics by Don Black and Charles Hart, directed by Trevor Nunn.

It was an unexpected choice of material for Lloyd Webber, though he has clung as tenaciously to this work as to any other. 'I can't remember girls having an enormous part in my early life but my first true love inspired part of *Aspects of Love*,' he once said. 'She is very well known but she never even knew I was in love with her and I still don't think she knows today.' Nor will he come clean now, though I suspect it might have been a little local, unfulfilled infatuation on that trip with Tim to Pau.

Garnett's hero, Alex Dillingham, becomes infatuated with the teenage daughter, Jenny, of an actress, Rose Vibert, with whom he had an affair twenty-one years previously. Jenny is also Alex's half cousin, and her father, George, is vaguely outraged; but when George married Rose, he was senior to her by forty years.

Being twenty years older than a woman you marry is not exactly the same as seducing a minor, even though Jenny is completely smitten with Alex. 'Love Changes Everything' was the chart-topping song of the show, but love cannot always excuse everything, though neither Garnett nor the musical made any moral deductions from the characters' behaviour. As Trevor Nunn says, the book 'wickedly and brilliantly poses aspects of romantic love which are more and more difficult to remain sympathetic with . . . and all these affairs are pushed a little further than we like our comfortable notions of love to be.'

Garnett saw himself as both George and Alex, and the characters have mirror image qualities. Like George, Garnett, born in 1892, loved his food and his wine, the throw of the dice. A botanist and close friend of D. H. Lawrence, he was a conscientious objector during the First World War and a prolific writer after it, producing a now largely forgotten output of novels and short stories.

A cheerfully bisexual, twice-married character, he scandalised even some of the other free-thinking 'Bloomsberries' by marrying the daughter, Angelica, of his lover, the painter Duncan Grant. Angelica's mother, also Grant's lover, was Vanessa Bell the painter, herself married to Clive Bell, and the sister of Virginia Woolf. The latter was particularly outraged by Garnett marrying a woman young enough to be his daughter (he was forty-eight, she twenty-two) – she didn't seem to mind about the incestuous side of things – but the marriage was successful and produced four daughters. One of these, Amaryllis, was a beautiful, haunting, troubled actress whom I got to know a little around fringe theatres in the early 1970s. Tragically, she committed suicide before her career took on any shape or substance.

One of the problems with *Aspects* as a musical was the lack of a defining shape to the libretto beyond placing Alex and his recurring hit tune at the centre of it. Although it contains some of Lloyd Webber's most beautiful music, and seems to breathe the very air of the French countryside around Pau, it has an arbitrary, undramatic structure, unlike, say the earlier *Evita* (which lacks narrative drive but not structure) or the later *Whistle*. No librettist is credited, presumably because he didn't want the flak.

Black and Hart had written the lyrics on an equal 50/50 footing, Hart recognising that Black was the better ideas man and a good initiator, so most of the titles were his. Hart did a lot of the filling in, what he calls the drudgery. They enjoyed each other's company and wrote most of the first act down at Lloyd Webber's villa in Cap Ferrat, finishing the rest in London. Someone, not Hart, described to me the sensation of working with Lloyd Webber as being permanently on red alert, and Hart felt that on *Aspects*: 'It's hard to relax with Andrew in the same room. He's a very dominant personality and perhaps because I'm sponge-like I found a lot of that rubbed off on me, and I got quite wired. Don never gets wired. We didn't quite get it right, but I never felt the production swamped the work, actually. If anything we were too faithful to the book when there was no need to be; it's not as if anyone came to the theatre knowing it.'

Hart reckons that the problem of conveying internal thoughts – a key feature of the novel – was never properly addressed, resulting in too much sung dialogue. The point about people singing, in operas or musicals, is that they do so because mere spoken words are no longer adequate to convey meaning, or passion, or despair. (Ignoring for the moment Voltaire's contentious remark that anything too silly to be said can always be sung!) The continuous music of *Aspects* is, I think, continuously interesting: mellow, supple, wistful, nostalgic. The subjects are transforming love, memory, and sensual pleasure in a daisy chain of liaisons dangereuses.

Garnett's fiction charts these shifting amours in five evocative sections. Alex the soldier falls for Rose the actress playing Ibsen's Hedda Gabler in Montpellier and later Natalya Petrovna in Turgenev's *A Month in the Country* in Paris; the show changes the first role to Ibsen's much younger Hilde Wangel in *The Master Builder* to help the passage of time between the two performances and Alex's ageing process. All three stage characters are notable ball-breakers.

Later, Alex's uncle Sir George Dillingham is involved with an Italian socialite, the Marchesa Giuletta Trapani, in Venice, and Rose sets off to win George back. The musical makes George a plain painter and Giuletta a plain sculptress, whose works conform to the popular idea of the avant-garde in echoing Allen Jones (submissive ladies frozen in hardware, sofa lips) and the chaotic, colourful monumentalism of Eduardo Paolozzi. Ensnared by Jenny, Alex makes a sexual tryst in a hay loft – at George's funeral – with Giuletta.

In a really effective dramatic innovation, Lloyd Webber, Black and Hart wrote 'Anything But Lonely' ('There's so much in life to share, what's the sense when no-one else is there?'), a swelling, defiant valedictory for Rose, who emerges strongly as the most victimised character in the piece. And the funeral wake itself, a climactic flash point in the action, became a cross-rhythmed tango, brilliantly choreographed by Gillian Lynne, where George's last will and testament of explosive joy is fulfilled.

The show generalised the implicit theme of impossible love made suddenly real. And, interestingly for a composer who himself had married a much younger woman (as indeed had his father, and his brother Julian, not to mention his director, Trevor Nunn), much was made of the poignancy in age gaps and the weightiness of prior commitments.

When *Aspects* opened in April 1989, everyone was familiar with Michael Ball singing 'Love Changes Everything', which had already risen to Number Two in the charts. When it slipped to Number Three, RUG instigated a Mother's Day campaign in the tabloid press with the slogan 'Take Michael home to Mummy', and the record was reinstated at Number Two, though it never made the top spot. Audiences were even more familiar with the song by the end of the show. But it is quite wrong to suppose – as some critics have – that it is a) the only good song in the score, or b) that it crops up any more frequently than any other musical motif. The charming ballad 'Seeing is Believing' – an expression of transforming love with distinct echoes of Richard Rodgers – and the sensual 'Other Pleasures' – which opens with the same four-note, augmented seventh phrase as 'What would you do' in Kander and Ebb's *Cabaret* but which then soars to its own logical melody – are just as recurrent, and thematically underpin the entire score.

The show is less through-sung than through-composed. An objection to the repetition of a good tune with differing lyrics and diminishing returns was brilliantly posited by Mark Steyn, who wondered in his *Independent* review if the young Lloyd Webber would have been as impressed by 'Some Enchanted Evening' if it had popped up ten minutes later as 'Would You Like A Biscuit?'

But the older Lloyd Webber was certainly entitled to have a go at the integrated scoring of musical items and dialogue, in the manner of earlier twentieth century composers, notably Gian-Carlo Menotti in pieces like *The Telephone* or *The Consul*. And Menotti, like Lloyd Webber, was attempting to write in the 'verismo' or realistic vein of Puccini: real people in real situations.

One way of looking at Lloyd Webber musicals, in fact, is to see them increasingly as attempts to solve the problems of an eclectic, varied style of composition in the making of organically structured theatre works. The music in *Aspects* never stands still but curls round the narrative like wreaths of smoke, signalling a quite different way of writing to that of the barbarous recitative in *Superstar* or the segregated pastiche styles in *Starlight*.

Whereas *Superstar* and *Evita* were designed to get by without dialogue – were conceived in fact as integrated, coherent musical albums which *then* had to be imagined for the stage – *Phantom* and, to a greater extent, *Aspects* were written as theatre pieces within which contrasting musical experiments had to bed down within an overall musical scheme and sound world.

There is a lovely item, 'Chanson d'Enfance', sung in simple French, that begins with a descending major scale reminiscent of 'Angel of Music' in *Phantom*. But whereas that song builds to the requisite operatic robustness, this one has a second ten bars constructed on a typical bold Lloyd Webber interval leap of a downward sixth and a most tender, sweet and childish resolution. The item recurs, symmetrically, just as mother and daughter, Rose and Jenny, inspire rhapsodic spasms in George by wearing the same white and silver lamé dress.

Even difficult, private things in Garnett, like the ghostly slipper and the siren song, are not ducked. The latter yields a bewitching duet, 'Mermaid Song', that is woven into the several other main musical themes. The second act has great stretches of melodic lyricism followed by wittily banal foxtrot passages emanating from another Rodgers-like song, 'The First Man You Remember' ('I want to be the last man you'll forget').

This duet for George and Jenny does not fight shy of simple, even banal, lyrics, with dancing round the floor and walking to the door and young hearts missing a beat to rhyme with sweeping off my feet, evoking Groucho Marx's line of 'Ever since I met you, I've swept you off my feet.' And then there is the fine bacchanalian tango, where Alex meets Giuletta for the first time and another die is cast.

The London production, though running for three years, had an uphill struggle from the off in one of the West End's most cavernous and unsympathetic theatres, the Prince of Wales. Although the power and originality of the musical certainly came across, the production by Trevor Nunn was immensely busy, with a literal approach to the settings, and lots of chairs. There were endless scene changes, but Maria Bjornson's design supplied pleasant glimpses of mountain peaks through a series of slatted doors and a magically versatile grey brick wall. Still, this wasn't a patch on her *Phantom* work.

Nunn, too, had been promised something else: 'It had been really magical at Sydmonton, and Andrew was 100 per cent agreed to doing a small theatre version, completely non-technologically. It just didn't stay that way. Suddenly a requirement was coming through about the number of people needed in the pit, and the administration was saying that if we have that many in the pit we need a thousand people in the audience.' Lloyd Webber disputes this account, saying that the band was a good deal smaller than for most West End musicals including his own, and that the design was large and complicated mostly at Nunn's insistence.

Whoever claims who wanted what or why, the choice of theatre in the first place was simply one of brute economic expediency. If Nunn didn't like it, he could have resigned. If Lloyd Webber didn't like what Nunn was doing, he could have sacked him. Hindsight is always a potent adjunct to memory. The truth is, the venue of the Prince of Wales did not help the show. Although the auditorium is quite shallow, it is very wide and has a huge cubic capacity. Intimacy was hard to achieve, though many, including myself, felt they had a darned good try. Nunn's final verdict was that *Aspects* 'emerged a more conventional musical theatre piece than it was intended to be'.

There was some larkiness in the original casting, prophetic of larger problems ahead on *Sunset Boulevard*. At a party in the South of France thrown by songwriter Leslie Bricusse – collaborator with Anthony Newley on *Stop the World – I Want to Get Off* – Lloyd Webber met, and was charmed by, the smooth and affable 61-year-old film star Roger Moore.

Moore had exactly the right debonair insouciance and the right wicked twinkle for George Dillingham, and would undoubtedly look the part. The small detail of Roger having little experience in musical theatre, and none at all of singing in public, did not deter Andrew from excitedly announcing that he was to play the role. A few weeks into rehearsal, with Moore taking singing lessons, growing a beard and giving interviews containing lines like, 'It's a tremendous challenge and it could be an even bigger one for the audience', he graciously withdrew, admitting defeat.

Moore was succeeded by Kevin Colson, who could not only sing superbly, but who gave a performance of great finesse and expertise, if not perhaps matching the charismatic (and box office) potential Lloyd Webber must have seen in Moore. Alongside him, the wonderful Michael Ball – who surely posseses the finest tenor baritone heard in British musicals over the past two decades; he had first struck out for stardom as Marius in *Les Misérables* – aged the seventeen years backwards then forwards.

The exchange deal on Sarah Brightman going to New York with *Phantom* necessitated American casting for Rose, and Ann Crumb, elegant and voluptuous, with cascading auburn tresses, certainly made an impact as the Stephane Audran of the French provincial stage.

Another American, Kathleen Rowe McAllen, was no less impressive as Giuletta, the femme fatale, a stunning beauty with a voice to match. Her progress in the musical was that of an extra moving centre stage, pivotal to all the shifting alliances, and indeed the encapsulating hit song which, shot through with contextualising, melancholic wisdom, becomes her personal epitaph.

The adaptation bumped the action of Garnett's pre-war merry-go-round into the post-war period, starting Act One nearly in the present of the 1960s and back-tracking to the Montpellier theatre in 1947, to a Parisian fairground, Giuletta's studio in Venice and a military camp in Malaysia. Act Two moved into the continuous present, from a Paris theatre in 1962 and then to the gardens at Pau for the anxiety-flavoured conclusion.

Charles Hart had worked at close quarters with Hal Prince and Trevor Nunn on his first two jobs. What was the difference? 'Hal was good at cutting to the chase, doing away with nonsense. In terms of putting a show together, what he does is just breathtaking. Trevor takes longer to express himself. Actors adore him, but you do have to persuade him to keep the running time down.

He's an extraordinary fellow, infuriating and likeable. *Aspects* was a great experience, but a very different one. And you know, at root, in many ways, Hal and Trevor are similar. And they are both, in different ways, geniuses.'

Ball, Crumb and Colson all went to New York for an opening at the Broadhurst Theater one year later, in April 1990. At a royal gala, the handsome lyricist Charles Hart was introduced to Prince Philip as the handsome actor Charles Dance. Maybe the slightly less handsome Don Black should have been introduced as the slightly less handsome Don Johnson, and if someone had passed off Andrew Lloyd Webber as a really handsome composer – but *who*? Charles Hart, perhaps? – the show might have run longer than its modest 300 performances. It closed in March 1991 without returning a dime of its $8m investment. Howard Kissel in the *New York Daily News* had opined the show was a fake, and Frank Rich reckoned it generated about as much heated passion as a visit to the bank.

'Andrew Lloyds Bank' as Gerald Scarfe, the cartoonist, dubbed him, had been busy trying to buy back the Really Useful shares. Going public he now reckoned to have been a terrible mistake, seeing himself chafing under the yolk of having to produce profits and mollify shareholders. But the Really Useful had been floated on the London Stock Exchange at the height of the expansionist boom in 1986. The crash of 1987, and a not wholly successful corporate agenda, had left the shares dipping if not exactly languishing. His mistake had been not appreciating the risks involved.

There were some minor irritations, too, such as a toilet-cleaning company in Ripponden, West Yorkshire, opening trading in May 1990 under the name of the Andrew Lloyd Webber Lavatory Services Cleaning Company. Like the most powerful of bleaches, ALW duly went right round the bend and successfully slapped a High Court injunction on them banning the use of his name.

He was also harassed by a nun called Sister Maria Gabriel who wanted him to write a score for her musical about the little heroine of Lourdes, Bernadette. She even turned up on the doorstep at his Belgravia home, prompting the composer to ask, along with his heroes Rodgers and Hammerstein, 'How do you solve a problem called Maria?' (There was indeed, eventually, a dire West End musical called *Bernadette*, written by two schoolteachers and financed by devout Catholics, that lost a fortune and even deprived post-preview audiences of the full candlelit glories of a miraculous grotto designed, according to one producer – as reported by Mark Steyn – to resemble a large, coiled turd; as well as the best 'worst' lines such as that of an angry mother shaking her fist at a radiant little Bernadette and howling, 'You've been down at that grotto again, haven't you?')

To keep the charitable side of things going, Lloyd Webber sponsored a programme of research into diabetes which investigated why one twin can develop the condition and not the other, remembering the life-or-death decisions his Uncle George had to take in the early days of insulin, when he was able to minister to only a quarter of those who needed it.

Between February and July 1990, through a series of deals and switches of personnel within RUG, Lloyd Webber wrestled back the company to himself. He bought out Robert Maxwell's 14.5 per cent, thus moving to control with 52.5 per cent of the shares. Other investors were offered 233p a share, valuing the group at £77m. A loan of £50m from Coutts the bankers, allowing him to do this, was to be paid back over the next five years. The shares were duly de-listed in October 1990.

The chief executive, John Whitney, was eased out

with a handsome pay-off after only eighteen months and replaced by Patrick McKenna, a high-flying accountant at Touche Ross who had looked after Lloyd Webber's personal tax affairs since the late 1970s. At the same time, Biddy Hayward left to form her own Theatre Division, taking 'Prince' Edward Windsor – who was learning fast; he now knew that, after putting sugar in the tea, it was a good idea to give the wet stuff a gentle stir with a spoon, and not necessarily a silver one – and four other RUG employees with her.

Within a year, her new company, Theatre Division, which started promisingly with a collaboration with the Almeida Theatre in Islington, had collapsed due to a mixture of inexperience and chronic under-financing. What Lloyd Webber would learn the hard way over the next few years was that, without Brian Brolly and Biddy, or people like them, he had no real theatrical nous or flair in the company, and the producing side of things, let alone the finding of outside projects, ground to a halt. As a result, his power base in the West End was weakened.

What both Brolly and Biddy would also discover was that without Lloyd Webber, or someone like him, being a producer was not really all that much fun or even worthwhile. Or financially rewarding. Once the decision to take the company to the Stock Exchange had been taken, it placed Lloyd Webber in a quandary for this reason: while liking the idea of being free to perform as an artist, he could never really cope with the idea of responsibilities to the shareholders. His greatest responsibility to them was his talent. But being an irrepressible ideas man, he would storm into the office from lunch and direct Brolly and Michael Sydney-Smith to go ahead immediately on the latest scheme he might have dreamed up, or the latest vision of rescuing the British musical theatre. Brolly would pour cold water on such proposals in order to wait for calm and that time of mature reflection that never really arrived.

Understandably exasperated by Brolly's perfectly reasonable tactics, Lloyd Webber had decided to create his own satellite company, funded obviously by the RUG, but in a curious *Alice in Wonderland* sort of way, not responsible to them. This was an impossible situation and the beginning of the rift with Brolly. Brolly had a duty to the shareholders. Lloyd Webber was the artist from whom all this wealth and plenty had derived; he was surely entitled to do what he thought was best. At the same time, Michael Sydney-Smith felt that Lloyd Webber's overwhelming sense of responsibility to the shareholders was such that he sought to escape it. He was terrified of failure on their behalf.

On one occasion Lloyd Webber insisted all the RUG directors flew to Paris for an emergency meeting. Were they going to go his way and allow him to form his satellite company, or not? On the way from Charles de Gaulle airport to the meeting in a Paris hotel, Michael Sydney-Smith shared a taxi with Lord Gowrie, the RUG chairman. The apprehensive Gowrie rehearsed his strategy. He said that sometimes in a company there has to be a divorce. 'And we know whom we have to support.' Andrew, of course, was the bride with the dowry. From that moment, Brian Brolly was out on a limb.

Looking for support outside the board for his idea of a satellite company, Lloyd Webber had turned to his trusted friend and new main ally, Patrick McKenna. Ten years younger than Lloyd Webber, he was a prototype Essex Man, born and raised there, living in mock Tudor splendour near Brentwood where he later built himself a palatial mansion. He was personable, cunning, efficient, and a brilliantly able financial planner. What he didn't know all that much about was theatre. For the moment that didn't matter. What he had was clout. At Touche Ross, he had handled the tax affairs of Annie Lennox, Cliff Richard, Phil Collins and Laurence Olivier.

McKenna was used to the big time. And just as Brolly had advocated the flotation, so McKenna suggested the buy-back of shares from the public. The pressures of the cost – £77m – were eased within a year in a remarkable deal he engineered with Polygram, the Dutch record group, who paid £80m for a 30 per cent stake in the company.

Polygram were one of the top three recorded music producers and publishers in the world. Their labels included Mercury, Polydor, Decca/London, Phillips Classics and Deutsche Grammophon, and their clients Elton John, Def Leppard, Dire Straits – and Andrew Lloyd Webber. They were also riding high on record sales of Luciano Pavarotti, and the Three Tenors (Pavarotti, Placido Domingo and Jose Carreras).

Lloyd Webber's contract with Really Useful was renegotiated, giving the company rights in his entire creative services until the year 2003, on top of the traditional income from his royalties. It was an inspired deal that, when the euphoria had died down and McKenna's aims were achieved, became an albatross round Lloyd Webber's neck. McKenna would go the way of Brolly: wealthy and humiliated. Like some wonderful tragic hero, Macbeth or Richard III in Shakespeare, Lloyd Webber first craved then dispensed with the company of political lieutenants less imaginatively gifted than himself.

The buy-back went nearly as planned except for one stumbling block. Stoll Moss Theatres, lately taken over by the Australian impresario and landowner Robert Holmes à Court, were the RUG's leading minority shareholder. They held a 6.6 per cent stake. Lloyd Webber needed a clear 95 per cent holding to take out the remaining shareholders under the provisions of the Companies Act. And Holmes à Court wanted the bargaining power to try and prise the Palace Theatre away from Lloyd Webber and add it to Stoll Moss's

Shaftesbury Avenue empire of the four great theatres along the avenue itself, as well as the London Palladium.

Battle was joined and the atmosphere unyielding. Then the most incredible and shocking thing happened. Quite unexpectedly, in September 1990, Holmes à Court collapsed of a massive heart attack in his garden. He died instantly, aged just fifty-three. He had been struggling of late to recover *his* vast losses in the Stock Exchange crash. His wife, Janet, perhaps surprisingly, took over his companies, including Stoll Moss, and proved a more pliable negotiatior. The Stoll Moss stake was bought out. Mission accomplished. Lloyd Webber said that McKenna's restructuring of the company had given him the confidence to feel 'that it will be my secure home in the forseeable future'.

Once more, he kidded himself that he could concentrate on creative work and not worry about the money. This delusion took hold alongside the harsh reality of his less secure home life at home. In July 1990, Lloyd Webber had issued another statement, chillingly similar to one he had issued in May 1983 when announcing his switching of horses from Sarah One to Sarah Two: 'It is clear to me that, with great sadness, I have to face the fact that my marriage to Sarah Brightman is at an end. My admiration for her as an artist remains undimmed.' Referring to a slim, fresh-faced ginger girl with a horsey background called Madeleine Gurdon, known to her friends as Gurtie, he added: 'I wish to confirm we have become close friends.'

In August he accompanied Madeleine to the Smiths Lawn Horse Trials in Windsor where she was competing. The retired jump jockey Charlie Mann, who had dated her on and off for a couple of years, said: 'Good old Gurt – I think they're made for each other and I hope they'll be very happy.' They seemed to be an established item already.

A few years later, Lloyd Webber would admit that it

had been extremely hard to make a successful marriage work when the other half was on stage performing every night, adding dolefully that 'she had played around a wee bit'. As Michael Walsh rightly observed, the British public never really got over the idea of Sarah Two being a Jezebel, although she never went all that far out of her way to disabuse them. There were persistent rumours of extra-marital affairs.

But as Arlene Phillips says, the one thing that is incontestable about Sarah Brightman is that nothing, absolutely nothing, comes between herself and her career: 'In Hot Gossip, for a warm-up, she would come in an hour before the warm-up. I don't know about having kids, but I do know that if Sarah had to practise, rehearse, or go for a singing lesson, that task would come before anything, regardless of its importance, that was happening in her life with Andrew.'

Talk of having children together early in the marriage had soon been forgotten. Andrew needed a wife and companion who could run his domestic life for him. He was congenitally incapable of doing it for himself. And he was desperately keen to have a second shot at being a family man. He loved small children and he had a lot to share with them.

In the summer of 1989, Lloyd Webber's friend David Crewe-Read met a vivacious redhead at a wedding party full of racing and country people around Newbury, Lambourn and Sydmonton. Madeleine Gurdon was an outstanding horsewoman and three-day eventer who had represented Britain at the European Championships of 1985 and had been runner-up on Midnight Monarch at Burghley, the toughest eventing course in the world, in 1988.

She and Crewe-Read shared a mutual friend, Lucinda Clifford-Kingsmill, also an event rider, whose family, strangely enough, had owned Sydmonton Court. Her father had in fact sold the place on to Lloyd Webber in

215

1975, partly because he was keener on drinking than on running the property. Crewe-Read had a well-trained, not to say roving, eye for a pretty woman, and he was much taken with Madeleine.

He took her round to meet his friend and neighbour Andrew Lloyd Webber just before Christmas, no doubt with a view to impressing her with his connections. Instead, something else happened. 'Sarah was away,' says Crewe-Read, 'and Andrew and Gurtie got on like a house on fire. She loved the sense of power that comes from older and wealthy men and was fascinated by him.'

There was also an extraordinary double coincidence that drew them together. Years earlier, Lloyd Webber had been watching television sport one Saturday afternoon with his daughter Imogen, then seven years old, when he saw this attractive young horsewoman going round Badminton. He remembered the cameras staying on her and a funny interview she gave afterwards in the pouring rain.

Then, in the mid 1980s, he had seen her on television again, this time in a charity event before the Grand National, when the event riders at Gatcombe challenged the jockeys to swap courses. Madeleine therefore went round the Aintree course, and at Becher's Brook, the most challenging of the fences, she gave another interview and said, on air, 'Do tell me where my hair and make-up is before I do this interview!'

This time, Andrew noted the name and, on an impulse, wrote a short letter saying 'Bravo!': 'I never got a reply, and she told me at that party that she never received the letter.' And because of the Clifford-Kingsmill connection at Sydmonton Court, Madeleine had a strong sense of her life having run in a parallel line of destiny to Andrew's.

At least, they had enough in common for her to become a regular dinner date on those occasions when he needed one while Sarah was away, which was a lot of the time. Madeleine was twenty-eight and coming off the peak of a tough riding career spanning ten years. She was ready to move on. 'I thought this was great,' she says, 'and a bit different from riding horses. We became really good friends before anything else happened. And we were both rather surprised.'

One of the things that recommended her to Andrew was that she knew next to nothing about his career or his musicals. She moved in the social world of such distinguished sporting friends as Lucinda Prior-Palmer, Mark Todd and Captain Mark Phillips. All she knew about him was that he was something to do with the musical theatre, in which she had no interest, and that he had bought some jewellery, including a Cartier bracelet, in the Duchess of Windsor auction.

A few months later, Madeleine spent a weekend in Venice with Andrew and a group of his friends. On the way back, she flew with him to Paris to see *Cats*. 'It was then,' says Crewe-Read, 'that Andrew and Gurtie understood there was more between them than just friendship . . . Andrew seemed besotted with her and she was fascinated and flattered by all his attentions.'

One of their first dates in public was Sir David Frost's summer drinks party at his Chelsea home in July 1990. Lloyd Webber had known Sir David since the early days of *Superstar* on both sides of the Atlantic, but the pair's friendship would become closer, with their respective wives and young children, over the coming years.

Madeleine Astrid Gurdon was the second of four daughters of Brigadier and Mrs Adam Gurdon of Burgh, Suffolk. The Brigadier, now retired, had served in the Black Watch, and could trace his family back to William the Conqueror. He had been posted in Hong Kong, Germany and Scotland before settling in Suffolk. Madeleine had left All Hallows Convent in Ditchingham, Norfolk, with one ambition: to ride for England.

Around this time, she was based in Middle Woodford, near Salisbury Plain, in the heart of the horse country. She was always completely bound up in her horses, but she had enjoyed a three-year affair with a property developer, Alfred Buller. And her last boyfriend had been Marcus 'Fluffy' Armytage – ironically, like Lloyd Webber, now a columnist on the *Daily Telegraph* – an old Etonian jockey who rode the 1990 Grand National winner, Mr Frisk.

They met when she was thrown from the saddle at Wincanton, and Armytage gallantly galloped over and picked her up. Their first date in a two-month fling was at the Pizza Hut in Newbury, so he must have guessed that the way to a girl's heart might not be through her stomach. He was obviously wrong: one cannot imagine Lloyd Webber whisking a girl off to the Golden Egg or the nearest doner kebab house. Or even being much help if she fell off a horse.

Madeleine's close friends were astonished when she took up with the composer. Simon Marsh, a cheery Old Harrovian who now manages all the Lloyd Webber horses, had grown up with Madeleine, sharing the same sort of background. Madeleine had lived for a time in the same house as Marsh (though never as 'a couple' apparently) and two other friends – Nick Wright and Nick Chain, both in racing – in a place called Top Farm House just outside Cambridge. Marsh was working on a stud in Newmarket while Madeleine was working for Sir Mark Prescott, breaking in yearlings and riding out, also at Newmarket.

Marsh went 'ballistic' when she told him about the affair. 'I said you must be mad. There was one of my best friends going out with a man who was in the papers every day and who had a very public life. She insisted I met him and we went out for dinner: Andrew faced with Madeleine and me and the two Nicks. He was absolutely terrified! So we had him on the back foot to start with.

And we got on instantly. I loved him. God knows what we talked about. It wasn't about horses and it wasn't about musicals.'

The divorce from Sarah Two went through on 5 November 1990 at 11 a.m. and at 6 p.m. on the same day, the engagement to Madeleine was announced. Sarah loyally went off to try and boost the box office as Rose Vibert, the woman who loses out in love, in the ailing *Aspects* in New York.

The marriage was at Westminster register office on 1 February 1991, with a religious blessing in Madeleine's home village of Burgh, in St Botolph's Church, two weeks later. She had indeed gone, according to one inventive caption writer, from nags to riches. There were four ushers: Marsh, the two Nicks and another racing chum called John Nesbitt. Guests were asked to donate to a forces' charity – the Gulf War was in full swing – rather than bring wedding presents.

The same request was made at Sydmonton, where a wedding party was cancelled because of atrocious weather and heavy snowfall. But there was a big party one week later. Julian Lloyd Webber played a new cello piece composed in honour of the bride, Michael Ball sang 'Love Changes Everything' and Elaine Paige gave the first semi-public performance of 'With One Look', Norma Desmond's transfixing aria from the forthcoming musical *Sunset Boulevard*.

Later in the month, after recording an interview at Sydmonton, Andrew and his new wife Madeleine Gurdon were guests on the second programme of a new *Talking With David Frost* series for the PBS television network; the guests on the first programme had been George and Barbara Bush. Their joint celebrity status was ratified.

Madeleine was a different sort of class act after Sarah Two. But one of the most striking things about her is her absolute straightforwardness. The horse she was most associated with as a young rider was The Done Thing, which she started out with at pony club. Long before she met Lloyd Webber, she had launched a country clothes company, also called The Done Thing, in order to keep her horses in straw. Her first client was an art dealer called David Mason who sponsored events at Gatcombe and other horse trials.

One of his daughters, like Madeleine, was an international two- and three-day eventer, and a family friend. When Madeleine turned up with a van-full of anoraks, jumpers and jodhpurs, the Mason clan, as well as their grooms, and the riders of other Mason-sponsored horses, gathered round and supported her cause.

When Madeleine wrote to Mason asking if he would sponsor her, he explained that he already had enough clients and couldn't take on any more. So she struggled on with her clothes business. 'She was always a very focused and determined girl,' says Mason, 'even at sixteen, when I first knew her.'

She carried on with the business after the marriage, and there was a series of offers in various colour magazines. But the publicity was a mixed blessing and, once pregnant with their first child, Alastair Adam (born 3 May 1992), she happily sold on the business. And when a bust-up ensued between David Crewe-Read and Andrew, Madeleine invited David Mason to meet Andrew and offer advice.

Crewe-Read had arranged for the purchase of a Lord Leighton statue, *Athlete Wrestling with a Python*, but the deal fell through and so did his friendship with Lloyd Webber. Shortly after, Millais' *Chill October*, a picture Lloyd Webber very much wanted, came to auction, and Lloyd Webber asked David Mason to bid for it on his behalf. He did so successfully, and soon replaced Crewe-Read as Lloyd Webber's full-time art adviser. As Mason was a full-time professional, with galleries in Duke Street, St James, and contacts all over the world, the art-collecting side of Lloyd Webber's life was soon established on a far more formal and professionally strategic footing. His great luck was that his new liaison with Mason coincided with many desirable paintings coming to auction because of the recession.

Madeleine's countryside interests and abilities as a hostess would transform life at Sydmonton. And indeed sharpen up Andrew's rural activities. Like Sarah Two, she was mad about cars. Sarah had favoured big strong Porsches. Andrew gave Madeleine a bright red convertible Mercedes. And while Andrew was a cat man, she preferred dogs. She had a little Jack Russell, Domino, who had slept in her bed before Andrew did.

Being around Lloyd Webber is not always easy – he probably has what one admiring colleague refers to as a multivalent personality; that is, his entire attitude to anything or anyone can depend entirely on what mood he is in – but anyone who knows anything about a certain kind of artistic talent and temperament knows also that such a personality goes with the territory. How could such a fiercely sensible and straightforward girl cope with this on a day to day basis?

'He's difficult because he keeps the pressure on himself all the time. Sometimes the easier option would be easier. And if he can make a drama out of a small problem, he will. He does overblow things in the nicest possible way, but if he could get the same result by not overblowing it, he won't! He has a gift for making things incredibly complicated and coming out the other side not smelling of roses. But he doesn't mean any harm to anybody and I don't think he's ever done any harm to anybody.'

Robert Maxwell certainly meant harm to Lloyd Webber. He was still pursuing his relentless litigation against Aurum Press, a division of the RUG, which had published the offending biography. In October 1989 he had threatened to blackmail Lloyd Webber and publish pictures of him dancing with young girls in nightclubs. It was all nonsense, but Lloyd Webber was anxious to avoid embarrassment, so in April 1991 he invited Maxwell to dine with him, Madeleine, and her parents, at Mark's Club in Mayfair. Lloyd Webber remembers the great fraudster, the size of a house, furtively ordering extra courses in between everything else they were eating.

According to Tom Bower, the author of the biography, Maxwell's cheerful conversation at dinner degenerated into yet more innuendoes and threats. He wanted £100,000 and an apology. Lloyd Webber was later advised by his fellow RUG directors, Bill Taylor and Keith Turner, to stand firm against this bullying, while Patrick McKenna advised capitulation for a quiet life.

Turner now says that the two sides had stumbled towards a settlement, but Lloyd Webber pulled out when Maxwell altered the wording at the last minute to imply culpability as well as apology. By October, the RUG and Bower had to prepare for the trial of Bower's action against Maxwell. Bower was summoned to the RUG offices in Greek Street and asked by McKenna why he shouldn't give in.

He stood firm – and so, in effect, did Lloyd Webber and his company. At the end of the month Bower went to Russia on other writing business. On 5 November 1991, Robert Maxwell was dead. He disappeared in still unexplained circumstances from the deck of his luxury yacht, the Lady Ghislaine, into the Atlantic and thus precipitated his legend and posthumous exposure as a fraud and villain of the highest and most odorous rank.

Lloyd Webber was let off the hook for the second time by the fortuitous demise of a shark-like magnate. In Holmes à Court's case, everything about him was above board. With the shady Maxwell, an awful lot, including his own bulk, was below. But the RUG had acted honourably and deserved the lucky break of Maxwell's mystery detour.

NINE

SUNRISE AT LAST OVER SUNSET

Owning the rights in your own work must be the ideal for any creative artist, but in the nature of the show-business beast, you more usually end up owned. The first half of the 1990s was a period in which Lloyd Webber set about defying these rules by assiduously re-acquiring the rights in one of his earliest pieces and producing his next big show entirely within the company designed to exploit him.

Even before Robert Stigwood had come along, *Joseph* had been sold by Tim and Andrew to the independent music publishers Novello for 100 guineas. When Novello had been acquired by Granada Television, Lloyd Webber kept in touch with Sir Denis Foreman, the chairman of Granada, reminding him of the little show that could still prove to be a big asset, and he was more than miffed when Granada sold on Novello without telling him. It was bought in the late 1980s by a small film music outfit called Film Trax and eventually they asked the RUG if they would be interested in buying *Joseph* from them, as they started to sell off various items in their catalogue.

Keith Turner negotiated a deal on behalf of the RUG costing £1m and soon afterwards heard from Tim Rice expressing dismay that he had not been offered his half share. The RUG directors felt that as Tim had resigned from the board, not without financial advantage to himself, and that the rights had been offered to the board, he was no longer part of the equation. Andrew says he abstained on the vote. There was nothing in writing from Andrew, but Tim had always, not unreasonably, understood that when the copyrights on their collaborations came up they would have an equal share. Andrew at first denied any such understanding but, after thinking it through, readily agreed as long as Tim paid half of what the RUG had paid to Film Trax.

The papers were drawn up and the business was well in hand when Tim decided to withdraw from the purchase. There was nothing much happening with the show and the price was more than he could afford at that time. Within a few months *Joseph* was relaunched in a spectacular new production at the London Palladium with pop teen idol Jason Donovan – an Australian TV soap star in *Neighbours* who was branching out – ensuring a siege at the box office. It wasn't long before Tim Rice changed his mind yet again about his half share in the once-little musical, but Patrick McKenna argued that, because of the Palladium success, the show now had a totally different value, and Polygram, as major shareholder in RUG, vetoed the request.

All of this annoyed Rice intensely, but as usual he presented a sanguine face to the world. 'In a funny way, I think I'm better off not having my share because I don't have to get involved in any of the productions, or run any risks. And I've also been able to be as awkward as I like – I still have an artist's veto – and all I've done since then is collect the royalties.'

And moan quietly to Elaine Paige about another source of irritation. She found their differences amusing, but refused to get involved. 'Tim is this bright and breezy chap most of the time, but sometimes he hides behind it a bit and I think he can be, and has been, hurt.

Deep down he gets quite cut up about things. You have to have that in your character and nature to be creative, and Tim is no different from any other writer.'

Which just goes to demonstrate how a charming, innocent collaboration could become, in time, a source of resentment and enmity between the two people who wrote it. *Joseph* had become a popular stalwart of school, college and touring productions around the world. In Britain, the producer Bill Kenwright had a version (fairly tacky, when I saw it) on the road for years on end. But it had never been a West End hit.

But on 12 June 1991, a production costing £1.5m had opened to an advance at the box office of £2m and climbing. The cast album went straight to the top of the hit parade, as did Donovan's beguiling, Caribbean-flavoured version of 'Any Dream Will Do', and the show broke all Palladium box office records before it closed in January 1994. When Donny Osmond led the American cast in the same production, *Joseph* was discovered anew on that side of the Atlantic, too.

Like Topsy, the show had growed and growed in a remarkable display of what Milton Shulman called theatrical parthenogenesis – the development of an egg without fertilisation. The twenty minutes at Colet Court had stretched to forty at Edinburgh, an hour in the West End and now this two-hour, camp extravaganza dreamed up by director Steven Pimlott and designer Mark Thompson, talented scions of the subsidised theatre and opera stages.

It was certainly fun, of a sort, but the garishness rather outstripped the charm of the material. Pimlott's brief was simply to make a framework for Jason Donovan at the Palladium, and both he and Thompson could not believe their luck in being let loose in the home of vaudeville, scene of countless revolving farewells at the end of television's popular *Sunday Night at the London Palladium*.

A great, gilded, pyramidical set opened like a giant's Bible and belched forth a hectic parade of mincing shepherds, Egyptian dummies who looked as if they had stepped off a frieze in the British Museum, stuffed sheep, revolving architectural models and a slave gang in white plastic mini-skirts who carried on like a Mediterranean chorus line of over-worked gay waiters. Jason Donovan sported a blond wig and a glorified white loincloth and exuded enough pouting primness not to disappoint his fans or gain too many enemies. Not satisfied with apotheosis in his chariot of gold, he was strapped to a platform and catapulted towards the dress circle while his rainbow cloak trailed out behind him like a huge tent straining in a high wind.

Pimlott, who regards the work as the *HMS Pinafore* of the Rice/Lloyd Webber oeuvre in its brightness and freshness, and in its joyous sense of discovery of what the two young men could do, wanted a new duet for the narrator (who was superbly sung by Linzi Hateley) and Joseph. 'There's a crucial moment when Joseph has the choice of forgiving or not at the turning point of the story, and I wondered if they might not have a little moment together. But it wasn't to be.'

The robust simplicity of the piece has guaranteed a new life for *Joseph* and Rice has even indicated that now he would be prepared to write a new song for the proposed video production starring Donny Osmond. 'The show just works and everyone loves it. And I can almost watch it as if I hadn't written any of it.' The Palladium version proved Lloyd Webber's claims for its indestructible quality, what he called 'a strong core to the piece that makes it possible to hang anything on it, like an umbrella stand.'

There had never been a musical, as opposed to a pantomime, running like this at the Palladium, and even Lloyd Webber had been sceptical of its chances of success. All fears were confounded with a hit of extraordinary proportions, personal fortunes for the director and designer, and a net profit, by the end of the run, of nearly £4m. A hefty proportion of this went to the Palladium owners, Stoll Moss, who had fixed themselves a good investment deal in exchange for the buy-back of RUG shares after the death of Robert Holmes à Court.

Steven Pimlott became the latest post-Nunn director to have a hit and make a killing. He bought a well-appointed home in the Essex countryside for his wife and family, though he denies that he never need bother about working again. 'The biggest liberation, as a director, is that I don't have to choose the work because of what it will pay me. I have since discovered that I don't enjoy directing opera as much as I used to. I never stopped to think about it before because it was paying the fee. So it has been absolutely life-changing.'

This effect of association with Lloyd Webber on colleagues' material lives is a running balm, or sore, depending on luck and circumstances. Choreographers Arlene Phillips and Anthony van Laast have had their reputations enhanced and transformed. Gillian Lynne had an impregnable reputation before she had anything to do with *Cats*, but she would never have been able to take an indefinite rental on a top floor New York apartment with amazing views of the East River and the whole sweep of Manhattan, nor own a property in the Caribbean, before that windfall.

Before *Cats*, BC, she had been involved in four shows on in the West End, earning several hundred pounds a week in royalties, and was so busy she had borrowed £1,000 to hire a full-time secretary. After Deuteronomy, AD, it was pay-back time. In sharp contrast to the pleasure and ease new wealth gave an experienced trouper, the impact on a newcomer, like lyricist Charles Hart, as the *Phantom* bandwagon got rolling, was more complicated. His first job left him floored with a fortune, and he became like one of those troubled, mildly tragic Lottery winners who are not at all sure that getting lucky was the best thing that ever happened to them.

In keeping with his family background, Hart lives in a magnificently renovated tiny club theatre at Notting Hill, west London. Two blue plaques on the outside wall, either side of a brilliantly concealed new garage, declare the pedigree of the place: 'Here stood the Mercury Theatre 1931-87, founded by author and playwright Ashley Dukes (1885-1959) as a new stage for Plays by Poets'; and 'Here was the Birthplace of British Ballet, home of the Ballet Club and the Ballet Rambert founded by his wife Dame Marie Rambert (1888-1982).'

In the body of what was the theatre downstairs there are bedrooms leading off a curvilinear hallway, a snooker room, a garage. Upstairs, on what is effectively a new floor altogether, a central living area – topped by a brilliantly conceived kitchen – with grand piano, musical and audio gizmos, art deco furnishings and carpentered music cupboards, is set off with appropriately Gothic '*Phantom*-ness' by the ecclesiastical wooden arches.

Rambert's daughter, who lives a couple of doors down the street, had sold the place on to a property developer and Hart bought it from him six or seven years ago. 'There's far more money than I would ever know how to spend.' Some of it he gives away, some he invests, but he keeps no other properties except the house in the country he has bought for his parents. His one palpable luxury is a small aeroplane that is garaged at Maidenhead. 'Perhaps it was only a problem in my own mind, but there was a problem. I didn't feel friends were hanging around because of the money, I just felt awkward about it. So I lost touch with some of them. Of course it's lovely to be able to take friends to dinner, but you have to be careful not to create a hierarchy where you are constantly putting yourself at the top.'

Hart hopes that in ten years' time he will have surprised himself, in some way. Meanwhile, he has turned down some commissions because he was determined to do both music and lyrics, produced a fairly good song cycle – which Lloyd Webber presented at Sydmonton – added new words to Heinrich Marschner's nineteenth century Gothic opera *The Vampyr* for an extraordinary *Phantom*-meets-*Rocky Horror* BBC2 production by Janet Street-Porter and the late Nigel Finch, and worked with fellow composer Howard Goodall on *The Kissing-Dance*, a musical version (with very good stretches) of Oliver Goldsmith's *She Stoops To Conquer* which the National Youth Music Theatre premiered at the Brighton Festival in May 1998.

'Now I am laid back,' he says. 'It was a struggle at first because I felt a pressure on me to live up to something. It's funny when you're a writer: your world can feel very small and can involve very few other people. In fact I find it rather lonely, increasingly. On top of which I've always been a bit of a maverick. I never really wanted to mix that much with it all.'

Not worried about talking himself out of a future job, the modest Hart finds it surprising that Lloyd Webber has never written lyrics and suggests a reason. 'On *Aspects*, he had a very clear idea of what he wanted each bit of music to say. He'd play through and improvise a kind of text that didn't fit, or he'd talk a story over the music. But he'd never suggest words that would fit exactly. Musicians avoid this. You have to shake off your inhibitions to write lyrics. I certainly found it really embarrassing, when I started, in a way that I never found writing music embarrassing.'

There was another victim of the boom years, in the sense that the recession kicked in too early. In February 1992, Sarah Two's father, Grenville Brightman – a spry, dapper, grey-haired Barry Norman lookalike – was found dead in a fume-filled VW Golf (there were pills and whisky bottles nearby) in a wood near Tring, Hertfordshire, not far from the family home.

Aged fifty-seven, he had been divorced from Sarah's mother for five years. And his business was down the tubes. His two property firms had reported debts of £10m. Not even Sarah's divorce settlement of a reported £6m could have helped; and anyway, she had vowed never to touch that money. She talked for the first time about this tragedy five years later: 'If he thought it was the right thing to do it was, and I've only ever had good feelings about it . . . he was a very intense man who might have had a lot of anger in him. He was also very shy.'

In this post-divorce period, Sarah Brightman rebuilt her career first by performing the music of her former husband all over the world in concerts, and then by striking out in her own considerable right. There is always a colourful, dramatic element in her life, and true to form she suffered the further misfortune of losing most of her possessions and personal effects in the 1995 Los Angeles earthquake: everything, except her burgeoning art collection, was in storage in a warehouse crushed into oblivion by a collapsing motorway bridge.

Although she keeps a flat in London, she is now based in Hamburg, where she lives with an aristocratic German record producer, Count Frank Peterson. With Andrew's encouragement, she started collecting paintings and soon entered the market on her own, acquiring some fine British work by, among others, Stanley Spencer and Laura Knight. At the ripe old age of thirty-seven, she remains unrepentant about never having had children. And she hit the jackpot in 1997 when her single, 'Time to Say Goodbye', recorded with the blind Tuscan tenor, Andrea Bocelli, a protege of Pavarotti, went to the top of all the European charts.

The manner in which this success was achieved was

typical of her determination. Having moved to Germany, Sarah found it impossible to break into television, and nobody played her records on the radio. She was caught in a pincer movement between classical music snobs and pop snobs. So she found a song to introduce a popular boxer, Henry Maske, in a televised fight. She was not allowed in the ring, so she had herself suspended in wires above it. 'It was bizarre, it was a risk, but it worked. Twenty-two million people saw me.' The coup gave her immediate access to the radio waves, and she followed up with the tenor and the huge hit. The record sold nearly three million copies and won five platinum discs. In Germany, it became the bestselling single of all time.

Later that year she returned to Britain on tour and ended with a sell-out concert at the Albert Hall. In what James Rampton of the *Independent* called the most surprising moment in an evening almost monotonously awash with show-stoppers, Sarah beckoned on a sheepish-looking man in shirt-sleeves to play the piano. 'I'm so glad you could come,' she gushed. 'I only live round the corner, so I'd not much excuse,' replied her former husband. And she hoisted her bottom on to the piano where she perched like Michelle Pfeiffer in *The Fabulous Baker Boys* while together they gave an early airing to the title song of *Whistle Down the Wind*. For the encore, Andrea Bocelli (and a massed choir) joined her on stage to reprise their great hit song, and she was greeted, Rampton reported, 'by the sort of standing ovation, whooping and hollering the venerable Albert Hall usually only witnesses at the Last Night of the Proms'.

As the next big show, *Sunset Boulevard*, approached the starting blocks at the Sydmonton Festival of 1992, Sarah performed and recorded an anthem written by Lloyd Webber and Don Black for the opening of the Olympic Games in Barcelona. 'Amigos para siempre'

('Friends for Life') summed up her new relationship with Andrew, and she still looked as though she meant it as she sang the glutinous item with Jose Carreras, the Spanish tenor who is to Placido Domingo what, in golfing terms, Jose Maria Olazabal is to Severiano Ballesteros: a second-choice maestro just lacking the final personality punch, but undoubtedly a maestro in his own right.

These occasional compositions will make an interesting anthology one day. Lloyd Webber had supplied two television theme tunes for the World Cup competitions of 1978 and 1982. The first, for the tournament in Argentina, had a suitably *Evita*-ish flavour, the second was based on the Jellicle Ball in *Cats*. Now he feared a defeat at the polls for John Major's precarious Conservative government. A Labour victory would almost certainly instigate punitive taxation, a fate he had been spared by Mrs Thatcher's reforms. So he went public in endorsing Major and advised on the choice of his campaign music, a stirringly orchestrated rondo by Henry Purcell.

Rod Argent worked with Lloyd Webber on this commission, having previously refused an invitation to write an anthem for the Labour Party. Somehow, Argent's political affiliations emerged in the media, and heated headlines appeared in the Tory press about how Lloyd Webber was working with Red Rod from the Red House – his address in Bedfordshire. In the event, Labour under Neil Kinnock snatched defeat from the jaws of victory and, for his services to the arts, Lloyd Webber was knighted in the June 1992 Queen's Birthday Honours. When he arrived at Buckingham Palace in the presence of Her Majesty, the band struck up 'Love, Look Away' from Rodgers and Hammerstein's *Flower Drum Song*. 'They could at least have played "I Enjoy Being A Girl",' he remarked, resorting to his camp Cameron Mackintosh-style intonations.

That was at least a more upbeat, life-enhancing number from the same musical. It could have been worse. They might have given him a quick burst of 'Fan Tan Fannie'.

At the end of the year, RUG bought a half share of James Nederlander's Adelphi Theatre in the Strand, a house with a fine musicals pedigree, and an art deco interior dating from 1930 when the impresario C. B. Cochran presented Jessie Matthews in *Ever Green*, a musical play by Benn Levy with songs by Rodgers and Hart. The company spent £1.5m on a major refurbishment, re-named the main stalls bar for Jessie Matthews, and hung an array of photographs of the vivacious star around the walls.

It had always been an ambition of Lloyd Webber to create a vehicle in which Sarah Brightman could celebrate Jessie Matthews, whom she much resembles. Richard Rodgers was clearly as keen on Jessie as Andrew was on Sarah, and he felt a strong pull towards her for this reason. Publicising *Evita* on the BBC World Service in Bush House one morning, Lloyd Webber appeared on the same arts programme as Miss Matthews. He hadn't quite clicked into her identity until, as he squired her politely up the Strand afterwards towards Charing Cross, they passed the Adelphi and the penny dropped.

'Good God,' said Andrew, 'you had your biggest success, and your biggest scandal there [she fell in love with her co-star Sonnie Hale, and during the resultant, sensational High Court divorce case between Hale and his wife Evelyn Laye, another great star, the judge described her as 'a person of most odious mind'] . . . can I take you for a late lunch?'

She quickly said she did not want to talk about any of that and disappeared into the underground station, home to suburban Pinner on the Bakerloo and Metropolitan Line. She died in 1981, riddled with cancer, a sad and lonely, mostly forgotten, major star of the century.

Eight years later at Sydmonton, Sarah Brightman performed a wonderful Jessie Matthews cabaret and soon afterwards, in a Royal Variety Show paying tribute to legendary British musical artists, gave her spirited version of Jessie's great hit, 'Dancing on the Ceiling', high kicks and all. Lloyd Webber was in the audience, sitting near the still aggrieved Evelyn Laye, who turned in her seat and exclaimed to Sheridan Morley, 'Has that fucking bitch come back to haunt me again?'

Jessie Matthews was no Norma Desmond, having quietly accepted her lot and subsided into obscurity, but Lloyd Webber had bumped into Jessie just as Joe Gillis in Billy Wilder's great film *Sunset Boulevard* accidentally stumbles across the self-deluding, half-forgotten movie star who is still planning a comeback.

Lloyd Webber had turned the 1950 black and white movie over in his mind since first seeing it in the early 1970s. When he enquired after the rights, he discovered that Paramount, the studio who owned them, had sold them to Hal Prince – who, when Stephen Sondheim declined an invitation to work on an adaptation, asked Lloyd Webber to collaborate with him on turning Norma into a Doris Day figure of the 1950s. Lloyd Webber didn't fancy that idea much and let the matter go for a while. He talked to Tim Rice about it, but Rice says he never cared enough about some old movie actress going back to her film studio, or at least not as much as he did about somebody dying of cancer having failed to become president of her country.

A few years later, while contemplating *Phantom*, Lloyd Webber had lunch with Christopher Hampton to see if he would be interested in working with him. Hampton thought the idea a boring one and predicted failure with it, and started telling Lloyd Webber how he had been trying to get the rights to *Sunset Boulevard* for a possible libretto for David Pountney at the English National Opera.

Hampton had recently been in Los Angeles working on his brilliant and funny play about escapism, idealism, émigrés and Brecht in Tinsel Town, *Tales From Hollywood* – which ended, in homage to *Sunset Boulevard*, with a screenwriter narrating his own death by drowning in a Bel Air swimming pool – when it occured to him with a blinding conviction that Wilder's film, 'with its larger-than-life characters, its mood of hermetically sealed nostalgia and its emotional extravagance' was perfectly suited to musical adaptation.

Hampton wrote to Billy Wilder who replied in a letter dated 8 February 1983: 'Of course I am thrilled by your and the English National Opera's interest . . . However you must understand that although I am co-writer and director of the picture, I don't own any part of it. Nor do I have any control of the rights. Call it injustice or a cruel booboo of the capitalist system, the sole possessor of the property is Paramount Pictures. If you can straighten out the legalities with Paramount, and if they ask for my blessing, it will certainly be given.'

Over that lunch, Hampton discovered that the studio had been stalling him because they were in negotiations about those rights with someone else. Lloyd Webber. So Hampton asked Lloyd Webber if, when he got round to having a go, he would get in touch. By the time he heard about the project again, Lloyd Webber had come across Amy Powers, a twenty-eight-year-old lawyer writing lyrics for CBS Records, and the first draft performance of *Sunset* at Sydmonton in 1991 had been given with her words. Lloyd Webber had taken another flyer on an unknown talent, but things did not work out as well as they had with Charles Hart on *Phantom*.

Steady Don Black was called up once more and by the next year's Sydmonton showing, a fully fledged mini-staging by Trevor Nunn with Patti LuPone as Norma and Kevin Anderson as Joe Gillis, Amy Powers had disappeared and Black had been joined by Hampton.

Hampton, when invited to come aboard, had said he would not do so without writing the lyrics – he saw no point in working on a musical otherwise – and Lloyd Webber simply said that Black was already doing them and that Hampton should have lunch with him and sort it out.

He did, the two got along well, and they decided to do the whole thing together, book and lyrics. Black had never written a book, Hampton had not written lyrics, but had written poetry when younger and had translated some of his favourite French poets like Rimbaud and Verlaine (one of his finest plays, *Total Eclipse*, charted that particular friendship, prompting one critic to suggest that Verlaine's problem was that he was always chasing Rimbaud).

Owing to Hampton's commitment to other film projects, he could only work part-time on *Sunset*. The compromise involved Black and Hampton working together for the first week of each month in Lloyd Webber's house at Cap Ferrat and showing the composer their work at the end of each day. The music had mostly been written, though they did ask Lloyd Webber to write something for a scene in which Norma was looking at an old movie so that they could write a lyric about the beginning of cinema. The remarkable anthem 'New Ways to Dream' came back to them overnight.

Hampton enjoyed the freedom of the exercise, finding that writing to a preordained metre was easier than having to make the choice of one. And Black was impressed by his new colleague. 'He's obviously a very clever man, and it wouldn't surprise you to find him quoting Spinoza when he came round for a cup of tea. The main thing was that he said when you deal with a masterpiece, as this screenplay was, you don't mess with it. He knew a perfect operatic plot when he saw one. The torrid, emotional songs like "We Never Said Goodbye" and "The Perfect Year" he said were more my game.'

They were, and Black could even rewrite the lyrics of the first for Barbra Streisand when she began her sensational 1994 tour launch in Madison Square Garden, New York, as a thank-you to her for taking 'With One Look' – 'With one look I'll ignite a blaze, I'll return to my glory days' – into the charts as a single. Hampton did more work on the drugstore songs for Hollywood hopefuls, and the atmospheric second act opener for the cynical Joe, 'Sunset Boulevard'.

These items tapped into his tart and nauseated *Tales From Hollywood* mode and packed a neat punch, with good detail and clever rhymes in a swirling, driving rhythm: 'Sure I came out here to make my name, wanted my pool, my dose of fame; Wanted my parking space at Warner's. But, after a year, a one-room-hell, a Murphy bed, a rancid smell, wallpaper peeling at the corners . . . Sunset Boulevard, headline Boulevard, getting here is only the beginning. Sunset Boulevard, jackpot Boulevard, once you've won you have to go on winning.'

The structure was built round a few strong pillars. Black describes how Lloyd Webber has the tunes, and knows what he wants the songs to do. 'He likes to have not necessarily hits, but he likes them to *land* theatrically. To do the job. To call him a composer is not quite right. John Barry and Henry Mancini are song-writers. Andrew is much more a theatrical dramatist. He doesn't just play you a tune. He will say – for instance, in *Sunset* – Norma looks at Joe from the top of the stairs – and he's playing away at the piano – she turns round, then we move to G Minor, and he will play a few dozen more bars before we get to the tune. He sets it all up.'

Another contender for the role of Norma, Meryl Streep, was in the audience for the Sydmonton try-out and was reduced to tears by Patti LuPone's performance: tears of emotion and also tears, perhaps, of realisation that she could never match such a burn-out. It was not too far off what LuPone was about to achieve on the

West End stage, with what showbusiness writer Victor Davis described as 'her rattlesnake vitality, enormous elastic mouth and a voice that can break your heart'.

Black recalls the sunny Saturday morning at Sydmonton not just for the power of that performance but also for an instance of Lloyd Webber's self-knowing sense of humour. People are kept on their toes with him around, never more so than in the tension-filled build-up to a complicated Festival production. 'Everyone had been going mad. We were starting at eleven. And at five-to, he just looked at me and said, "I think there's time for one more tantrum" . . . he knew he was getting every-one in a terrible state, but that was marvellous. And of course he does get the best out of people.'

LuPone was undeniably laying claim to the part, though it was hard to see, even then, and without a grotesque make-up, why Kevin Anderson's almost contemporary Joe Gillis would object so much to sleeping with her. Admittedly Norma is only fifty years old, in the movie and the musical. The pertinent line, 'Nothing's wrong with being fifty, unless you're acting twenty', had been changed to 'Nothing's wrong with being your age . . .' Why? Lloyd Webber says that in Hollywood everyone *is* over fifty, so they felt they had to leave the issue a little more open to interpretation.

But the creepiness of the story lies in Norma's entrap-ment of Joe first as a gigolo and then as a messenger for her unperformable script. And she has to come across as a battered, crazed, bizarrely unattractive old crone, as Gloria Swanson certainly did on celluloid. As one theatre director said to me, 'Well, I'd do it with Patti LuPone. So the central thing about the movie was gone. Even if she does sing the bollocks off it.' And LuPone certainly did that.

She had won her Broadway reputation, and a Tony award, as Evita on Broadway in 1980. Her great grand aunt had been the coloratura soprano Adelina Patti, for whom she carried her Christian name. Of all Lloyd Webber divas, LuPone is the most brilliantly articulated as a singer, with a full open-chested belt when needed and a distinctive, dreamy quality in her upper register.

As the critic Matt Wolf remarked, her Evita had 'a delicious, come-hither sneer', something he felt eluded both Elaine Paige, and Madonna in the movie. And for all the plausible objections to her personification of an embattled, obscene old crone, Wolf is correct in saying that she walked an extremely taut tightrope between camp and pathos.

The story is almost *Phantom* 'Mark Two' in this respect, with another garish old creative spellbinder muscling in on a burgeoning love affair between Joe and his scriptwriter sidekick Betty Schaeffer, the successors to Christine and Raoul. The Gothic mansion on the Boulevard is the equivalent of the Phantom's lair, and is represented in Lloyd Webber's writing by the rancid fumigations of sexual anguish and despair seeping upwards not to the Opera, but to the romanticism and jive and bebop in Schwab's drugstore.

The extremities in contrast between fresh and stale air were expressed in the stunning musical contrasts in each location on New Year's Eve. The party with no guests in the mansion, where Joe dances a sad and poisonous tango with Norma, dissolves into the exultant, optimistic mambo riot ('We'll be down on our knees outside Grauman's Chinese') to which he flees, joining in the company of his friends, the hungry actors, prentice writers and under-employed composers.

As the show went forward to the Adelphi, there were slight ructions over the orchestrations and wobbles over the preparations. David Cullen, Lloyd Webber's regular collaborator on the orchestrations, was told by RUG that he wasn't needed this time, which upset him greatly. He loved the film noir music in *Sunset* and knew exactly what was needed.

'It was a great show for my particular technique of combining real instruments and synthesizers to make a very large sound. In the end, we didn't have a big band there but it sounded very big.' On the brink of the production schedule, Lloyd Webber decided he needed Cullen after all, and Cullen was so relieved that he agreed to a contract on post-recoupment royalties. Unluckily for him, the show never recouped its investment despite running for three years.

'If I had my way,' Cullen says, 'the orchestrations would be solely credited to me, because composers always have an input to the job and I don't think Andrew's is any larger. But I've come to accept it. On *Sunset*, they rang up and said Andrew wanted his name to precede mine on the orchestrations credit and I said, "Fine, I'll agree if you multiply my royalties by a factor of four." They didn't agree to that, but they could have done because it wouldn't have cost them anything: there *were* no royalties!'

Minor tiffs with RUG aside, Cullen is a modest, unassuming collaborator who admires Lloyd Webber inordinately. 'He has pushed things along enormously, hasn't he? I think his greatest gift to us has been the integrated musical, in that there is definitely now an almost operatic musical evolvement. Something that has been an introduction to one song will come back as the middle eight of another song, and it all sounds organic.' There is no better example of this than *Sunset*.

Hampton had misgivings about the scale of the production Nunn and designer John Napier were conceptualising. 'None of this was antagonistic. We just had different views. Andrew was pretty pleased with it as it stood so he let me defend it while Trevor came up with various suggestions, some of which were dotty, some of which weren't. Rehearsals were like a movie, with countless people milling around all the time, so they weren't much fun.

'But all the way through, Andrew was saying he should get someone else to produce it. He was finding it a strain doing both things. And it all got to the stage where more money was spent than could possibly be recouped.' A lot of this was to do with extravagance, but also with a vast over-spend on the budget by a production team hubristically out of control with self-confidence. The RUG were sole producers, the profits in the company were sky-high and the advance at the Adelphi box office was rocketing towards an unbelievable £5m mark.

Then another hitch. Ten tons of stage scenery started moving around of their own accord. The latest electronic valves which controlled the hydraulics were discovered to be reacting to every passing radio transmission from taxis, motorcycle couriers, even chaps on mobile phones. The opening was put back by thirteen days while the problem was expensively sorted out.

At last it was looking good, and on the delayed first night of 12 July 1993, it looked, and sounded, amazing. The big theme climbed out of the pit like the monster it prefigured, rising like heat from a swamp, swaggering alongside instant evocations of John Barry's *Goldfinger* theme, the 'Warsaw' Concerto and the sticky pudding gorgeousness of Tchaikovsky's 'Pathètique' symphony. It struck an immediate chord, this sound, and pinpointed a crucial quality: Lloyd Webber's most melodic music sounds familiar even when you've never heard it before, and even when it is obviously not obvious. This was dark, sour, insinuating, smelling of anguish and despair. There were echoes of the painful 'Ingemisco' in Lloyd Webber's *Requiem*.

Norma's mausoleum-style palazzo, as designed by Napier, was a baroque domestic cathedral, studded with spooky, wall-high inlets and alcoves, Moroccan arches, an organ, candelabra and, to start with, a dead monkey. When Joe is chased in off the road by the hoods wanting

241

their car back, Norma takes him for the monkey's undertaker. He thinks he's the man with the casket; Joe rhymes if the ape wasn't dead he would ask it. About Norma.

LuPone swept on almost immediately to sing 'With One Look' in dark glasses, glittering toque and cape. And she instantly expressed a resonant irony at the heart of the piece. Norma, closely modelled on the actress who actually played her in the movie, Gloria Swanson, was a relic of the silent movie era. With speech, in her book, the art form dwindled. She stayed big while the pictures got small, as the line goes.

And here was a silent goddess blasting our ear drums with a noise that would break the sound barrier. She was like the rusty diesel train who wins through in the high-tech setting of *Starlight Express* while advocating old values and the Nietzschean triumph of the individual will. Norma celebrates her power over an audience, her people in the dark of a cinema auditorium, by exhibiting just that power herself on a brightly lit stage. Having usurped the show's narrator, she turns on him savagely before the last bars have faded: 'Now, go!'

Compared to a sequence like that, the show had a lot that was less concentrated, an impression partly created by the elaborate scene changes and the literal attention to the film. It was never clear, for instance, why we had to see the actual car chase that delivers Joe to Norma's den, but having decided that we should, the production found no way of showing this apart from running the excerpt from the film itself. Which looked more like an admission of defeat than an act of homage. There was, though, a tremendous vigour to the music at this point, panning out to the big tune.

There is something in Tim Rice's view that, admirable as an adaptation though *Sunset* is, it adds zilch to the film. 'It would have been more interesting to have the story from Norma's point of view. We only have Joe's word for what happened. The story of the car chase might have been a pack of lies invented by Joe as an excuse to break into Norma's. You could have taken the story of the film and told it differently, a bit like the Jesus and Judas swap around we managed in *Superstar*.'

Attempts to lighten the mood of the piece were just as unsuccessful, in a clothes-fitting scene where Norma clowned as Chaplin and in a parallel second act number with a troupe of masseuses. Some of these weaknesses were addressed in the course of the run, and quite drastic changes after the Los Angeles premiere, all of them for the better, were incorporated after Lloyd Webber took the unprecedented action of closing the show in London for a fortnight.

London had been treated to another musical about Hollywood in the same period a few months earlier, when *City of Angels*, with music by Cy Coleman, lyrics by David Zippel and book by Larry Gelbart, had opened at the Prince of Wales. In New York, where the show ran for three years, I thought it was one of the best musicals I had ever seen. I still think so, but I'm never moved when I try and remember the songs.

Sharp and witty, Gelbart's libretto fed off Raymond Chandler and the Hollywood careers of battered writers F. Scott Fitzgerald and William Faulkner; the *doppelgänger* tradition of unhappy author and enslaved fictional character was developed to dizzying new theatrical heights. The writer Stine appeared in Technicolor while his private dick, Stone, inhabited a black and white 1940s movie. Each was in thrall to the other and, just to keep things complicated, both were stuck in the tale of a governing movie being made of the book by Stine in which Stone stars.

Like Sondheim, the show attracted reviews dripping with relief that musicals could still be civilised and sophisticated unlike so many much cruder examples of the genre. You might even say the show was aspiring to the condition of art, so much better a condition in critics' eyes than a desire to lift you out of your seats and shake you by the ears and livers. But however much the critics raved, the London audiences resolutely stayed at home. *City of Angels* enjoyed a *succès d'estime* and was a total flop. As George S. Kaufman once said, a *succès d'estime* is a *succès* that runs out of steam.

Like both *Phantom* and *Aspects, Sunset* is primarily a story about thwarted, intense romance, the gruesomeness of Norma's attention-seeking suicide bid, and her final, humiliating loss of her wig, directly comparable to Erik's exposure when the mask is ripped off. The heartbeat of these love-seeking monsters corresponds exactly, you feel, to the music gushing through the main geezer's geyser.

When it comes to the more anaemic romantic clinch between Joe and Betty, in a fine scene on the back lot of the studio, Lloyd Webber produces a classic romantic duet in the style of Rodgers and Hammerstein – 'Too Much in Love to Care' – which is far more melodically evasive but which has everything else: structure, good lyrics, passion, dramatic effectiveness.

The particularities of the lush melodies in *Sunset* derive from bold usage of open fifths, augmented fourths and sevenths, creating a harmonic equivalent of tropical decay and splendour. In the film, not only did Gloria Swanson appear as 'herself' disguised as Norma, but so did other luminaries of the silent movie era such as the director Erich von Stroheim as Max the manservant and, more fleetingly, Buster Keaton, H. B. Warner (who played Christ in Cecil B. DeMille's *King of Kings*) and the beautiful Anna Q. Nillson.

Max in the musical has some great moments of revelation, as when he reminisces about old Hollywood and takes the main tune simply, and unexpectedly, into a rising major-key resolution on the couplet, 'I've seen so many idols fall, she is the greatest star of all.' The condition of helpless emotional slavery is enriched when he reveals his identity as the great director Max von Mayerling (i.e., von Stroheim) – contemporary of D. W. Griffith and DeMille – who was actually the first of Norma's husbands when she was a mere girl of sixteen. His final task is to guide her through her last scene, a grim parody of her momentarily triumphant return to the studio earlier on.

He calls for lights, camera, action. Norma appears at the stop of the stairs, where the only lights are the popping of newsmen's flash bulbs below. But the illusion is complete: 'Just us and the cameras and all you wonderful people out there in the dark. And now, Mr DeMille, I'm ready for my close-up.'

Awash in fatuous dreams of her ludicrous Salome movie, and dressed to the nines in red streamers and clunking jewellery, she staggers down the staircase for her final call, still 'mad about the boy', still in search of the oblivion of either death or applause, whichever promises the greater recognition.

LuPone caught exactly the terror of a mind going dangerously adrift but also the reckless self-belief that carried her forward to the next gesture, the next cheap shot at fame, the next bid for unqualified sympathy. And then it all comes crashing down. In a most extraordinary way, the rollercoaster tragedy of this experience was reflected in the events surrounding both the continuing life of *Sunset* and the rapidly amassing fortunes of the Really Useful Group.

TEN

NORMA STRIKES BACK, THE BUBBLE BURSTS

There were two good reasons for opening *Sunset Boulevard* in Los Angeles before New York. First, it was a perfect homecoming and a chance to restore Norma Desmond in her natural habitat. Secondly, it neutralised the effect of the traditionally hostile New York critics, or at least kept them at bay for a while.

In fact, the *New York Times* had already passed judgement in London. Frank Rich mingled with the crowd at the Adelphi Theatre opening and informed his readers that Patti LuPone was miscast and unmoving as Norma Desmond.

'Glenn Close is not an actress,' Maggie Smith once said, 'she's an address.' Almost everyone else begged to differ. Including Christopher Hampton, who had worked with her on his film of *Les Liaisons Dangereuses*. He kept recommending her for the LA production of *Sunset*, but there was scepticism over whether she could sing or not, even though she had won a Tony for appearing in a musical, *Barnum*. So she was flown over on Concorde to audition.

When she arrived, Lloyd Webber took Hampton aside and told him that he had made two dinner arrangements for later in the evening: a table for half a dozen or so at his favourite local Italian restaurant, Mimmo d'Ischia, if the audition went well; and a table for two – Glenn

Close and Hampton – at the Four Seasons if it didn't. Hampton was horrified to realise that he had been detailed to take her out to dinner and explain why she couldn't have the part. Greatly to his relief, they all went to Mimmo d'Ischia.

Close had a remarkable triumph at the Shubert Theater in Century City, LA, less than a mile away from the real Sunset Boulevard, giving a mega-watt acting performance that swept away any lingering doubts about her vocal qualities. She never sang it as well as Betty Buckley or Elaine Paige, or indeed Patti LuPone, but most of those who have seen all versions proclaim her the most dramatic diva of all.

The show was much tighter, there was a new song ('Every Movie's A Circus') in the drugstore and a much darker tone prevailed. The first night party was held on a sound stage in the original Paramount Studios, where the movie was made, and the audience and revellers included Ronald Reagan, for whom William Holden – Joe Gillis in the film – had been best man at his wedding to Nancy.

Meanwhile, Patti LuPone was informed in London that she had in effect been sacked from the Broadway opening to which she had been contracted. She was not about to go quietly into that dark last night of her nine-month London run. It was a difficult situation, but she was not to blame. Backers for Broadway were cowed by the Rich reservations, and Glenn Close had taken LA by storm.

Paramount, who were putting up $6m of the ridiculously extravagant $12m Broadway budget, wanted Close in the saddle, or they were out. It was, said Lloyd Webber, 'as simple and as difficult as that.' Unless, of course, he insisted on having LuPone. But this was not exactly a Sarah Brightman in *Phantom* situation. And sometimes these nasty things happen in showbusiness.

Lloyd Webber now says that, in retrospect, LuPone had been 'quite difficult with everybody' but there was no love lost on either side. On the night Glenn Close opened in Los Angeles, Patti LuPone was 'off' in London. The Paramount people took this as another sign of volatility and risk. Those first night pictures of composer and star hugging each other in triumph soon turned to ashes. A financial settlement of a million dollars was reached and Lloyd Webber sent flowers but not an apology, leading LuPone to declare that Lloyd Webber had no feelings and was 'major bad karma'.

She milked her last night for all she could, even though the set broke down as she finished 'As If We Never Said Goodbye'. During the twenty-minute delay that followed the malfunction, the rumour in the bar was that she wasn't coming out until Lloyd Webber gave her another million. 'I said to the cast, "We are going out in a blaze of glory; there is no sadness here, only triumph," and I said it to them as much as I was convincing myself not to cry.'

As Close was confirmed to open at the Minskoff Theater in New York in November, a replacement had to be found for her in Los Angeles. What happened next was even more sensational than Norma's comeback. It was an invisible comeback, a phantom exaltation. Faye Dunaway, star of *Bonnie and Clyde* and Roman Polanski's *Chinatown*, was cast in the role, then sacked before she even opened. The entire Los Angeles production was closed down so that most of it could move, with Close, to New York.

When approached about the role, Dunaway had worked hard at singing lessons and auditioned successfully for David Caddick, the musical director, and Lloyd Webber in the Bel Air Hotel, Los Angeles. Everyone was happy, and a contract drawn up: $25,000 a week for a thirty-week run, plus five per cent of the weekly gross above $700,000 – a possible additional $13,000 a week assuming full houses. At the end of May, Dunaway met Trevor Nunn in New York and he became worried about the time available for rehearsals.

The actress was finishing work on a prior film commitment and Nunn had just seen Betty Buckley into the London production, with the changes, over an intense rehearsal period of several weeks. And Buckley was a hardened musical theatre pro. As time passed, the songs were lowered to suit Dunaway's range. With a 5 July opening looming, Nunn confessed when asked that, with two weeks to go, he could not guarantee that Dunaway would be 'musically ready'.

Lloyd Webber was shocked and dismayed; he had come across to Los Angeles not for this, but en route to see the Omaha production by Anthony van Laast of his *Requiem* as a ballet. Nunn reported that Dunaway wasn't making progress, that she couldn't hold pitch and that the outcome would almost certainly be embarrassing. A meeting attended by David Caddick, Peter Brown the publicist, Nunn and Lloyd Webber concluded that swift measures were in order.

A week later, it was regretfully announced that the show would close, but there were obvious legal implications in a statement issued by the RUG that Dunaway 'would not be able to play the role of Norma Desmond as previously announced'. Several contradictory statements and disavowals on who finally took the fateful decision did not clear the air. Dunaway fired off a few return salvoes and Lloyd Webber then released to the media a confidential letter in which he claimed he was acting in her own best interests and protecting her from a critics' roasting:

> Faye, I can completely understand your hurt and anger . . . but I know the right decision was taken. I think it has been most unfortunate in the way it has appeared in public. . . I hope this adequately

explains how very upset I am about the whole situation and also the way it has been handled. There is really nothing more I can say other than to hope that our paths cross one day in happier circumstances where my regard for you can be shown more fruitfully.

The response was a 37-page lawsuit filed by Dunaway's lawyers at Los Angeles Superior Court alleging that Lloyd Webber's real motive for closing the show was financial. With weekly overheads running at around $650,000, the Los Angeles production was still some $6m short of recouping its investment, despite playing to full houses for six months. Closing the show and transferring the cast to New York, it was alleged, saved the huge cost of rehearsing a new cast for Broadway.

This was a mistake. The integrity of the RUG was impugned on the basis of an implied motivation that had nothing to do with Dunaway's ability to deliver a satisfactory performance. The case could only rest on whether or not the RUG had acted unreasonably vis-à-vis the chances of her doing just that. RUG reacted robustly and Dunaway issued a further personal statement: 'I hope that I am the last in a long line of artists who have come to this man's productions in good faith and have suffered great personal and professional injury at his hands.'

This was another mistake. The discreetly handled departure of Roger Moore from *Aspects* and the less fortunate termination of Patti LuPone's Broadway contract hardly constituted a line of any sort, let alone a long one. RUG hit back with a 123-page court document which referred ungallantly to the case as 'the plight of an over-50 actress'. There was only one sensible conclusion to this sordid affair, and that was an out of court settlement, with a big pay-off for Dunaway –

perhaps in the region of $2m – and signatures on both sides promising not to bad-mouth each other again.

It was all entertaining, knockabout stuff, even though it didn't do all that much for Lloyd Webber's peace of mind or, he later concluded, his health. The whole episode he now describes as 'the blackest period in my whole life in theatre'. He came, he says, very close to 'chucking it all in'. Nothing was worth doing with these sorts of upsets. On top of that, just before Glenn Close had opened, his mother had died, aged seventy, of cancer in London, and he had dashed back two days later for the funeral. He was only sorry that she had not lived to see the triumph of *Sunset* in its home town.

He loved Jean and she had always been supportive of his efforts in later life. But the distance placed between them by her closeness to John Lill and other proteges in Harrington Court had always left its mark, and theirs was not the cosiest of mother and son partnerships. But he came to admire her steeliness and her honesty. She was never swept away by her son's fame or fortune and never changed the way that she lived.

A defining image would be of Jean standing in a sea of tuxedos at one of Andrew's first nights wearing a dowdy beige overcoat, basic spectacles and her hair bunched at the back in a rubber band. The unaffected frugality of her presence cut through the back-slapping noise and brouhaha like a knife through greasy butter.

By the time *Sunset* reached New York, the critic who had started the whole domino diva effect, Frank Rich, had changed jobs on *The Times* and had been succeeded by an altogether mellower writer, David Richards, who gave Lloyd Webber his first outright enthusiastic notice in that paper. Richards loved the show and he loved Glenn Close: 'The musical allows [her] to give one of those legendary performances people will be talking about years from now . . . the actress takes breathtaking risks, venturing so far out on a limb at times that you fear it will snap. It doesn't.'

But the curse of Norma struck again – she was far more disruptive a character, it was turning out, than the Phantom at his most vengeful. When Close took a twelve-day break in March, the box office takings were adjusted by a well-meaning RUG New York executive in order to disguise a drop in receipts. Close was furious and released her letter to Andrew: 'You and your people have made me and my colleagues feel that *all* you care about is the money.'

As Oscar Wilde might have nearly said, to have alienated one Norma Desmond could be regarded as a misfortune, but to have alienated three was beginning to look like suicidal carelessness. Lloyd Webber could justly say that he knew nothing about what had gone on in New York, and the matter was quickly and amicably patched up. The executive responsible offered to resign, but was forgiven and fully reinstated. Lloyd Webber and Close remain bosom buddies to this day.

Although *Sunset* opened on Broadway to a record-breaking advance of over $30m, and gleaned a review like that in *The Times*, it still failed to turn into a long-runner like *Cats* and *Phantom*. Which proved that Rich had a point when he said that the all-powerful *Times* critic was not, in the end, all that powerful. People tended to end up going to see what they wanted to see. And, as the RUG was coming to realise the hard way, there was a limit to the appeal of *Sunset*.

Mel Brooks had once told Christopher Hampton, at a meeting to discuss an ailing musical about the Rothschilds that neither was directly involved with, that there were two kinds of show, a family show and a hard-nosed show. In a family show about the Rothschilds, he said, the audience wants to see the walls of the ghetto come down. 'But Mel, historically . . .' stuttered one of the authors . . . 'Don't give me historically,' yelled back

Brooks. 'I pay fifty bucks for the tickets, I pay twenty bucks to park my car, there's the baby-sitter, there's the goddam restaurant. I am *entitled* to see the walls of the ghetto come down.'

Hampton and others were coming to the conclusion that *Sunset* was a hard-nosed show. It had a strong appeal to a large, but limited, audience. The RUG assumed that *Sunset* was going to be another *Phantom*. The company was unstoppable, as Patrick McKenna supervised an accelerated earn-out on *Phantom* – by issuing licences for productions in Europe that Brian Brolly had hesitated over – and the surprise phenomenon of the rejuvenated *Joseph*. In 1994, Lloyd Webber's personal earnings were shown as £12m, his fortune estimated at £385m.

The luck went their way, too. Four routine audits of licensees in Canada and the United States delivered back to the company not the expected few hundred thousands of dollars, but millions. In the 1991 deal with Polygram, there was an accelerated payment due for their entitlement, conditional on the results achieved up to 1994.

And, at that time, neither Polygram nor McKenna believed it was achievable. But with *Joseph* and the audits, the company did hit those targets. And at the end of the 1995 financial year, the group reported that profits had soared by 800 per cent to £46m. This was a truly astonishing performance by any standards, and at this point Patrick McKenna was looking to double the size of the company over the next five years.

In this mood of optimism, the company decided that it would produce, exclusively and independently, *Sunset* in those markets with partners who were theatre builders. Thus, in 1995, a £25m glass-fronted, 1500-seater theatre rose up in green fields at the confluence of the Rhine and the Main rivers, adjoining a 187-room hotel in a complex built round a lake. The site was surrounded by forests, at the end of an autobahn a twenty-minute drive away from Frankfurt. Nobody knew where it was. And as Lloyd Webber now admits, '*Sunset* was a great production but it simply wasn't the sort of show you could stick outside on a web of motorways, in the way we did very successfully with *Starlight*. It needs a big city buzz around it. It's a metropolitan show.'

The *Sunset* development was handled for the RUG by its new head of theatre division, Kevin Wallace, a dapper, guarded Irishman who had been working for the company in Germany and Switzerland; and funded by a hotel group hoping misguidedly for cultural tourist trade. Wallace had been heading for a career in Irish parliamentary politics as a member of Garret Fitzgerald's (now John Bruton's) Finna Gael party but was diverted by a spell at drama school in London. He was now fully enmeshed in theatre politics, and enjoyed the cut and thrust of the RUG's stated ambitions of owning and operating theatres in Europe.

At the same time, across the Swiss border in Basle, a similar operation funded by city businessmen was purpose-building a theatre for *Phantom* and ceding all production rights to the RUG with an option to put in more Lloyd Webber shows should *Phantom* come a cropper. (Although *Phantom* had been co-produced originally with Cameron Mackintosh, he held no producing rights in the show outside the English-speaking countries.)

The omens were good, as long as the theatrical properties could sustain the investment. At this time, in January 1995, there was reason to suppose that *Sunset* might do as well as *Cats* and *Phantom* in Hamburg (running since 1986 and 1990 respectively) and *Starlight* in Bochum, a smash hit since 1990. These three shows had all been licensed to the one entrepreneur, Fritz Kurz, whose Stella company had broken through a hostile, heavily subsidised theatre culture, to prove what nobody thought possible in post-war Germany: that musicals could be commercially successful.

All three of those shows are running still. *Sunset*, managed and produced by the RUG alone, isn't. A conclusion may be drawn two ways: the RUG either overestimated its own ability to handle the German market; or badly overestimated the appeal of *Sunset*. Something of both, most likely. And proof, surely, that the ownership and exploitation of copyrights, on which the wealth of Lloyd Webber's company is founded, is a tricky business. *Phantom* managed solely by the RUG in Basle was a comparative disaster, closing within two years after sustaining 'substantial weekly running costs' and losing over three hundred jobs.

Even *Cats* and *Phantom* could have gone wrong in Hamburg if they had not been handled by a man with the particular, ebullient genius of Fritz Kurz. By the time *Cats* opened in Hamburg, the show was already a huge hit in Sydney, as well as in New York, and productions were running in Tokyo, Vienna (where Gillian Lynne had discovered Ute Lemper and cast her in the small role of Bombarulina), Budapest, Oslo, Los Angeles and Toronto.

But Germany was different. Kurz, a London-based, American-educated entrepreneur from Stuttgart, invented himself as Germany's lone commercial theatre producer. 'In Germany,' he says, 'you have to build a theatre each time you do a musical.' He had been introduced to the RUG by Michael Sydney-Smith, whom he had met at the Sorbonne in 1973.

Kurz secured – rent-free from the state – the disused, cavernous Operettenhaus on the Reeperbahn, Hamburg's red light district, and saved it from becoming a parking lot. Then, having convinced the RUG board that he was their man, and that he should have the licence to produce *Kattzen*, he initiated the first credit card theatre bookings service in Germany – opening up thirty telephone lines –

and set about publicity with a most un-Teutonic, American-style enthusiasm.

Lloyd Webber viewed this operation with amusement and suspicion. To which he soon added alarm when Kurz chartered a rackety old propellor-driven Viscount aeroplane from Richard Branson to ferry the composer and his crowd over to Hamburg for the premiere. There was no catering on board and a furious and increasingly claustrophobic Lloyd Webber, egged on by Cameron Mackintosh in 'school's out' vein, wanted to leave the plane before they even took off. One of Kurz's imposing aristocratic sidekicks, Count Peter von Recklinhausen, locked all the doors and said that it was impossible to turn back.

The composer's black mood hardly abated on arrival when shown to a suite in the Atlantic Hotel in which Adolf Hitler was reputed to have stayed. Mackintosh shouts of 'Adolf slept here' and 'Vee haf vays of making you money' only made things worse. With room service hastily summoned, the *stürm* clouds lifted *und* drinks were *drang* as he and Mackintosh jumped on a table, left index fingers over upper lips, right arms flung in the air, and vented their fury on the Führer.

At which exact point the deeply unamused hotel manager and a team of flunkeys arrived to take the maestro's inside leg measurement: he had not brought a dinner jacket and was being provided for by his hosts. Nothing would induce Lloyd Webber to attend a civic reception in the Rathaus, where the Queen's cousin, Lord Lichfield, was on hand to take photographs for the souvenir brochure. But the performance at the ice-cream and champagne premiere pleased him greatly. And he was impressed by Kurz's efficiency, marketing skills and organisational flair. Whereas about 30 per cent of the London *Cats* audience travels from outside the capital – from the Home Counties and Greater London – the figure in Hamburg is 80 per cent. These people have to be identified, targeted and bussed in.

Within a week, the RUG issued Kurz with the licence to produce *Starlight Express* in Bochum, a small Ruhr town with a potential audience of twenty million people within a two hours' travel radius. Still, he risked being thought of as a lunatic similar to the obsessive hero in Werner Herzog's *Fitzcarraldo* – 'Fritzcarraldo'? – who drags a steamship over a hill to build an opera house in the middle of the Peruvian jungle. The clever thing – and the difference – was that Kurz was acting on a detailed socio-economic survey of a district that was actively seeking regeneration.

The state and the city built the theatre, and Patrick McKenna supervised the business plans. Kurz and McKenna arranged a system of contracts and small investment based on the London way of doing things. And Kurz's brother organised the bus operation, selling seats to individual bus companies which ticketed outings from schools, factories and community centres all over the Ruhr valley and even into Belgium. All of these outlets depended on repeat bookings – birthday treats, office outings, and so on – to ensure the longevity of the run. Even today, *Starlight* in Bochum remains a favourite outing for sports teams and visiting business parties.

The Ruhr district was a traditional steel and mining area, now hit by the recession and unemployment. The state wanted to move into the modern, post-industrial age and *Starlight* became an agent, or at the very least, a symbol of that desire. A local firm produced all the lasers for the show. Ironically, *Starlight* itself celebrated a vanished age of steam railways in the power and speed of modern electric and diesel engines. Trevor Nunn and John Napier were offered a new kind of space with ramps and an amphitheatre, so the cast could skate through the entire audience; there was not that merely partial involvement, depending on where you are sitting, that sometimes takes the edge off *Starlight* in London.

The Lloyd Webber invasion of Germany became seriously controversial with *Phantom*, for which Kurz wanted to restore and re-build the Old Flora music hall in a slightly rundown, though attractive and bohemian, district of Hamburg. He raised the money and hired the man who had built the Bochum theatre to begin the task. But he was thwarted by a local residents' campaign, and violent demonstrations – 'Kill Kurz' slogans were painted on billboards – forced him to a halt, leaving a huge hole in the ground and another huge hole in his pocket.

Undaunted, he fought back against extreme political pressures and found another site, the 'New Flora', incorporated as part of a development project just a couple of hundred yards away across a four-lane motorway. (By this time Kurz and his company Stella had lost an entire $8.8m investment on the Broadway production of *Carrie*, a dreadfully misguided and inadequate musical based on Stephen King's great novel, which he had first tried out under the auspices of the Royal Shakespeare Company, still anxious to find another *Les Misérables*.)

Phantom opened there on 1 July 1990, with the Wagnerian tenor Peter Hofmann taking a break from Bayreuth. The box office advance was immense. The bookings were unprecedented. But the locals, bolstered by the political activists and cultural nay-sayers, made it a night to remember in more ways than one. Next day's Hamburg newspaper had three pages on 'Der Phantom-Skandal', with photographs of molested first-nighters, ranks of policemen with helmets and riot shields, and angry demonstrators blocking the streets and theatre access. Lloyd Webber was asked to enter the theatre by the stage door but he refused, marching bravely through the mayhem at some considerable personal risk.

In the following year, 1991, Fritz Kurz left Stella, and his partner, Rolf Deyhle, an impresario and businessman who had been drafted in by the banks when the financial health of the company was threatened by the *Carrie* debacle, took over completely. Since then, Stella have built two theatres in Stuttgart for Cameron Mackintosh's *Miss Saigon* and Disney's *Beauty and the Beast*, but these ventures have not proved as successful. And the boom time of ten years ago is thought to be fading.

The failure of *Sunset* was undoubtedly part of this, but you also feel that the particular dynamism of a man like Kurz is the missing factor. Not putting *Sunset* out to other investors proved a costly mistake and the idea of negotiating with people in the Nevada desert, Los Angeles, over an entertainment complex there was soon scrapped. The quest for a greater share of profitability in all projects led to this erosion of outside investment and made the company vulnerable to losses which they considered unthinkable.

Bill Taylor, the RUG's finance director and later successor to his friend McKenna as chief executive, admits mistakes were made. '*Sunset* did no good at all to our image as producers. It did well on Broadway, recouping 97 per cent of its investment, but that is not a success by our standards. The Los Angeles investors lost money because, although there was an override from New York to them, it didn't amount to very much. And a subsequent major US tour, costing ten million dollars and starring Betty Buckley, lost money in every single territory apart from Chicago. This was a serious setback. We badly misjudged the market.'

The company's view that *Sunset* could be another *Cats* or *Phantom* was seriously misguided. And yet there were many who counted it among the best of all Lloyd Webber's shows. Taylor noted a pattern. 'It always played very well and invariably received good reviews. But it hit a wall and dropped away after nine months. The word of mouth was good, but not good enough.

And the show didn't have the same depth of audience. It's not a children's show, obviously. It's a complex story, with complex, not particularly attractive, characters.' In other words, definitely hard-nosed.

Bad news like this was gleefully seized upon in some quarters to prove that Lloyd Webber was all washed up. Because he was the originating source of all the company's activity, his status as an artist was continuously muddled with his image as a businessman. This was not something he could complain about, necessarily, but it didn't help when it came to considering the work. Or at least, in the media, it didn't.

A rumour emerged in 1995 that the RUG might be interested in acquiring the ailing *Express* newspapers. Lloyd Webber's friend Sir Nicholas Lloyd, who had lately resigned from editing the daily title (his wife, Eve Pollard, edited the *Sunday Express* for a time), had told him that he never had enough money to hire decent journalists. But his colleagues on the RUG board pointed out that, as they all knew nothing about newspapers, the venture would be foolhardy.

In response, Mark Lawson opined in the *Guardian* that Lloyd Webber, with Richard Branson and Jeffrey Archer, embodied the Thatcherite theory of the acceptable uses of art, and that in all three cases the art was almost incidental to other ambitions. 'In his post-Rice shows, Lloyd Webber achieved,' he said, 'a sort of theatrical Esperanto, the first artistic global franchise. Every one-horse town in the world now has Coca-Cola, McDonald's, CNN and a Lloyd Webber show.'

The accusation was fair on the grounds of the RUG's avowedly cloning policy of the shows. And of course this kind of comment crept increasingly into criticism which in turn assumed a blandness in the work itself where usually none existed at all. It was a self-inflicted image problem, and many of the frustrations that boiled over two years later, as the Really Useful cracked open and losses of £10m were announced (in 1997) following two years of profits in excess of £30m, were part of Lloyd Webber's own difficulty in reconciling his artistic identity with his need to build empires.

There were also local repercussions following the new production style instigated by McKenna. The ticket agencies in London had enjoyed a high old time in the 1980s thanks to Lloyd Webber and Mackintosh, and McKenna thought he should re-write the rules of how the facts of everyday theatre life worked on the ground. So he cut the agencies out of the equation. This was an unnecessary move, because if *Sunset* had been a huge hit, the RUG would have made a lot of money anyway, losing well under ten per cent of that net income to the agents.

But it was also an unwise move, for the agents then simply removed their operation to other shows and *Sunset* undoubtedly suffered, losing block bookings to, say, *Miss Saigon*, which struggled on through rocky periods at the box office, easily outlasting *Sunset* which closed after three and a half years.

By the time *Sunset* closed in London they were running out of Normas. Everyone in the world except Boy George had played the part. Elaine Paige had scored a triumph in the role in New York, though the stage carpenters had been compelled to add three inches to the stairs because she proved partly invisible while descending them – 'With One Look', she disappeared behind the bannister.

Paige had been knocking 'em dead as Edith Piaf when *Sunset* came round the first time, but she stood in for a few weeks when Betty Buckley (who had taken over from LuPone) had to go into hospital, and then succeeded her in her own right, playing for nine months in London and several in New York, her debut there. 'It was wonderful, and well worth the wait. They went wild, and I was shocked and flabbergasted.' She found the role as challenging dramatically, though not musically, as Evita.

'All that emotional stuff in Andrew's music is so exhausting. And in *Sunset*, it's up and down that bloody staircase in heavily beaded, very heavy dresses. No laughing matter, believe me.' Well, no, but it might have been with Boy George. And it nearly was with Petula Clark, who was the last London Norma.

On the last night, 5 April 1997, the Adelphi front rows are packed with Pet Clark fans cheering every little gesture and curious intonation. At one point, she even flaps at them to sit down during an ovation. The cheap garishness of this performance made her resemble, in her final Salome costume, a transvestite geisha.

The music still soars and thrills, and the ensemble numbers are as tight and as evocative as ever. The score will live, no question. But the clumsiness of the staging becomes more of a problem with weaker performers. The opening effect of a body floating in a pool is still brilliant. And the arrival back at the studios surely loses impact by being played side-on, not full to the audience as the gates are breached. The clunkiness of the plotting in the second act, the pale echo of *Phantom*-ness about the piece, was disguised originally by the electrifying performances of LuPone and Kevin Anderson.

At the curtain calls, Pet declines her fans' request for a chorus of 'Down Town', and gracefully thanks everyone involved. Nunn, Black and Hampton sidle on sheepishly from the wings. No sign of Lloyd Webber. Nunn starts to speak, and after a few minutes you fear he might never stop. But he does, by pulling an extraordinary stunt.

From the stage, he greets Patti LuPone in the stalls. She acknowledges the applause. She is in town to make a London comeback as Maria Callas in Terrence McNally's *Master Class*. And, who knows, to exorcise the troubling, troubled ghost of Norma Desmond.

ELEVEN

MODERNISM AND THE MUSICAL: SPOT THAT TUNE

An American critic called Joe Queenan published an abrasively entertaining book in 1998 – *Red Lobster, White Trash and the Blue Lagoon* – in which he woke up one morning and decided to make a tour of low-grade popular culture. After years of writing about high-falutin respectable popular culture – Igor Stravinsky, Henry James novels, Satyajit Ray movies – that nobody less intelligent than himself cared about, he decided to turn his ferocious, unforgiving gaze on the cultural phenomena that appealed to the downtrodden, burger-scoffing, crimplene-contained masses. Books by Danielle Steel. Tony Orlando and the Osmonds. CDs by Michael Bolton.

And *Cats*. The fearless one enters what he calls 'the fiendishly vapid world of Andrew Lloyd Webber' and discovers something much worse than he expected. Nothing, he declares, had prepared him for 'the epic suckiness' of *Cats*, not even his alleged familiarity with the composer's 'curiously mesozoic pop music'. He recounts the relief with which he listens to the reprise of 'Memory' because all the other songs are so awful.

Everyone's entitled to their opinion, and we can't help what we feel. Critical reactions mean nothing without the passion to articulate them. Similarly, criticism is about measuring achievement, and the experience of criticism in the performing arts must at least involve a degree of participation, if not submission. Coming out with your prejudices confirmed is easy. Witless abuse – I know, I've done it – is even easier. And staying at home, metaphorically and literally, is the easiest thing of all. Having set sail on what he describes as a Sea of Poop, Queenan returns to his brainy high ground, his integrity intact, totally convinced, like Odysseus, that he would have been a whole lot better off pulling the duvet over his ears and leaving the door shut.

Even intelligent theatre practitioners make glib assumptions about the nature of Lloyd Webber's musicals because they don't tally with their own preferences. The young director/performer Phelim McDermott was interviewed in the *Independent* about a marvellous deadpan musical adaptation he made of the *Struwwelpeter* cautionary stories for children. He elaborated on his interest in improvisational theatre to create a new form of 'theatrical biography', using an audience member's story as a basis for a performance. He admitted an element of therapy was involved. 'I'd rather say it's just story-telling, which is the basis of therapy anyway. That's probably why therapy exists, because in society story-telling has been lost, really: it's been turned into *Cats*.'

You can hear the tone in the voice. But of course there is a story in *Cats*, and it's one of selection, redemption and celebration. The narrative framework was devised as a means of containing the T. S. Eliot material in exactly the same way as McDermott and his colleagues devised a narrative in their show – one of an unloved, freakish child in a repressive household – to contain the different stories of Heinrich Hoffmann. The gap between *Struwwelpeter* and *Cats* is one of style, not content, of an attitude towards populism, not towards the value of the material itself. *Cats* aims to please many, *Struwwelpeter* aims to please not so many. The schism occurs in the assumption that to do the first necessarily impugns your integrity and scuppers your credibility.

Julian Lloyd Webber, now an internationally renowned soloist, fulfils his virtuoso promise in a busy career. Rarely have two musical siblings been so prominently successful

Original cast members of *Starlight Express*, including Stephanie Lawrence (*seated, front*), with choreographer Arlene Phillips (*seated, far left*), and ALW flanked by director Trevor Nunn (*left*) and lyricist Richard Stilgoe

ALW receiving an honorary doctorate from President George Bush in 1990

Snapped at a recent Sydmonton Festival after the Sunday afternoon croquet competition: ALW; PR executive Matthew Freud; Really Useful Group director Bill Taylor (with cup); the former Conservative cabinet minister, John Selwyn Gummer; and Simon Marsh, manager of all the Lloyd Webber horses

The world premiere of *Cricket* in 1986 at Windsor Castle marked a brief reunion of Rice and Lloyd Webber. The short piece, later repeated at Sydmonton but never professionally presented, was commissioned by the Queen's third son, Prince Edward, to celebrate her sixtieth birthday. Prince Edward worked briefly for the Really Useful Group as a production assistant in 1988. He is pictured second left with Her Majesty and Prince Philip, cast members Sarah Payne and the late Ian Charleson, Rice, ALW and director Trevor Nunn

ALW with film director Alan Parker (*left*) supping Guinness and planning the next shot in an Irish pub in Budapest where much of the location work on *Evita* took place

Sarah Brightman and Michael Crawford sing the music of the night in *Phantom of the Opera* at Her Majesty's in 1986. The show still plays to packed houses in London and New York, and both Brightman and Crawford have gone on to develop spectacular solo singing careers

(*above left*) Michael Ball and Ann Crumb in the first production of
Aspects of Love at the Prince of Wales in 1989

(*above right*) ALW with (*from left*) his friend and advisor Peter Brown,
his father-in-law Brigadier Adam Gurdon, and long-term colleague
Anthony Pye-Jeary outside McCarthy's public house in Fethard,
County Tipperary

Trevor Nunn, director of *Sunset Boulevard*, listens to ALW making a
point in the build-up to the 1993 opening. In the stalls of the
Adelphi Theatre, lyricists and co-librettists, Christopher Hampton
(*front*) and Don Black, keep their counsel

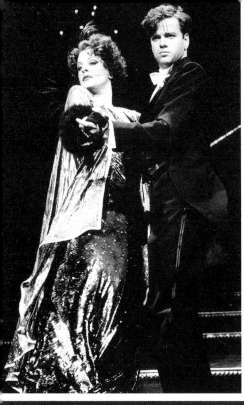

Patti LuPone and
Kevin Anderson dance
a New Year tango in
the original London
production of *Sunset
Boulevard*

Petula Clark is latest in
a line of distinguished
Norma Desmonds in
Sunset Boulevard,
following Betty
Buckley, Glenn Close
and Elaine Paige. But
the curse of Norma
may have caused a
downturn in the
fortunes of the Really
Useful Group

ALW and Madeleine with Alastair, aged one week,
at Sydmonton in 1992

Veronica Hart as Candy and Dean Collinson as Arnos sing
'Tyre Tracks and Broken Hearts' and long for escape in
Whistle Down the Wind at the Aldwych in 1998

ALW keeping afloat in the sunshine with Alastair (*left*), Bella and
Billy at home in the pool in the South of France

Trevor Nunn underestimated the size of this problem of how your work might be so easily despised because of its broad appeal: 'I was fascinated by what we mean by populism, and how it might be possible to do a work with a hidden underlay, and for a populist audience still to get it. It seems to me it works.' Which explains the longevity of the show's run. The fact that Japanese tourists flock to *Cats* does not in itself contaminate the original undertaking, though it does for people like Joe Queenan. Innocent audiences might first be seduced by the publicity and the hype. But that doesn't form their responses once they are inside a theatre.

I've seen *Cats* several times, and I don't honestly think it's a less worthwhile evening in the theatre than your average night out at the Royal Shakespeare Company. But we all, to a greater or lesser degree, have a problem with the sadly conflicting notions of serious theatre and popular entertainment.

No-one's reputation defines this appalling and regrettable rift between high and low culture more vividly than Andrew Lloyd Webber. The popularity of his work guarantees the contempt of critics who take themselves more seriously than the work they review. And what has been justly described as 'the culture of contempt' has ratified the Midas of Musicals as chief villain in our daily work and play. To a quite extra-ordinary degree, the very mention of a Lloyd Webber musical validates a response of sanctioned sneering, knee-jerk knocking and politically correct lip-curling. This mobster mockery, of course, is an aspect of metro-politan cultural snobbery of the sort that has always surrounded opera and light entertainment.

Duke Ellington once said that there were only two kinds of music. Good and bad. It is one of Lloyd Webber's favourite aphorisms. And it is an understandable source of pain to him that the critical consensus mostly consigns him to the second category. Not infrequently his name is taken in vain by other artists on the basis of this consensus. It is all tied up with his success, and their envy, as if somehow he's got something he doesn't deserve by underhand means. The phenomenon almost constitutes a subculture in itself. It is not cool to like Andrew Lloyd Webber.

In a recent British film, *Shooting Fish*, a charming, fresh but ultimately derivative amalgam of *Shallow Grave*, *Four Weddings and a Funeral*, and *Bonnie and Clyde*, the young con artists sting four free tickets to the new Lloyd Webber musical. The poster says 'Dogs', with a critical puff ('A barking good show'), while inside an audience of Japanese tourists sleep on each others' shoulders to the soporific accompaniment of an *Evita*-ish theme playing in the background.

It's open house on Lloyd Webber in the theatre itself, too. In Phyllis Nagy's *The Strip*, one of the best plays presented at the Royal Court in recent years, a redneck mass murderer exasperatedly tries to remember where he has heard before Yvonne Elliman's beautiful recording of 'I Don't Know How to Love Him' – 'I know it comes from some fucked up Limey musical thee-a-ter thingamajig with a band of hippies humping Jesus . . .'

In the same year as *The Strip*, 1995, the Young Vic presented Martin Crimp's contemporary version of Molière's *The Misanthrope*, in which the creepy theatre critic Covington offers a helping hand to the disaffected, intolerant Alceste:

'We critics are artists too:
perhaps you don't realize just how much I could do for you.
Who knows – it might even reach the stage
where I could get you on to the front page
– like a Lloyd Webber musical – or some other natural disaster . . .
(*Laughs at his own joke.*)
OK, OK, you're wondering what I'm after . . .'

And in David Hare's *The Blue Room* (1998), a new version of Arthur Schnitzler's sexual daisy-chain *La Ronde* in which Iain Glen played, in one of the ten playlets, a dim and conceited playwright, and Nicole Kidman a cocaine-sniffing model, the playwright asks the model if she ever goes to the theatre. 'My aunt took me to *The Phantom*.' 'I said the theatre!'

This is fairly amusing and also fairly obvious. Less amusing and a lot more angry is the denunciation of William, the keyboard player and pop song writer hero of Jonathan Coe's novel *The Dwarves of Death*, who is enmeshed in a drugs and murder mystery and subjected to a catalogue of hideous experiences: urban alienation, romantic rejection, humiliation and physical violence. And, worse than any of these, a new Andrew Lloyd Webber musical.

This paragon hails from Sheffield, like Jarvis Cocker, though nothing he says or does suggests he has an ounce of Cocker's talent. But like Jimmy Porter, he does have a gift for spiteful and entertaining invective. And he fancies himself as a music critic. He yearns for a beautiful middle-class girl called Madeleine – the novel was published in 1990 – who cares about old people and makes him take her to see *Phantom of the Opera*.

He reckons that to accuse Lloyd Webber of stealing tunes is to make him more interesting than he is, though he can't resist showing off his anorak-like nerdiness in declaring that one of the cadences in 'Think of Me' sounds exactly like Puccini's 'O Mio Bambino Caro' (goodness me, the man's a marvel, a musical Sherlock Holmes) and that there is a recurrring phrase ripped off from Prokofiev's *Cinderella*.

That I cannot vouch for, though I do know that Prokofiev's *Cinderella* is one of Lloyd Webber's favourite pieces – he was shivering with pleasure on hearing the score beautifully played at the West End opening of Matthew Bourne's brilliant 'London during the Blitz' staging of the ballet in October 1997 – and that Prokofiev once deduced there were a million tunes still available to people who were inclined to go looking for them.

Equally certainly, the same notes – from C to C, there are only thirteen on the keyboard, eight white and five black – do come round every now and again and often in the same order. The orchestrator David Cullen says, 'Andrew has this terrific melodic gift, and I do very much resent people criticising him for borrowing and stealing. He's in the business, generally, of writing very simple melodies. Not simpler than the average pop song but simpler than most show songs, perhaps. If that's what you are doing, you're going to come closer to other things. There aren't that many notes.'

Rod Argent considers that Lloyd Webber's melodies may sound simple but in fact often have extremely unusual constructions and unexpected interval leaps. 'Half the time these days you hear a song like "Memory" played wrongly. There's a wonderful little bar with two extra quavers in it that most people even out to 4/4 time. The original is like speech, really elegant. It's not a complicated song at all. The joy of it is that it sounds totally natural. And that's a gift.'

As Julian Lloyd Webber says in a spirit of fraternal solidarity, 'It's impossible to avoid quoting other bits of tunes when writing tonal music. But Andrew's become so neurotic about this now that he gets everything checked out. You can hardly blame him when obscure people from Denver, Colorado, keep coming out and saying they wrote the same tune as his years before.'

The widow of a composer of a 1940s song called 'Bolero Blue' wrote into the Really Useful Group pointing out that 'Memory' was a steal of her husband's variation on Ravel. The company wrote back sternly and said 'Nonsense' and she was never heard from again. But the obscure guys in Colorado have had a bit of a field day, two of them in particular proving the verity of the old adage that where there's a hit there's a writ. Lloyd Webber twice found himself on the end of these nuisance suits.

Everyone from Irving Berlin to Jerry Herman, who wrote *Hello, Dolly!* and *Mame*, has had this problem. Jule Styne, composer of *Gypsy* and *Funny Girl*, once demonstrated to Herman how 'Oh, You Beautiful Doll' is the old favourite 'I'm Just Breezing Along with the Breeze', note for note. He also discovered that one of his own songs, 'Ride on a Rainbow', is the exact same verse of Jerome Kern's 'All the Things You Are'. And Herman himself discovered by chance that the first eight notes of 'The Way He Makes Me Feel', a song by Michel Legrand in the Barbra Streisand movie *Yentl*, were identical to the first eight notes of his own song 'Ribbons Down My Back', written many years earlier. Not for a minute did he contemplate a court action. The notes had just come round again.

In the mid-1960s, an unknown songwriter filed a complaint that the opening notes of the *Hello, Dolly!* title song were the same as in one he had written. The two songs subsequently diverged completely. The hill-billy tune had been published and recorded, but Herman had never heard it and, as he says in his autobiography, it was hardly being sung all over nightclubs in Manhattan. The case never went to court.

Melodies come to Herman all the time, as they do to Lloyd Webber. Herman's method is to let them hang about and, if they don't go away, he starts to write them down. 'This is just my own little theory, but if I have to really *work* to remember a melody that I was all excited about, I say it's not worth keeping. I will throw it away, like you throw a fish back into the sea if it isn't good enough to make a meal.'

Melody hangs about Lloyd Webber, too, much as mist hangs over Connemara or wisecracks hang around

Jackie Mason. It seeps from every pore, and his friends will tell you that when he plays a new tune at his piano, or on his magical Yamaha Clavinova, he is beatifically transported to a state of rhapsodic radiance. Like Jerry Herman, when tunes refuse to go away, he does something about them.

The idea that he might be trawling through obscure catalogues of unperformed but previously published songs is as ridiculous as it is impracticable. And if you live with a head full of music, especially in the twentieth century, you are very likely to have residual echoes of anything from jazz to rock to classical bumping into each other.

You don't hear Beethoven without also hearing Mozart, Puccini without Verdi, Shostakovich without Glazunov. Music invariably incorporates what happened before. And any composer worth his salt is clearly influenced, consciously or unconsciously, by the music he loves. Steven Pimlott refers to this as 'the old Brahms syndrome'. Told that the last movement of his First Symphony sounded just like Beethoven, Brahms replied, 'Any fool can see that'.

But this unconscious process is quite different from the alleged habit of reproducing someone else's notes on a stave, as if anyone had a copyright on them anyway. In 1988, an amateur songwriter called John Brett claimed that the title number of *Phantom*, as well as 'Angel of Music', had been plagiarised from the tapes of songs he had composed and sent to Elaine Paige and Tim Rice on 29 July and 7 August 1985. Lloyd Webber's songs, unfortunately for him, had been performed at Sydmonton on 5 July 1985. The High Court action was dropped before it was due to be heard in July 1991.

The *Phantom* theme was also the cause of a 1990 suit lodged by an unknown American composer of liturgical music, Ray Repp, claiming it was plagiarised from a hymn he had written in 1978. Repp was a former seminarian now working part-time in a clothing shop. Lloyd Webber lodged a counter-suit – not a serious counter-suit, but an action designed to stop the case proceeding – claiming that another song of Repp's was pinched from 'Close Every Door' in *Joseph*. That counter-suit was thrown out by the courts, so the case had to proceed to trial.

The peculiarity of the American legal system meant that lawyers in Chicago who had invested so many hours of unpaid time on the case needed to fight to the death in a sort of legal poker game for either a) a share of the damages awarded or, more likely, b) their share of a settlement when Lloyd Webber threw up his hands and said he'd had enough of it all. Lloyd Webber offered to drop his counter-suit if Repp dropped his appeal against *his* case having being thrown out, as it was, in 1994.

Repp refused, and the case came to court in New York yet again at the end of 1998, where the jury finally ruled that Repp's claim against Lloyd Webber on the plagiarism issue was groundless. The composer played his theme on a piano in court, explaining how he had composed the tune with Sarah Brightman by his side in Sydmonton. Afterwards, he said, 'I have been thoroughly vindicated. This is a victory not just for me but for all songwriters who have been plagued by contingency lawyers. Perhaps we will now see the end of these money-grabbing, spurious cases.'

On the day of judgement, Tim Rice stood up for his old buddy in an impassioned letter to the *Daily Telegraph*, who gave it pride of place: 'Even though in most cases there is no chance that the accused could have heard the allegedly stolen copyright material, it is often easier for the hit-writer to pay the accusers to go away . . . I have suffered in this way at the hands of such unscrupulous writers, and have reluctantly come to the conclusion that even the most ridiculous claims are not worth the potential costs of defending them.'

Lloyd Webber had taken an important stand on behalf of his colleagues. But underpinning the media coverage of it all was the familiar, rancid, unabated dislike of his music, notably in a piece in the *Observer* by Peter Conrad, who referred to 'the stupefyingly banal tunelets' in *Phantom* and, after listing bona fide creative magpies in history such as T. S. Eliot and Stravinsky, granting them the immunisation of postmodernism, fell on Lloyd Webber's courtroom submission that he tried not to listen to other people's music around the house or even in his own chauffeur-driven car for fear of unwittingly acquiring new ideas: 'Lloyd Webber listens exclusively to himself, which is my idea of aural hell. Great composers steal, minor composers borrow. Only those without talent fret about being original.'

The Jonathan Coe character in *The Dwarves of Death* develops his rant against Lloyd Webber beyond the plagiarism issue: 'Musical ideas which appear new to Lloyd Webber's mind were simply common currency among the composers of fifty, sixty, seventy years ago. It's no wonder that he gets nutters sending him tapes of their own compositions and saying that he's plagiarised them: dull minds think alike, and anybody with half an ear for melody could churn this stuff out.

'And then he jumbles it all together with no concern for style, for period, for genre – bits of pastiche operetta lead into passages of stupid rock music (complete with drum machine) and an absurd Gothic-sounding organ (actually a DX 31) endlessly plays the sort of chromatic scales which are every kiddy's idea of what the sound-track for a horror movie should sound like. And then the audience laps it up. They love it. I just cannot this phenomenon.'

Most of this fictional reaction is meaninglessly subjective, but you never expect the character in a novel like this to be somehow undermined by the idiocy of his own droolings. And the novelist himself, when quizzed by the

Guardian three years later, had no way of explaining his proxy anger. 'It's so annoying to see someone overrated and making so much money, isn't it? Without you being able to see what's so good about it. I think it's also a kind of rage that people, writers and musicians, people like me feel, because we genuinely do think we're better than him, but the financial evidence is so glaringly to the contrary.'

Dream on, baby. What is sad about this, apart from the arrogance, is the sheer weight of material envy, rather than intelligent analysis, informing the attitude. Presumably Coe will feel more relaxed once he has sold – as he undoubtedly will – a couple of his fine novels to the Hollywood film studios. It's only a matter of time. And will we think of him as a worse writer when he hits the jackpot?

Do people, including myself, who enjoy Stephen King's novels, think any the less of him because he made so much money out of selling them as films? No. Call no man happy till he's wealthy, by all means. But if it's any consolation at all to Coe and co, one of the most attractive things about Lloyd Webber is the constant air of edgy, dissatisfied unhappiness he exudes. Indeed, that is a crucial part of his creative personality.

Of course, the operatic pastiche derided by Coe's William in *Phantom* is deliberate and exact, and the common currency of composers referred to is the old chestnut of the post-Puccinian Italian *verismo* composers often warmed up by the serious opera critics. It's the only way in which they know how to write about him. Lloyd Webber, said Hugh Canning of the *Sunday Times* when *Sunset* opened, 'is the Francesco Cilea *de nos jours*. And like Cilea, whose *Adriana Lecouvreur* still enjoys the advocacy of ageing divas in Italy and America, Lloyd Webber is a one-tune-per-show composer.'

Without specifying which tune he means, Canning

then sneers at Lloyd Webber's Puccinian melodic hints and harmonic tints, as if such touches were an indecent assault on the public rather than an affront to his own pulsatingly fine sensibilities. And what is usually meant by this kind of 'one tune' accusation is merely an admission you have heard it before you enter the theatre.

Ever since he started, Lloyd Webber has pored over other composers' musical theatre scores to see how they work. As Cameron Mackintosh says, 'He is a great respecter of craft . . . Andrew will plot every single note from the outset to the play-out in a theatrical arc. He likes to build what he calls an unsinkable boat, constructing and butting everything together.'

Cultural ring-fencing is a favourite pastime of the arts panjandrums, as well as the critics. The usually sensible Brian McMaster, director of the Edinburgh Festival since 1992 and, before then, the head of Welsh National Opera, accused Lloyd Webber in 1994 of 'totally patronising people by creating the impression that opera is not for the man in the street – musicals are.' Similarly, I once heard the opera director Peter Sellars take almost hysterical exception to the suggestion that the musicals of Stephen Sondheim aspired sometimes to the condition of opera. 'Stephen Sondheim does not write operas,' bristled the impatient stager, pronouncing 'operas' as 'opperahs' with a drawling Southern twang – 'Mozart writes opperahs!'

And that was that. The term defines the quality of the experience and implies a superior quality in music. George Gershwin's *Porgy and Bess* is undoubtedly an opera but one which the composer never wanted to see performed in an opera house. Lloyd Webber replied to McMaster's strictures by pointing out that many operas were popular entertainments until opera houses became the home of the cultural elite and the rich, 'a situation which is happily changing'. He went on to say that the massive increase in public interest in opera during the past decade had been influenced by 'the groundswell of often almost completely sung works in the commercial theatre', citing *Les Misérables* and Sondheim's *Sweeney Todd* as well as one or two of his own.

It was a just point, and one surprisingly missed by David Pountney, the former director of Scottish Opera and English National Opera (with whom Maria Bjornson had worked for years), when he appeared as the castaway on BBC Radio 4's *Desert Island Discs* in February 1998. Speaking of opera and contemporary composers, he complained that 'the music has moved away from the audience', and that this detachment of composers, and of painters for that matter, was an increasingly acute twentieth-century problem.

This closing out of an audience is precisely the opposite of what Lloyd Webber does, or at least attempts. His music seeks out punters, makes them experience pleasure in tunes and harmonics, and aims always for theatrical effect. The falling chandelier in *Phantom*, the descent to the sewers, the colourful masked ball, the cod Meyerbeer operatics – all of that is excitingly musicalised while the central love story is turned up full throttle in the romantic numbers.

The musician in Coe's novel who complains of Lloyd Webber pressing too-familiar musical buttons in *Phantom* is missing the point. That is exactly the element of populist, eclectic genius in what he does. The unfamiliar can be safely left to Harrison Birtwistle. The trouble with Lloyd Webber's quest to draw from all sources and mix classical with rock is that he leaves himself open to attack on all sides.

In part, he asks for it. Julian Lloyd Webber reckons that people can too easily acquire a false impression of his music from endlessly hearing the hits taken out of a show's context and done to death. ' "Love Changes Everything" is not the best song in *Aspects*. And you don't hear the wonderful introduction to "Wishing You

Were Somehow Here Again" unless you go and see *Phantom*.' And if you do hear it, you don't listen to it if you're a character in Jonathan Coe.

When *Sunset* opened, the jazz musician and broadcaster Steve Race was moved to write to *The Times* in May 1997 after the paper reported that the composer 'who has spun vast wealth from reinventing some of the under-appreciated melodies of Haydn, Handel, Purcell, Faure and Puccini, last night worked a similar miracle . . .' Race declared that he and many colleagues in the music profession were fed up with these snide remarks: 'He is neither Sondheim nor Gershwin, but he is a fine stage composer in the tradition of Lehár, Romberg, Friml and – yes – Ivor Novello: a true theatre man, whose work delights millions of music lovers worldwide. His one crime is to have made a vast amount of money for himself, for the arts and for Britain. Unforgivable!' So should we be thinking Lloyd Webber, light opera, after all?

Superstar seemed at the time to suggest a coming together of rock and theatre music in a way that *Phantom* obviously doesn't. And *Evita* reflects the shift in percussive rhythms that took place in jazz and rock in the 1970s. The drummer John Hiseman says that *Evita* still sounds modern because 'it is firmly based in the standard way to play funky drums, in a mixture of jazz, white rock and Latin'.

Both *Superstar* and *Evita* are characterised by the sort of switching rhythms and jumbled-up time signatures that reflect a restless oscillation between a kind of modernism and a desire to be at the frontier of rock. 'Everything's All Right' in the first is a beautifully spun melody in lilting, elusive 5/4 time, and it has the same kind of hypnotic effect as Borodin sustains in the second movement of his Third Symphony, also written entirely in 5/4.

Hiseman points out that the jazz rock groups of the

mid-1970s, including his own Colosseum, made a point of mixing time signatures in just the same way Lloyd Webber does throughout *Evita*. *Cats* has something of this in its most energetic sections, and the *Requiem*, a piece that never sounds as blandly imitative as its detractors suggest, has a 7/4 section in the middle, with drums, which Hiseman says is immensely challenging and always difficult for the conductor.

But in the mid-1980s, popular music split into a thousand fragments, with techno, rap, garage, acid house, retro and post-punk cutting all links with the continuum of Beethoven, jazz, the Beatles. There is even now a fashion for playing instruments badly in pop because playing them well is both un-cool and beyond the capacity of the performer. *Starlight Express*, Lloyd Webber's most emphatically pastiched score, is perhaps an acknowledgement of all that – with Southern blues claiming the place of the true religion among the heretical sects of pop, folk and street rap – as he then departs into the romantic operatic hinterland for *Phantom* and *Sunset*.

The other factor is that any artist sets out his stall in a certain period, say from the age of eighteen to the early thirties and, as Hiseman says, creates a bubble within which he then moves onwards taking the audience with him. I think there is something in this, but you do note that Lloyd Webber rather goes out of his way, almost wilfully, exactly like the film maker Mike Leigh, to produce a piece of work as different as possible from the one that preceded it.

'Andrew has created his own world,' says Hiseman. He and his wife, saxophonist Barbara Thompson, have worked with every kind of distinguished musician, but she says she has never worked with anyone like Lloyd Webber. 'He's absolutely unique. You've got to remember there are a hundred pubs in London alone at the moment with everyone bashing out the same four chords. That's basically what's going on. Andrew is alone.'

The high-risk strategy has on the whole paid off, but you can appreciate the composer's bemusement at the constant accusation that he is peddling safe and predictable pap when you can just as equally argue that he has not had a copper-bottomed hit since *Phantom* in 1986 and yet shows no signs of creative abatement or a withering of enthusiasm for the writing process. Whatever else Lloyd Webber is doing, he is not standing absolutely still – like, say, his contemporary, Willy Russell, author of *Educating Rita* and *Blood Brothers* – nor is he retreating from the commercial fray.

That probably annoys the also-rans more than anything else. The pop and rock world has had an increasingly ambivalent relationship with Lloyd Webber over the years, as unsympathetic as Coe's hero to the cause of a popular musical theatre. And this reaction intensifies as pop fragments and *Phantom* flies backwards. An Australian folk pop group of that era, Crowded House, begin a noisy song called 'Chocolate Cake' with a lyric of pleasantly impudent asininity: 'Not everyone in New York will pay to see Andrew Lloyd Webber, may his trousers fall down as he bows to the Queen and the crown; I don't know what tune that the orchestra played, but it went by me – sickly, sentimental. Can I have another piece of chocolate cake, Tammy Baker's got a lot on her plate; can I buy another cheap Picasso fake, Andy Warhol must be laughing in his grave.'

Elvis Costello, too, has a song, 'God's Comic', which maintains the right-on tone of disapproval in defining the epitome of middlebrow culture as listening to Lloyd Webber's *Requiem*. This still sounds like passive, harmless sneering compared to the heartfelt noise of hate emanating from the lyrics of Roger Waters, formerly of Pink Floyd, on his apocalyptic 1992 *Amused to Death* album. As the world falls apart in 'It's A Miracle', an earthquake disrupts a performance of a despised operetta by Lloyd Webber, and the piano lid (not the chandelier) crashes down to break the composer's fingers.

Around the same time, the Master of the Queen's Music, Malcolm Williamson, reacted angrily when he learned that Lloyd Webber, and not he, had been invited to write something for the Queen's fortieth anniversary celebrations. (As it turned out, Lloyd Webber had not been invited to write anything, either.) Williamson dismissed his rival as a cabaret composer whose absolutely fatuous music was melodically poor and harmonically crude, the work of a man using every meretricious trick in the book to make a fast buck.

Lloyd Webber's music was everywhere, he said, 'but then so is Aids'. That was one insult too far, but he charged on nonetheless, defining the difference between good music and Lloyd Webber as the difference between Michelangelo and a cement mixer. 'The comparison only breaks down to the extent that there is an element of creativity in a cement mixer.' He added injury to insult by dismissing poor old Bill Lloyd Webber as a man who wrote 'abysmally unsuccessful oratorios', and one whose bootlaces his own son was not even fit to tie. Why stop there? 'At least his brother Julian can scratch the cello, although he does that badly.'

The brothers kept quiet, but one of the newspapers asked Ned Sherrin to comment on the spat. Malcolm Williamson had written the score for a 1959 musical, *No Bed For Bacon*, which Sherrin had penned with his friend and colleague Caryl Brahms. It had been a disaster: 'We wanted to use an unknown composer, and the music publishers Boosey and Hawkes recommended Williamson. He is a very bizarre man with whom I hope never to socialize or work again. In the pub after the opening night he poured a pint of beer over Caryl's head. I just feel sorry for the poor Queen. I hope he doesn't treat her in the same way.'

The matter died down. But only until the following August, when Williamson completed one of the most spectacular about-faces in the history of critical analysis and commentary. After delivering the manuscript of his fourth piano concerto to a pianist friend in the Savoy Hotel, he crossed the Strand to see *Sunset Boulevard* in the Adelphi.

Within a few days he went public again: 'Andrew has opened the flesh of the mind . . . this music is immortal.' Well, blow me down with a feather, tickle my toes with paprika. The man was possessed with critical remorse and eating not only his hat but his entire wardrobe. 'It is technically musically marvellous . . . it also has spiritual and philosophical depth to it. *Sunset Boulevard* is a huge question mark asking: what is reality?'

What, indeed? Wherever reality was, Malcolm sounded as if he was losing his grip on it. And turning out to be not much better a music critic than William in the Coe novel. Still, Lloyd Webber accepted the compliments with a good grace: 'It's wonderful when another musician enjoys your work. My father introduced me to Malcolm's liturgical work when I was a boy and I always admired him a lot – it hurt me to be so criticised by him.'

Even that big hand of friendship could not put Malcolm off the scent. He had got religion in a big way and shuffled along to see Phillip Schofield in *Joseph* at the Palladium. He came out declaring that 'Close Every Door To Me' was a ravishingly beautiful aria. Which it is. And not only that: 'one of the most beautiful of our time'. It was now the moment for Malcolm to draw himself up for his final pronouncement, complete his recantation and swallow the very last shreds of his vest and underpants: 'Andrew's music must be taken every bit as seriously as the most significant developments in opera from *The Magic Flute* to Benjamin Britten.'

Well, I don't see why not. It would make a change from not doing so. Even John Lill, who dislikes conventional rock music – he used to like Bill Haley and Winifred Attwell – thinks Lloyd Webber deserves a great deal of his success. 'It's the everyday rock stuff that is meretricious, treating people as sheep and marketed to make money. Andrew has done a great deal of wonderful work in introducing people to a classical element in music. Whatever you say about him, his music is always good music. It's not nasty and it's not exploitative. He always has good themes and interesting harmonies.'

It is fair to say that Lill is not a modernist, let alone a post-modernist. You could hardly expect a pianist who still communes with Beethoven and Brahms to care all that much about the music of Harrison Birtwistle or Luigi Nono. Nono's a yes-yes to the avant-garde, but to Lill he remains just a Nono. 'So much pretentious noise under the label of modern music I now find instantly repugnant. There is a basic structure – harmony, rhythm, melody – and you have to have those three things. It's as natural as to live, to breathe, to sleep. Music has to be about the bending of the rules, not the breaking of them. Evolution not revolution.'

This is certainly a conservative view, but a prevalent one. Even a great champion of modernism like Sir John Drummond, another former director of the Edinburgh Festival and former head of BBC Radio 3, will not go to the stake for Birtwistle. Asked on *his* BBC radio desert island what would be the one record he would keep of the eight nominated, he followed a spirited rant against the philistinism and sheepishness of concert-goers who wallow in Mozart and steer clear of Peter Maxwell Davies by choosing the sextet from *Cosi Fan Tutte*.

This theme was taken up, as it happens, by Julian Lloyd Webber in a speech he gave in February 1998 at the World Economic Forum in Davos, Switzerland. He spoke of 'the new führers of the classical music establishment' who operated in unspoken agreement that new music had to sound a certain way. Like, for instance, the way of Stockhausen. He cited the pushing aside of composers like Samuel Barber, Aaron Copland, Malcolm Arnold, William Walton and even Britten himself. These 'forty years of madness' dated from 1945 to the early 1980s.

Today, Lloyd Webber junior is more optimistic that composers like John Taverner, John Adams, Gavin Bryers and James MacMillan are writing music that is both accessible and untainted by any compromise with integrity. And are recognised for so doing. He reckons his brother deserves better treatment than he usually gets. He did once tell a music magazine that if he goes somewhere to play the Shostakovich or Honegger concertos, the last thing he wants to hear is some cretin banging on about whether or not he likes *Starlight Express*.

But he accepts all that as part of the chore of being Andrew's brother. 'What the music critics fail to acknowledge is the fact that a lot of his music is extremely clever. We're not talking about three-minute pop songs by any means, and they never admit that. The snobbery is often there just because he's successful. Puccini got exactly the same treatment in his day. He gets a much better press abroad, and I don't mean New York. Obviously, I travel a lot, and I pick up on what people think about Andrew – whether I want to or not! – and the basic opinion is that he's like some sort of god.'

Julian's defence of the old-fashioned view that music should reach as many people as possible had political overtones. He predicted a new dominance in classical music emanating from the Far East, noting that the seven orchestras in Tokyo, for instance, are mostly on a par with their Western counterparts. Fewer children in Britain are taking up musical instruments in the way his generation did almost as a matter of course in schools. And that, combined with the force-feeding by the media of a culture that is 'pop, pop and more pop' will herald a serious crisis in both performing and listening standards before long.

Julian started his campaign, I think, with a need to reassert his own father's reputation as a composer. But it grew into something else, and it runs parallel to Andrew's concern about standards and opportunities in the musical education of our children. There was a magisterial response to the speech in the pages of the *New York Review of Books*, where the concert pianist and academic Charles Rosen took a view of the argument diametrically opposed to John Lill's.

Rosen averred that Julian's dislike of recent contemporary trends only proved that modernism still had a role to play. His dislike of the modern style, suggested Rosen, possibly derived from his dismay that his father gave up writing music just as the English musical scene was opened up by Sir William Glock – visionary music director of the BBC and architect of the modern day Promenade Concerts – to all the latest international movements.

He also challenged some of Julian's assertions about the availability to listeners of the works of Copland and Barber and said that the example of what happened to great figures of the past like Josquin and Monteverdi – forgotten for centuries, then revived – taught us that 'the art that is tough and that resists immediate appreciation . . . has the best chance of enduring and returning.' Accessibility was not a criterion of excellence, or even value.

And he summarily denied that any of the composers mentioned by Julian Lloyd Webber actively sought to alienate their audiences. 'On the contrary. Composers, artists and writers have always wanted popular success – but on their own terms. Music has indeed become less whistleable or hummable. I have heard friends whistle or hum tunes by George Gershwin or Harold Arlen, but I have never heard anyone whistle a tune by Andrew Lloyd Webber; perhaps I move in the wrong circles.'

This sly shift of argument, with its twin imputations that Lloyd Webber does not operate as a composer on his own terms, and that the right people don't know his tunes, brings us full circle to the snobbery station. Rosen simply cannot resist spoiling his defence of modernism by taking a cheap shot and pleading a preference for rarefied atmospheres. The theatre is no place for such elevated sentiments, and one can at least concede to Rosen the possible disparity that must inevitably exist between music composed for attentive, concentrated listening and music designed to pin people to the back of their seats in a theatre.

And what does music set out to achieve, anyway? In a thoughtful *New Yorker* response to the subject in the course of a reappraisal of Leonard Bernstein, David Denby referred to an article by the American avant-garde composer and teacher, Milton Babbitt, happily comparing the work of serious academic composers to that of researchers in advanced physics.

David Cullen, who studied at the Royal Academy of Music with the composer and occasional cabaret singer Richard Rodney Bennett, reports that his old teacher just about tolerates him these days as an ex-pupil who went to the bad by working with Lloyd Webber. 'Richard has a song about what cabaret performers should charge for singing different types of song. He starts fairly cheaply with Leonard Cohen and Bob Dylan and builds up to the most expensive, which is anything from *Phantom* or *Les Misérables*! A lot of classical composers dislike Andrew, and I always say, look, if you sit down with the idea of writing something entertaining for the average public, you're not going to come up with a twelve-tone symphony.

'There is also this feeling among musicians that there are all these simple melodies floating around that anybody can write down, but we have an agreement that we'll aim a bit higher. And they feel he is sort of letting the side down. I think this will eventually turn around. People sneered at the Beatles for the first decade or so. Then suddenly jazz groups started playing their stuff and they became accepted.'

Approval by the cognoscenti continues to evade Lloyd Webber. But no audience I have ever sat with at *Cats* or *Phantom* reacts as indolently as either those Japanese tourists in *Shooting Fish* or the platoons of gawking midwestern Huckleberries and legions of Farrah Fawcett lookalikes so vigorously despised by Joe Queenan on his maiden voyage over the sea of sappiness. Those guys are there because the shows slake a thirst for goosebump-inducing musical theatre that most contemporary 'serious' opera dutifully scorns.

Partly this is to do with the instant excitement of the sound, the organ anthem in *Phantom*, the swooping synthesizers in *Cats*. Guided and abetted by colleagues like Rod Argent, David Cullen, and his regular record producer Nigel Wright, Lloyd Webber becomes a jumpy, proactive tiger in the jungle of new music technology, mixing tracks in three stages in the studio, relentlessly chasing down imperfections and sending off his Clavinova disks for Wright to start recreating in the studio before he comes tumbling in behind them.

'It's a wonderful instrument, this Clavinova,' says Lloyd Webber fingering a tune he wrote last night. 'Although it's basically a machine created for people playing in piano bars, Wagner would have loved it and certainly would have worked on it. You can do all the arranging and scoring on it. I often get up in the middle of the night, record a few ideas, and see what they sound like in the morning. It's just a different way of writing them down.'

Cullen still prefers writing out full scores for the bigger shows, spreading out the sheets over the floor of his Sussex house so that he can see them all at a glance. The trouble with computers is the need to keep scrolling down the screen to see just a fraction of what you've done. Lloyd Webber will have played through the complete score for two or three days on a cassette recorder, then followed up with quite detailed indications of what should happen, sometimes on the back of an envelope. 'He's such an intelligent guy, so quick and definite about what he wants. An awful lot of our work is done over the telephone. And who on earth else likes opera, pop, even the old British musical-style tinkly music, and the new rock sounds, as much as he does, and could even begin to try and put them all in the same show? But he can and he does. And, what's more, in my view, it all sounds part of the same show, too.'

'The thing about melodies,' says Lloyd Webber, 'is that you can use them in a theatre show but they are not important unless they are in the right dramatic context. Even "Some Enchanted Evening" would not be so good in the wrong show in the wrong place.' I ask him where he gets the gift. He looks puzzled. 'The interesting thing is, I don't quite understand why other people haven't got the knack of melody.'

Joe Queenan comes home from *Cats* feeling thoroughly dejected. 'In the back of my mind, I'd expected the show to fall into that vast category occupied by everything from bingo to Benny Hill. You know: so bad, it's good. But *Cats* was just plain bad. Really bad. About as bad as bad could get.'

He revises that theory of badness by cueing up a Michael Bolton record. The mindset behind the choice of material to poke fun at is never going to change. That would be asking too much. But, I sometimes wonder, who gets the best deal? The experience of art is a kind of transaction between a state of innocence and a pre-arranged statement that takes advantage of it.

You get nowhere if you don't even go halfway. The girls on that train station who were going to *Cats* because it was on the tourist's itinerary were not necessarily the same girls who emerged from the show two hours later. Maybe they were. But equally maybe they weren't. And maybe they also like Stockhausen. Somebody's got to.

TWELVE

AN ENGLISHMAN'S MEAL IS HIS CASTLE

PAINTINGS AND CHURCHES

Andrew Lloyd Webber is a mixed-up, misplaced Victorian. Temperamentally, he is a passionate conservative who loves rock and roll; a devotee of High Victorian architecture beguiled by the mysteries of suburban developments in Hounslow; an inveterate gastronome with a penchant for fresh garden peas ('cooked quickly with a hint of mint'); a theatrical high-flyer with a taste for the irredeemably vulgar.

If it is true that only odd or abnormal people work in musical theatre, Lloyd Webber certainly qualified early by exhibiting an indomitable desire to own Pre-Raphaelite paintings. When most of us in his generation were hoping to be train-drivers or footballers, he was planning a nationwide campaign to save derelict castles.

And he was haunting King's Road antiques shops in search of seriously out-of-fashion Victorian paintings. As a schoolboy, he saw Lord Leighton's *Flaming June* for sale in a shop in Fulham. The price, which he could not afford, was £50. Its value, thirty years later, is more like £10m.

Today, he has one of the best private art collections in the world. By sheer coincidence, his two *Sunset* collaborators have lived in houses occupied by two of the artists he most admires. Christopher Hampton used to live in William Morris's house in Hammersmith, while Don Black's Kensington abode has a blue plaque on the outside wall informing us that William Holman Hunt lived there.

In fact, Hunt's studio is now Black's dining room, and when Lloyd Webber first visited for dinner, Black told him he was going to see something he hadn't seen for years. Lloyd Webber's ears twitched: what was it he hadn't seen for years? 'Blank walls.'

There are no blank walls at Sydmonton, where most of the collection is kept. Plans to build a modern Gothic glass and iron tower designed by Rod Hackney to house the collection were quietly dropped a few years ago. The composer now owns around 250 important paintings, well over half of them acquired in the past seven or eight years.

The Andrew Lloyd Webber foundation is a charity administered by his adviser, David Mason, and retains, in pride of place, virtually as a gift to the nation, two paintings together worth £30m: Canaletto's topographical curiosity *The Old Horse Guards from St James's Park* (1749) and Picasso's portrait of one of his closest friends in Barcelona, *Angel Fernandez de Soto* (1903). These acquisitions moved the collection on to a new plane, and out of the strictly defined area of Pre-Raphaelite speciality.

The first was the most significant: the painting, a glorious social document, was saved for the nation, drawing a resounding vote of gratitude from Nicholas Serota, director of the Tate Gallery. The Tate's offer of £6m had been rejected by Viscount Harris, heir to the Earl of Malmesbury, whose family had owned the work since 1757, and he would certainly have sold it abroad, probably to Giovanni Agnelli, the Italian car magnate and art collector, had not Lloyd Webber intervened and paid £10m.

He had nostalgic reasons for doing so, as the view represented was one of his schoolboy routes around Westminster. You can see the leisurely populated Parade with the Admiralty building, the spire of St Martin's-in-the-Fields, the entrance to Downing Street and the brick of the Old Horse Guards building which was demolished soon after Canaletto painted it.

The large canvas – it measures three feet by eight feet – is full of interesting detail, including one Lloyd Webber had not spotted when he bought it: two men in the middle distance are almost certainly urinating against a wall.

A small side issue was raised by Alan Bennett in his 1997 diary, reporting the anecdote passed on by the composer George Fenton that the painting had been paid for by Access Card in order to earn the air miles – 'enough presumably to last him till the end of his days. Such lacing of extravagance with prudence has since become so common that Christie's have now suspended credit card payments altogether.'

The Picasso, a masterpiece of the Blue Period, was bought in New York in 1995, partly to celebrate winning seven Tony Awards for *Sunset* (he won seven, also, for *Cats* and just six for *Phantom*). Angel de Soto was a fervent half-Catalan patriot described by Picasso as 'an amusing wastrel', and is portrayed in a haze of pipe smoke, large glass on the table. His heavy-lidded eyes are enlarged and endowed, in the art historian John Richardson's phrase, with the painter's own obsidian stare.

Richardson also recounts in his great book on Picasso how, in their impoverished Barcelona heyday, the inseparable friends shared a studio and indeed their one and only pair of gloves. When they went swaggering on the town, each kept one bare hand in a pocket while gesturing conspicuously with the other gloved one to the passing parade.

Part of the deal with the charity commissioners is that these two pictures must go out on loan for at least three months of each year, but in practice they go out for much longer than that. And galleries around the world have tours booked into Sydmonton twice or thrice a year. 'They write in, and so long as we know who everyone is . . .' says Lloyd Webber, sounding slightly miffed that he's done all this, built up this amazing collection and still has to have round the clock security in his own home.

When at Sydmonton, the Picasso hangs next to Edward Burne-Jones's *The Challenge of the Wilderness*, a remarkable painting by any standards, which is also blue, a colour that predominates in the late, strange pictures of this artist. It is a study in drapery, with three garlanded trumpeters stepping out in an almost abstract array of creased and broken folds in their garments. It is also curiously unfinished, thus suggesting an even more emphatic tone of modernism.

It is now known that Picasso saw this picture, and others of Burne-Jones, whom he admired. In being years ahead of the Pre-Raphaelites swinging back into fashion, Lloyd Webber had spotted the roots of modernism and surrealism – first noted, he is quick to point out, by Wyndham Lewis in 1948 – as well as taking delight in the gorgeous tints and white-skinned, red-haired ladies of the brotherhood.

'It's a funny thing,' says Lloyd Webber 'how art divides in interesting ways and then comes back. My father's music, you see, is outside of its time in the sense that he is like a very late Pre-Raphaelite when Cubism is at its height. The parallel isn't exact because he was writing a long time after Burne-Jones painted, but you can now see that all the links between Burne-Jones and Picasso are taken seriously when they were a joke forty years ago.

'My father was writing in a way that the musical

establishment could not possibly take seriously at that time. It is tragic, but entirely understandable. And in the same way, Pre-Raphaelite painting became unacceptable when women won the vote and emancipation kicked in; people no longer thought it appropriate to see languid maidens lolling about replete with latent sexuality.'

The Fall of Lucifer is another extraordinary Burne-Jones and not one you would necessarily think of as being typical of the artist's work. It is a long, tall picture, departing angels piled on top of each other in their sculpted blue cloaks, exuding anxiety. 'We know all the young Catalans went crazy about this picture,' says Lloyd Webber, 'and if that isn't the beginning of Cubism, well, come on . . .'

The art critics caught up with him in late 1997, when a revealing exhibition at the Tate, *The Age of Rossetti, Burne-Jones and Watts*, pursued other parallels with the European symbolist movement, though the fully emancipated Waldemar Januszczak, art critic of the *Sunday Times*, remained unconvinced that a Rossetti heroine was anything other than 'a lightly clothed sexual vacuum into which all the painter's desires rush.'

That may be true, but who cares when you see the glorious, fleshy-lipped goddess, *A Vision of Fiametta*, modelled by Marie Spartali? Spartali was one of Dante Gabriel Rossetti's main muses and herself a painter who painted under her married name of Stillman. Securing this work was a triumph of cunning and skulduggery – there are only a few Rossetti oils in private collections, worldwide – but it still bugs Lloyd Webber that he lost out on the magnificent *Proserpine*, which John Paul Getty snapped up for a song when the stock market crashed in 1989.

The acquisition of *Fiametta* was a brilliant inter-national coup. David Mason had forty years' experience, having opened a gallery – MacConnal Mason and Son – with his father, a banker, in 1957. The father and son business – David and his son – continues to this day, operating out of two freehold buildings in Duke Street, St James, one with a flat above which, he says, comes in handy 'after an evening with Andrew during the week!'

Mason was asked by Andrew and Madeleine to sort out the mix-up over some of the commissions arranged by David Crewe-Read. He sorted out what he could in three weeks and went off to his boat, telling them to let him know if they needed any more help. 'But I seriously underestimated how focused on the whole art business Andrew was.' Within a few months, seventy per cent of his working life would be spent on Lloyd Webber's collection. It still is.

Mason has had a varied and interesting career. Apart from the consuming activities of his galleries and his horse trials, he was a tireless campaigner – though he never mentions it – in the thalidomide babies case against the Distillers Company (he was awarded the OBE for his work in that area), and a presenter of *The Antiques Road Show* on BBC television. And he knew all the tricks of the trade. At a sale of porcelain in 1992, by lurking outside on the telephone and using eight people planted in the auction room, he bid successfully for ninety-two of the ninety-nine lots at a cost of £700,000.

His brief was to protect and improve the core of Lloyd Webber's Pre-Raphaelite collection, but also to buy masterpieces in other periods. Hence the Picasso, and later acquisitions of Landseer, Alfred Munnings, most recently Stanley Spencer. His nose is sufficiently educated to know what to go for even when he doesn't much like it himself. With Mason by his side, Lloyd Webber has become one of the top ten art collectors in the world. And they are now buying a lot of modern work straight from the artist.

Going through the catalogues, Andrew spotted that *A Vision of Fiametta*, one of those few major privately-owned Rossetti oils, had been sold at Christie's in 1965 for just under £4,000 to a man called David Rust. Mason tracked his address to Washington, where he lived in retirement. He had worked for the Washington National Gallery. Six weeks after Mason fired off a letter, the same letter came back, with Mason's name stuck over the address with Sellotape and one sentence scrawled across the bottom of the envelope: 'What's your best offer?'

Lloyd Webber yelled at Mason to get on a plane, but when Mason rang Rust, he was told there was no sale, he wasn't interested. Still, he took a flight on Concorde and found the house – 'slightly rickety, nothing special, a bit like *Sunset Boulevard* in fact, with an old swimming pool at the back'. Rust only had a few pictures – he had sold any really good ones he might have had – but *Fiametta* was his favourite.

Mason hit him with a big offer. No deal. Rust started to talk about his divorce and his daughter. He went to the fridge and brought back a can of Diet Coke which they shared. Anyway, he said, the capital gains tax on the picture would be enormous. Mason said he would pay this bill. And what he wanted in dollars Mason would pay in pounds. Still no deal.

Mason flew back to London, where *Sunset* had gone into rehearsal. Mason insisted on dragging Andrew away for five minutes to talk to Rust on the telephone. Then Mason talked to him again, and made an even bigger offer. This floored Rust but he kept fighting for half an hour until he caved in. He said he was going to Europe for three weeks and would ring when he returned. 'When are you going?' asked Mason. 'The day after tomorrow.' 'I'll be over tomorrow to pick up my picture.'

Mason hurriedly got Bill Taylor to authorise a bank draft for untold millions – 'He thought I was mad and must be going to gamble everything away in Las Vegas, or something' – and Sir David Napley, Lloyd Webber's lawyer, knocked up a contract. Mason jumped back on to a Concorde, drove to Washington, parked a lorry with porters round the corner from Rust's house, went in and placed the bank draft on the table.

Two hours later, Rust was still counting up the noughts on the end of the cheque, and still saying he hadn't quite decided one way or the other. But in the end, Mason walked out the door with *Fiametta* under his arm as the hired lorry drew up. 'The picture's in the lorry. I'm in the car behind with a driver and we follow this truck containing this priceless painting through the roughest part of Washington. And we keep losing the bloody van. Then we get pelted with stones and shouted at by all these kids in the black area and the van driver's black and he's shouting back at them. We get to a warehouse and I supervise the packing for two and a half hours, go back to the Four Seasons and telephone Andrew, waking him up in the small hours. 'What the hell's going on?' '*Fiametta*'s coming home.'

Mason knew that the painting would not be allowed in the body of the Concorde, so he found the baggage supervisor at the airport and gave him three hundred dollars. 'I bribed him, sure, and went out on the tarmac with him. The picture just fitted into the nose of the aircraft. I unpacked it at Heathrow, drove straight down to Sydmonton, unpacked it there. Andrew took one look and burst into tears.

'People have their gods, their devotions. It can be music, it can be money. Andrew's god is art, and the music is a means to the art. But with David Rust, who I knew would sell within an hour of first meeting him, money is his god. I had to promise to have a copy of *Fiametta* made for him so that he could hardly tell the difference, and we agreed never to divulge how much we paid.'

This swashbuckling activity is a new side of Lloyd

Webber, a sporty side even. Tissot's *The Captain and the Mate*, one of his costume pieces and probably Tissot's most famous picture – the two sailors are taking their leave of their ladies on deck and the scene somehow conveys a novelettish interior among the rigging and the horizon – was part of a divorce settlement for 'a mega-wealthy, very famous person in New York' which Madeleine first heard about through their New York neighbour Blaine Trump.

Lloyd Webber says they were rung up. 'David and I, frankly, got totally pissed in Green's and sent through a completely derisory offer. I rang David when I got home and said, bloody hell, we'd better withdraw that offer. This was a Friday. On the Monday, we heard that the offer – for that one, and another Tissot – was accepted. She just wanted the paintings out of the house.'

At the end of 1994, Lloyd Webber bought four wall-high tapestries by Burne-Jones that illustrate the Arthurian legend of Sir Galahad in pursuit of the Holy Grail. Costing £842,000, the purchase established him in the public and professional mind as the most powerful buyer of Victorian art since the American oilman Fred Koch.

Interestingly, Koch was the (for a while) anonymous donor who funded the Royal Shakespeare Company's third auditorium in Stratford-upon-Avon, the Swan, a wonderful, warm, all-wooden neo-Elizabethan arena that opened in 1986 as Trevor Nunn's legacy to the company he had run for nearly two decades.

One of Lloyd Webber's most requested pictures for loans and exhibitions is Millais' *Chill October*, which Van Gogh got very excited about. It certainly gives the lie to the accusation that Millais went completely commercial in later life. This landscape was painted in Scotland, near Perth, and shows the wind sweeping across the picture with birds flying into the full face of the glowering gust. Lloyd Webber becomes stock still with renewed wonder as he gazes into the lake and the dark trees. He yearns for its return whenever it leaves Sydmonton.

Another one very close to his heart is Richard Dadd's *Contradiction* – he vows never to sell it – and he declares himself 'absolutely and utterly in love with' Holman Hunt's *The Morning Prayer*, a very small – twelve inches by six – portrait of gorgeous perfection. You can sense that Lloyd Webber is as happy as he'll ever be when contemplating the best of Burne-Jones and Millais and, boy, does he have enough of them to keep going.

In the vast stairwell at Sydmonton now hangs the proud picture of *The Prince of Wales* by Joshua Reynolds, formerly lodged in the stately home of Brocket Hall. 'I thought it would be fun to have a good Reynolds here, because the Pre-Raphaelites called him Sir Sloshua! And of course there is now the association of Madeleine and the horses.' The prince sits astride his magnificent white steed looking out with an amused, amusing grin.

This masterpiece was a picture specifically bought to fill a space in the house caused by the removal to another resting place on the first floor of Millais' art nouveau-style *Design for a Gothic Window*, conceived as a riposte to the decorations in William Butterfield's All Saints Church in Margaret Street, where Bill Lloyd Webber had been the organist and where he had married Jean. Lloyd Webber's ownership of this exuberant stonework is not only a testament to his belief that Millais was 'by far the greatest' of the Pre-Raphaelites, but a resonant resume of his life, background and interests.

All Saints was the great controversial church building of the 1850s, described by John Ruskin as 'the first piece of architecture I have seen built in modern days which is free from all signs of timidity and incapacity.' It was the first important building where brick was used decoratively, and was acclaimed by the architect and writer G. E. Street as 'not only the most beautiful but the most vigorous, thoughtful and original' of all the Gothic Revival churches.

Millais came up with his rival window design on a famous holiday with Ruskin – they allegedly worked on about twenty designs on wash paper – but the surviving stone arches, with their fluting angel faces and gracious, curving lines, comprise the only remnant anyone has ever traced.

'I knew about the piece when I was in Fulham, but it cost about £800 and I couldn't afford it then,' says Lloyd Webber. 'It was bought by Jeremy Maas, the first dealer to do anything with the Pre-Raphaelites, a pioneer in the 1960s, in fact. Like me he's a member of the Savile Club and he said he couldn't get the thing into his house and so, years later, he let me have it for a couple of thousand. It means a great deal to me.'

The Millais window also demonstrates a deep-seated passion not just for the churches themselves but for what goes on inside: spirituality, music, decoration, design. Lloyd Webber buys the whole package and decided to do something about locked churches in 1994, when he founded his Open Churches charitable trust with a £1m donation.

This fund pays for certain churches, previously locked, to be open for both worshippers and sightseers – the two can easily be thought of as the same thing – for several hours in the daytime. Lloyd Webber was inspired by a remark of the great architectural historian Nikolaus Pevsner, who said that his entire work on the Buildings of England series 'would be rendered pointless if fine churches were not freely accessible at a reasonable hour'.

There are 3,000 Grade 1 listed churches in the country, and half are kept locked between services. The idea is to return these churches to their communities, and Lloyd Webber's father-in-law, the monocled Brigadier Gurdon, who administers the trust from an office in the Really Useful headquarters, wants to underline this point by suggesting that all the church bells in the land should ring in clamorous celebration come the millennium.

Addressing the Lambeth Conference of bishops at the University of Kent in Canterbury in July 1998, Lloyd Webber outlined his plans: 'We have invited every Christian place of worship in the UK to hold a fifteen-minute service at noon on Saturday 1 January 2000 and to herald that service with a celebratory peal of bells.

'We have also invited every secondary school in the UK to write a prayer to celebrate the two-thousandth anniversary of the Birth of Christ and the arrival of a third millennium. This prayer will then be read at every cathedral, church or chapel service taking place as part of the millennium celebrations.' Lloyd Webber and the Brigadier also announced a recruitment drive to enlist and train 5,000 new bellringers in time to chime for the big day.

The first church opened by the trust on a daily basis was St James the Less in Westminster, where a memorial tablet to the actress Sybil Thorndike, a deeply devout woman, reveals that her father, the Rev Arthur Thorndike, was an archdeacon there. Like Laurence Olivier, she was a clergyman's child. And she and Olivier were the two actors, in Tyrone Guthrie's view, who best combined protean ability and star quality. Must be something to do with genuflections in the genes. Certainly, both were as capable of majesty and grandeur as of hilarious, self-immolating comedy turns, and Guthrie put this down to a kind of energy allied to spiritual freedom. And of course Thorndike was Shaw's ideal Saint Joan, a woman who obeyed the voice of God and appalled his representatives on earth. Who burned her to death.

The Open Churches scheme operates exactly as English heritage does: money is put up when the church also raises some. 'If you put up the whole lot,' says Lloyd Webber, ever the practical conservative, 'there's not much of an incentive for them to get their act together as a community. And that's what it's all about, really. What you want is someone inside that church who's not only going to open the doors, but who actually wants them to be open.'

Lloyd Webber and the Brigadier had instant success with their campaign. By April 1998, citizens of Liverpool, where only six places of worship are nowadays kept open, were boarding buses to find them. No-one is advocating full-scale Christian renewal. Indeed, one of the 'churches' is the oldest synagogue in Britain, the Bevis Marks synagogue in the City of London, opened for the first time ever to the public. Lloyd Webber is merely interested in facilitating those few quiet, reflective moments in the day when you might take a break and look at something of architectural value.

This seems to me an undeniably worthwhile thing to be doing, and a wonderful example of civic responsibility in action. The same can be said of Lloyd Webber's ownership of theatres, although there is a more obvious financial feedback for him. But the restoration of the Palace Theatre's facade has been a great service to London, as has the ownership and renewal of the Adelphi and the New London.

And when Paul Gregg's Apollo Leisure – whose Apollo Victoria has been kept warm by *Starlight Express* these past fourteen years – spent £15m on restoring the long-derelict Lyceum, Lloyd Webber rode in gallantly to support the rescue act with his *Jesus Christ Superstar* revival.

Henry Irving's beautifully renovated theatre, latterly the home of Mecca ballroom dancing and pop concerts, had been earmarked by the Royal Opera during the rebuilding of their nearby Covent Garden home. But they changed their minds at the last minute, and then the English National also scorned an opportunity to take up residence when the Coliseum closed for renovation.

In marked contrast to the tone of much media comment on Lloyd Webber's activities, Simon Jenkins, a former editor of *The Times* and a columnist on the *Evening Standard*, applauded this latest move to keep the grand theatres of London alive: 'To survive they need the crash of music and the crush of humanity. They need the spirit of vaudeville that inspired their builders. Like big churches they need big congregations and that means popular shows. The streets and services of the West End need them, too. A theatre is a dream machine for making money – or for losing it.'

The options ahead are all of Lloyd Webber's own making. He has already received and rejected a substantial bid for the Canaletto. There is no intention of selling the Picasso. But the Canaletto *might* one day be sold on the condition that it stayed in this country. 'One could raise, say £15m and what you could *then* do with the National Youth Music Theatre, for instance, would be pretty extraordinary. The future of everything is through schools and music, and it's so dreadful that the present government seems hell bent on cutting back on music in schools, especially in primary schools . . .'

Since his earliest days Lloyd Webber has talked about the moral commitment of his talent, and he always believed that he shared this attitude deep down with Tim Rice. They are not, nor have they ever been, trivial or self-indulgent citizens, like so many others in the pop, rock and theatre world, and I think both deserve a lot more credit than they get for what they do.

'The one thing my father brought me up to believe,' says Andrew, 'is that everybody is responsible in the end for the positive use of his or her best qualities. I have never moved from that view. As artists, as well as people, we have a moral duty to defend a free society such as we have in Britain. And we should respect that liberal and democratic tradition for what it is: a great privilege.'

Don Black has a lovely remark Little Richard let slip about Elvis Presley: that he got what he wanted but he lost what he had. 'I've always admired this about Andrew: that he doesn't want to lose what he had. He likes to step back into reality.' So, however many canvases he acquires, you'd have to say that there will always be the bigger picture. And that is to be applauded.

And duly was, when the music of the knight became the music of the lord with the announcement of a life peerage in the 1997 New Year's Honours. Later gazetted as Baron Lloyd-Webber of Sydmonton in the county of Hampshire, the composer's name appeared on the same list as the triumphantly retiring artistic director of the Royal National Theatre, Richard Eyre (knighted), the redoubtable novelist and sometime collaborator Frederick Forsyth (CBE), and all-round showbusiness wag, wit and compère Ned Sherrin (CBE).

HORSES AND LANDSCAPES

The first horse Lloyd Webber owned, or part-owned, was named after his nemesis in New York, Frank Rich. The horse, a four-year-old gelding, was bought by a syndicate including Robert Stigwood, Cameron Mackintosh, Anthony Pye-Jeary and Lord Delfont, at the Doncaster sales for 25,000 guineas in May 1991.

Gelded of course means castrated, the natural condition of a critic according to Brendan Behan, who said that critics were like eunuchs in a harem: they watch people doing it every night but they can't do it themselves. Not only did Frank Rich have no balls, he was even transformed into a winner by having no voice: he won a big race at Uttoxeter in November 1993 after having his tongue strapped down to prevent him making all sorts of horrible sounds, including gurgling.

When horses are named after someone, permission must be sought and the theatrical consortium copied an old trick of the Broadway impresario David Merrick who, when one of his shows was trashed by the critics, invited people with the same names in New Jersey to see his show and reported their enthusiastic quotes in his advertising.

Pye-Jeary confirms that a certain Mr Frank Rich who lives near Slough was consulted on the horse's christening and his permission obtained. 'A very strange looking horse it was, too. But he was a no-lose in the fun stakes. If he fell and failed, it was poetic justice. And if he won, we were cheering him on and winning as well.'

Within a few months of their marriage, Madeleine had awakened a new interest in her husband. Horses, as far as Lloyd Webber was concerned, were strictly for the birds. The very thought of sitting on one made him feel dizzy. But soon after the marriage Madeleine started converting the stables and fencing off fields to make paddocks on some of the best grazing land in Britain. The Watership Down rabbits were soon challenged for supremacy by the new Watership Down stud.

The landscape on the 4,500 acre estate has been revitalised without losing the utter serenity of the place. Lord Carnavon, who sponsored the excavation of the royal tombs in Thebes, is buried on nearby Beacon Hill. There is a sense of god's own rolling country, of timeless beauty hanging round the fine old oaks and cedars and the ever-changing colours of the hedges and foliage.

When Peter Brown took President and Mrs Reagan down to the estate, the president asked how much of it was Andrew's. 'As much as you can see,' said Brown. 'Gee,' said the president, 'I thought things in England

were very small. My ranch back home is only 860 acres.'
He was impressed.

The stables were converted from old farm buildings, the dilapidated asbestos barns were demolished, and an extra yearling yard added which Mark Todd, the international eventer friend of Madeleine's, rented for a couple of years. There is also a big new barn for young foals or sick horses. The paddocks spread away, a lush green carpet either side of the main avenue of huge limes that leads so dramatically from the front lodge to the main house.

Raising brood mares is a long-term business, but the Lloyd Webbers struck lucky early on. With Madeleine's old friend Simon Marsh installed as the overall manager of racing and breeding horses, they pursued a policy of buying the best mares they could, selling the colts and raising the fillies. In October 1997 at Tattersalls, they sold two home-bred yearlings for 500,000 guineas and 625,000 guineas, an extraordinary achievement for so young a stud.

One of the mares involved was Darara, whom Marsh snapped up at the Goffs sale in Ireland for 470,000 Irish guineas (she has already earned back twice that amount) in a manner similar to David Mason bagging the porcelain. Marsh bamboozled the rival stud's bidders, who thought they had a straight run at Darara, by hiding in a small office leading off the main auction room and topping the bids. When they reached their limit and could not reach the boss – he was playing golf in Barbados – they lost out, but later bought the yearling Darara was carrying for half a million!

The racing side of the operation is the fun side, the silly money. There have been several winners already at Cheltenham, a meeting where even leading owners wait a lifetime for a winner. Marsh says that Cheltenham is always a particular pleasure because of the huge Irish contingent and the 'crack', or talk. 'One year Andrew disappeared to the loo and he'd gone for a long time. You have to worry about him in a public place, because he could easily get completely lost.

'He suddenly reappeared with a big grin on his face: he'd fallen in with an Irish crowd who'd come over to see his horse Black Humour and wanted to pay their respects and sympathies because it had been withdrawn, injured in training. He'd had a drink with all the lads, talked about all his horses and not a bloody word about *Starlight Express*. He loves that.'

What is interesting about this is that Lloyd Webber has gone as thoroughly into the horse business as he has into painting. He tends not to do things by halves, and it was his insistence to Marsh that they should aim right for the top and not mess around that has provided Marsh with what he calls 'a phenomenal opportunity'. At the same time, the finances seem to be more stringently controlled than they were by the Really Useful during the *Sunset* period.

'The thing about Andrew,' says Marsh, 'is that for every one of his passions – wine, art, music – he's probably more knowledgeable than the people advising him. But not horses. Yet! He's got a fine brain and he doesn't miss a trick. He takes it all in. If I tell him something he'll often come back at me on it six months later. But I talk to Madeleine two or three times a day, because there is so much going on, and Andrew does see this as her domain.' The couple also now share a five per cent stake in their local Newbury racecourse.

Marsh is based in Lambourn, about half an hour's drive from Sydmonton, where the racing fraternity includes the distinguished trainer Charlie Brooks, another close friend of the family. But when he arrives at Sydmonton he is acting lord of all he surveys, conferring with Terry Doherty, the stud groom, on the latest news on the horses, how their feet are falling, how they look and feel.

The Lloyd Webber colours are pink and grey diamonds. The flat racing horses run in the name of the Lord, the jumpers in that of the Lady Lloyd-Webber. And the triumphs are, as so often in sport with animals, tinged with tragedy. One horse, Al Mutahm, was destroyed after severing a tendon at Newbury. Another, Joe Gillis, fared no more fortunately than his namesake in *Sunset Boulevard*: he dropped dead of a heart attack a furlong from the finish at Kempton Park.

The saddest loss, though, was Raymylette, who won seven races and died during an operation for combating cholic and intestinal trouble. Madeleine and Marsh had found him on top of the windiest hill in Cork, courtesy of a bloodstock agent called Johnny Harrington, and had fallen in love with him. 'He'd lived on this hill all his life so he was a bit ropey, but he was a big lovely chap and he ended up being probably the best racing horse we've had.'

The Irish connection led to the purchase in 1995 of another home, Kiltinan Castle in County Tipperary, Kiltinan. Having done for Frank Rich, surely Lloyd Webber wasn't aiming in retrospect to kill the long dead Ken Tynan? This was almost an impulse buy after Andrew and Madeleine turned up for Marsh's wedding; his wife Jane's family lived next door to the castle, just outside the village of Fethard.

The seven-bedroomed castle was built by King John in 1215, damaged by Cromwell in 1649, but later restored. It came complete with a 230-acre stud farm. The elderly American lady, a retired fashion magazine editor, who owned it, was an old family friend of Jane Marsh and indeed gave the wedding party a lawn meet before they all went hunting on the morning of the ceremony. Lloyd Webber considered the castle the most beautiful place he had ever seen. When the merry hostess popped her clogs a year later, the Lloyd Webbers were in Los Angeles but quickly made an appropriate offer.

Some of the fifty-odd horses are kept in Ireland, some in America, some in Sydmonton. And some are with trainers. From Madeleine's point of view, the racing world gives another dimension to their lives and replaces her former eventing career. 'It's something we can do together. If you go eventing, it takes all day. Racing is social and enjoyable, and it only takes up three or four hours in the day.'

One of the consequences of a new sideline in journalism – his Saturday column, 'Matters of taste' on the back page of the *Weekend Telegraph* – was a sharpening of Lloyd Webber's views on rural life. Marriage to Madeleine and the bestowal of the peerage also converted him into a most effective and influential spokesman on architectural and country matters.

Ironically, the more land he owned, the more inviolate he wanted it to become. Weekend flyers and their noisy, single engine propellor planes were an increasing annoyance. He has probably shaken a metaphorical fist at Charles Hart flying over Hampshire in his proceeds from *Phantom*.

Nor were country walkers terribly welcome. In May 1996, Lloyd Webber lost a five-year battle to stop hikers and ramblers cutting through a little lane on the estate. But a government inspector rejoicing in the ambivalently walker-friendly name of Ron Amblin – an anagram of No Ramblin' – ruled against Lloyd Webber's request for a re-routing of the path.

Having offered Middle England 'New Ways to Dream' in his musicals, Lloyd Webber now exhorted them through his newspaper column to rise up and save the countryside. 'The only reason I would ever leave England,' he says, 'was if the quality of life here became so much a travesty of what it was and what I'd hoped it to be. For me, the tragedy of the rape of Middle England is that ordinary countryside is so easy to violate and yet so difficult to argue for.'

It is difficult, perhaps, to wax passionate about the countryside around, say, Milton Keynes, but that is precisely what Lloyd Webber does. He lambasted the government announcement in 1997 that they intended to build 4.4 million new homes by 2016 and plonk them in the middle of what is left of the English countryside, 383,000 acres of it to be precise. 'In addition, there will be all the new pylon lines, new roads, the light pollution that you will see at night-time from miles around, all the trappings needed to finally turn England into a suburban hell.'

Lloyd Webber admits that while the population is not getting materially bigger, and family units considerably smaller, there is a growing need for accommodation as young couples can afford to buy property, single parents look for new homes, middle-class types seek second boltholes. And we all live longer. But he advocated renewing all the empty property and derelict land in urban areas. And he turned his verbal weaponry on plans to build a fake new market town at Micheldever in the heart of rural Hampshire.

Celebrating two interesting churches, St Mary's by George Dance, and St Michael's at Stoke Charity, he derided Eagle Star's 'heinous' proposals: 'Speaking of charity, much play is made by Eagle Star of "affordable housing". This is, in my opinion, an example of that insidious trick of offering a sop to planners as a "planning gain". Eagle Star is after a profit. It wants to make it out of the last swathe of truly unspoilt country-side between London and Southampton.'

This exemplary radicalism was no whit abated by the time the country folk themselves organised the Country-side March in London on 1 March 1998. This rally was confused in the public mind with the emotive issue of fox-hunting. Lloyd Webber would probably support a move to ensure that hunting was carried out as humanely as possible, though he witnessed at first hand the need to control foxes after a flock of baby lambs was cruelly ravaged by them on Watership Down.

But the main issue was that 'government townies are setting out to control the countryside from central Government, a countryside that they do not understand or really want to.' He also joined the protest against the government ban on beef on the bone following the panic in the farming industry over infected cattle. 'That this Government could be so patronising to its people that it will not allow them the choice to buy their beef as they want it is an insult to the nation's intelligence, quite apart from being a body blow to the rural community. So I shall be out marching and, like others from Hampshire, I shall be marching with particular thoughts of Micheldever.'

These concerns run deep. A few weeks later I was leaving the Adelphi Theatre where *Cats* the video was being filmed on the stage. I was amazed when Lloyd Webber suddenly related exactly what had happened to this building over the years, where the old bar area – now an amusement arcade – had once been. He has a remarkable sense of layers of history, of architectural accretions down the years.

And not just on notable public buildings. 'The greatest book to be written would be about High Streets in England, and in particular what lies behind the facades at the level of the first storeys. It's behind there that you find the old Georgian houses. You see this as you go through Hounslow, for instance.

'You might say, what on earth could there be of interest in Hounslow? Well of course, there's masses. It isn't necessarily great architecture, it's more all the features of topographical interest. And what remains of an England that was visible and fully evident only seventy years ago.'

PASS THE WINE AND THE DICE

George is memorialised in *Aspects of Love* as a sensual man who lived for the moment and took pleasure in food and drink. Lloyd Webber has long been a serious foodie and a connoisseur of fine wine ever since that outing to Camden Passage with Aunt Vi. He first went public on this important aspect of lunch in January 1996 when invited by the *Sunday Times* to write a couple of guest 'Table Talk' columns in the absence of A. A. Gill.

One of the more galling aspects of life for a working journalist is the endless parade of artists currently invited to show us how good they are at doing our job with the obviously implicit corollary that we would be no good at doing theirs. A. A. Gill was a hard act to follow, but Lloyd Webber took to it like a duck to water, from the very first paragraph: 'I now have two fond memories of Upper Street, Islington, north London. The first is Marlowe: the Musical at the King's Head, in which the dying Marlowe passed his plume to Shakespeare with the words: "It's up to you now, Willie." The second is the sweet-cured fish, pickled onion and watercress I had last week at Euphorium.'

In three sentences, the tone is established, and the setting of Islington as a current mecca of theatre and food. There is appropriate anecdote, the key flavouring of 'plume' and the clearly stated interest in unusual items on the menu. And it moves along quickly. Newspapers go in for too much celebrity journalism these days, but when it's this good, who can blame them?

Lloyd Webber was perhaps proving a point to Tim Rice, who had long established himself as an outstanding cricket writer on the same paper. But like other theatre practitioners turned occasional journalists – Peter Hall, Richard Eyre, Sue Townsend, David Hare – he was also building a different kind of bridge with his public.

And as he was not known as a writer, he would reveal even more of himself than people knew already. It was a relief to discover, for instance, that he could be funny about himself. On a trip to La Scala in Milan, he visited La Scaletta, a restaurant where olive oil is king. 'Sadly, there was Muzak: Glenn Miller and later, worse, me . . . The Muzak then piped out an almost actionable version of "The Music of the Night".

'I assumed this was by some local artist and asked who it was. The artist was not local. If I revealed all I would be in Feuds Corner [a *Sunday Times* feature of head-to-head animosities] in a big way. Happily, the sliced back of rabbit jolted me back to Elysium. It was accompanied with yellow and red pimentos that had been reduced to such concentrated sweetness that my prejudice against peppers was overcome entirely.'

Food writing is a growth industry in the journalism of conspicuous consumption. One often feels that the public prints are groaning under the weight of their table testers, people eating themselves to death in order to make sure they know where the next meal's coming from.

Indeed, as if to acknowledge the inherent dangers in the lifestyle, Lloyd Webber started his next column with a reference to Jay's, his local bar in Fethard, Tipperary, as the only pub he knew which boasted both a restaurant and an undertaker's.

The joy of Jay's is contained not just in the food, but as an indicator of the composer's new double status as a welcome outsider perhaps known for something other than for what he's known elsewhere: 'Conversation stops in the bar if a stranger walks in: my face was vaguely known, so the locals concluded I was a race-horse trainer. This was fine, as only a priest can make a more important contribution to society in these parts.'

When A. A. Gill returned after two weeks, Lloyd Webber was snapped up by the *Telegraph* to write his own monthly food column which almost immediately became the weekly back page pulpit on the *Weekend* section. He was not confined to matters of restaurants, but that is usually where he begins and ends. Although Peter Brown in New York initially advised Andrew against taking on this extra work, the chore proved to be a welcome break from the grind of everything else.

And having another string to his bow took his mind off the job in an agreeable manner. It encouraged a more systematic approach to an already ingrained habit of lunching and dining out. And, most importantly, it gave him an autonomously organised extra-curricular activity at a time when the Really Useful under Patrick McKenna was going full steam ahead (in the wrong direction), without consulting him all that much.

Having sought freedom from the everyday running of the company, Lloyd Webber found himself after *Sunset* increasingly distanced from what was going on. Frankenstein's monster was up and running, and the boss did not even have an office in Tower House. Yet again, he had ingenuously found himself taken for a ride on his own merry-go-round.

The *Telegraph* column was a prop of independence in his own kingdom. And people enjoyed reading it. When Andrew and Madeleine were in Washington for the opening of *Whistle Down the Wind* Peter Brown suggested a drinks party with his friend the British Ambassador, John Kerr. Instead, Kerr wrote back insisting on hosting a Saturday lunch.

When the Lloyd Webbers and Brown arrived, they found not the usual eight or ten guests, but a full three-dozen turn-out of the Washington political and cultural elite. At the end, Brown said how kind of Kerr it was to have gone to all this trouble and invited so many important people. 'Not at all,' said Kerr, 'I'm a great fan of Andrew's column in the *Telegraph*. This was the least I could do.'

The articles appeared illustrated with pleasant water-colourish daubs of tablecloths, wine glasses, plants, waiters and customers, often with views of countryside or South of France landscapes or sea views (interestingly, Lloyd Webber never visits the really great restaurants of Paris, which is a little like an English soccer correspondent never covering a match at Old Trafford or Highbury).

Odd Proustian flights of autobiography peep through, as when the contemplation of a sautéed John Dory with *sauce vierge* reminds him of the sensation when he first visited Aunt Vi's house next door to La Mortola's famous gardens near Ventimiglia. 'I'll spare you the corny old routine about the first time I drank in the fabulous scents that only a Riviera garden can provide. Actually, my aunt assured me that they were partly caused by the cat having sprayed a heavily flowering rosemary bush. But this *sauce vierge* tasted like an enchanted garden.'

Similarly, a visit to the Riva restaurant in Barnes with Tim Rice prompts memories of visiting a Puccinian tenor friend of his mother's, Freddie Peckover (the real name, he thinks, of the reasonably well-known singer Alfred Picaver), in nearby Castelnau and of hearing there his first ever Puccini – 'Ch'ella mi creda' from *The Girl of the Golden West*. And round the corner was Olympic Sound, where many a recording session, including those for *Superstar* and *Evita* had been enjoyed and endured.

A new Wodehouse-ian jauntiness creeps in. Having been reported – wrongly – as teetering on the brink of leaving the country should New Labour win the forthcoming May 1997 election, an advertisement in the *Sun* newspaper had suggested that Lloyd Webber avail himself of the services of Thomson's Holidays.

'The gist was that if you want to quit our fair shores, this mob were the top chaps to help you.' Having declared that he hates beaches, even hates the sun – and that the Thomson holiday brochures represent his idea of 'Hades-on-stilts' – Lloyd Webber indulges in a spot of comic dialogue and ends on a decent remark about the Thomson guys sending him a cruise brochure that looks rather 'spiffing'.

A better, quieter application of the style was seen in the volley fired off at Rule's, the plush restaurant in Maiden Lane that was an outstanding theatrical haunt until the rebirth of the Ivy and the Caprice: 'There are no burgundies at all. For a place that puts so much store on its game, this is somewhat dumbfounding.'

Visiting Marco Pierre White's new Oak Room in the Piccadilly Hotel (now Le Meridien), Lloyd Webber waxes lyrical about taking tea with pater and listening to an orchestra playing medleys from *The White Horse Inn* and *The Merry Widow*. The Wodehouse strain intensifies: 'Next morning the sun was shining. No subterranean den this lunchtime was Webber's motto as I decanted myself into the motor and headed for parts west . . . I decided the midday nosebag should be partaken somewhere I would never usually go to. Quails in Cobham seemed just the ticket.' This paragraph might be usefully condensed as 'Drove to Surrey for lunch.'

This fit of 'Plum' duff writing was no doubt brought on by the re-working of *Jeeves* as *By Jeeves*. This involved the writing of a new song, 'It's a Pig', which had serious gastronomic consequences. To survive the task, Lloyd Webber charged his trusty companion, Pye-Jeary, with lunching with him on pig for an entire week. 'We attempted,' reports the pork-prone partner, 'to eat every bit of pig that we could. We failed only with the tail and anything to do with the genitalia. But apart from that we had ears, snout, obviously every form of trotter available, and everything more or less in the middle, the head, and so on. We managed it. But you can imagine that not many people would want to do that.'

Offal, liver, kidneys, heart, all are grist to the Lloyd

Webber digestive mill, and there is usually a fine duodenum on offer in Gerrard Street that gets the old juices pumping. The Aroma restaurant, a Chinese dive also in Gerrard Street, serves a stew of fish lips, sea slugs and duck webs that is a particular favourite. Pye-Jeary is the inevitable companion on these outings. Madeleine announced her New Year's resolution in January 1997 as, 'To ignore Andrew's requests to taste obscure food, for example, fried pig's ears, sea slug stew and any sort of offal.'

One *Telegraph* column in praise of peas consumed by the plateful in Mark's Club with David Frost was backed on the page turn by a Pet of the Week item featuring Cameron Mackintosh's dog Hugo, a big Rhodesian ridgeback who accompanies the impresario and his partner, the photographer Michael Le Poer Trench, everywhere they go: 'He suffers,' said Mackintosh, 'from an unusually sensitive stomach. He likes a nice shepherd's pie and he's quite partial to cod or turbot. Sometimes I go to the fridge and I'm not sure if it's Hugo's food or mine.'

Making a dog's dinner, or a pig's ear, come to that, of eating out was not on the agenda. Whereas Lloyd Webber could easily have come across as just one more bistro bore in the press gallery of chomping chumps, he communicated deftly as a discriminating, expert and sympathetic creature with strongly held, mostly reasonable, though conservative, views. It was very good public relations. And no other food writer was going to describe Sir Terence Conran's noisy new Bluebird restaurant as 'the gastronomic equivalent of eating at a Gary Glitter concert.'

When it comes to wine, another oversubscribed journalistic growth area for bores, snobs and social climbers, Lloyd Webber is no less secure but a little less convincing if only because the vocabulary of wine writing is so ridiculous. He is good on blatant marking up in restaurants, excellent on tributary subjects like hangover cures. But when he considers his own vaults at Sydmonton he suddenly turns into an oenophiliac Doctor Dolittle, a babbling recluse in a world of his own. 'There's nothing I like more than tottering down to my wine cellar last thing at night. I give the magnums a pat, talk to the Burgundies, caress the Trocken-beerenausleses and leave with a gentle "bye-bye boys" to those naughty tannic young Côtes Roties. I like particularly a secret small bit of the cellar at the back where wives, children *et al* can't find me.'

Pye-Jeary is usually around for any serious action on the cellar front, too. He goes dewy-eyed at describing a small party Lloyd Webber gave for his *Whistle* lyricist Jim Steinman's fiftieth birthday in 1997. He called up all the '47s. 'Oh dear, oh dear, there were some specials there. A very jolly evening, I seem to remember, with just a few people getting really stuck in . . . you'd think of Jim Steinman as a prince of darkness, with his long grey hair and been-up-all-night demeanour. But he's surprisingly, almost overwhelmingly nice, and he really knows his wines.'

Really knowing your wines is a badge of honour to be worn proudly when around Lloyd Webber, but he is usually tactful enough to play his knowledge low key with lesser obsessives. When he put up his cellar for auction at Sotheby's in May 1997 he was only selling about half the stock – 18,000 bottles – but soon after-wards started buying like crazy again. The Bordeaux vintages in the sale were described in the catalogue as 'a hedonist's paradise which surpassed even themselves and made truly mythical wine'. The Sotheby's specialist rated this the greatest collection that had ever come to auction: 'If Bacchus had a cellar, this would be it.'

The sale made £3.5m, way beyond the pre-sale esti-mate of £2.7m. The owner's initials had been stamped on all cases, a security precaution advised by a judge on the occasion of the bankruptcy of the London Wine Company in the early 1970s, in which Lloyd Webber was badly caught out. The stamp also added to the market value, appealing to smart buyers like Barrie Lavin, an Edgware-born sommelier who spent £282,000 at the sale and promptly freighted the lot off to the Mojave desert. He was buying for a Las Vegas casino with an upmarket tasting policy that sells on re-corked bottles at a bargain price to customers in the hotel bar next door.

It must seem odd for someone as pernickety as Lloyd Webber to see his carefully constructed cellar divided up among snob collectors, who are probably less genuinely interested in wine than he is, and gambling holiday-makers who most certainly are. A good eye for detail in this sort of gathering was evident in one of his best and most disdainful *Telegraph* passages aimed at connoisseurs of the antics of music B-list executives gathering in Cannes for a pop business conference: 'As we speak, crates of Bacardi, lager and Coke are being loaded into the bars of the grand watering holes on La Croisette. Prices are being hiked. Recipes for intolerably sweet cocktails are being revised for this annual ritual of open credit card slip grockle-fleecing. Wannabe Spice Girls are squeezing into their PVC. Pubescent Vanessa Paradis lookalikes are perfecting their pouts. Manufacturers of medallions and chest wigs are rubbing their hands in rapture and the purveyors of Clarins instant tan are positively rampant with glee.'

With friends in the music business like Lloyd Webber, what did these mini-execs want with enemies? On another Cannes pop-fest occasion, Lloyd Webber had opened a door in the Majestic Hotel to find in a purple haze of smoke 'a massively overweight record label chief dancing naked on a table while two nymphettes massaged his thighs . . . [and] . . . the Bacardi and Cokers roared on every gyration.' Here was the puritanical younger Andrew who disapproved of Tim Rice's bed-hopping in *Superstar* rock concert days. But here was also someone who has taken his own fair share of stick looking very much more than capable of giving it back. Good for him.

Back on the ranch at Sydmonton, in October 1998, Lloyd Webber initiated a serious dispute over the merits of 1982 clarets and was moved to open a selection of his own and throw them on the mercy of a gathering of oenophiles including Serena Sutcliffe of Sotheby's, star chef Marco Pierre White, Matthew Freud the PR mogul, Lindsay Hamilton, the Pimlico wine merchant, and John Walsh, columnist on the *Independent*. Seventeen different clarets were decanted three hours before the tasting. 'The consensus,' Lloyd Webber reported in his column the following Saturday, 'was extraordinary. Every bottle was hugely tannic to a greater or lesser degree. We started with Montrose (weak), La Lagune (shallow, New Labourish, going nowhere), Ducru-Beaucaillou (actively horrid, I had to wash my mouth out with water) and Grand-Puy-Lacoste (chemical).'

Things improved with the Château Margaux, 'a very fetching feminine bobby-dazzler' and the Château Latour, a well-made 'mega big boy', a serious stayer. This would be saved for his children's twenty-firsts, but John Walsh was not hanging around. One sip, and he began to tingle from head to foot: 'It lay on my tongue like a dream, spread itself languorously to the corners of my mouth, and took off in a million directions at once. "Bloody hell," was all I could say. The wine merchant looked up. "Incredibly long finish," he observed. "That's the secret. That's where the money is." And I only realised that it was the best wine in the world because, for the first time, all the adjectives deserted me.'

In his new side-line of journalism, Lloyd Webber was also subject to the perilous vagaries of the new technology. He was loaned a state-of-the-art dictaphone by the *Telegraph*. (And no, he had not heard the one about the office secretary who, when asked if she used a dictaphone, replied that, thanks all the same, she used her finger.) The marvellous machine backfired on him badly when attending the first night of Darren Day in Cliff Richard's old movie-onto-stage pop travelogue *Summer Holiday* in Hammersmith.

The thing went off in his trousers, spewing forth insider information on whether or not he should part with the vintage Latours at a forthcoming wine sale. It took him an age to press the right button, giving the surrounding customers the confusing notion that the sight of Darren Day in his gleaming white Y-fronts was causing consternation in the great composer's nether regions. 'I don't think it was Darren's inner thighs that set the thing off,' he confesses, 'but the sight of all those cuckoo clocks that suddenly sprouted on the bus route.'

FAME AND FRIENDSHIP, HEALTH AND HAPPINESS

What is he like, then? David Mason was asked this question by the *Los Angeles Times* and said he was like Rasputin: 'He knows what you're thinking before you do; he is almost psychic in this respect. And he is alarmingly quick and a bit frightening. He rang up when this appeared in print, yelling and screaming that the article said he was like Rasputin, and I said, "Well, Andrew, you are", and he said "I know, but I don't want to read it in the bloody papers!"

'He can be your best friend and your worst enemy, the nicest guy in the world and the nastiest. I have the same relationship, if you like, with my wife. That's what meaningful relationships are like. But it's impossible to see him in black and white. He's a very complex fellow.'

Showbusiness is not always a pleasant game and dirty tricks are not unknown. But when people have reason to be upset with Lloyd Webber it usually boils down to matters of etiquette. And this stems from innate shyness. The soothing telephone call, the explanatory apology, are not in his repertoire. But neither is deviousness or undue malice. What you see, on the whole, is what you get. And that simply is not true of most theatre producers and impresarios.

He cares less about reviews than what he sees as acts of betrayal by colleagues who have used his company to feather their own nests. Retribution in such cases is swift and merciless. But as Madeleine says, he will trust colleagues and be quite naive sometimes in so doing. Big decisions he fully understands and approves – such as taking the company public, and later, having bought it back, selling a thirty per cent stake on to Polygram – he regrets and complains about. The sale to Polygram remains a sore point, and he grimaces still at the realisation that, while it was done to ensure that the company had no debts, a side effect was to boost the income of a chief executive whose salary was directly related to profits.

In the wake of the *Sunset* collapse, Lloyd Webber found himself in a company that had been showing profits of £30m suddenly expecting losses of £10m. And he felt helplessly imprisoned by the fact that, in a few years time, the Really Useful could be in the majority grip of Polygram. He would be owned lock, stock and barrel. The company shed staff in London and closed offices abroad, and in May 1997 Patrick McKenna departed and the personnel in London was overhauled. Bill Taylor took over as chief executive and Lloyd Webber moved back into the office.

Having worked hard to talk Polygram out of their option to move to control early in the next century, Lloyd Webber and his new personal and business manager, John Reid – Elton John's manager for twenty-eight years, and an experienced fixer in the music business – found themselves having to deal with Seagram, the Canadian drinks and entertainment group, who acquired Polygram in May 1998.

Suddenly the gloom clouds lifted when the head of Seagram, Edgar Bronfman, turned out to be a big musicals man and assured Lloyd Webber and Reid that there would be no question of Seagram moving to fifty-one per cent control of the company in 2003. Lloyd Webber was confident, too, that his first right to buy the Polygram stake in his company would apply also with Seagram.

That confidence, and patience, bore fruit in April 1999 when a delighted Lloyd Webber announced that he had bought back – for $75m, or £47m – the 30 per cent Polygram/Seagram stake. He was now, for the first time in his life, in full control of all his work.

With his new show going into production and the morale higher in Tower House than it had been for some time, Lloyd Webber's own mood shifted accordingly. The hounded, unhappy man of the early part of the year became liberated with the onrush of creative energy and the tingle factor of an approaching first night.

John Reid says that Lloyd Webber is similar in some ways to Elton John. Both are intensely shy, both don't know how to relax. And both, in different ways, have created public personae that are larger than life, Elton with his extravagant stage acts and lifestyle, Andrew with his old-style Barnum and Bailey showbusiness drum-beating.

In the early days of his partnership with Tim Rice, Lloyd Webber certainly took the back seat in affairs of publicity and ready quotes in the press. But he learned quickly and by the time he flew the coop with *Cats* he was as adept as anyone at the flashy soundbite and well-timed gesture.

He married Sarah Two in time to meet the Queen at a royal gala for *Starlight Express*. And his fiftieth birthday gala not only successfully upstaged Cameron Mackintosh's celebration of thirty years in show-business, but also achieved peak-time television exposure and a most convenient free advertising plug for the upcoming *Whistle*.

Mackintosh had out-manoeuvred him on *Sunset* by managing to have coach party bookings diverted to his own productions of *Oliver!* at the Palladium and *Miss Saigon* at Drury Lane. The Really Useful had made a terrible error by cutting out the party booking agents in an act of hubris and greed for which Lloyd Webber carried the can but blamed Patrick McKenna. It is inconceivable that he did not know what was going on. In the end, Madeleine's hostess skills came crucially into play when she and Andrew hosted a dinner for the aggrieved agents to make reparation. 'It was all a terrible mix-up,' says Lloyd Webber. 'I was unaware of the extent of what was going on. But to be fair to Patrick, he did at least appoint Kevin Wallace to the head of the theatre division, for which I'm eternally grateful.'

His wife has also worked hard at keeping the extended family of two Sarahs and all children in touch with each other. What about her husband? Does he never shut the door on work and business problems? 'Oh, sure! If anything, it gets worse when he gets home! He talks about whatever's in his head. We live and breathe whatever we're up to; or rather, whatever he's up to. And most of the time it's the most exciting life. We're doing fascinating things and meeting amazing people. And Andrew always loves going out to dinner!'

But is he happy? His brother Julian ponders the question. 'I wonder quite what drives him still. He's always restless. I'm not surprised he's been ill lately. He's lived life very hard for a very long time. He must have the constitution of an ox. I know what it's like flying all the time. He'll go to LA for a couple of days and you wonder, was that really necessary? It's not as if he's giving a concert, like me, is it? It's because he always has to keep moving, keep doing something. This is something which eventually, physically, will take its toll. I can't see him ever changing.'

The mystery illness came to a head in December 1994 when Lloyd Webber was treated in hospital for an ulcerated oesophagus. The inflammation of his throat had been brought on by a previous treatment for a recurring tropical disease. He now says he felt 'ghastly' all the way from *Aspects* to *Sunset*, trying allergy treatments and various medications until, when *Sunset* was opening in New York, a specialist conducted various tests on him.

Within two hours, he was told he had been overtaken for several years by an amoeba feeding off his dietary system. *And* getting fat on all those sea slugs and pigs' trotters. Two years ago, in New York again for the tenth anniversary of *Phantom* and assailed by the latest in an endless round of colds and irritating illnesses, another doctor told him that this amoeba had vitiated his immune system and that in situations of stress he became even more vulnerable to its effects.

The only cure is a complete rest of nine months or so, and this he might take in the forseeable future. Or he might not. Madeleine has insisted that the three young children – Alastair, William and Isabella – stay in school in London, so there is more of a domestic routine organised around holidays and half-terms.

Peter Brown thinks that Madeleine is the best thing that ever happened to him. 'She's an enormously good influence. And having this young family a second time round gives him a chance to be really interested in his children. Which he is. The first time, when Imogen and Nicholas were small, he was too busy making a living and making a mark to pay much attention to them.'

Lloyd Webber takes Alastair to football matches, often to Loftus Road to see Queen's Park Rangers, whose owner, Chris Wright, chairman of the music publishing and film group Chrysalis, is a racing friend. Does Alastair support QPR? Dad isn't too sure. 'I think he's with Chelsea now, or maybe Arsenal. Chris Wright has a horse with Madeleine, so Alastair appeared there as a team mascot for a cup match with Chelsea. And he came off the pitch saying he supported the visitors. I didn't help much by saying afterwards that I thought QPR were basically a third division side. But it's all good fun, and we have a great time.'

Superstar, *Evita* and *Sunset* all initiate discussions on the power of celebrity, the accident and maintenance of fame. Jesus is as much a victim of his own reputation as of Judas's betrayal. Evita manipulates her role in the national iconography to both appease and soar above the masses ('And as for fortune, and as for fame, I never invited them in, though it seemed to the world they were all I desired; they are illusions' runs one verse in the hit song). And Norma Desmond tries to make a deal with the public in a defiant comeback as a star whom no-one remembers.

Lloyd Webber himself has been famous for years and finds it difficult to walk down the street without being embarrassed. He long ago gave up driving a car because of cheery and not so cheery hoots and 'Wotchas' from other motorists. But he does sit in the back of a car, and indeed will do so even to travel just fifty yards down the road from a theatre to a restaurant.

Rod Argent in his Zombies days (daze?) describes the period of his life between the ages of nineteen and thirty as one of arrested development: 'You become the centre of the universe and, wherever you go, people react to you in an unreal way. You don't analyse it, you just accept it. When I met Andrew, he was already famous and he always struck me as someone with his feet on the ground to an extraordinary degree.

'He still does. And he's still shy. But I think he has

now woven a protective cocoon around himself to the extent that it's harder to get through to him now than it was.' Tim Rice certainly concurs. He says he would happily work again with Andrew if he could get through the six secretaries. Rice himself does not have a big producing company to run, but he has a busy life and gets by with one loyal secretary.

Lloyd Webber declares that he never understands these protestations when Tim can, and does, get hold of him whenever he likes on his private line. Tim is also adept, he reckons, at using the excuse of business appointments to back out of tricky work situations. When Nigel Wright was producing the new *Superstar* album, Tim insisted that he should be on hand for one or two tracks on which he particularly wanted to be involved. On the day in question, he told Wright that he was returning from New York for some crucial meetings that he could not postpone and that the recording session would simply have to wait until he turned up. Wright got as much done as he could with the cast and the musicians, but by four o'clock in the afternoon, there was nothing else to do but sit and wait for the lyricist's arrival. So, with the musicians moving happily into over-time, the entire personnel removed to a room with a television to watch the final session of play at the Wimbledon tennis championships. After a few minutes, the cameras scanning the crowd zoomed in on a box that contained a clutch of celebrities, including Sir Tim Rice! Nothing was said when, two or three hours later, Rice duly reported to work, but a few giggles were stifled as he apologised for being unavoidably detained elsewhere.

Famous people find it easier to get along with other famous people than with unknown types. They need to bask in each other's glow on an equal footing. The celebrity pact becomes a celebrity pack and the pictures in newspapers do not lie about this. Michael Caine really does hang out with Roger Moore. It saves a lot of trouble and you don't have to waste time being deferential to each other, or impressed. And the deal ensures a reflection of your own fame in the mirror of your friend's.

Thus the easeful companionship Lloyd Webber finds in the company of Sir David Frost. They go back a long way. 'Frostie' as both Andrew and Tim Rice call him, interviewed the emergent duo on both sides of the Atlantic in the early days of *Superstar*. 'I count him,' says the TV interviewer, who has cleverly managed a graceful career journey from satire in the sixties to mainstream showbusiness and political interrogation, 'as a real close friend. Somebody I would feel at a moment of real need very happy going to . . . d'you know what I mean?'

The two titans and their families are neighbours, country-style, at weekends. The Frosts have a retreat a short drive from Sydmonton, halfway between Romsey and Stockbridge. So Sunday lunch is often a fixture. Sir David and Lady Carina, daughter of the Duke of Norfolk, have three boys in their early teens who enjoy the company of the Lloyd Webber younger brood, and the adults' friendship has intensified as a result.

They also manage a foursome for dinner in London once a month. And the two chaps will often have a short-notice lunch at somewhere like Mark's Club or the Connaught. Do they sometimes have a spontaneous night out and a good dinner? 'Yes, and indeed a bad dinner,' says Sir David. 'In the cause of his column we have had one or two disasters, notably at the Hotel de Paris in Monte Carlo, where they were pushy and rude and did all the things that spoilt restaurants do when they are accustomed to unquestioning tourists, I suppose. Andrew wrote that up brilliantly.

'One of the things about friendship is that you don't really analyse it. One of the truths, I suppose, is that it is instantaneous and emotional. And loyalty is part of it.

Andrew is a very funny man and when he's on song he's simply hilarious.

'He's had more than his fair share of bitching from the press, quite apart from the reviews. The Australians call it the tall poppy syndrome. But I think he's come to terms with that. Of course everyone is more sensitive than they appear. Tony Jay [the comedy writer and co-author of BBC TV's *Yes, Minister!*] once said that all any author wants from a review is six thousand words of closely reasoned adulation.'

Frost reckons that Lloyd Webber has overcome the adversity of harsh opinion and has worked out for himself that, on the whole, 'it's better to be Andrew Lloyd Webber than be stuck on the outside looking at Andrew Lloyd Webber'. He also admiringly pinpoints the direct relationship Lloyd Webber has forged with Middle England and Middle America. 'I think it's to do with aspiration and dreaming. That line in *Sunset Boulevard*, "We taught the world new ways to dream", could have been written just for Andrew. It reminds me of a phrase Bryan Forbes wrote in a movie I produced in the mid-1970s, *The Slipper and the Rose*, starring Richard Chamberlain and Gemma Craven.

'It was about the legend of Cinderella being brought up to date, and at one point Gemma as Cinderella asks Annette Crosbie as the Fairy Godmother – who is turning carrots into horses for the gold coach – how she does it. And Annette says, "It's a trade secret, actually, but it helps if you dream . . ." And that's what Andrew is in tune with. People's dreams.'

Julian reports how his brother becomes very emotional about his own [Andrew's] music, and very emotional when he hears his father's music. 'I played the Elgar concerto a few years ago at the Festival Hall with Yehudi Menuhin conducting, and for an encore we did "John 19:41" from *Superstar*. Madeleine says he was in total floods of tears.' And Nigel Wright, the record producer, recalls being with Andrew when he rose from his seat, entirely overcome, on first hearing Elaine Paige sing 'With One Look'.

Before *Whistle* was previewed at Sydmonton, the director Gale Edwards stayed in the house for a week. She awoke in the small hours one morning and heard a distant piano. 'I crept from the guest room down the great oak staircase in a dressing gown. The door was ajar and there was Andrew in his dressing gown and pyjamas, and without batting an eyelid he said, "Come in Gale, what do you think of this?" And I sat with him until dawn while he tried things out. He was excited, lost, frightened, in need of opinions. It was one of the most wonderful hours of my life.

'And I felt I could die happy because I'd been at the workface and seen how it works. I felt privileged to stand there and see it, and be a part of it. I felt I saw through some kind of window into Andrew's soul. And he was not a celebrity or a world famous composer. Just a man at a piano searching for the right tune. And at that moment I felt such undying admiration for him.'

THIRTEEN

IT'S A PIG, IT'S MADONNA,
IT'S A WRAP

In March 1996, *Starlight Express* had been running twelve years. The faithful audience on that anniversary included a man called Steve Starlight – who had changed his name from Steve Lane – and who hailed from a place called Westgate-on-Sea. Also present was a Kentish postman, Alan Newman, who had spent £21,000, he estimated, on seeing the show 750 times. Shortly afterwards he got married and stopped going.

During its eight-year West End run, *Evita* took £23m at the box office and was seen by four million people. One of them, Mrs Maye Briggs of Romford, Essex, made quite a contribution to that total income. She saw the show 330 times.

Which makes you wonder whether or not hit shows depend on the kindness of strangers, or just strange people. They call it the repeat audience in the trade. This phenomenon lay at the heart of the Andrew Lloyd Webber success story. No show runs unless people who need people – the funniest people – send in the people.

These folks keep the flame alight. Bob Martin, a retired printroom manager from Eastleigh, Hampshire, was a *Cats* groupie who developed his obsession seven years after the opening night. 'I always go up on my own,' he says. 'I've been a loner most of my life. But I've got to know everyone involved in the show. They're a great bunch. I've got this running joke with the front-of-house staff, who pretend my ticket's stolen or forged. Or they say I'm banned from the theatre.'

One would rather, on the whole, people watched Andrew Lloyd Webber musicals than make a nuisance of themselves in the community. But with fans like these, you begin to have second thoughts. Mr Martin goes to see musicals to keep the actors happy. Having spotted them once, he follows them around. 'I've seen *Crazy For You* nineteen times, *Les Misérables* seven times, *Me and My Girl* nine times. *Cats* has widened my life, given me a new direction.'

Is this really the secret of *Cats'* success? A rest home for weirdos? The composer railed against the implications of accepting the European social chapter by itemising the difference of *Cats* costs in April 1997: in Hamburg, *Cats* had a cast of forty-five, in London of twenty-five; the backstage musicians numbered twenty in Hamburg, four in London; ticket prices were double the London cost in Hamburg, backstage staff triple.

In June 1997, *Cats* became the longest running show in Broadway history, after lagging behind *A Chorus Line* for fifteen years. The similarities with Michael Bennett's ground-breaking dance audition piece – in one case a dance job was on offer, in the other a place in cat heaven – were itemised by Peter Marks in the *New York Times*, who then suggested that the experience of sitting through the show was like a trip through the time tunnel back to 1982. The show had become an artefact, he averred, and was no longer a living work.

But how could you possibly tie *Cats* to a date? When I revisited *Cats* in its 'seventeenth phenomenal year' at the New London, I felt an audience, including fourteen nice ladies from Osaka, responding to the show as if they had just discovered it. The earth, and the rubbish tip, moved for them. And for its producers. By May 1999 the show had taken over £100m in London alone and been seen by over eight million people.

If *Cats* is a vaudeville, it is also about a process of selection, just as *Superstar* and *Evita* are about the questioning of one person's right to take an ascendant place in a society he or she is avowedly representing. *Starlight*, too, is a hymn to individuality in the rat race. By the time the show reached its tenth anniversary in March 1994, it had become the second longest running show in British musical theatre history behind *Cats*, a position it holds to this day.

Even more so than *Cats*, however, *Starlight* is constantly reworked by its production team to take account of changing street fashions in music and nostalgia. It is clearer now that the show is a fantasy of a small boy sent to bed by his mother with the injunction to put away his trains. On my last visit, on school half-term, the place went crazy. The races are tighter and meaner, and the final reduced to just four participants. Several new songs were added in 1992, notably 'Make Up My Heart' for Pearl and 'Next Time You Fall in Love' (with lyrics by Don Black) for Pearl and Rusty.

Lloyd Webber's musicals are timeless, or lost in space nostalgia. They do not appear to address the real world any more than do *The White Horse Inn* or *The Desert Song* in a previous generation. They are about his music and the incidental stories of Jesus, Evita, the Phantom or whomever. Or are they? The symbiotic relationship between Jesus and Judas in *Superstar* was redefined by Gale Edwards in her superb late 1996 revival at the refurbished Lyceum Theatre as a sarcastic, taunting shadow play.

You suddenly saw where the idea of staging the showdown between Javert and Jean Valjean in *Les Misérables* had come from. Judas saw himself as the true victim, and his suicide was followed by his own resurrection on the road to Golgotha.

John Napier designed a tiered, Roman colosseum on

the stage, where paying customers reinforced the gladiatorial aspect of the show. Caiaphas and the high priests descended on a gantry in steel and cobalt costumes, in textured contrast to the soft orange and brown tunics of the antagonistic religious sect. The debauchery of Herod's court – a place of writhing catamites and sudden flames – matched the barbarian bombast of hysteria and betrayal in the second act.

And Zubin Varla – a mesmerising young actor who had already made his mark with the Royal Shakespeare Company – presented Judas as a warped, Iago-like malcontent who perfectly expressed the show's central thesis that Jesus was both frail and impenetrable as man and myth. How could such a creature be trusted, let alone loved? This was a perfectly reasonable question to ask.

A sceptical age which has forgotten about faith is turning to the tasteless public confessionals of the new messianic gurus on daytime television. Oprah Winfrey, Ricki Lake and Jerry Springer encourage a spirit of rabid revivalism and emotional hysteria among their audiences of desperate non-believers. The new harshness of *Superstar* lay in its absolute refusal to buy that sort of false comfort while pointing out the dangers of cultish spirituality. The show wasn't a Christian rock musical at all. It was a statement of agnostic cynicism.

No such new meanings were yielded by the re-working of *Jeeves* earlier in the same year as *By Jeeves*, a show dedicated to the memory of David Land, who died in 1995. In later years, Land had bought the Theatre Royal, Brighton, running it as the last privately owned theatre in the country. At his memorial in March 1996, Lloyd Webber and Tim Rice paid their respective tributes from the stage he loved so much, performed 'Any Dream Will Do' at the piano together and led the chorus of 'Land of Hope and Glory'.

Land used to drive Lloyd Webber nuts from time to

time and never displayed, as far as Lloyd Webber was concerned, all that much in the way of theatrical acumen. But he was a big-hearted enthusiast who had the invaluable knack of keeping a sense of proportion and a sense of humour. Both these qualities Rice also brought to Lloyd Webber's music, and you might say that these were qualities he could do with a little more of today. There are signs of their return, certainly, in *Whistle*, which is probably Lloyd Webber's rockiest and most impassioned score since *Superstar*.

And as a holiday from the grandiose obsessions of *Sunset* the return to Wodehouse proved a welcome break. Alan Ayckbourn had approached Lloyd Webber with a view to re-working their collaboration and presenting it as the opening show in his spanking new Scarborough theatre.

Ayckbourn's admired colleague and mentor Stephen Joseph – an actor, director and writer, son of the publisher Michael Joseph and the actress Hermione Gingold – had been memorialised in Scarborough with a theatre-in-the-round in a converted school hall. When Joseph died in 1967, Ayckbourn left his job in the BBC radio drama department to run Joseph's theatre and to live in his house, a rambling Victorian vicarage in the old part of the town.

The pair had kept in touch ever since their famous fiasco. The new theatre was housed in the revamped 1936 Odeon cinema opposite the station, enticingly proclaimed with blue and pink neon strip lighting on the exterior. Inside: peachy pink walls, art deco friezes, brightly lit bars, a gift shop, an elderly audience and a fairly average restaurant.

Scarborough's an odd place, the northern equivalent – with a much more dramatic coastline and superior beaches – of Frinton-on-Sea or Worthing in the south. Ayckbourn once said that, apart from visiting his theatre, there was nothing to do there except get drunk and buy shoes. But a combination of local fundraising (Ayckbourn himself had pitched in with nearly half a million) and money from the government-backed national gambling Lottery had created an impressive new facility.

The official opening coincided with the Scarborough premiere, on May Day 1996, of *By Jeeves*. Lloyd Webber sat happily in the audience with Sarah One and his first child Imogen to his right, Cameron Mackintosh to his left. They gurgled with pleasure throughout like schoolchildren on an end-of-term outing. For both men, this was a return to the kind of paradisiacal British musical comedy theatre they had in fact erased from the play lists. The composer was deliberately trying to retrieve, or reinvent, his past. And Madeleine was in the Portland Hospital in London, about to give birth to their third child, Isabella.

The party had taken over a posh boarding house in the town. In the restaurant after the show, the kitchen had caught fire and Lloyd Webber led the troops back to his lodgings where he improvised a meal from the fridge. He then led them all back again to the hosed-down restaurant for desserts and coffee and stayed with the company until the small hours. What had he seen in the show that was different from the 1975 version?

Quite a lot, really. Apart from the crucial down-scaling exercise advocated by Ronald Bryden in his *Plays and Players* review, there was a new sense of making the most of modest resources and it was a most definite one-in-the-eye for the mega-musical jeremiad wallahs.

The narrative was tightened beyond all recognition – by Ayckbourn – moving even further away from *The Code of the Woosters* and incorporating other Wodehouse elements, but no aunts, alas – into a knock-about farce of mistaken identities, low-budget scenic gags and the ingenious pig hunt. The framing device was now that of Bertie losing his banjo and having to improvise a show, whereas before he had merely snapped a string on the instrument.

Jauntiness reigned. And reined: 'The secret with men, of course is, you treat them a bit like horses' trilled Honoria Glossop in 'That Was Nearly Us'. The lyrics were the funniest since the Rice days, the stomping jollity of it all a carefree throwback to the sort of silly musical theatre – Dorothy Reynolds and Julian Slade's *Salad Days* the prime example – that had first inspired Mackintosh and made him want to work in theatre.

Andrew had rejected the genre in the rock revolution, but was still surprisingly susceptible to the wiles of Julian Slade and Sandy Wilson. The lilting melody of 'Half a Moment' was as good an operetta-style song as he had written, and the pig chase prompted a silly, charming comic number of the first order with superb lyrics from Ayckbourn which even incorporated the stage directions: 'With a badly bruised libido, exit Wooster tres rapido.'

The patter numbers speeded up and were brilliantly executed by Steven Pacey as Bertie and Malcolm Sinclair as the avuncular, super-cool Jeeves. As Lloyd Webber sat watching 'Travel Hopefully' in which Bertie expressed his philosophy en route to Totleigh Towers, bumping into Bingo Little on a charity walk for hedgehogs, he must have thought that his innocent, charming melody from the long-lost Barnardo musical had come full circle in the ecology madness of the day.

'This plot is thicker than Mulligatawny, Jeeves,' was the sort of line Ayckbourn spun through the relationship, dapper daftness pitted against stoical reason. And the overall flavour caught something profound in the type of British theatre Lloyd Webber had otherwise renounced. Amateur, sentimental, jolly. He was plugging into the enemy ethos again, wallowing in friendly fire. 'I was quite resigned to the fact that we might not move the show beyond Scarborough. It was done again, really, as an act of love, and of faith in Alan and the new venue. As Isabella was being born, I stayed up there for several weeks and had a lovely time looking at buildings in Whitby and other remote parts of Yorkshire during the day, while Alan was slogging away in the theatre. We met up in the evenings and reviewed what was happening. It was a lovely time, like a holiday.'

The show was ecstatically reviewed, transferred to the Duke of York's but ran for only eight months. Which only goes to show that the maestro of mega-musicals is as subject to the winds of change as anyone. And as subject to the vagaries of the industry he has personally transformed: 'It's blindingly obvious to everybody except an imbecile that there are now no great tunes in pop and no great tunes in musical theatre.'

Present company excepted. Our leading theatre song-smith cannot get radio air time for his tunes, unless recorded by Celine Dion, Boyzone, or Tom Jones. This is a serious problem. Even the apparently lost cause of Willy Russell's *Blood Brothers* – now a ten-year West End hit – was only freakishly rescued back in the mid 1980s when Terry Wogan broke the mould by playing 'Tell Me It's Not True' on his early morning breakfast show.

Theatre's out, as far as the wireless is concerned, and 'every ounce of the day I hit record companies who tell me they are not going to record one of my songs because it comes from a musical . . . and I keep saying my songs are not that bad at the moment . . . my musicals are always supposed to be about spectacles . . . when I did *Tell Me On a Sunday* it was about a girl sitting on a stool singing songs.'

By the time *Evita* became a film everyone knew the songs, the show, and the people who had supposedly nearly been cast in it. Alan Parker, the eventual director, listed some of them: Raquel Welch, Ann-Margret, Bette Midler, Liza Minnelli, Olivia Newton-John, Pia Zidora,

Meryl Streep, and Elton John (as Che). He had been invited by Robert Stigwood to make the film but had mumbled that, after *Fame*, he wanted 'out' from musicals. When he changed his mind, fifteen years later, Michelle Pfeiffer was on board but unwilling to leave Hollywood with two young children.

Parker, who had directed such contrastingly magical musical films as *Bugsy Malone* and *The Commitments*, inherited a script and half a project from Oliver Stone, the latest director to be involved after a putative litany including Richard Attenborough, Ken Russell, Herb Ross, Alan Pakula and Franco Zeffirelli: 'By May of 1995, I had finished writing my script – which called for 146 changes to the original score and lyrics – and so, like a mailman offering his leg to a couple of hungry Rottweilers, I sent my first draft to Andrew and Tim. Fortunately, they liked it very much.'

Less fortunately, it was tough getting them to work together on the song Parker needed for Perón and Evita at the end. But the result, 'You Must Love Me', sung by Madonna after Perón has carried her upstairs weak with cancer and dying, deservedly won an Oscar, a plaintive, moodily exact ballad for voice and treated piano that expressed Eva's defiant love and Perón's fears for the worst.

Madonna had written to Parker demanding the part. She said that only she could understand Eva's passion and pain and that she had not written this letter of her own free will: 'It was as if some other force drove my hand across the page.' These thoughts she confided to the readers of *Vanity Fair* which published her *Evita* Diaries, complete with an on-set fashion shoot, in November 1996: 'Last night I dreamed of Evita. I was not outside watching her, I was her. I felt her sadness and her restlessness. I felt hungry and unsatisfied and in a hurry. Just as I had earlier in the helicopter, suspended over the earth, on the way to meet President Menem. As

I gazed down on all of B.A., my mind started drifting. I tried to imagine how I would react and what I would do if, like Evita, I knew I had cancer and I was dying. I could finally understand the feverish pace at which Evita lived during her last years. She wanted her life to matter.'

Madonna looked the role in her sheath-like costumes and brown contact lenses, and her empathising became interwoven with the reality of her own stardom and isolation on location in first Argentina, then Budapest, then London. She shares celebrity dreams with Sharon Stone, chides her accountant for sending flowers on Valentine's Day ('I am mistrustful of flowers from people who make a percentage of my gross income') and declares that, like Evita, she will never apologise for her behaviour – or reputation as a 'bad girl' or 'fallen woman' – when a bishop in Budapest refuses the crew permission to shoot inside his basilica: 'The bishop can kiss my ass. I'm not grovelling for one more person in the name of this movie.'

She had already done her bit by sweet-talking President Menem into allowing her to sing 'Don't Cry For Me, Argentina' on the balcony of the Casa Rosada in the historic Plaza de Mayo, Buenos Aires. The Péronist, star-struck Menem had complimented Madonna on her physical similarity to Evita, whom he had met as a young man. She noted how his eyes hardly strayed from her bra strap.

But he had also condemned the musical as 'an absolute and total disgrace'. And there had been a vociferous campaign against Madonna, thought of by many poor Argentinians who revered Evita's memory, as a perverse, anti-religious Madonna, a virtual symbol of prostitution. With the arrival on set of heart-throb Antonio Banderas to play Che, the press started speculating on the competition Madonna offered to Melanie Griffiths, his girlfriend: 'Everyone knows I would never date a man who wears cowboy boots,' snapped the icon in her diary.

Economic imperatives, as well as Madonna's seductive skills, won Menem round on the balcony issue. A week after her first unofficial meeting with the President, she was summoned to an official one along with Alan Parker, Antonio Banderas and Jonathan Pryce (who was to play Juan Perón). According to Parker, they all sat nibbling the President's famous pizza when, after much small talk and diplomatic tap dancing, Madonna suddenly said, 'Let's cut to the chase here. Do we have the balcony or don't we?' Menem smiled and nodded, 'You can have the balcony.'

Parker was slightly miffed by this development. He had spent a large amount of money having the balcony rebuilt back in London. But he had to cave in to Menem's caving in. The film would bring a lot of work for extras and allied trades. And even the British task force of Alan Parker and his crew – during the Falklands War, the British troops were always referred to as the task force – were eventually made to feel welcome. There was no problem filming in the countryside, in the town of Junin where Evita grew up and at Chivilcoy where her father's funeral took place.

The film makes much of Evita's humiliation as the bastard daughter of a landowner. Her impoverished mother was the landowner's lover and bore him five children. They were banned from the funeral but allowed to say a quick farewell at the wake. In the film, the young Evita gatecrashes the church ceremony and is pulled away from the coffin. The traumatic memory of this funeral is interleaved with the sombre majesty of her own twenty-six years later.

Madonna was even working on that side of the movie, even though it didn't involve her. 'Forgot to mention Menem's daughter,' she told her diary, 'who also attended the meeting. A thin wisp of a girl who seemed very fragile and very sad. She held her father's hand through the whole meeting and they kissed and whispered things to each other in a very intimate way. I was mesmerized by them.'

The beauty of the cinematography, the cleverness of editing sequences to pre-recorded songs, the sheer detail and scale of the film, all conspire to disguise the fact that *Evita* is a theatrical artefact. Its structure is accumulative, not organically emotional. Parker's sterling attempts to fly in the face of the evidence of the kind of creative energy informing the piece itself only underlined the fundamental fatuity of the exercise.

Jonathan Pryce complained in an interview that his quest to play 'multi-dimensional' roles on film received a setback with the cardboard cut-out figure of Péron: 'You could have put a pair of scissors around Juan Péron in *Evita*, but that isn't mine or Alan Parker's doing. That's the part as written.'

No it wasn't. It was Pryce's mistake to look for depth where none existed and where his function as a character was merely that of being there in attendance and singing songs. That is quite a lot, and demands a different sort of art from that Pryce was prepared to offer. He is such a good actor, however, that despite himself he came up trumps. Especially at those moments when he just had to be astonished, or baffled, by what Madonna was doing in the opposite shot.

She had a similar, but more telling, effect on Banderas, whose generic Che became a critical quick-change Everyman in every scene, and a rivalrous lover. He and Pryce's eyes meet across Evita's coffin at the end and when Banderas kisses the glass top, Pryce stares back in cold puzzlement. It's a great moment, and the credits roll to a reprise of 'You Must Love Me', the new song.

One weakness of the story was always that Evita's illness was unrelated to anything she had done – and nothing is made of her uterine cancer stemming possibly from a history of sexual promiscuity. But the study in stardom was certainly reinforced by Madonna's glowering and very beautiful performance, and given many new layers, even if the singing of the role was hugely inferior to either Elaine Paige or Patti LuPone on stage. The religious side, the Madonna element, was notably well conveyed. And by stealing 'Another Suitcase in Another Hall' from Péron's rejected mistress, she extended the sexual vulnerabilty of the role.

The more real and historically authentic the film becomes, the further it actually moves away from its very 1970s, Latino-rock musical source. So instead of crowds of rioters, mourners, 'descamisados' (the shirtless) and trades unionists on the march demanding a new Argentina, you feel they should be agitating for a new kind of musical film, or at least something different from what they are saddled with.

Mark Steyn hit an even more cynical note than usual in demanding 'a reproduction of that famous Madonna photograph where she's hanging bare-bottomed over the wall, only this time with sensibly logoed *Evita* knickers painted on, and her saying, "Now Eva Péron."' But he was surely more than half-right in saying in his *Spectator* column that whatever the film's defects as a portrait of Evita, 'it works brilliantly as a definitive autobiographical record of Madonna'.

By the time she arrives in Budapest, Madonna is pregnant. And by the time she is home in New York, she's sick and tired of being the other woman. Danced off her feet, rehearsed into the ground, manhandled by actors playing military police, bursting at the seams with a new life impatient to start. 'Have I solved the riddle of Evita? Have I answered all the burning questions? Why was her country so passionately divided, for and against her? Why did she evoke such a strong response in people, then and now? Was she good or bad? Innocent or manipulative? I'm still not sure, but I know one thing – I have grown to love her.'

Tim and Andrew had gone through their usual wobbliness over writing the new song. 'Why are you at my side, how can I be any use to you now? Give me a chance and let me see how, nothing has changed . . .' Péron is waiting for news of the worst, but Rice was reiterating an old problem. It had been an odd year for them.

Well, for Tim, anyway. 'I was told that I had to be involved in the *Superstar* revival and when I said that I didn't like the poster they said it was too late . . . and I said, well, I was getting involved. And in the end, apparently, one is not to be involved.' He missed the first night on a pre-booked walking holiday in Lowestoft and although he admired the production, he suspected the whole thing had been put together 'rather badly, financially, because it was so expensive'.

Similarly, he felt the whole business of the *Evita* film was shrouded in confusion. 'Suddenly Andrew was in Budapest for the filming, and I knew nothing about it. There were one or two tiny changes made to the lyrics by Alan Parker that I wasn't told about and that I thought were pointless.

'And when it came to the London opening, Andrew said we simply had to go in together and that we would knock Madonna off the front pages. And I said, why would you want to do that, she's far more interesting to everyone than we are? And of course the wonderful irony in the end was that we were both upstaged anyway by a couple of dykes who had used the premiere to come out in public – Simon Ward's daughter and her chum!'

It also amused Rice that Evita was now a name on everyone's lips but that had been the opposite of the case when they started work on the album and the stage show. 'And yet when the movie came out, some guy called Tom Shone in the *Sunday Times* – and I can't remember whether he liked the movie or not – said that the object in writing the show had been merely to put bums on seats. It was totally untrue that Eva Péron had somehow been a commercial idea we had latched on to.

'The show is accurate once you accept that they didn't sing and that Che is not necessarily Che Guevara but an Argentinian anti-Péronist. The only thing everyone can be agreed about is that Eva Péron wanted to be famous, wanted to be a star. And in Argentina, being a film star was no great shakes, whereas distinction in politics was.'

Rice's estranged wife Jane was finally so incensed by the endless accreditation of *Evita* to just one of its authors that she fired off a letter to the *Daily Telegraph*: 'It would be helpful if journalists from all newspapers who write about *Evita* would not refer to it as an Andrew Lloyd Webber musical. It happens over and over again, and it is exasperating for everyone (including Andrew) who knows that it categorically is *not* an Andrew Lloyd Webber musical.

'It was Tim Rice's idea in the first place; all the initial research in 1974 was done by him, and every word of the show was written by him. *Evita* has become hugely successful as a result of the collaboration of Tim and Andrew. When it first came out it was known as a Rice-Lloyd Webber musical. It still is.'

When their song was nominated for an Oscar – which it duly won – Rice expressed doubts on the subject of how welcome this might be while addressing a cricket dinner: 'I have picked up two Oscars with great men in the past but the prospect of picking one up with Andrew Lloyd Webber leaves me with mixed feelings – a bit like watching your mother-in-law driving off a cliff in your new Ferrari.'

Oh dear. Maybe Lloyd Webber had this lodged in his mind when he said that working with Jim Steinman on *Whistle* had the distinct advantage of never bringing cricket into the equation: 'Jim has got something of the

Tim Rice about him in that he loves his charts and his rock 'n' roll. But the difference is Tim likes to play cricket and I can't see Jim or me on a cricket field. Much as I think Tim is an absolute genius lyricist, it's wonderful to work with someone who is *so* big – the number one songwriter in America last year.' (Steinman wrote Celine Dion's chart-busting 'It's All Coming Back To Me Now'.)

Touché. Jane Rice had been on that research trip with Tim and she had seen how, over the years, Andrew had taken the initiative in publicity, had grown to relish the sport of it all and hone the one-liners, while Tim was happier backing away from the spotlight. Rice's daughter Eva showed signs of replacing him there, starting a rock band, launching a career as a model, and writing a book. 'She's very like what I was at that age, trying anything and seeing what happens.' His son Donald is studying in Edinburgh and plays the piano 'quite well'.

This Scottish connection led Sir Tim – he was knighted in 1994 – to buy the 33,000-acre Dundonnell estate, near Ullapool, in the Highlands, and its ten-room, eighteenth-century house. He had been over-whelmed by the beauty of the estate, which includes the mountain An Teallach, several crofting townships and a salmon river. His fiefdom would be as impressive, though less extensive, than Andrew's. And there was a delicious theatrical connection.

The estate was bequeathed by Alan Roger, the last of three outrageous bachelor brothers, to the son of his Chinese manservant, who had put it on the market. The contents of their Highland home – antiques, camp clothes and bizarre furnishings – had already been sold on.

They included the sequinned ballgowns worn by Bunny, the designer and dandy who was the best known of the trio. He was said to have climbed An Teallach wearing pink tights. And he claimed to have marched through enemy lines in the war wearing a chiffon scarf and carrying a copy of *Vogue*.

One cannot really see Tim and his cricketing cronies carrying on in the same sort of style. But there will be famous parties, for certain, even if David Gower, the former England cricket captain and a great buddy of Rice's, appears in slightly more conservative garb than Bunny Roger's.

The affair with Elaine Paige had lasted eleven years while Tim dithered over divorcing Jane and giving Elaine what she wanted: a home with him and a family. He never did, and Elaine terminated the relationship. She never talks about her private life, but Paige is at least as cut up about the split between the two colleagues. 'I do wish they were working together again. They were something special and fantastic together.

'There's been nothing else coming along behind them, has there? Andrew is the most brilliant tunesmith. He does something to you, strikes a chord. And Tim is the same, the way he puts a slant on things, surprises you with language.' Paige is a big star, a dignified diva, but there is something inexpressibly sad behind her eyes, too. Something has gone from her life, and you feel it will only burst through when she sings. 'It's been an interesting road to travel and I feel privileged that I was there at the beginning. It was something, that start of a new era. Though of course we didn't think of it that way at the time. I've been fantastically lucky to have had these roles – and I include *Chess* which is as good as any of them, probably too sharp, too clever – in the modern era of musical theatre. I can't see how it can get any better. So I carry on with my recording career and my concerts and hope something good comes along again.'

The creative liaison of Eva Rice and Nick Lloyd Webber developed further towards the end of 1998, when the youngsters announced that, as a result of playing the same venues in their respective bands, and meeting socially for the first time since infancy, they had written a few songs together. Following in their fathers' footsteps, Eva wrote the words, Nick the music. Eva described her own band, Replicant Saints, as 'Blondie with a Nineties twist', while Nick described his own, Morgan's Baby, as a bit more obscure – 'we produce an eclectic mix of sounds, which are perhaps less easy to swallow.'

Tim's life took another intriguing twist when it emerged in December 1998 that he had become a father again. He sired a baby girl with his new partner, twenty-eight-year-old interior designer Nell Sully, and was reported to be as pleased as Punch. But still there was no indication that he would divorce the ever-loyal Jane Rice, who has always insisted that she has a very convenient way of life which she does not wish to change. This news must have caused another stab of pain to Elaine Paige but, like Tim, she has consistently maintained a dignified public profile on her private life, refusing to comment when she must have been screaming inside.

Charles Hart feels a little distanced from it all now, too. He has fallen off the Really Useful's internal mailing list and was more or less excluded from the tenth anniversary bash for *Phantom* in New York. In a twenty-nine page anniversary section in the showbusiness bible *Variety*, Hart's name did not even appear once. Not in one advertisement, one congratulatory message, one column inch of craven editorial.

'I don't really mind,' he says. 'I'm sort of used to it. And I know it's not really Andrew. It's the others. I accept what goes with all that stuff, those machinations, it's par for the course. If you go into this game you play by the rules. I'm not really in touch with Andrew any more, and not at all with Cameron. I'm a bit of a maverick, I suppose. I never really wanted to mix that much with it all.'

It is nonetheless fairly extraordinary that the lyricist of one of the most successful musicals of all time should feel so downgraded. The numbers game alone told a story, said *Variety*, as grand as any opera: $2.6 billion in worldwide ticket sales, an audience of 108 million in twelve countries and eighty-five cities, and still the hottest ticket in New York and London, indeed wherever *Phantom* plays. The Broadway production alone had used 791,250 gallons of shot powder, 1,688,000 pounds of dry ice and 26,540 bulbs in the chandelier. The Phantom had made 8,350 journeys to his lair and the conductors had burned off 718 pounds of body fat. On 27 October 1998, the show played performance number 5,000 at Her Majesty's in the Haymarket, and still the chandelier had not fallen on anyone's head in the stalls.

Always an expensive show to produce, *Phantom* is equally demanding to maintain, and very few Phantoms, one imagines, have set about the role with the terrifying thoroughness of Michael Crawford, who springboarded from his success in London and New York to a secondary, highly remunerative career touring internationally, and playing Las Vegas, with *The Music of Andrew Lloyd Webber*. Certainly the Phantom I saw at the beginning of 1998 had skimped on the prosthetics of his face mask to the extent that, when revealed, his make-up made him look like Bart Simpson covered in chocolate. And the acting needed more rigorous attention in the great second-act trios between Christine, the Phantom and Raoul.

Cameron Mackintosh never had any producing rights in *Phantom* outside of the English-speaking ones. So the productions in Germany, Scandinavia and South America are wholly in the Really Useful's domain. With the copyright on *Cats*, the future of the company, even after the scares over *Sunset*, is secure.

The last big expansionist throw of the dice under

Patrick McKenna was the Battersea Power Station project, which McKenna described at the time as 'the single most exciting development that we're potentially involved with.' In partnership with three other big players, Really Useful aimed to create the largest cineplex in Britain, with sixteen to twenty screens, as well as indoor theme park attractions, restaurants, nightclubs and sports arenas. But when McKenna disappeared, so did these Disney-style ambitions.

After the changes, concentration reverted to the copyrights rather than showbiz mogulism. A chastened and leaner Really Useful under Bill Taylor started looking at the future life of Gale Edwards' *Superstar* revival around the world. The *Cats* video, with Elaine Paige as Grizabella and John Mills as Gus the Theatre Cat, was in the can. It was shot with sixteen cameras, four of them shooting all the numbers as master shots and every number done with reaction shots as if in a real movie.

Lloyd Webber may have upset his original *Cats* collaborators, Trevor Nunn and John Napier, by not involving them, but he was thinking ahead in terms of a permanent video-related enterprise with David Mallett, the video specialist and director, and Nigel Wright, the producer and sound engineer.

'Except for Mungojerrie and Rumpleteazer, I don't think any of the actors look directly to camera in the old-fashioned theatrical sense,' says the composer. 'It's an extraordinary technique, and it's great for dance, too, because if we need a wide shot on dance we've got it and if we need to come in close, we can pick the instant. The cutting is done in a contemporary way, so it's a little faster than in the old movies, but it stays on the performer always.'

Evita had to be counted a success as a film, but there was no subsequent sense of the floodgates opening for musicals on celluloid. There should have been a

Phantom film years ago, and Keith Turner even thought that the company had missed out by being so late with *Cats*. But these decisions always had to be balanced against the theatrical life of the musical, and both *Cats* and *Phantom* as theatrical properties continue to be the bedrock of the company's wealth and of Lloyd Webber's fortune.

The Really Useful has several million pounds of routine pre-tax profits in any one year. Turner sums up: 'Okay, some of the more interesting European markets have now finished. But there are still three *Phantom* companies in America, and two *Cats* companies. The company will now have to work harder at getting a production up and running in Brazil, but at least that can be looked at again now. If we literally did nothing from tomorrow, you would see, at a conservative estimate, £50m of pre-tax profits for at least the next five years.'

The drive of the mid 1990s was to maximise profits and diversify in a Disney, corporate sort of a way when there were more sensible diversification plans on offer, for instance a closer relationship with the Rodgers and Hammerstein estate. There was also a notable lack of any theatrical production beyond Lloyd Webber's own output, the sort of show like *Daisy Pulls It Off* or *La bête*, that did so much for the company's good name in the theatrical community at large. Plans were in progress to make a *Joseph* video in Toronto starring Donny Osmond and maybe *Sunset* starring Glenn Close. *Aspects of Love* was being talked about in terms of a new British touring production, and a video beyond that with a re-worked script by Jeremy Sams.

At the same time, journalists speculated on the end of the mega-musical, a trend that was always more to do with the scale of promotion and worldwide market penetration than with the actual size of the stage spectacles. There are Spielbergian scenic moments in *Cats*,

Phantom and *Starlight*, but they are not ludicrously extravagant or even theatrically overwhelming. *Song and Dance* and *Aspects* were intimate evenings misrepresented to a large extent in large theatres. *Phantom* and *Sunset* aspired to the condition of romantic opera.

The staircase and split scenery of the latter were as extravagant as anything in Lloyd Webber ever became. *Whistle* would get down and get even simpler. *Superstar* and *Evita* would always be seen to advantage in stark, Brechtian stagings, *By Jeeves* was a college romp boiling down to banjoes, for heaven's sake, while *Joseph*, however much it was dressed up, would always remain a kids' delight.

The main difference is one of philosophy. The tendency from *Phantom* onwards was to pay the cost of whatever the costs were while confident in the assumption that the money would come back through the box office. As Disney and Livent became players in the Broadway musical with shows like *Beauty and the Beast, The Lion King* and *Ragtime*, that philosophy widened further to acknowledge the fact that the cost of such shows could never be counted back through the takings, but would be absorbed by the corporation. No show would have to account to a single production budget.

Such an approach was obviously unrealistic for the Really Useful. Kevin Wallace categorically declared that not only did they not have the luxury of that approach, they did not *want* the luxury. *Whistle* when it came to London would be costed at just £2.3m, and the figures worked out on the projected box office receipts of a particular auditorium that had been chosen as best suited to a particular piece of work. And outside investors were back on board.

The production of *Whistle* in Washington DC at the beginning of 1997 cost in excess of $10m. It received lukewarm reviews and was withdrawn from Broadway, where the investors were paid off to the tune of $7m by the Really Useful. The Broadway co-producers, Jujamcyn, lost out, but the show had not yet entered that critical phase where the Really Useful could have been charged huge penalties for not going to New York.

Lloyd Webber was determined that nothing like the *Sunset* debacle would be repeated and that costs should be strictly controlled in London. 'I'm not having people sending round scores by bike; they can ruddy well get on a bus. I'm taking half royalties on *Whistle* until we recoup, and so is everyone. And then we have a sliding scale. If we are playing to 90 or 100 per cent audiences, we get full royalties, and if just fifty per cent, 50 per cent royalties and so on.' The projection was that *Whistle* at the Aldwych would take about forty weeks of playing to capacity audiences to recoup.

The new slimline RUG was having no truck with unnecessary trucks. On *Whistle* in Washington, Lloyd Webber had discovered a boiler under the stage that had been installed to heat the baptismal font, because the regulations required water of a certain temperature if a child was going to be immersed. The requirements also entailed a hole in the middle of the stage and a cost of $170,000.

A similar hands-off approach on the *Superstar* production resulted in huge extra expense, to the retrospective chagrin of the composer. 'When we started, we all thought it would be marvellous if we could stage the musical in an amphitheatre with the audience all around. Everyone agreed, but what nobody told me was that, because of the regulations, it would cost about a million quid. If they'd told me that, I would have said, forget it.'

Throughout all of these upheavals and changes, Patrick McKenna and Lloyd Webber were not really speaking. Bill Taylor, diplomatically refusing to apportion blame, rightly says that, 'it was impossible for this company to run while divorced from its main shareholder and its main contributor of assets. It was a ludicrous situation that had to change. Now that Patrick is gone, Andrew is no more involved in the day to day business than he was. But he is much better informed. So I don't give him surprises. I want him to know exactly what we are up to, and why.'

Also during this period, Madeleine proved herself not only a talented hostess, but an increasingly important associate in Andrew's life. Unlike either Sarah, she took an active interest in the business side of things and was often forthright in her opinions, most of which Andrew heeded. And she was taken more seriously among her former racing and riding colleagues. In October 1988, she joined the board of the Newbury Racecourse, with chairman David Sieff declaring that the business would benefit from her extensive experience.

The house in Eaton Square was at last sold at the beginning of 1998, when Victor Kozeny, a 34-year-old Czech financier who made a £300m fortune during his country's post-Communist privatisation windfalls in the early 1990s, secured the purchase. Madeleine and Andrew looked forward to the more suitable and much cosier premises around the corner in Chester Square, with a knocked-through top floor across three houses that was ideal for the children.

Less happily, in July, Julian and his second wife Zhora announced that they had been separated 'for some months', that the separation was amicable and involved no other parties. The demands of the soloist's life had taken their toll for the second time. It seemed only a few weeks – it *was* only a few weeks – since the couple had been seen jiving happily away to the music of Julian's beloved Bobby Vee at his brother's fiftieth birthday bash. Julian's first wife, Celia, had said that living and working with her husband was like being inside a big pressure cooker. She just had to get out. Who knows what goes on? Madeleine, you felt, would surely stay the course.

In June 1998, a week before the first preview of *Whistle* in London, Cameron Mackintosh celebrated his thirty years in musical theatre with a royal gala, *Hey Mr Producer!* attended by Her Majesty the Queen and the Duke of Edinburgh at the Lyceum Theatre. The two contemporary composers to whom he owes most, Lloyd Webber and Stephen Sondheim, share the same birthday and shared, on film, the same piano in an item devised by Sondheim which wedded the tunes of 'Send in the Clowns' (from *A Little Night Music*) and 'Music of the Night' from *Phantom*.

Their subject was Mackintosh himself: 'Isn't he rich? Isn't he square? Isn't he working the room, somewhere out there? Send in the crowds. Acts on his whims, took a big chance, seeing his anagram said: Cameron, Romance. He went to France. Send in the crowds.' The tune shifted to 4/4. 'Night time falling, Cameron keeps calling. Posing questions, questions with suggestions . . . Suddenly appearing, always interfering, But here we are and cheering as we might, the man who flogs the music of tonight.'

As the applause followed, Lloyd Webber and Sondheim appeared in person from either side of the stage and embraced in the middle. It was a magical moment. The impossible dream team of box-office bonanzas and intellectual credibility. Lloyd Webber is the composer who sets out to be challenging while remaining popular, Sondheim the composer who wants to be more popular while never ceasing to be challenging. And their respective works will forever represent a sort of polarisation in musical theatrical endeavour in the second half of the twentieth century and define the parameters of an endless debate about the values of an art form when the mood of an audience is to take its entertainment lying down.

Lloyd Webber is reluctant to be drawn on the nuts and bolts of the future of musical theatre beyond saying that the big corporations who have entered the market place in the past five years might well provide splendid spectacles on their limitless budgets but are courting danger by operating as businesses first and creative organisations second. 'Theatre is not a business you can quantify. In the end there are no rules at all. The other day I had lunch with Cameron and he said, "You know, when they've decided they've had enough and gone away, you and I will still be here." And we will.'

FOURTEEN

THE HALF-TIME WHISTLE

Where do new musicals come from? Out of the air and along the breeze, battered into shape by a chance encounter, a random idea, and very often a whole skein of distantly related factors. Composers from Puccini to Richard Rodgers have stored their tunes for the right occasion, hoping it will come along. The first was always having trouble with his librettists. The second was luckier in having two long-term literary colleagues, Lorenz Hart and Oscar Hammerstein.

Lloyd Webber's Hart was Tim Rice, with a splash of Richard Stilgoe; his Hammerstein, Don Black, with support from Charles Hart. Alan Ayckbourn and T. S. Eliot have chipped in, too. His collaboration with Jim Steinman on *Whistle Down the Wind* was the most unexpected of all, and the history of their project as circuitous, and finally triumphant, as any in the catalogue. The two – dubbed Ermine and Leather on a New York morning TV show – had come close to working together on *Phantom*.

If there is any one theme running through all of Lloyd Webber's works, it is a quest and a yearning for the spiritual dimension in life. (I exclude only *By Jeeves* from this general categorisation.) I hear church bells in the rock and roll, the liturgy in the levity and the agony in the ecstasy. And in Steinman's epic ballads on Meat Loaf's *Bat Out of Hell* albums, you hear another version of the same search for spirituality beyond the material life. These 'power ballads', as they have been called, tell of tyre tracks and broken hearts, escape into glowering red sunsets, messages of love and death, dreams of redemption and memories of suppression.

So did the new musical. But how come? Just as *Phantom* was prompted by another enterprise based on the same story, so *Whistle* first lodged as an idea when, in 1993, the National Youth Music Theatre, of which Lloyd Webber had just become an active patron and prime sponsor, presented a charming version of Mary Hayley Bell's novel at the Edinburgh Festival fringe.

Lloyd Webber found the lyrics and music of talented newcomer Richard Taylor charming, and tailor-made for the young performers. The piece was very faithful to both film and novel. He put it on at the Lilian Baylis theatre, an adjunct of Sadler's Wells, and invited other producers to take a peek.

Nothing happened, but the musical has since been revived and looked very well at a Cheltenham Everyman performance I saw in the summer of 1997, mobilising local children alongside professional actors and creating a plausible world of pre-Christmas ritual among the stones, bricks and haystacks of a superstitious country village.

There was a fine second act opening of a school nativity play – a metaphorical summation of the story – played against a background of adult scepticism. This was a gem of choral and dramatic arrangement and betrayed the best of Stephen Sondheim's influence. Some of the off-kilter romantic tunes and fill-in blather, alas, betrayed the worst. But there were some wonderful chorales, and a governing musical intelligence was at work to cover the bitty fusions between scenes.

The central theme – how would people react if Jesus came back? – was beautifully expressed, vigorously and without sentimentality. This would not be a facet of the grown-up panic in the Lloyd Webber/Steinman version, which moved Swallow into a different area of inter-action by making her two or three years older than her thirteen-year-old self in both the NYMT and Cheltenham versions. Richard Taylor and his librettist Russell Labey had not secured rights in the novel, only permission to do their version. That permission stands, their version lives on. But Lloyd Webber had seen a different way forward and thought he would have a go.

Mary Hayley Bell, the wife of John Mills, published her book in 1958. The story came to her, she says, out of the blue, with a beginning, middle and end. She wrote it, and set the action, around the family's farm in Sussex, and the three children – Swallow, Brat and Poor Baby – who find a criminal hiding in the barn and take him to be Jesus, were recognisably modelled on the Mills' young trio of Juliet, Hayley and Jonathan. The story is told by ten-year-old Brat, an inspired mediating voice – years before Adrian Mole – between the acuity of childish observation and the absurdity of adult behaviour. Swallow is twelve, Poor Baby seven.

The cloudless idyll is darkened with rumours of civil unrest beyond the hedgerows, and of dangerous men lurking in dark lanes and barns. The children form a com-munity of resistance to protect their new charge – some of them come from as far afield as Dorking! – and achieve a sort of victory over the policemen and firemen who chase the convict from the burning oasthouse and barn. There is a sign of the cross. When Brat goes to bed there is darkness all around, but she knows they are not alone.

The subsequent 1961 black and white film was pro-duced by Richard Attenborough, directed by Bryan Forbes, scripted by the reliable Yorkshire firm of Keith Waterhouse and Willis Hall, and relocated (and indeed shot) in the Lancashire dales. Alan Bates was the man on the run and Hayley Mills, the original Brat, became my generation's ideal best pretty friend growing into pre-sexual girl-next-door as the sainted Swallow.

There was some pretty good music on the soundtrack, too, by Malcolm Arnold, one of the 'unfashionable' composers Julian Lloyd Webber wants to restore to favour. Maybe that stiffened his brother's resolve. Meanwhile, *Sunset* came along, and a year after launching that show in New York, Lloyd Webber renewed his old friendship with Jim Steinman over dinner: 'People associate this rock and roll legend with Meat Loaf. But his real loves are theatre, food and wine. Dining with Jim is hazardous as he orders everything on the menu. This is not because he is greedy. He has an ordering disorder. Once he hosted a party of six and he told the waiter to bring one of everything. There were at least ten starters and twenty main courses. The waiter was surprised. "One of everything?" he queried. Jim thought deeply. "Yes, you're quite right to ask. We'll need six of everything."

The rumour of a movie remake of *Whistle* came up over the various desserts and Steinman immediately bit. He then insisted Lloyd Webber meet his screenwriter friend Patricia Knop – whose film credits include $9\frac{1}{2}$ *Weeks* and Jacques Demy's *Lady Oscar* – who became excited about doing a draft.

'By now,' Lloyd Webber wrote in the *Sunday Times*, 'Jim and I were thinking of Louisiana as a possible location. Swamps, the freeways that bypass the dirt-poor towns, the strange religious sects such as snake-handlers, who preach that if you are bitten by a serpent and survive then you are a true believer in Jesus, plus that pervasive background of rock 'n' roll, all smelt very beguiling.'

Investigations into the remake rumour led nowhere except to a script doing the rounds of the studios about three children in smalltown America who find a killer in the garage who tells them he is Father Christmas. At this point the composer wrote to Bryan Forbes to ask if he would sell him the remake rights and a deal was happily struck. The work went ahead. Brian Gibson, the director of *Breaking Glass* and *Wilde Time*, was brought on board to point the cameras.

The Louisiana Bible-belt in the 1950s suggested to Steinman the world of Faulkner and Tennessee Williams, the world of Southern gothic, and into this was introduced what the London director Gale Edwards later called a more modern, Sam Shepard-like view – 'the notion that if you cut loose, hit the freeway, burn up the road, you will find happiness. It's the view that in momentum there is freedom, while in stasis there is death.'

Jim Steinman knew all about Sam Shepard, the great modern American playwright of rural superstitions, blasted families and heading on down that highway. As a student at Amherst College in New England, Steinman wrote a show called *The Dream Engine*, a three-hour epic rock musical featuring killer nuns and a fifty-five-minute nude scene.

Steinman's loud and kinky sound of music drew him to the attention of the late Joseph Papp, founder of the New York Shakespeare Festival at the Public Theater where Shepard had been a key playwright, and where the epochal musicals *Hair* and *A Chorus Line* had been launched. Papp teamed Steinman with Michael Weller, a fine playwright known here for plays like *Cancer* and *Loose Ends* in the 1970s (he also wrote the screenplay for Miloš Forman's not half-bad movie version of *Hair*).

At the auditions for their first and only show, *More Than You Deserve*, an overweight Texan christened Marvin Lee Aday, but generally known by his high school nickname of Meat Loaf, lumbered in, opened his massive lungs and rolled his eyes into his head, convulsing his hands in great eloquent, spasmodic motions.

'I thought,' says Steinman, recalling in an *Independent* interview what was later defined as one of the ten most important encounters in the history of rock music, 'this is the most thrilling freak I've ever seen. And

I also thought, this is a true Wagnerian Siegfried.' The result was a farewell to theatre and the 1977 release of *Bat Out of Hell*, the third biggest selling rock album ever.

Steinman, who was told by a fortune teller when he was seven that he had 'an incredible need to astonish' is today one of the great vampiric figures of rock. He sleeps most days, wakes at night. He lives alone in a small rented house one hour from New York. And he is prone, despite the genial exterior, to the blackest of depressions. He is much more like Andrew Lloyd Webber than you would think.

Steinman does not, overall, enjoy good health. He missed the Vietnam war by being diagnosed borderline schizophrenic. And he takes pills four times a day to ease the constant pain caused by poor dental surgery that allowed his adult teeth to grow sideways into his gums over milk teeth that never fell out. 'I am conscious of pain a lot,' he told Spencer Bright in the *Sunday Times*. 'I've lived with it since that operation. I don't know how that affects me. I don't want to sound morbid about it – people live with a lot worse – but I think it has affected me in some ways quite deeply.'

As a result of the Sydmonton preview in July 1995, the planned film suddenly became a more likely stage show. Brian Gibson, hired on a 'pay or play' agreement, received his fee anyway. Lloyd Webber and Gale Edwards, who had staged Patricia Knop's screenplay with some explanatory narration and slight changes for theatrical purposes, went to New York and looked at theatres.

Then Edwards went to Lloyd Webber's house in France to begin rewriting. Hal Prince, having got wind of Gale Edwards' mini-triumph in the tiny church chapel, urged Lloyd Webber to go ahead, preferably with him, Prince, at the helm. Flattered by this approach, Lloyd Webber decided to drop Edwards and go with Prince, and to open the show in Washington. It would run there for six weeks and open on Broadway around Easter 1997.

Gale Edwards was philosophical. 'That was disappointing. I always felt *Whistle* was a gentle, psychologically motivated piece and the last thing it needed was showmanship, or overblowing. Hal is a legend and a genius, with an impeccable track record. Nevertheless, it really didn't feel like the right territory for him. But there you are. If you flirt with this world of commercial musicals – and it is only a flirtation of mine, because most of my work is in classical theatre – you have to be aware of the kind of world that it is.'

She had plenty else to get on with, and never fell out with Lloyd Webber. She was working on an Australian musical, *The Boy from Oz*, and revived both *Superstar* for Lloyd Webber and *The White Devil* – in a tremendous and sensual production – for the Royal Shakespeare Company.

Steinman and Lloyd Webber got along famously throughout the whole Washington preparation period, and continue to do so, differing only over the composer's preference for precise rhymes as opposed to Steinman's for no rhyme at all. Lloyd Webber had his way. 'He's the boss,' said Steinman, 'in the sense that he's the producer, but I couldn't ask for a nicer collaborator, really. He's very demanding and intense – but then I am, too.'

Reports on the premiere are wildly varied. Inside the Lloyd Webber camp, they justify in hindsight the decision to axe the show before Broadway and start again in London. The fault lay not in the material so much as in the treatment. But the *Washington Post* was unequivocally dismissive, commenting savagely on 'tuneless whistle' and 'burning but no fire'.

Benedict Nightingale of *The Times* and Sheridan Morley of the *Spectator*, who both hopped across to

Washington, were more enthusiastic, the first finding the show attractive, touching and engrossing, while Morley admired the wonderful designs and 'one of the most truly heartbreaking scores' he had ever heard. Morley also identified the perception problem for an audience now expecting lush romanticism à la *Phantom* but finding themselves sitting in front of 'a downbeat show of considerable danger, intelligence and cynicism.'

This was the first time Lloyd Webber had premiered a show in America since *Superstar*, so it was in every sense a Second Coming, with all the concomitant dangers of misapprehension, confusion and outright rejection.

In the update of his book on the composer, Michael Walsh berated the show's writers for confusing their picture of historical Louisiana with incorrect regional details, and joined the *Washington Post* man in scoffing at a score which omitted any hint of blues, jazz and ragtime in favour of 'a tinny, generic country-western and 1950s rock sound.' And he stood on another American high horse in laying into Benedict Nightingale for liking the show, having earlier declared that British drama critics were hopeless, musically illiterate individuals guilty of misunderstanding the great man's stuff.

Mark Steyn, who has maintained an intriguingly cool and balanced view of the composer's work over the years, not unmixed with more personal animadversions, admired the seriousness of the drama – 'a surprisingly vivid examination of the need for religion and spirituality among farming folk eking out a hard existence in a poor southern nowheresville.'

Steyn also admired Patricia Knop's book, noted the number of laughs won by many numbers and welcomed Lloyd Webber's return to traditional musical theatre values – in the division of labour between composer, lyricist and librettist – after years of trumpeting the virtues of 'through-composed' musicals. 'Coupling the Wagner of rock with the Puccini of pap could have been lethal,' he wrote in the *Daily Telegraph*. 'Instead, it seems to have sharpened both guys up. Lloyd Webber has returned to his rockier roots. Meanwhile the stricter disciplines of theatre writing have inspired Steinman to some of his best work in years.'

Whether or not the show was a turning point, it was certainly an attempt to do something new, something different and certainly something unexpected. The Washington audiences were full, and a decent profit was made. But Lloyd Webber was only 70 per cent happy with the show, which was about 70 per cent more than Jim Steinman was. Steinman thought the production sucked, was unmoving and was hurriedly and carelessly cast, and that all of this happened because 'everyone involved was doing a lot of other things at the same time'.

Nigel Wright felt that having 'some superfluous Aunt living in the house, looking after the kids, removed the emotional chunk of a one-parent family struggling against all odds. You lost the sense of the kids wanting Mum back and Dad wanting a woman in the house . . . the day Andrew was introduced to the House of Lords [by Lord Owen and Lord Archer, formerly David Owen, the Foreign Secretary, and Jeffrey Archer the politician and novelist] Anthony Pye-Jeary and I accompanied him there and went back afterwards to his music room. We sat and listened to the Sydmonton tape. We realised how simple it was and how far it had been over-cooked and over-stretched.'

The company repaid the investors in full and decided to start again. Lloyd Webber took advice on this from his lawyer friend John Eastman, the late Linda McCartney's brother, who advised him to be capricious and follow his heart. Like other close friends, says Lloyd Webber, he 'felt that if at this stage in my career I couldn't pull a production, then the whole reason for having a production vehicle was a waste of time. Hal and I parted company with, I am happy to say, no hard feelings.'

Gale Edwards had declined an invitation to visit the show in Washington. But when Lloyd Webber asked her to take charge of the London premiere, she laid down her conditions. She insisted on dealing more extensively with the racial issues. She wanted no-one from the Washington cast. And she wanted more emphasis on the Americanisation and the notion of the freeway to nowhere.

Not for nothing had she worked with Trevor Nunn. Her entire involvement, such as it was, in top class musical theatre, was down to Nunn, who had selected her as his co-director for the Australian premiere of *Les Misérables* when John Caird was unable to go to Sydney. 'When Trevor was directing *Les Misérables*, if you turned down the volume he could have been directing *King Lear*. I am not saying the two works of art are comparable. But the way of approaching them is the same, the same process, the same attention to detail.' And the same lack of dance numbers.

Having started with song and dance in his Shakespeare, and moved on to *Cats* and *Starlight*, Nunn had gradually expunged terpischorean movement from the modern British musical. 'The baleful influence of *Les Mis*,' Wayne Sleep calls it. Any choreography in *Whistle* would only involve the small kids whirring their arms around while they sang optimistically about ruling the world – admittedly this was more graphically entertaining than Harry Secombe singing about what he would do if *he* ruled the world on the election hustings in *Pickwick* (1963) by Wolf Mankowitz, Leslie Bricusse and Cyril Ornadel, but it hardly constituted show dancing to rival the explosions of Jerome Robbins or Agnes de Mille, let alone Gillian Lynne.

This is why *Chicago* was so rapturously received when the Broadway revival came to London in

November 1997. The audience was audibly gasping for all those sassy dance routines, that glimpse of stocking, the delirium of movement to music. Musicals were becoming not exactly hard work, but a lot grimmer.

Subsequent revivals of *Show Boat* and *Oklahoma!* – the first by Hal Prince, the second by Trevor Nunn, both with brilliant and intellectually pertinent choreography by the new queen of the chorus line, Susan Stroman – reminded us of what we were missing. Great shows with emotional uplift and physical take-off.

Edwards considered the piece already had the first and provided the second with a stark but imposing hydraulic design by Peter J. Davison, a great, jagged unfinished curvilinear freeway that expressed two main aspects of the show: the freeway to nowhere; and the upper and lower worlds of the redneck, God-fearing Louisiana community above, led by an angry sheriff, and the Mississippi mud flats below, where children recreated their own religion and indeed their own god.

These two worlds don't talk to each other. If they did, the kids would know there was a convict on the loose, and there would be no show. The book was by now credited not only to Knop, but also to Lloyd Webber and Gale Edwards.

Edwards in particular saw Swallow as a girl on the cusp of womanhood, the troubled centre in a wheel of men, whose spokes converged with varying degrees of threat. 'There's her father, whom she must learn to love in a different way now her mother's dead; there's the man in the barn for whom she becomes an agent of salvation and sexual possibility; and there's the boy next door who has been her heart-throb but who has now hit sixteen and got spunky on his motorbike. This Amos is now hanging out with Candy, whose currency is sex, and with whom he is presumably having a physical relationship. Swallow's crush on him was as the boy next door, the James Dean myth.' It had been her invention at Sydmonton to have this dramatic moment of hesitation on the nearly-kiss between Swallow and the Man in the big duet, 'Nature of the Beast'. And for the London show, Edwards was reunited with the same protagonists, the American baritonal tenor Marcus Lovett (who had taken over as both the Phantom and Alex in *Aspects* on Broadway) and the sweet-voiced Lottie Mayor, who had been around musicals for a few years, in *Oliver!*, *Aspects* directed by Gale Edwards on tour, *Martin Guerre* and even the dreaded *Bernadette*.

James Graeme, the father at Sydmonton, was also repeating his role. And there was further reassurance for the composer in the presence of John Turner, who had appeared in the original *Jeeves* and as Péron in succession to Joss Ackland in *Evita*, making his fourteenth West End appearance in a musical and lending his gravity and considerable voice to the sheriff.

The rehearsal period was intense but joyful. Lloyd Webber declared at the end of it that he had never known such a happy one. He hugged and kissed his creative team after the final, raucous run-through in the Borough school hall, unashamedly allowing tears to roll down his face as he moved among the actors with trays of champagne and orange juice.

The tense period between the rehearsal room and the opening night was spent acclimatising to the Aldwych Theatre and embarking on the previews. There was trouble with the hydraulics, necessitating the cancellation of a few previews, and indeed the teething problems continued a little into the run. The musical supervision was as expertly handled as ever by Michael Reed, but the musical director, Simon Lee, was mysteriously replaced at the last minute by Christopher Nightingale.

Lloyd Webber sat with his colleagues in the splendid new megarestaurant Bank, just along from the Aldwych Theatre, discussing last-minute changes, sipping not a few glasses of 'rather good New Zealand chardonnay' and swapping favourite stories of the previous few weeks. 'Mine is of an audition with a load of children from the Sylvia Young Stage School, all of whom were wearing identical sweatshirts with Sylvia Young School advertised prominently on the front. Gale wanted to rough the kids up and told them to take the sweatshirts off. Underneath they were wearing identical Sylvia Young School T-shirts.'

The show, which opened at the Aldwych on 1 July 1998, had been overhauled and re-written, two songs dropped, three or four new ones written. It was tighter and shorter and the tricky plot in Act Two was tightened up, though not, as it proved, sufficiently for some people. There remained a slight problem area when Swallow goes with Amos to meet the train – a fantastic effect, looming suddenly out of the dark, that had been part of the Washington production – and collects the package containing the gun for the Man. How had the unidentified emissary known where to drop the package when the Man had been on the run from the penitentiary for forty-eight hours and could not possibly have got any messages through?

But this plot development took Swallow into the dark with Amos, accelerated her quasi-sexual dilemma and released Candy – who had been told to leave town by the sheriff – into the role of a vindictive betrayer. The atmosphere of the show's second act became increasingly hysterical as the hunt gathered force, the snake charmers invoked a wrestle with the devil, and the children closed ranks against the adults. The first act finale had a stomping, stamping adult counterpoint thrillingly laid over the children's beautiful, lyrical 'No Matter What', one of Lloyd Webber's most haunting pop tunes, as the kids bring the Man presents in the barn.

Musically, there had been nothing as adventurous on the West End stage for years, and yet the cries of critical dismay – bordering on the downright rude and insulting – were unprecedented even in the annals of Lloyd Webber critical maulings. Publicity had been low key, but the minute a Lloyd Webber show appears on the horizon, the usual suspects appear to explain why they hate his work and deeds.

The *Independent on Sunday*'s classical music critic Michael White trotted out the old saw about imitation Italian *verismo* and registered his gut reaction, self-confessedly intuitive rather than analytical, fuelled by outrage 'that so small a talent could have made it quite so big'.

Sondheim, White averred, was the nagging thorn in Lloyd Webber's side, 'the industry standard by which his work will always be judged and found wanting.' By White maybe, but not by most people, who are perfectly capable of distinguishing between the two types of genius represented by each composer and deciding which of them they wanted to go and see in the theatre.

Casually dismissing Lloyd Webber's use of the leit-motif as haphazard and pretentious, and accusing him of drawing on a reservoir of one or two tunes that flow *ad nauseam*, White flounced off over the drawbridge to his little moated castle of operatic respectability and approved bonne bouches and gewgaws. He may be writing just about *Phantom* and I suppose *Sunset* – he had not seen or heard *Whistle* or, as far as one can tell, any other of the musicals – and he is delivering this bilious jeremiad before the new show has even opened.

And up went those good old cultural Keep Out signs again: 'The likelihood of a Lloyd Webber score finding its way into the National Theatre or ENO is (mercifully) small and almost certainly unnecessary: if Lloyd Webber is possessed of one great skill, it's the ability to sell his products, market his ideas.'

Critics are entitled to pillory artists, that is an important part of their role, but why should denigration precede the evidence and comment on the merely material sideshow? It always came down to this. The success was what really upset snobs like White. There was very little hype and pre-publicity to *Whistle*. It received several good reviews, a few more hostile ones, and was never setting out to be any kind of blockbuster. But people wanted to go and see it. Houses were full and the company expected to be in residence at the Aldwych for several years.

Fifty per cent of the London capitalisation was recouped five months into the run and tickets were put on sale into the new millennium. No-one had expected a box-office smash with this show, but Lloyd Webber was well pleased with its solid performance. A lot of work had been done since the Washington opening, and Cameron Mackintosh embarked on a similar campaign of retrieval when he withdrew *Martin Guerre* from the West End, after one re-vamp, and relaunched a tougher, meaner show at the West Yorkshire Playhouse in December 1998.

Blockbuster ambitions were in temporary abeyance. Whatever misgivings critics might express over *Whistle* or indeed *Martin Guerre*, the early production history of both shows at least demonstrated that both Lloyd Webber and Mackintosh were still doing what they believed in, and doing it with all their heart and might.

From the opening, rousing chorale in the church, the audience at *Whistle* knew it was listening to proper music, music that challenged as well as gave pleasure, music that expressed a dramatic situation from one scene to another, music that soared, or rocked, or strung along with the children, or expressed the most intense emotional dilemmas.

As an eclectic composer par excellence, Lloyd Webber melded various styles and genres into his score. He has always done that. There are different types of song in every musical from *Show Boat* to *Follies*, but only Lloyd

Webber is accused of indiscriminately trying to please all sorts of people by writing different types of song.

Maybe the trouble is that he wears his emotionalism and his sentimentality on his sleeve. There was no holding back in the naked power of the operatic trio 'A Kiss is a Terrible Thing to Waste', one of his finest ever compositions, in which Swallow is bitten by Amos and stalked by the Man.

The number sounds more like Jim Steinman than Jim Steinman – in a Meat Loaf number like 'You took the words right out of my mouth, it must have been when you were kissing me' – and was stirred to an extra-ordinary pitch of overlapping intensity by three people at a point of crisis. Formally, it had echoes of the second act trio in *Phantom* but musically it was entirely new.

Similarly, 'Nature of the Beast' was in a Gothic operatic mode unprecedented in the canon, and the simple beauty of 'I Never Get What I Pray For' and Swallow's 'If Only' proffered touching statements of the children's loneliness and aspiration, as well as thematic material cleverly reworked into the rest of the show. There is a lot of contrapuntal writing in the score, many pre-echoes of songs that come round later, and there are plenty of strange time signatures.

The townspeople's bar-room atmosphere was strongly reinforced in one of the new songs for London, 'Cold', in which the big black singer Edward is happily encouraged to sing the blues for as long as it suits the white majority. And like the other items, this became part of the quilting and patterning in both the under-scoring and link music.

The idea of escape dangled before Swallow by Amos is expressed in the driving biker number, 'Tyre Tracks and Broken Hearts', again a classic Steinman scenario, in which Amos and the impatient, kittenish Candy profess their intention of getting out of this place if it is the last thing they ever do, more or less.

The raw metallic orchestrations, with the vicious drumming and screeching voices, struck one reviewer, Nicholas de Jongh of the *Evening Standard*, as evocative of a mild day in Pinner circa 1972. They struck this one as more like an authentic approximation of the small-town frustrations of kids on the skids than many a trite and overpraised new play on the London fringe. We shall just have to take the soigné Mr de Jongh's word for the excitements of Pinner in the first flush of his post-pubertal social awareness phase.

Most critics had problems with the larger children's chorus, notably 'Long Overdue for a Miracle' and the exuberantly simple 'When Children Rule the World', which did indeed sound to the corrupted ear like a United Children of Benetton advertising jingle.

But exuberance has its place in this musical, and the children must be allowed. Before gathering round the manger with their Christmas gifts for the Man, he regales them with a stomping, picaresque story of gambling and wild living in the tale of Annie Christmas, a ballad of immense spirit and vivacity, reprised more darkly in the second act for a limited audience of Swallow, Brat and Poor Baby.

The title song, one of sinuous, supple tenderness and delicacy, establishes the sadness and the susceptibility to change early on of both Swallow and her father. When it returns at the end, it is as balm after the storm and the fire, with the single parent family reinforced by the experience of the Man passing through and strengthened for the hard life ahead.

Had Lloyd Webber come full circle to the primal questions of faith, belief and friendship that he and Tim Rice had first, and more flippantly, addressed in *Superstar*? Had he come out the other side of his romantic phase, and was this paring down to essentials something to do with the sizing down of his company's activities?

Only time will tell. The will to work, the determination to experiment, the desire to succeed and to reach a wide audience – all seemed in place in this unexpected and remarkable piece of new musical theatre. One song, 'No Matter What', in which the children declare their loyalty to, and faith in, the new visitor in defiance of religious and educational dictates of the adults, became a surprise Number One hit single when released by the group Boyzone in August 1998. A sweet and melodic item, with a catchy beat and instant freshness, the song stayed at the top of the charts for three weeks, and was re-recorded by Boyzone in an even more attractive version when an album of songs from the show was released with contributions from Tina Arena, Donny Osmond, Tom Jones, Boy George, Elaine Paige, Michael Ball, The Everly Brothers, Meat Loaf and Bonnie Tyler.

The Boyzone single was a big hit right across Europe, but an unseemly row developed when the price of the single in Britain was cut to one penny below the minimum necessary for it to be registered in the charts. This was done allegedly to facilitate the quick journey up the listings of Boyzone's next song, not written by Lloyd Webber and Steinman. The composer was furious, claiming that his own record company, Polygram, had ruined his chance of having the bestselling West End show single of all time.

Once again, Tim Rice joined his old partner in the public prints. Rice and Lloyd Webber wrote to *The Times* on 9 December 1998, thirty years after their first big success together, to bemoan the sharp practices in a record industry they had helped to sustain over a long period and to defend the virtue of single records. The ambitious young Turks had turned (almost) into grand old men of the establishment.

'Albums may generate more income, but in the long term the downgrading of the individual hit song will be disastrous for our music industry. The Beatles opened up the world of British music with wonderful songs, and no-one complained if nine or ten tunes were selling simultaneously.'

For the artistic puritans, professional rivals and the culture police, Lloyd Webber's campaign to marry popular modes of entertainment with serious affairs of the heart – and serious methods of composition – will always be unsettling and contemptible.

But the most successful and widely applauded musical theatre figure of our time could at least rest assured that, halfway through his life, he had achieved so much that annoyed the hell out of some people and gave deep pleasure and theatrical sustenance to untold millions beyond them and across the world. He had made his mark, and his unprecedented fortune, this Midas of the Musicals. His reputation, like that of *Cats* itself, was surely 'now and forever'.

The boom years were over. This much was certainly reflected in the harsh and unforgiving world of *Whistle Down the Wind*. The hunted, haunted Man was no longer a superstar, not even a superstore, but a transparent shop-soiled window of lost opportunity, unfulfilled potential and spiritual yearning.

There was still a long way to go. And if Andrew Lloyd Webber were to find new ways to dream, the right people to help him, and the time and inclination to do so, he could still be surprising us and, who knows, himself, for many years to come.

POSTSCRIPT

Something changes every day in Andrew Lloyd Webber's life, and not just his collaborators. He lives in a permanent state of flux. Sometimes this is creative and really useful flux, sometimes it is not. Two very big things happened within a few months of the first publication of this book.

He wrote, work-shopped and more or less finished, a brand new musical, *The Beautiful Game*, with the comedian and writer Ben Elton, author of *Popcorn*. You might conclude that as Tim Rice was enjoying such huge success with *his* Elton (John) – their musical version of the Disney film *The Lion King* was a smash hit of 1999 in London, playing round the corner from *Whistle Down the Wind* in the Lyceum Theatre – then Lloyd Webber was certainly entitled to go out and find an Elton of his own, Ben.

And just as we tiptoed apprehensively into the new millennium, it emerged in the second week of January that Lloyd Webber's Really Useful Group, in a 50-50 partnership with NatWest Equity Partners – a venture capitalist city firm owned, until recently, by the National Westminster Bank – had bought control of the Stoll Moss group of theatres, about one third of the major West End houses, including the Theatre Royal, Drury Lane, and the Palladium, for £87.5m.

It is hard to assess which event was the more astonishing or unexpected. Lloyd Webber himself had told me around Christmas that he fully expected to be outbid for Stoll Moss. And maybe he was. Still, Janet Holmes à Court, who had run Stoll Moss since her husband Robert's unexpected death in 1990, preferred, I think rightly, to think of her theatres enjoying the supervision of a fully committed theatrical outfit, and of a fully committed impresario, as opposed to the possible vagaries of fortune, or asset-stripping, of a larger, less engaged, entertainment conglomerate. After all, only weeks earlier, Paul Gregg's Apollo Leisure group, owners of several London venues, including the Lyceum, and of several large and important venues around the country – a total of twenty-three venues – had been acquired by the American-controlled giant SFX Entertainment group for $259m.

The West End power games could be entering a phase of unprecedented volubility. The new company, Really Useful Theatres, would have control of a dozen major West End houses. Lloyd Webber's old friend and rival, Sir Cameron Mackintosh, had acquired the beautiful Albery and Wyndham's theatres for £7m in October 1999. These were added to a portfolio of ownership including the Prince Edward, the Prince of Wales and the Strand – as well as the lease, at some time in the future, as a result of a pre-existing property sale, on the Queen's and the Gielgud, two of the Stoll Moss group on Shaftesbury Avenue.

Increasingly, it looked as if the owners of theatres would become their own producers. And just as Lloyd Webber was landlord to the long-running Cameron Mackintosh hit, *Les Misérables*, at the Palace, so he would double up in this capacity as Mackintosh's long-delayed presentation of *The Witches of Eastwick* shaped up for a Drury Lane opening in the summer of 2000.

It is true that Lloyd Webber and Mackintosh are both theatre romantics, and both are undoubtedly committed to the fate of new work. But they are also locked in a battle for control, as well as one of healthily pulsating egos. At the time of his purchase, Lloyd Webber flatly refused to be drawn on any statement except one of good intentions, and there is no reason to disbelieve him when he says that theatres should be kept 'in the hands they should be kept in; not in the hands of pen-pushers and number-crunchers.' The managing director of NatWest Equity Partners, however, sounded a slightly different note when he told *Time* magazine that 'not only are the assets themselves attractive, but the demand for live entertainment is increasing, and there is also a trend toward convergence between filmed entertainment and theatrical entertainment.'

Nobody serious in the theatre seriously believes the last part of that statement, despite the glorious theatrical transformation wrought by the brilliant Julie Taymor on the Disney film of *The Lion King*. It seems much more likely that Lloyd Webber will use his pre-eminence to set up new projects among younger artists with managements and writers he admires. And if that proves to be the case, the next ten years could be very interesting indeed.

As the theatrical community gathered for the Olivier Awards in the middle of February 2000, Lloyd Webber told me that he really saw no point in continuing to work in the theatre unless he did things that both challenged himself and surprised his audience. One such challenge had been issued by Ben Elton, who had asked Lloyd Webber why he never set any of his musicals to a contemporary theme, and proceeded to wax eloquent about a television documentary on the subject of a football team in Northern Ireland.

Lloyd Webber was hooked. The soccer team was Star of the Sea, which blossomed in North Belfast at the end of the 1960s shortly before the Troubles erupted so tragically in that unhappy province. The team comprised lads from Protestant and Catholic (and indeed Mormon) family backgrounds. They dominated youth soccer right across the country and were defeated only twice in their two peak seasons. The idealism behind the team was swept away on a rising tide of hatred and bigotry culminating in the tragic events of Bloody Sunday in Derry in 1972 and the aftermath of a disastrous decade.

The team was managed by a Protestant. The players included a Protestant lad who later served five years in prison for armed robbery, a Catholic whose brother was shot dead in the street, another Protestant who was sentenced to seventeen years in prison for terrorist activities – and, most famously of all, Bobby Sands, the Catholic hunger striker, sentenced to ten years for terrorist offences, who died in 1981 in the Maze prison after starving himself for 66 days. In that period, he was elected to parliament and after his death became a folk hero in the Catholic Republican community. Young Bobby with a shining face was the team's left back.

A Beautiful Game does not refer to any of these characters or incidents, but takes the situation as the basis of a musical drama arising from issues of religious differences and sectarianism. There are several haunting ballads and a beautiful song for a young girl that is a re-working of the aria, 'The heart is slow to learn', originally conceived for the now-shelved sequel to *The Phantom of the Opera*. This is a brave and almost certainly experimental project which nonetheless taps in to many Lloyd Webber recurring obsessions of faith, hope and charity for children, dissent in the community and the healing, possibly redemptive, power of love. The show will be awaited towards the end of 2000 with as much anticipation and excitement as any blockbuster musical. And one thing is certain: this is not a block-buster musical, any more than was *Whistle Down the Wind*.

The novella that Frederick Forsyth had written with a

view to a *Phantom* sequel was published separately, no hard feelings all round. It was announced that *Cats*, the longest running musical in Broadway history, would close in June 2000, two months after the re-opening there of *Jesus Christ Superstar*, the show with which Lloyd Webber, and Tim Rice, had made their controversial, career-launching New York debuts back in 1971.

Lloyd Webber regrettably ceased his generous financial support for the National Youth Music Theatre. Julian Lloyd Webber announced that, after the collapse of his second marriage, he was closely involved with Roz Hamandishe, a 27-year-old, Zimbabwe-born recruitment consultant whom he had met in a wine bar and had then seen on a video recording of the television programme *Blind Date*.

Andrew expressed an increasing enthusiasm for Indian music (and, for that matter, Indian food) and appeared as the final guest of the twentieth century on BBC Radio 4's *Desert Island Discs*. He chose a funny revue sketch about food featuring John Cleese and David Frost, and music by Prokofiev, his father, Richard Rodgers ('Some Enchanted Evening'), the Beatles ('I Wanna Hold Your Hand'), Elvis Presley ('Hound Dog'), Shostakovich (the cello concerto) and himself ('Pie Jesu').

His book choice, in addition to the Bible and Shakespeare, was Simon Jenkins's magisterial new survey of English churches, and his luxury, so that he could have fun cooking anything he was clever enough to catch, was a herb garden. And we faded out with a strange, poignant image of the musical Midas in a rude loincloth rubbing a couple of sticks together to knock up a cheap meal, unattended and unremarked, miles and miles away from the hubbub of Shaftesbury Avenue . . .

SELECT BIBLIOGRAPHY

Black, Don, and Hampton, Christopher, *Sunset Boulevard* (Faber, 1993)

Eliot, T. S., *Collected Poems 1909-1962* (Faber, 1963)

Ganzl, Kurt, *The British Musical Theatre, Volume Two* (Macmillan, 1986)

Ganzl, Kurt, and Lamb, Andrew *Ganzl's Book of Musical Theatre* (Bodley Head, 1998)

Goodwin, John (ed), *British Theatre Design* (Weidenfeld & Nicolson, 1989)

Green, Stanley, *Broadway Musicals* (Faber, 1987)

Herman, Jerry, with Stasio, Marilyn, *Showtune* (Donald I. Fine Books, 1996)

Lloyd Webber, Andrew, with Eliot, T. S. and Napier, John, *Cats, the Book of the Musical* (Faber, 1981)

Lloyd Webber, Julian, *Travels With My Cello* (Pavilion, 1984)

McKnight, Gerald, *Andrew Lloyd Webber* (St Martin's Press, 1984)

Main, Mary, *Evita: The Woman With the Whip* (1952, Corgi 1977)

Mantle, Jonathan, *Fanfare* (Michael Joseph, 1989)

Parker, Alan, *The Making of Evita* (Collins Publishers, HarperCollins, 1996)

Perry, George, *The Complete Phantom of the Opera* (Pavilion, 1989)

Rice, Tim, and Lloyd Webber, Andrew, *Evita* (Elm Tree Books, 1978)

Richmond, Keith, *The Musicals of Andrew Lloyd Webber* (Virgin, 1995)

Rodgers, Richard, *Musical Stages* (Random House, 1975)

Sleep, Wayne, and Search, Gay, *Variations on Wayne Sleep* (Heinemann, 1983)

Sleep, Wayne, *Precious Little Sleep* (Boxtree, 1996)

Steyn, Mark, *Broadway Babies Say Goodnight* (Faber, 1997)

Suskin, Steven, *More Opening Nights on Broadway* (Schirmer Books, 1997)

Walsh, Michael, *Andrew Lloyd Webber* (Viking, 1989, updated Abrams, 1997)

INDEX